Henry VIII
AND
HIS RABBIS

Henry VIII AND HIS RABBIS

How the King Relied on Jewish Law
to End His First Marriage –
and Why He Failed

JERRY RABOW

AMBERLEY

First published 2025

Amberley Publishing
The Hill, Stroud
Gloucestershire, GL5 4EP

www.amberley-books.com

Copyright © Jerry Rabow, 2025

The right of Jerry Rabow to be identified as the Author of this work has been asserted in accordance with the Copyright, Designs and Patents Act 1988.

ISBN 978 1 3981 1990 1 (hardback)
ISBN 978 1 3981 1991 8 (ebook)

All rights reserved. No part of this book may be reprinted or reproduced or utilised in any form or by any electronic, mechanical or other means, now known or hereafter invented, including photocopying and recording, or in any information storage or retrieval system, without the permission in writing from the Publishers.

British Library Cataloguing in Publication Data.
A catalogue record for this book is available from the British Library.

1 2 3 4 5 6 7 8 9 10

Typesetting by SJmagic DESIGN SERVICES, India.
Printed in the UK.

EU GPSR Authorised Representative
Appointed EU Representative: Easy Access System Europe Oü, 16879218
Address: Mustamäe tee 50, 10621, Tallinn, Estonia
Contact Details: gpsr.requests@easproject.com, +358 40 500 3575

Despite what you may have heard, writing is not a solitary endeavour. It's just that, at times, it can become a very selfish one. This book is dedicated to my wife, Lola. Through her loving sacrifices, patient understanding, and unreserved support, she has become the co-author of this book – and of my life.

CONTENTS

Genealogical Tables 9
The Tudor Timeline 11
List of Illustrations 13
Preface 15

Part I: An England without Jews 21
  1 The Jews of Early Medieval Europe 23

Part II: Henry's First Two Decades of Marriage to Catherine of Aragon 29
  2 Henry VIII's Marriage to Catherine of Aragon 31
  3 Henry VIII's Children 42
  4 Henry VIII and Anne Boleyn 46

Part III: Henry's Quest for an Annulment 65
  5 Henry's Biblical Arguments for an Annulment 67
  6 Henry's Legal Strategies 80
  7 Henry's Christian Theological Strategy 99
  8 Why Henry's Christian Sources Failed 117

Part IV: Henry Turns to the Rabbis 127
  9 Henry Turns to Jewish Law 129
  10 Henry's Rabbis 142
  11 Henry's Search for Additional Rabbinic Support 159
  12 Why Jewish Law Failed to Help Henry 175

Part V: The Great Matter Ends	183
13 Henry's Final Tactics	185
14 Why Henry's Quest Failed	195
Afterword: Henry Crafts the Tudor Dynasty	203
Conclusion: Who Was Henry VIII?	211
Appendix A: Summaries of Henry VIII's Love Letters to Anne Boleyn	216
Appendix B: Canon Law Governing Annulments: Consummation and Public Honesty	222
Appendix C: Responsum of Rabbi Jacob Raphael	232
Appendix D: The King Who Married Six Wives	238
Appendix E: The Tudor Succession	244
Acknowledgements	256
Notes	260
Bibliography and Online Resources	325
Index	341

Henry VIII's Claim to the Throne
(Line of Descent from Edward III)

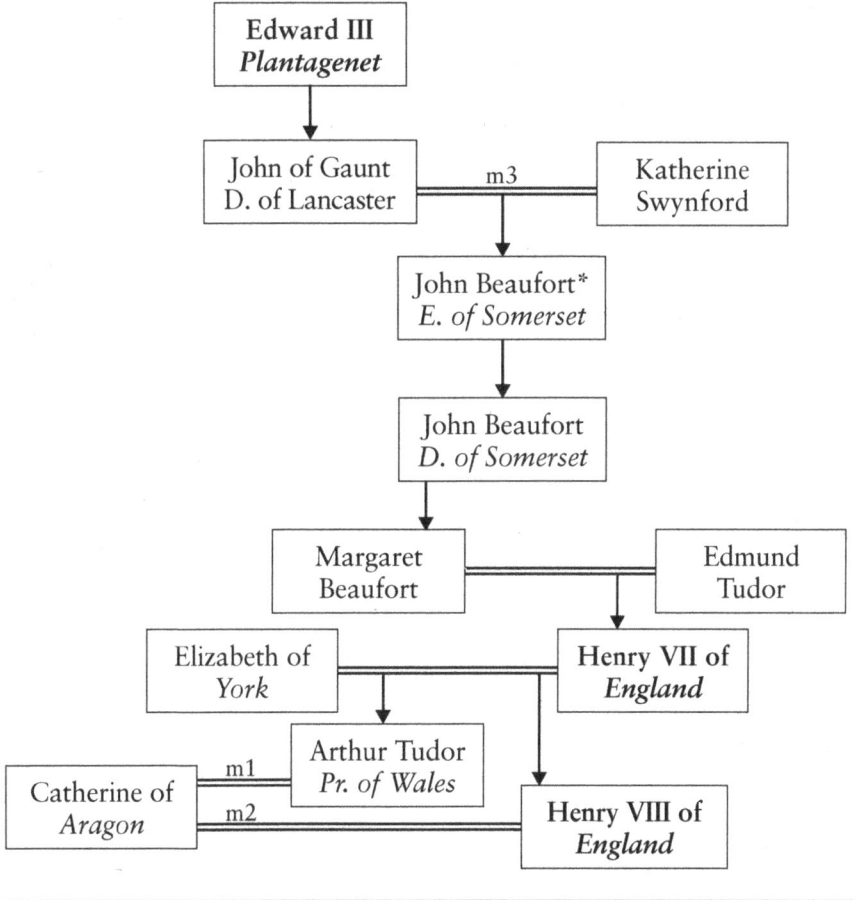

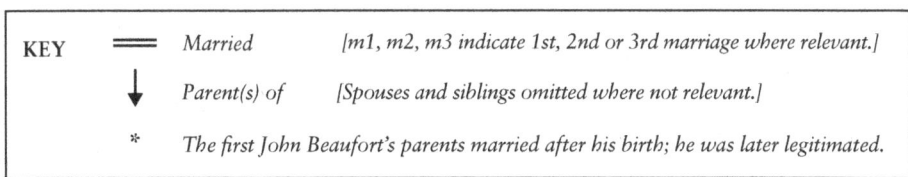

```
        Edward III
        Plantagenet
             │
             ▼
    John of Gaunt ═══m3═══ Katherine
    D. of Lancaster         Swynford
                  │
                  ▼
            John Beaufort*
            E. of Somerset
                  │
                  ▼
            John Beaufort
            D. of Somerset
                  │
                  ▼
    Margaret ═══════════ Edmund
    Beaufort              Tudor
                  │
                  ▼
    Elizabeth of ═══════ Henry VII of
    York                  England
                  │
                  ▼
Catherine of ══m1══ Arthur Tudor
Aragon              Pr. of Wales
           ══m2══ Henry VIII of
                  England
```

KEY	═══	Married	[m1, m2, m3 indicate 1st, 2nd or 3rd marriage where relevant.]
	↓	Parent(s) of	[Spouses and siblings omitted where not relevant.]
	*	The first John Beaufort's parents married after his birth; he was later legitimated.	

Henry VIII's Wives and Their Desceendants

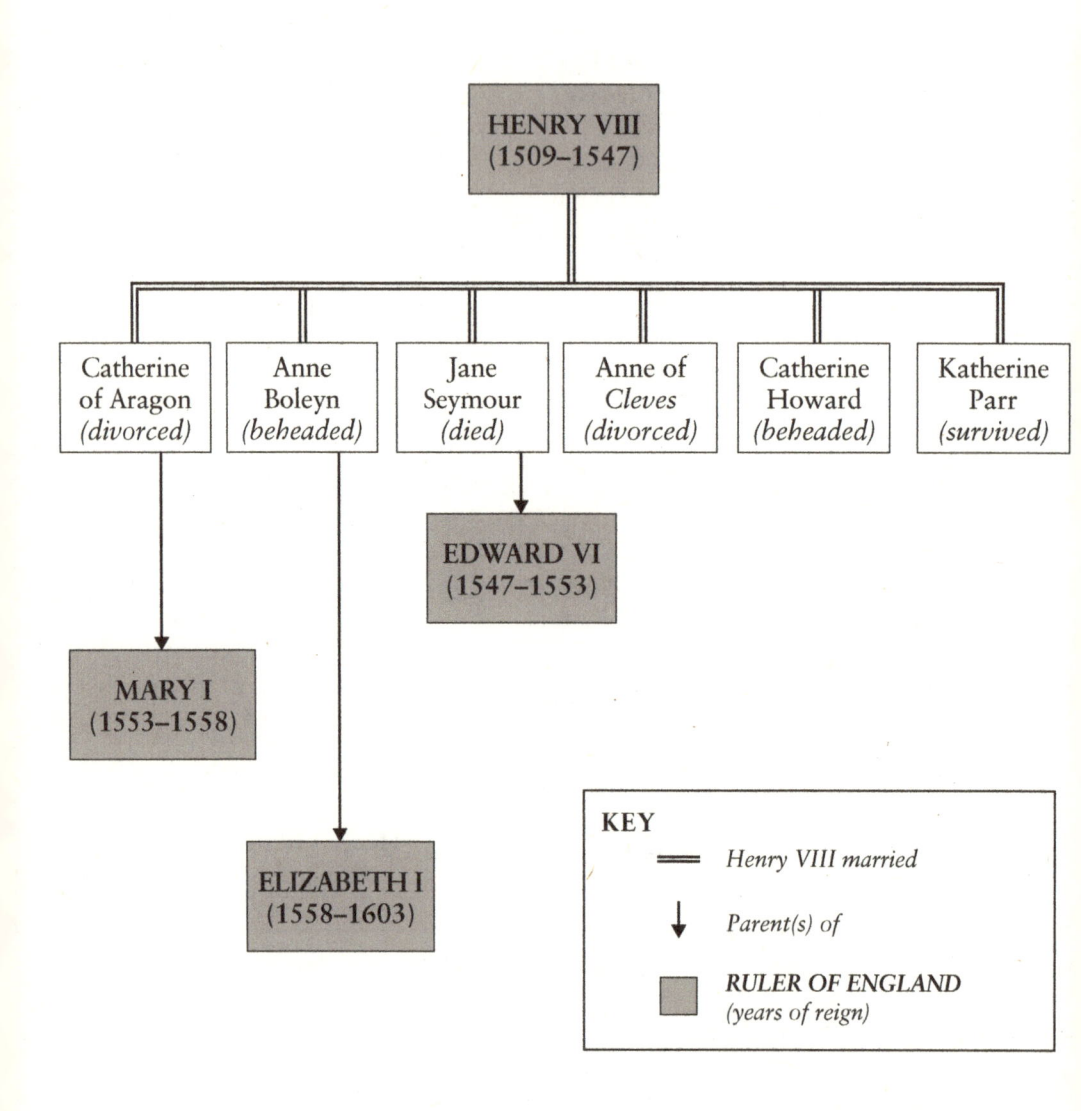

```
                    ┌─────────────────┐
                    │   HENRY VIII    │
                    │  (1509–1547)    │
                    └────────┬────────┘
     ┌────────┬────────┬─────┴──┬────────┬────────┐
Catherine  Anne     Jane      Anne of  Catherine  Katherine
of Aragon  Boleyn   Seymour   Cleves   Howard     Parr
(divorced) (beheaded)(died)  (divorced)(beheaded) (survived)
    │        │        │
    │        │        ▼
    │        │   ┌──────────┐
    │        │   │EDWARD VI │
    │        │   │(1547–1553)│
    │        │   └──────────┘
    ▼        │
┌────────┐   │
│ MARY I │   │
│(1553–  │   ▼
│ 1558)  │ ┌──────────┐
└────────┘ │ELIZABETH I│
           │(1558–1603)│
           └──────────┘
```

KEY

═══ *Henry VIII married*

↓ *Parent(s) of*

▢ *RULER OF ENGLAND (years of reign)*

THE TUDOR TIMELINE

1485   Henry Tudor defeats Richard III to become King of England, founding the Tudor dynasty for the House of Lancaster.

1486   Henry VII marries Elizabeth of York. They will have two sons, Arthur and Henry, and two daughters, Mary and Margaret, in addition to three children who will die in infancy.

1501   Prince Arthur marries Catherine of Aragon.

1502   Prince Arthur dies after five months of marriage, leaving no children.

1509   Henry VII dies. Prince Henry succeeds his father to the throne as Henry VIII.

1509   Henry VIII marries Catherine of Aragon.

1516   Catherine gives birth to Princess Mary. She will be their only child to survive infancy.

1533   Henry VIII's marriage to Catherine is annulled and he marries Anne Boleyn. They have one child, Princess Elizabeth.

1536   Anne is executed for adultery and treason. Henry marries Jane Seymour.

1537   Jane Seymour dies after giving birth to Prince Edward. Henry will marry three more times, but he will have no further legitimate children.

1547   Henry VIII dies. Prince Edward, aged nine, succeeds his father to the throne as Edward VI, subject to a regency.

1553   Edward VI dies. His cousin Lady Jane Grey is declared queen, but that situation lasts for only nine days.

1553   Princess Mary wins the people's support and becomes Queen of England as Mary I. Over her reign she will lose her popularity.

1558   Mary I dies. Princess Elizabeth succeeds to the throne as Elizabeth I.

1603   Elizabeth I dies having never married or produced an heir, making her the last of the Tudor dynasty. She is succeeded by the Stuart King James VI of Scotland as James I of England.

LIST OF ILLUSTRATIONS

Fig. 1. King Henry VIII.
Fig. 2. Catherine of Aragon.
Fig. 3. King Henry VII, with Elizabeth of York.
Fig. 4. King Ferdinand and Queen Isabella of Spain.
Fig. 5. Anne Boleyn.
Fig. 6. Thomas Wolsey.
Fig. 7. Henry VIII's armour at ages fifty-three and thirty-six.
Fig. 8. Pope Clement VII.
Fig. 9. Pope Julius II.
Fig. 10. Emperor Charles V.
Fig. 11. Castel Sant'Angelo, Rome.
Fig. 12. Scene from Shakespeare's *King Henry VIII*, Act 3, Scene 1.
Fig. 13. Trial of the marriage of Henry VIII.
Fig. 14. John Fisher.
Fig. 15. Thomas Cranmer.
Fig. 16. Pope Saint Gregory I and Pope Innocent III.
Fig. 17. Signature line of Rabbi Jacob Raphael's Responsum.
Fig. 18. Thomas Cromwell.
Fig. 19. Thomas Cromwell, detail from Fig. 18.
Fig. 20. Jane Seymour.
Fig. 21. Edward VI as a child.
Fig. 22. Lady Jane Grey.
Fig. 23. Queen Mary I.
Fig. 24. Queen Elizabeth I.
Fig. 25. Mary Queen of Scots.
Figs 26–28. Rabbi Jacob Raphael's Responsum.

PREFACE

Why Another Book about Henry VIII?
Many aspects of the Tudor dynasty in sixteenth-century England, particularly regarding Henry VIII, have become the subject of a vast amount of scholarship. This has been especially the case since the twentieth century, when historians H. A. L. Fisher, G. W. Elton, and others launched what can be called the modern period of Tudor historiography (the writing of history). It therefore seems fair to ask at the outset if yet another Henry VIII book is really needed. I would respond that after five hundred years, recent historians who are concerned with the early Tudor era are still disagreeing, and their disciples are still finding room to revise – or reverse – the conclusions of prior teachers and predecessors.

In addition to the academic efforts driving current interest in sixteenth-century English history, there is also today's great engine of public enthusiasm, sometimes bordering on celebrity fandom, which continues to increase the popular fascination with Henry VIII and all things Tudor. Enthusiasts now eagerly share their discoveries, speculations, and fascinations about the entire century of Tudor dynasty monarchs, along with their royal spouses and lovers, supporters and enemies, and national responses to political and military challenges, both domestic and foreign. Today's Tudormania employs all of the new media channels of expression and connection, including books, websites, podcasts, newsletters, guided tours to relevant historical sites, conventions, costumes, souvenirs, historical calendars, and curated lists of research resources. The result is a seemingly endless stream of more books by professional historians and amateur devotees, producing both non-fiction histories and hybrid works of historical fiction, with some prominent authors alternating between these two genres.

Cautions about Reading Tudor History

Having more historical writings does not necessarily produce better, more valid historical understandings. In the modern era of critical thinking and psychological analysis, most readers of popular history, as well as academic scholars, are aware that history is not simply an accounting of facts. Writing history is a human endeavour and subject to inevitable human shortcomings. For the history of Henry VIII in particular, we must be wary of the effects of commentators' religious, philosophical, political, and other biases in their selection of the people and events upon which they focus, as well as in the analysis and interpretation they offer.

We might generally presume that the more a work of history relies upon contemporaneous and direct source material, the more likely it is that we will be able to understand what really happened. However, unless the reader is careful, just the opposite may apply to sixteenth-century Tudor history. Most early Tudor original sources came from amateur, non-academic writers who wrote before the development of modern standards and procedures for writing history. Reading such sources requires extra vigilance against uncritical acceptance of anecdotes that might be based upon gossip, superstition, or partisan bias.

Henry VIII was a powerful and ultimately brutal monarch who was extremely sensitive about his reputation both within his realm and throughout the western world. In reading the early sources, we should therefore also carefully evaluate whether the ambitions and fears of witnesses, writers, and publishers of the time may have coloured some early accounts. Some observers, and even participants, may have been especially eager to please the king or his supporters and successors. Incurring the royal wrath could, and often did, prove fatal. Therefore, some early Tudor royal history sources that speak favourably about Henry VIII may be especially unreliable.

With regard to Henry VIII's first divorce, which is the focus of this book, we must be especially careful to examine the early sources for indications of religious bias. We know that none of Henry

Preface

VIII's arguments, threats, and pleas over six years could convince Pope Clement VII to free him from his marriage to his first wife, Catherine of Aragon. The king finally concluded that, to achieve his desired marital dissolution, he must resort to taking a monumental step. Henry removed England from the Roman Catholic Church. He replaced the pope with the ruling King of England as head of what would eventually become the Church of England.[1] This was a momentous act, marking one of the preliminary steps of the English Reformation. Because this breach between Rome and London was largely an outcome of Henry's quest for the dissolution of his first marriage, we must expect that particularly the early chronicles and histories of Henry's annulment and the events leading up to it may vary widely depending upon whether they were written from a Catholic or Protestant viewpoint.[2]

For Tudor history, we have unique access to many contemporaneous and near-contemporaneous documents preserved as official records of state or as early published histories that have been saved in library archives. Because they were created before the development of modern standards of historiography, however, such a multitude of these materials is both a blessing and a curse. I have tried in this book to present relevant extracts from the official records of early original documents rather than relying primarily upon later historians' analyses and conclusions. Nevertheless, we should remember to read even original or official documents with critical attention to possible distortions and biases.

Principal Sources for Early Tudor Documents

The largest collection of official Tudor documents accessible in the British government archives for the beginning of the reign of Henry VIII, the period most relevant for this book, is *Letters and Papers, Foreign and Domestic, Henry VIII*, Volumes 1–11, covering the years 1509–1536. These volumes are conveniently available at British History Online at: *https://www.british-history.ac.uk/series/letters-and-papers-henry-viii*.

However, the *Letters and Papers* collection presents some significant research problems. It does not primarily contain complete original documents, but rather subsequently prepared official summaries of original documents, including varying amounts of direct quotations, excerpts, and translations. These summaries were prepared in the late nineteenth and early twentieth centuries. In addition, the dates attributed to some items do not always appear in the original document and may be inaccurate. Furthermore, some of the original documents referred to may be copies of final versions retained by the author, or perhaps merely drafts which may or may not ultimately have been revised or actually sent by the author. Such problems are not as prevalent in the similar, smaller collections of typically translated documents located in the series of *Calendar of State Papers-Spain*, and *Calendar of State Papers-Venice* for the same period, available at British History Online at https://www.british-history.ac.uk/series/calendar-state-papers-spain and https://www.british-history.ac.uk/series/calendar-state-papers-venice.

The ready accessibility of these documents does seem to have cleared up some matters, but it has unfortunately unleashed additional and deeper disputes about other facts and their interpretation. The resulting increase in uncertainty is not restricted to merely peripheral background details. Some of the most central elements of Henry VIII's character and motives remain unclear.

The Focus of Our Story

Henry VIII was born on 28 June 1491, and died on 28 January 1547; he reigned from 1509 to 1547. This book does not attempt to examine issues of character and motivation over the entire period of Henry VIII's fifty-five-year life or over his thirty-eight-year reign as king. Instead, we will focus upon the six core years, 1527 to 1533, of what Henry called his Great Matter – the struggle to end his marriage to his first wife, Catherine of Aragon.

The major aim of this book is to explore how it could be that, in a Catholic England that had no Jews, Henry's final attempt to convince the pope to annul his marriage to Catherine relied upon Jewish law and its interpretation by contemporaneous rabbis. The answers to this puzzle are explored and explained as follows:

PART I: AN ENGLAND WITHOUT JEWS begins with a brief sketch of how the vast majority of the Jewish people left their homeland in the Land of Israel (Canaan/Palestine/Judea) by the end of the first century CE, gradually settling throughout much of Europe and Asia. Our specific interest is to understand how the Jews first settled in England in the eleventh century, one thousand years after the ancient

Preface

Roman conquest and destruction of Jerusalem in 70 CE. We'll also explore why, after continually residing in England for over two centuries, all Jews left England in 1290, two hundred years before the birth of Henry VIII.

PART II: HENRY'S TWO DECADES OF MARRIAGE TO CATHERINE OF ARAGON examines Henry's first twenty years of marriage to Catherine of Aragon, including how Henry became King of England, how he came to marry Catherine of Aragon, the developments in their marriage and family life, and Henry's early relationship with Anne Boleyn.

PART III: HENRY'S QUEST FOR AN ANNULMENT analyses the specific strategies that Henry adopted in his historic effort to terminate his marriage. With the help of original documents, we deconstruct the complex web of forces that converged to frustrate Henry's series of attempts to convince the pope.

PART IV: HENRY TURNS TO THE RABBIS assembles the evidence of what may be the most unexpected and fantastic development occurring in this epic struggle between London and Rome. Henry VIII's final attempts to convince Pope Clement VII to dissolve the marriage did not depend exclusively upon Catholic law, but eventually came to rely upon Jewish law, as interpreted by the rabbis. We will also investigate why those final arguments by Henry, based upon Jewish authorities, failed.

PART V: THE END OF THE GREAT MATTER concludes with an overall analysis of these six years of controversy and their ultimate consequences for Henry, Catherine, Anne Boleyn, and the remaining years of Tudor rule in England.

Henry and His Rabbis

Mainstream historians do not contest the basic fact that Henry and his agents sought opinions from Jewish scholars and rabbis to support his petition to the pope for an annulment. However, Tudor histories have seldom bothered to examine closely the role played by Jewish law and the individual rabbis consulted by Henry in the divorce matter. Except for a few sources, most references by those relatively few historians who even mention Henry's attempts to rely upon Jewish law seldom devote more than a single phrase or sentence to this issue.[3]

We will review some of the generally neglected historical evidence to illuminate the surprising details of this unique intersection of the worlds of Judaism, Catholicism, and Protestantism that occurred in the early Tudor era of the sixteenth century. The evidence considered will inform us about such diverse factors as England's flagrant and repeated resort to bribing the rabbis and Jewish scholars in Italy; the bitter conflict over the annulment question between two of the greatest rabbis in Italy in 1530; how the argument between these two rabbis can be traced to the previous appearance of two competing Jewish messianic figures in the early sixteenth century; and the overall lack of awareness by the English of the structure of Jewish law and custom. This last factor includes Henry and his advisors being totally unaware of some of the crucial cultural distinctions between the two major branches of Diaspora Judaism: Ashkenazi and Sephardi. The latter reference often includes the Mizrahi Jews who had remained in, or eventually settled in, the Muslim Middle East, and who generally followed many Sephardi laws and customs.[4] We will also consider the consequences of England's general ignorance of the then available books of Talmudic analysis and rabbinic commentary interpreting Jewish law concerning the central issues underlying Henry's annulment dispute. Finally, thanks to the remarkable survival in the British archives of the original formal opinion written in 1530 by Rabbi Jacob Raphael of Modena, we will examine a traditional form of rabbinic opinion making clear why Jewish law would not support Henry's cause.

PART I

AN ENGLAND WITHOUT JEWS

I

THE JEWS OF EARLY MEDIEVAL EUROPE

The Jews in England, 1066–1290

Jews as an identifiable group first came to England from France with William the Conqueror's successful Norman invasion of Anglo-Saxon England in 1066. Some of these Jews may have been formally or informally involved in financial administration for the Norman royalty and nobility. Following common patterns of Jewish immigration, most of the initial Jewish immigrants would have settled in small Jewish communities in London and a few of England's other population centres. The initial Jewish settlers would have been gradually joined later by family members or other co-religionists.

Unfortunately, it did not take long before England began to act upon the antisemitic beliefs that had for some time been expressed in continental Europe. Indeed, England soon became more than a follower in this, with ruthless government restrictions and deadly mob riots against its Jews in the twelfth and thirteenth centuries becoming examples for the rest of Europe.

A period of brutal attacks against the Jews in mainland Europe had begun in connection with the First Crusade in 1096, and continued to a lesser degree in the Second Crusade of 1144. To enlist Christian soldiers in these military campaigns, the Catholic Church offered economic benefits in this world and promised spiritual rewards in the next. The Church's recruitment rhetoric enflamed the

Crusade armies by calling on them to participate in the holy task of battling and destroying the infidels who were threatening the Christian way of life.

These exhortations were aimed at initiating Crusades to attack the Muslims in the Middle East. But it did not take much for the Christian armies who were about to leave on their long march to the Holy Land to realise that this calling could also apply to another infidel group living in the very midst of Christian Europe, often in the areas where the armies were formed or through which they marched. Therefore, the Crusaders conducted, or inspired the local Christian populations to conduct, vicious and deadly attacks upon Jewish communities along the Crusade routes to the Middle East.

The English were not significant participants in the First and Second Crusades. However, perhaps stirred up by the stories coming from the Continent around the time of the Second Crusade, England made an indelible contribution to European antisemitism – the Ritual Murder Libel (the 'Blood Libel'). The first significant use of these wild accusations to incite attacks against the Jews appears to have occurred in Norwich in 1144.

The Blood Libel is a bizarre legend that circulated widely among Christian communities in the Middle Ages. When a Christian child disappeared from a community in which there was some Jewish presence, or if the child was found dead, especially in springtime, the rumour of the Blood Libel would flood the local Christian community. Christians convinced themselves that the Jews must have kidnapped, tortured, and killed the child in a reenactment of the Crucifixion, and had drained the blood from the body to be used as an essential ingredient for making matzo, the ceremonial unleavened flatbread made for the Jewish springtime festival of Passover.[1] The original Blood Libel rumour in Norwich resulted in the alleged twelve-year-old victim becoming known as St William of Norwich, although he was never formally beatified by the Church.

The Norwich myth was detailed in a contemporaneous twelfth-century account written by Thomas of Monmouth, a local Benedictine monk. His story included many fabricated descriptions attributed to supposed witnesses. In the fifteenth century a new report repeated or elaborated the most inconsistent and irrational of these accounts as evidence of the event.[2] These reports of the

Blood Libel incident in Norwich served as a template for frenzied, hateful accusations against Jews by mobs and governments in other communities at other times. Amazingly, this fantasy has continued into the modern era.[3]

In the 150 years following the Norwich incident, the Blood Libel myth became a poisonous, if sometimes unstated, justification underlying other horrific and often deadly acts of antisemitic persecution of the Jews in more than a dozen Jewish communities in England.[4] The level of these atrocities in England intensified with the beginning of the Third Crusade in 1190. The English participated in this Crusade under the personal leadership of their popular, newly crowned King Richard I (Richard the Lionheart). A century of disaster for the Jews of England began when Richard's coronation ceremonies in London, in September 1189, triggered the Coronation Riot.

Richard had not personally exhibited extreme antisemitism, but the same cannot be said of others in his royal court and the leadership of the Church at that time.[5] At Richard's coronation banquet, the Archbishop of Canterbury, Baldwin of Forde, insisted that the Jewish congratulatory delegation, which had come to London for the event, be excluded from the banquet hall. When the crowd of commoners outside the hall saw the Jews being ejected, a rumour immediately circulated that their new king wanted the Jews to be forcibly converted or killed. The crowd turned into a murderous mob. The rampage against the Jews of the delegation quickly descended into several days of general rioting against Jews living in London, with burning and looting of their homes, and physical attacks and killings.[6]

Richard tried to restore order, but even his royal officers could not overcome the power of the mob. A few months later, as soon as the king had left England to lead the Third Crusade, the Coronation Riot was emulated in many of the other English cities with significant Jewish communities. The deadliest of these incidents was the massacre in March 1190 at York Castle, incited by some minor noble families who owed money to Jewish lenders. A reputed five hundred Jews took refuge in the Clifford's Tower building of the royal castle at York, but they lacked weapons and food to withstand the ensuing siege. Some of the Jews were killed by the mob, which did not allow any exceptions for Jews who were willing to choose conversion in a vain attempt to avoid death. As the walls of the tower were being breached, the remaining Jews followed the example of the ancient siege of Masada and killed their families and then themselves rather than being murdered by the mob.[7]

Expulsion of the Jews from England

During the 150 years following the unleashing of the Blood Libel legend at Norwich, The Jews of England suffered other difficulties in addition to attacks from rioting mobs. The Jewish communities in England were in large measure dependent upon indirect protection provided by the few very successful and wealthy Jewish moneylenders. At times, these men had some influence with the Crown, the nobility, and even the monasteries and churches, all of whom depended upon financing from the Jews. But at other times during this period, the Crown imposed confiscatory taxes upon Jewish merchants and moneylenders. Because of all the financial restrictions targeting them, the Jews of twelfth- and thirteenth-century England gradually became increasingly impoverished. The seemingly eternal question arose once again: Was it time for these Jews to seek a friendlier land?

In the end, the decision was made for them. In 1272, Edward I, son of Henry III, became King of England. In July 1290, King Edward proclaimed total banishment of all Jews from England, effective from 1 November 1290. There were perhaps 16,000 Jews in England at the time, almost all residing in Jewish communities located in seventeen towns. The harsh conditions of the banishment caused further economic hardship to the English Jewish community, which had already suffered great reduction of its wealth.[8]

This banishment not only remained in effect more than two centuries later, at the beginning of Henry VIII's reign in 1509, but continued through the entire Tudor dynasty and beyond, until the middle of the seventeenth century. Jews were finally allowed to return to England under the rule of Oliver Cromwell, Lord Protector of England during the Commonwealth period of 1653–1658.[9]

Thus, during the early sixteenth century, Henry VIII inherited and ruled an England without Jews – indeed, an England that had been without Jews for well over two centuries. This adds to our puzzlement that in 1530, Henry would turn to Jewish law and the rabbis of Italy for help in his final strategy to have the pope annul his marriage to his first wife and queen, Catherine of Aragon. To explain how this happened, we must begin by examining the background and circumstances of that first marriage of Henry VIII.

PART II

HENRY'S FIRST TWO DECADES OF MARRIAGE TO CATHERINE OF ARAGON

2

HENRY VIII'S MARRIAGE TO CATHERINE OF ARAGON

The Background of Henry VIII's Marriage

As seems to be true for so many aspects of England's sixteenth-century Tudor dynasty, the background of King Henry VIII's first marriage presents some unique complications. We must first consider several elements of that background so that we can understand the marriage. How did the Tudor dynasty begin? How did young Prince Henry Tudor become King of England? And how, as King Henry VIII, did he get to marry Catherine of Aragon?

How the Tudor Royal Dynasty Began

Ideally, the throne of England passes without conflict to succeeding generations of the royal house, following traditional rules. By the late Middle Ages, the English tradition for royal succession seemed well defined in many cases. The crown was to pass to the oldest legitimate son of the previously reigning king, or if that son was deceased, then to that son's oldest male descendant, or else to his oldest brother, etc. However, in instances where multiple distantly related claimants presented themselves as the next in line, the traditional rules were not always clear. In such cases, succession might end up being resolved by battle between armies supporting opposing claimants.

The Tudor dynasty began with such a battlefield coronation. England's long-running War of the Roses, contesting the rival claims between the House of Lancaster and the House of York, ended with the Battle of Bosworth Field in 1485. Henry VII, father of Henry VIII, gained the crown by leading his Lancastrian troops to victory over Yorkist forces led by King Richard III, who was killed on the field. Without this decisive military victory, Henry VII's underlying claim to the throne had been far from conclusive. He was a member of the Welsh nobility and only an indirect descendant of the Plantagenet King Edward III. Henry VII's royal lineage was additionally weakened because his claim relied upon Plantagenet royal inheritance through the Beaufort family line on his mother's side. That maternal line claim was further tainted because Henry's descent in the Beaufort line from Edward III was through Edward's grandson John Beaufort, who had been born illegitimate.[1]

Moreover, there were at that time several other nobles who could argue that they had a superior genealogical claim to succeed King Richard III.[2] Once crowned, Henry VII therefore moved promptly to consolidate his royal status. He expropriated the lands and wealth of his political opponents and redistributed some of that booty to reward his supporters and ensure their personal loyalty to him. He imprisoned or executed descendants of the Plantagenet dynasty who he feared could be potential claimants to the throne. He also definitively ended the War of the Roses (1455–1485) by marrying Elizabeth of York in 1486. This politically beneficial marriage merged the competing houses of Lancaster and York through the expectation that their joint male descendants would eventually occupy the throne of England in a new and combined royal line.

Catherine's Marriage to Arthur

While Henry VII's political marriage strengthened his somewhat questionable claim to the throne, he had to accomplish more if he wanted to establish a great Tudor dynasty for his heirs. Henry VII and Elizabeth had four children who survived to adulthood: Arthur (b. 19 September 1486), Margaret (b. 28 November 1489), Henry (b. 28 June 1491), and Mary (b. 18 March 1496). In 1489, before the future Henry VIII was born, Henry VII negotiated with Ferdinand II and Isabella, the monarchs of Spain, to arrange a political marriage similar to his own. The Spanish monarchs would unite their Spanish royal line with his English royal line through the marriage of their daughter Catherine of Aragon to Henry VII's firstborn son and heir apparent, Arthur. Both Catherine, born in 1485, and Arthur, born

Henry VIII's Marriage to Catherine of Aragon

in 1486, were infants at the time of their marriage contract in 1489. The agreement was not intended to be implemented for a dozen or more years, when Prince Arthur would have reached at least fourteen, considered at that time the age of majority for a male to enter into marriage.

In practice, such state treaties for the future marriages of children or infants were often revoked before they were ready to be implemented. The long waiting periods provided ample time for important circumstances to change. These changes could include new international alliances or wars, shifts in the wealth or international status of one or the other of the contracting families, the inability or unwillingness of the bride's family to fund the typically substantial dowry obligation, or simply a new belief by one of the families that they could find a better match for their prince or princess.

In this case, however, the contracted marriage continued to be seen by both Ferdinand and Henry VII as highly beneficial to their respective kingdoms. Thus, despite some delays and concerns during the lengthy period of betrothal, the marriage agreement of Arthur Tudor and Catherine of Aragon eventually culminated in their wedding.

In 1501, when Arthur was fifteen and Catherine was almost sixteen, the princess came to England. They married on 14 November 1501 in a grand royal wedding in London. By that time, Prince Arthur's younger brother, Prince Henry, was ten years old and was an attendant in the ceremonies. The people turned out in a large and enthusiastic show of approval of the match. Young Arthur, Prince of Wales, had not yet had much occasion to become admired by the public, but his mere existence as an almost-adult son of Henry VII embodied a promise to the war-weary kingdom of a peaceful and orderly succession to the throne. On her part, Catherine instantly won the hearts of the Londoners with her beauty, regal bearing, and somewhat exotic Spanish dress and customs.

Catherine also personified England's new alliance with Spain, offering to England worldwide trade benefits and an expanded political presence in continental Europe. It also did not hurt that Spain and England were already natural allies. They shared the same traditional enemy – France – which at that time was feared as the major political and military power in western Europe.

Not only were the English people happy with the new royal couple, but the wedding was an extremely important accomplishment for Henry VII. He was still deeply concerned with the tasks of consolidating his reign and establishing a Tudor dynasty for the future, and he reasonably expected that the new marriage would help accomplish all of that.[3]

Death of Prince Arthur

Suddenly, the fate of England, and indeed the fate of Christianity and the world, suffered a drastic and unexpected turn. The universal joy and optimism of the kingdom was abruptly cut short when, after less than five months of marriage, Arthur died on 2 April 1502. To this day, the cause of his death remains clouded in speculation and dispute. The historical record displays some uncertainty as to whether Arthur was a chronically sick boy or if he was healthy and robust at the time of his wedding. In any case, one of his attendants described the quick onset of a painful and extremely debilitating disease resulting in Arthur's death after less than a week. At this same time Catherine was recovering from what was likely the same severe illness. Many historians have concluded that Arthur probably died from the English sweating sickness. This was a highly contagious and often swiftly lethal infectious disease that periodically scourged England – perhaps an extremely virulent form of influenza or some related virus.[4]

Some other possibilities discussed as the cause of Arthur's death include tuberculosis or other forms of lung disease. Any of these infectious diseases may have evidenced a Tudor family susceptibility that could have been responsible for the later deaths, also as teenagers, of two of Henry VIII's future sons who survived infancy: Edward Tudor, who ruled as the boy-king Edward VI following Henry VIII's death, and Henry Fitzroy, Henry VIII's publicly acknowledged illegitimate son.

The phenomenon of celebrity gossip was apparently well established by the sixteenth century. Many in the general public could not resist speculating that the death of the fifteen-year-old newlywed Prince Arthur might have resulted from his excessive nighttime exertions as a bridegroom.[5]

Negotiations between Spain and England for a New Marriage

Despite the personal devastation felt by Catherine and the Spanish and English monarchs at Arthur's death, the same geopolitical and financial considerations that had initially motivated the marriage remained important. Moreover, the original marriage treaty threatened difficult legal and financial problems for both nations if the arrangement had to be unwound. A new political marriage arrangement between the ten-year-old Prince Henry, the new heir apparent to the throne of England, and the seventeen-year-old Princess Catherine could still promise a permanent alliance for resisting the French. Indeed, changes in some of the related circumstances after Catherine's first marriage seemed to make a marriage between young Henry and Catherine even more advantageous for both their nations.

On behalf of England, Henry VII was initially very insistent that Prince Henry be allowed to take his deceased brother's place under the agreement for the union of the Spanish and English royal lines. When Prince Arthur died, Queen Elizabeth had tried to console her husband by reminding him that they were still young and would go on to have other children, some presumably male, who could further ensure the Tudor dynasty.[6] Tragically, Elizabeth's assurances could not avert further disaster for Henry VII. In February 1503, less than a year after Arthur's death, Queen Elizabeth did deliver another baby, but neither the child – a girl – nor the queen survived more than a few days after the birth. This left young Prince Henry as the sole Tudor male heir to the throne.

With both his wife and older son dead, Henry VII must have seen that his hopes of extending his reign to establish a new Tudor dynasty had suddenly become gravely endangered. In that era, when miscarriages, stillbirths, and infant mortality were extremely common, the king's challenges for producing a line of male heirs to his throne were dire. He would have wanted the earliest possible implementation of a new Spanish–English marriage agreement in order to maximise the chancy business of having Prince Henry, the last direct Tudor male heir, produce a suitable male child to continue the Tudor dynasty into the distant future.

In addition, financial considerations may have further pushed Henry VII to seek immediate modification of Catherine's marriage agreement so that it would now apply to Prince Henry. The original marriage agreement with Arthur had called for a substantial dowry of 200,000 crowns to be paid to England by Spain. Up until then, however, only one-half of that dowry had been received, and the balance was now in jeopardy. Even worse for England's finances, upon Arthur's death the original marriage treaty might be read as requiring Henry VII to return to Ferdinand the half of the dowry already received.

England had not yet become a wealthy, dominant player in world trade. With the end of the feudal system, the English Crown was experiencing difficulties in relying upon repeated tax increases to raise the funds needed for domestic government and for the foreign wars endemic in the Europe of that period. Henry VII might have believed that Spain's supposedly unlimited wealth from newfound riches in the New World would provide an instant solution to England's fiscal challenges. A good start would be a new marriage treaty promising to England the full amount of Catherine's dowry if she married Prince Henry.

On their part, Ferdinand and Isabella shared England's view of the potential long-term political benefits to be gained by both nations from a marriage between Catherine and the new heir apparent to the English throne. However, when it came to finances, Spain's concerns about Catherine's dowry were the mirror image of England's. Where Henry did not want to face the possible obligation to return the half of the dowry already received, Ferdinand and Isabella took the position that they lacked the funds to pay the 100,000-crown balance of the dowry. Alas, Europe's widespread expectation that Spain would immediately receive enormous wealth from the Americas would continue in large measure to be an unrealised fantasy for another half-century.[7]

One measure of the extent of the fiscal problems facing both countries at that time is that, during several periods between her husband Arthur's death and her marriage to Prince Henry, Catherine was forced to live in miserable financial circumstances. At times, King Henry VII refused to allow her to reside at court. He also did not provide her with funds adequate to feed and support an independent residence appropriate for a young woman who was the widow of one crown prince and the promised bride of another. At the same time, Ferdinand would not or could not send funds to alleviate Catherine's financial desperation.[8]

Catherine had been seventeen years old when she became a widow. Because Prince Henry was then only ten years old, they could not marry immediately. A new marriage contract in 1503 between young Henry and Catherine specified postponement of the wedding at least until Henry reached the age of fifteen, on 28 June 1506.[9] In fact, the delay lasted more than the minimum three years from Arthur's death. The whole process of negotiation, renunciation, and renegotiation of the marriage agreement after Arthur died, including the time required by Spain to obtain and deliver the second half of the dowry, ended up dragging on for seven years.

Issues while Awaiting Prince Henry's Wedding
Negotiations with the Church for Approval of the Marriage
Second only to the financial issues between England and Spain over the dowry, the most pressing problem regarding the new agreement for the marriage of Prince Henry and Princess Catherine was not primarily a dispute between their fathers but between the two fathers on one side and the Roman Catholic Church on the other, specifically over whether Henry's marriage to his brother's widow was permitted by Church law.

It had been obvious from the moment of Arthur's death that any subsequent marriage of his younger brother to Arthur's widow would raise a serious question under the Church's extensive rules prohibiting incest – marriage between persons too closely related by blood or marriage. The specific biblical prohibition is expressed in Leviticus 18:16:

> Thou shalt not uncover the nakedness of [engage in sexual intercourse with] thy brother's wife: because it is the nakedness of thy brother.[10]

The Bible also recites a specific punishment for violation of Lev. 18:16, as declared two biblical chapters later, in Lev. 20:21:

> He that marrieth his brother's wife, doth an unlawful thing: he hath uncovered his brother's nakedness. They shall be without children.

In Chapter 5 below, we will return to examine the full significance for Henry VIII of these two biblical verses and their interpretation. At this point we can simply note that the prohibition against sexual relations between brother-in-law and sister-in-law expressed in Lev. 18:16 is surrounded by a group of verses in Lev. 18:6–18, all collectively referred to herein as the Leviticus Prohibitions. The verses in this broader group contain similar prohibitions for many other incestuous family relationships of blood or marriage. Over many centuries, the Roman Catholic Church had greatly expanded the scope of these incest prohibitions through interpretations that stretched the biblical rules to include distant degrees of relatedness.

Due to the common politically and socially driven patterns of in-marriage among the royalty and nobility of that era, the expanded Catholic interpretations of the Leviticus Prohibitions created frequent problems for the upper classes. Indeed, it has been observed that, during that era, it would be difficult to find any two noble families that had not developed some in-law ties over several prior generations. Fortunately, the Church was typically able to solve these problems for the nobility with a relatively simple procedure. If there was any possibility that a marriage might involve some *impediment* – the existence of any of the many possible violations of the Church rules regarding prohibited marriages – the proposed bride and groom would, almost as a matter of course, obtain a papal *dispensation*, an exception from the usual rules, which would authorise the prospective marriage.

Obviously, such a dispensation was especially important for young Henry and Catherine. The central purpose for Catherine's marriage to Prince Henry was the same that had motivated the prior marriage of Catherine and Arthur: the desire of Spain and England to join their royal lines through common descendants and secure a permanent alliance that could offset the power of France. Thus, the last thing that Henry VII and Ferdinand II wanted would be any possibility of a potential challenge to the validity of their children's marriage, since this could, in turn, question the legitimacy and fitness for royal succession of the future issue of that marriage.

It was the general practice of the Vatican at that time to grant such decrees of dispensation when requested, and paid for, by wealthy and powerful nobility. We can therefore imagine how readily a pope would want to issue a dispensation for the wedding of the children of two of the greatest Catholic kings of Europe. Thus, less than two years after Arthur's death, Henry Tudor, aged twelve, received a papal dispensation, dated 26 December 1503, from Pope Julius II permitting him to marry Catherine of Aragon despite her previous marriage to his older brother, Arthur.

Although not suspected by the parties at the time, this now-famous dispensation of Pope Julius would not ultimately be strong enough to resolve the issue of whether Prince Henry's marriage to Catherine of Aragon was free from challenge under ecclesiastical law. Indeed, we shall see later how Julius's dispensation would end up providing much of the fuel for the fiery end of Henry VIII's first marriage, ensnaring in its consequences many of the major political and religious powers of western Europe.

Prince Henry's Renunciation of the Wedding Treaty

Not everything went smoothly while the parties awaited the new wedding. By the time Prince Henry attained the age of fourteen, circumstances in England and Europe had changed. Spain was no longer presumed to have found an El Dorado of immeasurable wealth in the New World. King Henry VII appears to have concluded that since Catherine would not bring the hoped-for limitless wealth of Spain with her, she might not be the best available bride for Prince Henry. On 27 June 1505, one day before Henry's fourteenth birthday, the king had his young son make a private but formal and witnessed renunciation of the marriage contract on the ground that Prince Henry had never legally consented to it as an adult. This legal declaration apparently was not immediately disclosed to Catherine and her father.[11]

By this time, Henry VII's queen, Elizabeth of York, had died. While he was arranging for the prospective marriage of Prince Henry to Catherine of Aragon, he therefore began, actively but unsuccessfully, to explore the possibilities for his own marriage to a suitable – that is to say, a wealthy, young, and presumably fertile – member of European royalty. His motivation for this seems clear. If Henry VII were successful in seeking to remarry, not only would that have brought in another dowry to help with his perpetual financial problems, but it would also have offered the possibility of Henry VII himself having additional sons to further assure the Tudor succession.[12]

Henry VIII Reaffirms the Wedding Treaty

All of King Henry VII's schemes for improving the Tudor dynastic prospects came to naught. When Henry VII died as a widower on 21 April 1509, he left only his two daughters and his sole surviving son, Henry, Prince of Wales, who succeeded to the throne as Henry VIII. In one of the new king's first and most significant official acts after the death of his father, young Henry VIII announced that he was reversing his previous decision not to marry Catherine. Rather, he now formally reaffirmed their marriage agreement.

Henry VIII claimed that it had been his father's deathbed request that he withdraw his prior renunciation of the marriage contract. We must receive that explanation with caution. The new king would soon demonstrate that one aspect of his governance style was what we now call public relations. Henry VIII's public statement about his father's last wishes could have been one of his first attempts to tell the story about a political issue in a manner that he thought would enhance his public image.

The young king may have been motivated to reaffirm his marriage contract by the fact that Spain had finally shown that it was able and willing to pay the second half of Catherine's dowry due upon her wedding to Henry.[13] There also may have been a more personal, romantic motivation for Henry VIII's decision to marry Catherine. At that time, Catherine was widely acclaimed for her beauty and regal bearing. As a ten-year-old, Henry had been her escort for her triumphal wedding processional and ceremonies, and he perhaps had some limited contact with her at the palace since she had been widowed. Those youthful impressions might have attracted Henry to Catherine.[14]

The Wedding of King Henry VIII and Catherine of Aragon

Whatever the mix of personal, financial, and diplomatic motives might have been, it was as King of England that Henry VIII, about to turn eighteen, married Catherine of Aragon, aged twenty-three, on 11 June 1509 in a private ceremony that was publicly proclaimed four days later. Although Henry's wedding to Catherine had been private, it was followed in less than two weeks by a formal joint public coronation of the new king and his queen. The lavish ceremony was designed to project a sense of continuity and legitimacy for a dynasty that only a generation earlier had been founded through force of arms.[15]

The grand coronation ceremonies began on Saturday 23 June 1509, with Henry and Catherine's procession through London from the royal chambers in the Tower of London to the palace at Westminster.

The public ceremonies concluded the next day with their formal joint coronation in Westminster Abbey. For the cheering crowds that weekend in London, there were no theological concerns about the validity or propriety of Henry VIII's marriage to his brother's widow, nor any nationalistic reservations about Catherine's difficulties with the English language or her familial ties and loyalties to Spain. Catherine of Aragon was already beloved by Henry VIII's subjects. That popular affection would continue for her lifetime, even after she had been discarded two decades later by her husband.

In an uncanny repeat of the public wedding procession for Catherine's wedding to Arthur seven years earlier, London crowds once again expressed their joy and welcome, this time for the joint coronation procession of their new king and queen, Henry VIII and Catherine. Once again, the people felt that they had only to wait for this young couple to produce a male heir for the Tudor dynasty to achieve England's goals. Two decades of combined marriage negotiations had finally ended in the warmth of undiminished Spanish and English optimism.

3

HENRY VIII'S CHILDREN

Henry's Children with Catherine
At this point, we can glimpse the beginnings of the path of deeply ironic twists in the story of Henry VIII's first marriage. It had all seemed so simple at the outset. As soon as Queen Catherine could produce an heir who would be an acceptable future successor to the throne of England, the Tudor dynasty would begin to extend itself by a third generation – one that would fuse the royal bloodlines of England and Spain. The only problem was that, at this time, English tradition dictated that the successor to the throne of England had to be male. And while Catherine clearly cooperated in attempting to satisfy this condition, fate and nature did not.

Despite at least seven pregnancies in the nine years from 1510 to 1518, Catherine did not present Henry and England with a male heir to the throne. While there are varying accounts for her pregnancies, several recent historians agree that she had produced at least two stillborn children, two miscarriages, and three live births.[1] Unfortunately for the hopes of establishing an indisputable royal succession, out of those three live births, neither of the two male infants survived beyond a matter of weeks. The longer-lasting son, born in 1511, lived for fifty-two days – only long enough to be christened 'Henry', to be immediately celebrated, and then almost as immediately to be deeply mourned by the nation. The only child of Catherine and Henry to live beyond two months was a girl, Princess Mary (b. 18 February 1516; r. as Queen Mary I, 1553–1558).[2]

Henry's Other Children

During his marriage to Catherine, Henry also had affairs with aristocratic mistresses, generally already present at the royal court as attendants to the queen. In that era, affairs with mistresses were not unusual for men of royalty or nobility. Such relationships were generally regarded as an appropriate response to what were seen as the natural sexual needs of a husband. A common rationalisation was that failing to allow satisfaction of the husband's urges in that manner might cause him to resort to liaisons with poorer women or prostitutes. For the elite, taking a mistress was especially typical during a wife's perceived sexual unavailability when she was pregnant or for a substantial period after delivery – and Catherine was often pregnant.[3] For Henry VIII, at least one of these extramarital relationships produced an illegitimate child, and at least one other also may have done so.

Henry's Child with Elizabeth Blount

One of Henry's first mistresses, Elizabeth (Bessie) Blount, was a lady-in-waiting for Queen Catherine. Beautiful and talented as a singer, composer, and dancer, Bessie became the king's mistress in 1514.[4] In 1519, Bessie gave birth to a son who was named Henry Fitzroy. Henry openly acknowledged Fitzroy as his illegitimate son. The boy was the only illegitimate child ever acknowledged by Henry VIII – indeed, 'Fitzroy' means 'son of the king'.[5]

Always pursuing his dynastic ambitions, Henry's public recognition of Fitzroy as his son appears to have been an attempt to keep open the possibilities for Tudor male succession if needed. Henry's subjects might eventually regard his illegitimate son as an acceptable successor to the throne if he failed to produce any legitimate surviving sons. When Fitzroy was six, Henry elevated the boy to the peerage, bestowing on him a double dukedom as Duke of Richmond and Duke of Somerset, as well as additional honours and noble titles. In 1533, when Fitzroy reached the age of fourteen, Henry arranged for him to marry Lady Mary Howard, a member of one of England's great noble families.

Unfortunately, in 1536 Fitzroy died, leaving no heirs. He was only seventeen, and the cause of death is still uncertain. He may have died from tuberculosis, although there are various alternative theories. Possibilities range from the English sweating sickness to some familial genetic lung disease that may have also caused or contributed to the teenage deaths of Fitzroy's uncle Arthur and, soon after Fitzroy's own death, his half-brother Edward, born to Henry VIII and his third wife, Jane Seymour.[6] A few contemporaneous observers and some later historians have speculated that Fitzroy may have been fatally poisoned, presumably for political purposes.[7]

Did Henry Have Children with Mary Boleyn?

A few years after Fitzroy's birth, Mary Boleyn, Anne Boleyn's older sister, became King Henry's new mistress. This occurred while Mary was already married to William Carey, one of Henry's personal gentleman-attendants. During the period of her relationship with the king, Mary gave birth to two children: Catherine, in 1524, and Henry, in 1526. It is sometimes suggested that one or both of these children might have been fathered by Henry VIII, but there is very little evidence to support such a suggestion.[8] It is true that, during this period, Henry bestowed generous advancements upon both Mary's husband, William Carey, and her father, Thomas Boleyn. However, these gestures are explainable as no more than reciprocation for Henry's relationship with Mary, and as appreciation that these two men did not interfere with that relationship. His patronage did not necessarily have any connection to her children.

Moreover, when Henry had previously ended his relationship with Elizabeth Blount, he had settled her with some lands and arranged for her to marry a gentleman. This contrasts sharply with the fact that Henry made little or no provision for Mary Boleyn when he separated from her, and later he did not initiate any substantial financial assistance for her after the death of her husband, William Carey.[9] Finally, unlike the king's public recognition and ducal elevation of Elizabeth Blount's son, Henry Fitzroy, the fact that Henry VIII never acknowledged paternity of Mary Boleyn's son or daughter suggests that the king did not believe that he was their father.

In 1526, when Mary Boleyn gave birth to her second child, the king ended his relationship with her. By that time Queen Catherine was forty years old, and had endured at least seven pregnancies. Catherine no longer had the beauty of face and figure that initially had helped her to capture the hearts of the English people, and perhaps Henry's heart also. Sometime in the 1520s, her royal physicians advised Henry that she had begun menopause and was not capable of bearing further children.[10] Henry later stated that he had ceased having marital relations with her. Several modern historians place that cessation sometime before 1525.[11] Henry also later indicated that Catherine had developed some sort of physical condition or disease that made it impossible, or at least prohibitively unappealing, for him to have sexual relations with her.[12]

Thus, it is not surprising that Henry would promptly begin looking for a new mistress to succeed Mary Boleyn. What may have been surprising, however, was that he did not look very far. Sometime in 1526 or 1527, Henry began his pursuit of Mary Boleyn's younger sister, Anne.[13]

4

HENRY VIII AND ANNE BOLEYN

Perhaps Henry was expecting Anne Boleyn to be just one more pretty young woman at court in what was becoming a succession of dutiful mistresses – impetuously selected, chivalrously courted, enjoyed for a limited time, and then discarded for the next in line. If so, the king was in for a surprise. Anne may have learned something from observing the outcome of her older sister's relationship with Henry. Or perhaps she was just a very different sort of young woman.

The Boleyn Sisters
The Royal Court in France
Thomas Boleyn sent his two Boleyn daughters to complete their educations by serving as attendants to the Queen of France in the French royal court, where Thomas had served for a time as the English ambassador. However, the educations received there by the sisters appear to have included some rather special lessons. The reputation of the French court at that time included far worse faults than simply time spent in idleness marked by elegant dressing, dining, and dancing. The sexual activities there went well beyond the expected innocent flirtations or acting out the idealistic tropes of chivalrous and courtly but unconsummated love.

Mary Boleyn in France
Even in a court known throughout Europe for its widespread, frequent, and short-lived licentious affairs, Mary Boleyn had earned a special reputation in France for the number of her sexual encounters

with court nobility, and reputedly with court royalty.[1] Thomas Boleyn seems always to have been ready to use his daughters as tokens in the game of social advancement. So, when he summoned Mary back to England in 1520, he may have done so to arrange an appropriate marriage before her reputation for sexual activity grew to spoil all hopes of finding an acceptable husband.

When Mary returned to England, she became one of the ladies-in-waiting for Queen Catherine of Aragon. Thomas Boleyn was able to arrange for her to marry nobleman William Carey, but this did not impede King Henry. As discussed above, the king noticed Mary at court, and she became the royal mistress for approximately six years.

Anne Boleyn in France

In her turn, the younger Boleyn sister, Anne Boleyn, followed Mary to the French court and likewise earned a reputation for her time there. However, Anne's achievements in France were somewhat different from Mary's. It is not that Anne was immune to some participation in the sexual liaisons that were an expected feature of court service there. (After their eventual marriage, Henry VIII is said to have been amazed – and apparently, somewhat put off – by Anne's knowledge of special sexual techniques and positions.)[2] Anne's early reputation was based more upon other, more laudable personal qualities that she acquired or displayed at the French court.

Anne was renowned for her grace, wit, and refinement. Although small in stature, she moved and danced with elegance. And unlike some of her counterparts at the French court, Anne could converse intelligently in excellent French. She proved so desirable as a social companion that, after she ended one romantic affair and moved on to the next, she often maintained friendly relations with her former lovers.

Anne also paid great attention to her clothes. She often diverged from the prevailing styles to appear in gowns that were designed to emphasise her better physical attributes and disguise some of her less appealing ones. Some of her resulting style innovations, such as a high neckline and extra-long sleeves, were promptly adopted by others at court.

There seems to have been a large measure of agreement in the contemporaneous sources that Anne was not a great beauty according to conventional standards of the time, but that this was more than overcome by her physical grace, intelligence, and ability to attract men. However, any general agreement on her physical attributes stopped there. Descriptions differed wildly based upon the commentator's religion, nationality, and political views.[3] Even her eyes, which many acknowledged were her most outstanding feature, were alternately praised by her supporters as beautiful and expressive, or else denounced by her detractors as instruments of seduction or witchcraft.[4]

There were also disputes over whether she was relatively flat-chested, or if that appearance was simply the result of the design she chose for the bodice of her gowns. As we shall see below in Henry's famous Love Letter XVI to his then mistress Anne, the king seems unquestionably more than satisfied with her bosom.

Anne Returns to England

In 1522, Thomas Boleyn had Anne return to England. He first attempted to arrange a political marriage for her that would resolve the contested Boleyn family claims to the inheritance of the Irish title and Irish lands of Anne's grandfather, the Earl of Ormond – an inheritance also claimed by a cousin, Piers Butler. However, Thomas Boleyn's efforts to negotiate Anne's marriage to Butler's son, James, were not successful. By 1524 or 1525, she became, as Mary Boleyn previously had become, one of the ladies-in-waiting for Queen Catherine.[5]

Anne may have escaped from the proposed political marriage to James Butler, but soon after arriving at court, she began a romantic relationship with a young nobleman, Lord Henry Percy, heir to the Earl of Northumberland, the senior noble family in England. Percy, in training as a member of the household of the king's Lord Chancellor, Cardinal Thomas Wolsey, accompanied his master on frequent visits to the royal palace. These visits afforded Percy the opportunity to meet the ladies of the court. The one he noticed was Anne Boleyn.

It is not clear how far their physical relationship progressed, but at one point Percy and Anne may have privately exchanged pledges of betrothal. In that era, a pledge of betrothal was treated as more than a simple promise to marry. Betrothal essentially initiated the marital relationship, including legitimising a sexual relationship between the betrothed parties before their formal wedding, and prohibiting them from marrying any other parties.[6]

However, Henry VIII had also noticed Anne at court, and the budding romance with Percy was doomed. At the king's direction, Cardinal Wolsey intervened to block the young lovers' plans. Wolsey sent Percy off to enter into an apparently loveless marriage to Mary Talbot, daughter of the Earl of Shrewsbury. Anne remained available.

Marriages of the nobility during that era were often devices to merge two important families of royal supporters, or to elevate social or financial status as a reward to a loyal but minor noble family. Because of the importance of these political consequences, it was the king's prerogative to arrange or approve such marriages. Thus, it is entirely plausible that when Wolsey undertook to intervene in Percy and Anne's relationship at the king's direction, he might not have understood that Henry VIII wanted Anne for himself – only that that the king had other political marriage arrangements in mind for the younger Boleyn daughter.[7]

Even if Wolsey had known or suspected the king's full intent, however, no one could have imagined then that Anne would end up as Henry's queen, rather than just his next mistress, as had been the case with her sister Mary. Therefore, Wolsey could not have expected that he would eventually incur enormous personal cost for following Henry's orders to oppose Anne's romantic desires for Percy. Even as events moved forward, few alarm bells rang for Wolsey. Anne wrote several exceedingly courteous letters to him. However, it appears that in her heart she always remained his enemy. In large measure, the cause of her enmity was his interference with her young love for Percy. Many contemporaneous and modern historians attribute Wolsey's later spectacular reversal of fortunes to Anne's finally having achieved sufficient power to influence Henry so that the king would serve, at least in part reluctantly, as the instrument of her revenge on him.[8]

Henry in Love

With Percy out of the way, even if perhaps not fully out of Anne's heart and mind, Henry VIII was ready to begin his campaign of courting Anne Boleyn. Most early and modern commentators agree that, as this courtship progressed, Henry's passions were aroused by Anne to a far greater extent than by any of his previous mistresses. Indeed, it appears that in his relationship with Anne, Henry experienced, probably for the first time, a significant shift in the dynamics of power and control with one of his lovers.

Henry's Love Letters to Anne

Nothing promotes untrustworthy gossip more than a discreet but illicit romantic relationship, especially when a celebrity is involved. For an episode that happened some five hundred years ago, it would be sensible for us to despair of ever unearthing enough reliable, convincing evidence to help us understand what really happened. That is why it is so astonishing that we have access to a collection of the originals of seventeen intimate, sometimes passionate, love letters handwritten by King Henry VIII to Anne Boleyn during their early courtship years of 1527–1528. Because these original love letters have survived intact, they constitute a unique and invaluable historical treasure, a collection which provides direct insight into Henry's state of mind.[9]

Why Some Letters from Henry to Anne Were Written in French

Henry's early love letters to Anne – all of those currently attributed to 1527 and most that are attributed to early 1528 – were written in French. This represents about half of the total seventeen letters; the remainder are in English.[10] It could be that Henry's choice of French was simply intended to impress, allowing the king to show off his fine education to Anne, who had perfected her French while she was serving in Paris as an attendant to Queen Claude. Or perhaps it was simply that French was then already considered the language of love.

More likely, however, Henry used French in his early letters to Anne in a vain attempt to maintain secrecy about their relationship. In those times, important international diplomatic dispatches were often written in complex cyphers or codes. However, personal privacy for domestic correspondence typically relied upon direct delivery by a trusted messenger. For example, Henry entrusted Anne's brother, George, to deliver Letter XV to her – a letter that happens to complain about how details of the lovers' affair managed to become the subject of instant public gossip throughout London. But in that era, even a king's desire for privacy for his personal correspondence was often frustrated by the multiple levels of necessary servants, secretaries, and messengers. These functionaries all had access to documents while they were being written or delivered, and they were often bribed by political enemies of the monarch, or foreign ambassadors, to make copies or summaries. Since only those in the higher echelons of society would have been educated in a foreign language, Henry's use of French in the early letters to Anne may have been, to some extent, the equivalent of writing to her in a private code.[11]

Why the Letters Survived

If Henry was so insistent on secrecy, how is it that these extremely private letters survived to be published and read by the entire world? As with so many issues regarding the Tudor dynasty, there is no complete answer to this question. What we do know is that these original handwritten letters somehow made their way to the Vatican Library in Rome. Exactly how this happened remains a matter of speculation.

Some of Henry's letters refer to Anne's correspondence, although no originals or copies of Anne's letters responding to Henry have been found. This suggests that Henry or someone else with royal palace access destroyed the letters received from her as a matter of secrecy, or perhaps as a political expedient, or simply out of anger when Anne was eventually executed. But since Henry did not likewise destroy his seventeen letters written to her, we can assume that it was their recipient, Anne, who kept possession of those letters in some secure hiding place, perhaps at the Boleyn family seat at Hever. Since Anne would never have voluntarily given the letters to the Catholic Church – the religious beliefs of the Boleyn family were strongly allied with the new Protestant movement – they must have been discovered and secretly sent to the Vatican by someone else, without Anne's consent.[12]

The rest of the letters' history is well known. They do not portray the king's motivation for seeking an annulment as exemplifying his highest ethical behaviour. Therefore, the immediate English response to the discovery of the letters at the Vatican was to claim that they were Catholic forgeries. Later, however, near the end of the seventeenth century, the Vatican allowed the letters to be examined for authenticity by prominent Protestant bishop and Tudor historian Gilbert Burnet. After examination of the handwriting, Burnet conceded that the letters were authentic and not forgeries.[13]

Thereafter, the Vatican opened the letters to public scrutiny, presumably because they supported the Vatican's view of why Henry had led the English Church out of the Roman Catholic Church to annul his marriage to Catherine of Aragon. At the time of the annulment matter, Henry had repeatedly claimed that he acted from conscience because of God's prohibition against marrying his deceased brother's widow, a sin which was prohibited in Leviticus. However, the Vatican apparently felt that these letters proved that Henry was impelled not by moral principles or religious scruples but by his ignoble lust and passion for Anne. The Vatican hoped that revealing the contents of the letters would make clear to all that Pope Clement VII had been correct in refusing to grant Henry's request for an annulment.

However, if the Vatican thought that revealing the words of the love letters would end the dispute over Henry's motives in taking England out of the Roman Catholic Church, it soon learned otherwise. Despite the general acknowledgement of the authenticity of the letters, some Protestant/Anglican histories of the Great Matter have continued to claim that Henry's main motivation was his concern for the royal succession and the avoidance of civil war, and that his infatuation with Anne Boleyn, as graphically documented in the love letters, served merely as the trigger for his determination to marry that particular woman at that particular time.[14]

At the end of the eighteenth century, Napoleon Bonaparte's victories in Italy forced the pope to grant concessions to France, one of which was to allow France to take 500 manuscripts from the Vatican Library. These included Henry's love letters to Anne Boleyn. In Paris, the Bibliothèque du Roi (now the National Library of France) organised, translated, and numbered these letters, and the results were published. The original letters were later required to be returned to the Vatican after the fall of Napoleon in 1815.[15]

What We Can Learn from Henry's Love Letters

Even a cursory reading of Henry's love letters reveals several repeated themes that were obviously very significant to the king during this early phase of his relationship with Anne Boleyn. These themes include the language and tropes of courtly love; Henry's great pain at even the briefest separations from Anne; his frustration and hurt at Anne's initial unwillingness to commit to him; his longing for full sexual consummation, sometimes expressed in bawdy, explicit language; his reports on his successful hunts, some accompanied by gifts of venison; his concern for Anne's health during the sweating sickness season; and his irritation that details of their arrangements somehow became the topic of widespread gossip in London. Some of Henry's later letters, from 1528, reflect his increased confidence that his affections were reciprocated, and that Anne had committed to be his as soon as they could marry.

Indeed, in his later letters, Henry begins to treat Anne as his partner in managing his Great Matter to obtain the necessary annulment of his marriage to Catherine. He expresses optimism that the upcoming trial, to be held before cardinals Thomas Wolsey and Lorenzo

Campeggio at Blackfriars Hall in London, would swiftly provide that annulment. Anne would soon become his wife and queen. (See Appendix A for a summary of the principal themes in each of Henry's seventeen letters, together with a list of some of the conveniently available editions of the full texts.)[16]

While the letters have been authenticated as having been written by Henry, we must still consider the separate question of their honesty. Did Henry believe the things he wrote, or was he exaggerating the facts to please or persuade Anne? Examining the evidence, it seems likely that, while Henry VIII may have done many things in his public and personal life with the purpose of enhancing his public reputation, he wrote the love letters with the mistaken presumption that they would never be read by anyone other than Anne. Therefore, if the king's letters do contain some measure of insincerity, that would not have been caused by his concern for his public image, but would have been motivated solely by his desire to control the situation and obtain the physical relationship he sought with Anne.

Subsequent scholarship has dealt with the translation of the sixteenth-century French and English wording of the letters into modern English, although, not surprisingly, this has produced several alternative phrasings. A more significant challenge to understanding the love letters has been that not one of them is dated. Over the centuries, scholars have analysed and reanalysed the events described in the letters for clues to support at least approximate dates for the letters.[17] Those efforts allow us today to read the letters in a presumed chronological order. Thanks to this, we can deduce for ourselves the changing temperatures of the parties' respective feelings for each other during the course of this remarkable courtship. Because Anne's side of the correspondence is missing, however, her actions and attitudes over this period can only be inferred from Henry's letters.

Henry in Bed
When Did Henry and Anne Commence Full Sexual Relations?
Over the past five hundred years, historians and the general public have shared a great curiosity as to when Henry's lengthy courtship of Anne Boleyn resulted in commencement of their full sexual relations. There is still no universal agreement on the precise course of the sexual relationship between these lovers from the inception of

their relationship, probably in late 1526, until their purported secret marriage on 25 January 1533.

Nevertheless, certain passages in Henry's love letters can be read to indicate that, at least through the time of the last letter – number XVII, which was written around 8 October 1528 – Anne continued to be successful in refusing to engage in full sexual intercourse with the king before he was free to marry her and make her his queen:

> Letter I (pre-July 1527): ...by absence we are kept a distance from one another, and yet [our love] retains its fervour, at least on my side...
>
> Letter II (pre-July 1527): Consider well, my mistress, that absence from you grieves me sorely, hoping that it is not your will that it should be so; but if I knew for certain that you voluntarily desired it, I could do no other than mourn my ill fortune, and by degrees abate my great folly.
>
> Letter IV (pre-July 1527): ...beseeching you earnestly to let me know expressly your whole mind as to the love between us two. ... But if you please to do the office of a true loyal mistress and friend, and to give up yourself body and heart to me, who will be, and have been, your most loyal servant, (if your rigour does not forbid me) I promise you that ... I will take you for my only mistress, casting off all others besides you out of my thoughts and affections, and serve you only.
>
> Letter IX (15 June 1528): ... seeing my darling is absent, I can do no less than to send her some flesh, representing my name, which is hart flesh for Henry, *prognosticating that hereafter, God willing, you must enjoy some of mine, which He pleased I would were now.* [In James Orchard Halliwell's mid-nineteenth-century transcription of this letter announcing Henry's gift of deer meat from the hunt, Halliwell intentionally omitted the clause shown here in italics, because of its lewdness.[18]]
>
> Letter XVI (July 1528): ...wishing myself (especially an evening) in my sweetheart's arms, whose pretty dukkys [breasts] I trust shortly to cusse [kiss].[19]
>
> Letter VI (16 September 1528): No more to you at this present, mine own darling, for lack of time, but that I would you were in mine arms, or I in yours, for I think it long since I kissed you.[20]

Henry VIII and Anne Boleyn

These and other statements in the love letters, despite some of them being very explicit, have not settled the question of when Henry and Anne initiated full sexual intercourse. This persistent uncertainty will become more understandable if we examine King Henry's personality and style of ruling in the context of his times.

Henry's Personal Style for His Monarchy

Much like some of today's state rulers, Henry VIII was very focused upon the multifaceted image that he and his royal court projected to his subjects and to the other rulers of Europe. Henry was intelligent and unusually well educated, so his palace was much more than a gathering place for the idle nobility. Henry made his royal court into an international centre for the arts. He was an accomplished musician and composer, and regular features of his court included musicians, sometimes imported from Italy, as well as costumed dramatic performances and dances in which guests were expected to join the king and the nobles of his chamber as performers. Henry's court was also studded with visiting philosophers – educators from Cambridge, Oxford, and the Continent, together with learned English and foreign theologians. Many of these visitors admired the king and enjoyed their discussions with him.[21]

There was another quality that Henry also wanted to display to the domestic and international world – *strength*. Certainly, many monarchs entered into wars and forged alliances in part to demonstrate the strength of their kingdoms, but Henry went beyond the image of national strength. He wanted to demonstrate his personal strength and manly vigour. He started out with some natural advantages for this. He had an impressive figure in his early years, being unusually tall at 6 feet 1 or 2 inches tall, and broad-shouldered. And of course, he had started his reign just before he had reached the age of eighteen. Even after almost two decades of marriage to Catherine of Aragon, Henry was still a relatively young man.

Henry became an avid hunter, which we have already noted as one of the themes of his love letters to Anne Boleyn. The king often spent many hours riding long distances on his hunts. During the early part of his reign, however, Henry was probably best known for demonstrating his personal prowess and valour in the jousting tournaments that he organised, and which he frequently won. These jousts were not merely shows of pageantry. The participants faced significant risks, especially Henry VIII, since he competed against the best in every tournament. And his opponents were not expected to go easy on their king. In one joust, Henry suffered a lance strike only a few inches from his eye when he failed to close the visor of his helmet.

In light of his skills and love for jousting, it seems ironic that this sport contributed to the end of King Henry's image as a model of manly athleticism. In 1527, Henry began to suffer from a leg ulcer, from either a sporting injury or varicose veins. His physicians treated the ulcer but could not achieve permanent healing and closure, resulting in episodic cycles of worsening and relief. Then, in a jousting tournament at the beginning of 1536, Henry was knocked off his horse, which fell on top of him. The king remained unconscious for two hours. As a result of being pinned under the armoured horse, the king suffered new injuries to both legs, including the reopening of his leg ulcer. He never fully recovered. The wound continued to drain, with a recurring infection that caused intermittent episodes of foul odour and debilitating pain. Henry was so concerned about the potential public reaction to his incapacity that, for the period immediately following the injury, his condition was kept a state secret.[22]

Due to his injury, Henry was no longer able to exercise with regular hunting and jousting. This inactivity, together with his ever-growing appetite for huge quantities of unhealthy food and drink, cost Henry his former handsome figure. As he finished his life, he became increasingly corpulent. Because he was King of England, we have the record of his physical changes, not written on paper but in steel. His post-accident progress from extra fit to extra large can be measured today because he continually had to have increasingly large suits of armour made for him. He gained an estimated 100 pounds in his later years.[23]

Sexual Expectations in the Sixteenth Century
In the early sixteenth century, a major component of the concept of manliness was sexual prowess. Henry VIII did have several mistresses – Elizabeth Blount, Mary Boleyn, and Anne Boleyn – during this early period, and perhaps others. However, he appears to have had fewer extramarital affairs than would be expected for most European kings of that era. Certainly, at that time the English royal court by no means rivalled the reputation of the French court for the frequency of the monarch's sexual affairs.[24]

The Specifics of Henry and Anne's Relationship

Although there are reports that include sexual vigour as one of Henry's traits, the facts suggest that Henry might have suffered from some sexual performance issues.[25] In the 1536 treason indictments of Anne Boleyn, her brother George, and other alleged adultery partners, Anne is accused of having conversations with George's wife in which she mocked Henry's shortcomings in the bedroom.[26] Henry indeed seems to have waited an inordinately long time to consummate his relationship with Anne. So, exactly what was happening between them during those six years of courtship from 1527 to 1532? The majority view of historians is that during most or all of these years, Anne refused to have full sexual intercourse with Henry until only a few months before they were married.

Despite the king's previous sexual experience with his wife and mistresses, his love letters to Anne indicate more than a typical campaign of sexual conquest. His goal here was not merely a brief pleasurable liaison. Henry displays periods of displeasure, disappointment, and pain. These moods alternate with his romantic expressions of love and bliss. The letters indicate that he was deeply infatuated, perhaps deeply in love, with Anne. If we read between the lines, it appears that Anne was the cause of his oscillating emotions. She seems very much in control of their developing relationship. Her weapon in this uneven battle with her monarch was a single word, but not one that Henry was used to hearing: NO![27]

It is also possible that, at least during some later periods of Henry and Anne's premarital relationship, it could have been Henry who insisted upon sexual abstinence. When his negotiations with Rome appeared to have reached a critical stage, Henry would not have wished to risk spoiling his ability to obtain Pope Clement's annulment of the marriage to Catherine. Henry had claimed that annulment was required because his sense of morality was offended by the theological implications of the Leviticus Prohibitions that barred him from marrying his brother's widow. He would have feared that his lofty arguments would be seriously undercut if the pope became convinced that Henry's petition was motivated by carnal passion rather than the dictates of a royal Christian conscience.[28]

The situation may have been even more complex. Henry's love letters, especially Letter XVI, quoted in part above, indicate that by mid-1528 the two were spending time together in bed, with Anne at least semi-naked. They were engaging in some level of intimate sexual contact, although not necessarily full sexual intercourse.[29]

If we read the love letters closely in the presumed order in which they were written, they seem to be sincere. As previously noted, the letters' early florid, passionate sentiments and the later bawdy, crude attempts at humour may have been intended to present an exaggerated image of masculine virility and desire. Henry could have been attempting to impress Anne, or to persuade her, or simply to project the image of the man he wanted her to believe he was.

Perhaps the real voucher for the truth of Henry's love letters is not to be found in his expressions of love, but rather in the other parts of his correspondence that express his pain, confusion, impatience, and loneliness. Because the king reveals these weaknesses, we can perhaps also credit the sincerity of his expressions of manly desires. Although Henry's love letters may not tell the whole story regarding the couple's feelings and actions during 1527–1528, it is reasonable to read them as indicating that Anne was surprisingly successful in managing the affair by her strategy of withholding full, regular sexual access until she was certain that the king would make her his wife and queen.

Henry's Motivations for Seeking an Annulment
Henry's Desire for Anne Boleyn

We see in Henry's love letters how he ardently pursued his mistress. The letters also indicate how Anne countered Henry's campaign of love by insisting that she must become his wife and queen as a condition for continuing their relationship, and apparently also as a condition for full sexual relations. The six years that elapsed from the beginning of their active relationship until just before their ultimate marriage in January 1533 seem a very long time for an absolute monarch to pursue a mistress. Although Henry was only thirty-six in 1527, life expectancies in that era were relatively short.[30] The king's patience in extending this period of courtship – especially if, as it appears, full and regular sexual access to Anne was also being postponed – appears surprising.

It is commonly asserted that Henry's passion for Anne was a principal motivation – or as some believe, *the* principal motivation – for his seeking to end his marriage to Catherine. To the extent that such attribution of motive is accurate, the almost unimaginably lengthy royal courtship indicates Anne's success in capturing and keeping

Henry's affections, or, in the eyes of her critics, in manipulating him to make her queen. By 1527, as his ardour for Anne was burning brightly, Henry VIII undertook to have the Church annul his current marriage. King or not, Henry would be neither the first nor the last man to undertake a momentous, and ultimately impossible, task in the service of romantic love.

The love letters in their entirety indicate that, while Henry's passion for Anne was not always his sole motivation for seeking the annulment, it was his primary one.[31]

Henry's Concerns for Tudor Dynasty Succession

By 1527, Henry VIII had been married to Catherine of Aragon for eighteen years. She had undergone more than a half-dozen pregnancies, but their only surviving child was Princess Mary, born in 1516. Because Mary was the king's daughter rather than his son, she was not at that time recognised by English tradition as a potential successor to the Crown.[32]

As his first response to this problem, we have previously noted above that King Henry had publicly acknowledged paternity of his illegitimate son, Henry Fitzroy. The king elevated Fitzroy's status with noble honours in an apparent attempt to make him an acceptable successor. However, future public reaction to an illegitimate heir was difficult to predict. It was therefore uncertain whether granting Fitzroy noble titles, marrying him into a noble family, and eventually assigning to him some minor diplomatic duties would be sufficient to assure that the boy could peaceably succeed to the throne.

This risk to the orderly transfer of royal power in the absence of a legitimate male heir presented an especially grave concern to King Henry in 1527. It had been a decade since Catherine's last pregnancy. This suggests that by 1526 she was no longer fertile, or it at least confirms that Henry had by then ceased having marital relations with her, as he acknowledged several times.[33]

Certainly, Catherine was no longer the beauty she had been at the time of their wedding. Age, pregnancies, poor health, and family tragedies had all worked their transformations. There seems general agreement among contemporaneous observers and later historians that Catherine had lost her beauty by her mid-thirties and early forties. As early as 1515, Venetian ambassador Sebastian Giustinian reported that Queen Catherine was 'rather ugly than otherwise'. In

1519, the ambassador diplomatically tried to soften his report with a note of faint praise, observing that Catherine 'was 35 years old, and not handsome, though she had a very beautiful complexion'. At the same time, King Francis I of France was brutally less diplomatic, telling the ambassador, 'He [King Henry] has an old deformed wife, while he himself is young and handsome.'[34]

Later historians agree. In the nineteenth century, John Lingard quotes a 1531 report by Venetian ambassador Ludovico Falier finding Queen Catherine 'low of stature' and 'inclining to corpulency'. Recently, historian David Starkey observed, 'The decline in Catherine's appearance in her thirties was very marked.' And twentieth-century biographer Francis Hackett rather mercilessly describes Catherine's physical appearance at the time when Anne Boleyn caught Henry's eye: 'When Anne appeared at nineteen, he [Henry] was thirty-five, and Catherine was a sick and saddened matron of forty-one. ... Catherine was squat, white and dropsical.' So perhaps Henry simply fell out of love with his older, and in his eyes no longer sufficiently beautiful, wife.[35]

As previously noted, there are also several references in the record to Catherine having some particular but unidentified disease or physical condition that made Henry absolutely unwilling or unable to continue to engage in sexual relations with her. On 6 December 1527, Wolsey wrote a confidential letter instructing Gregory Casale (*Casali*), England's ambassador to the Vatican, to tell Pope Clement 'that there are secret reasons which cannot be trusted to writing, certain diseases in the Queen defying all remedy, for which and other causes the King will never live with her as his wife...'[36]

Almost a year later, Henry, or perhaps Henry and Wolsey together, similarly instructed the king's new agents in Rome 'to provide for everything, as well *propter conceptum odium* [on the principle of abhorrence] as for the danger that may ensue by continuing in the Queen's company, "whose body his Grace for marvellous great and secret respects is utterly resolved and determined never to use"...'[37]

For five hundred years, commentators have disagreed, many of them vehemently, over whether it was Henry VIII's love for Anne Boleyn or his dynastic concerns that drove him to end his two decades of marriage to Catherine. Perhaps this controversy can never be fully resolved so long as some insist on framing the question as an either/or issue. This was a complex matter and Henry VIII was a complex man. It could have been an irresistible conclusion for Henry to realise that terminating his marriage to Catherine could in a single stroke satisfy his strong desires both to advance his relationship with Anne Boleyn as well as to provide a peaceable royal succession for the Tudor dynasty.

Other Possible Motivations for Henry

Ironically, the asserted motivation for Henry's desire to end his marriage to Catherine that has received the least acceptance by both early and modern commentators is the one Henry claimed in his public explanations. Beginning with the first public disclosure of his intention to seek an annulment, Henry's justification was always that it was a necessity of conscience. The king claimed that he had finally realised that his cohabitation with Catherine was absolutely barred by the Leviticus Prohibitions. These moral scruples allegedly arose from Henry's recent study of the Bible, which he variously claimed had either occurred spontaneously as a result of his continuing theological studies, or else had been triggered by comments by the Bishop of Tarbes, Gabriel de Gramont. As discussed below in greater detail, some commentators have suggested that Henry's scruples originated following exhortations by his confessor, John Longland, or on the advice of the his chief advisor, Cardinal Wolsey.

However, even from the beginning of the King's Great Matter, the story of Henry's moral scruples has been derided by many commentators as a fabrication, an acceptable cover story that might convince the pope and the general public. One of the fiercest attacks against Henry's claims of acting from scruples came from theologian, and later cardinal, Reginald Pole. He was the king's cousin, and possessed his own Plantagenet descent from Edward III, which also gave him an indirect potential claim to the throne. Pole had begun his involvement in the King's Great Matter by helping Henry obtain support from French theologians. Pole later reversed his position and publicly announced, in an extraordinarily harsh treatise directed at the king, that Henry's drive for annulment and consequent reforming of the English Church were not motivated by the king's moral conscience, but by his base desire for Anne Boleyn: 'You, a man of your age and with such experience, are miserably burning with passion for the love of a girl.'[38]

Pole's stringent public attack on his cousin Henry appeared in 1536. However, an even clearer challenge to Henry's story of his supposed enlightenment from recent Bible study may be found in the wording of the significantly earlier June 1503 treaty between Spain and England reciting the terms of the marriage contract for the marriage of Prince Henry and Princess Catherine. The treaty expressly requires Ferdinand, Isabella, and Henry VII to obtain a papal dispensation for the impediment of affinity in the first degree between the prospective couple because of Catherine's marriage to Prince Arthur, which had been consummated.[39] It seems very likely that the terms of that treaty were known and understood by Henry VIII in 1509 when, after his father's death, he decided to marry Catherine.

Perhaps the best thing that can be said about Henry's claims of acting from moral scruples is that over time he may have been successful in convincing at least one person that this was his true and valid motivation. As the Great Matter progressed along its tortuous six-year path, it appears that Henry managed to convince himself that his cause was just and the annulment was required by God's law.

Discussion of Henry's several possible principal motivations for getting the annulment should not blind us from recognising that there were several possible secondary benefits that also might have influenced him. If your approach to divining human motivation is to follow the money, then you should note that very major financial benefits ultimately accrued to Henry from his pursuit of the annulment. The king's dispute with Rome concerning his marriage was resolved by the monarchy obtaining full control over the wealth of the Catholic Church in England.

This early step in reforming the English Church was relatively unique compared to the general Protestant Reformation that was then unfolding in some continental European nations. In England, the initial issue was not so much a matter of theology but of domestic control and unification of Church and State. Thus, among the first practical steps taken by Henry upon making himself the head of the English Church was the closure of many monasteries and churches of the Roman Catholic Church in England. He gained much from the resulting confiscation of immensely valuable Church lands, buildings, gold, silver, jewels, and funds.

The boldest aspect of this confiscation was that much of the wealth seized from the Roman Catholic Church went directly to King Henry in his individual royal capacity, not to the newly reformed English Church in its corporate capacity. Henry's rationale for obtaining these funds personally was that the principal function of these charitable institutions was providing hospitals, lodgings, meals, and other support for the poor. Since this type of charity was a royal obligation of state, Henry insisted that he must receive the funds and properties to support new royal charities for the poor.[40]

As real and valuable as these financial benefits were, however, it is difficult to conclude that Henry had the political shrewdness to have acted from the very beginning with design to enjoy the financial consequences that ultimately eventuated from his marital dispute. If this goal later did become a part of his motivations in the Great Matter, it is more likely that Henry had been schooled by the lessons he learned during the course of his dispute with Rome. Henry observed Pope Clement's acquiescence in the surrender of Church property in the German lands resulting from the efforts of Emperor Charles to forestall the Lutheran Reformation in the Hapsburg territories.[41]

Thus, it turns out that there was no shortage of possible motives for the king to seek the annulment. That the task required six years was not due to any weakness in Henry's motivation but to the fierce political and theological opposition that awaited the unsuspecting king.

PART III

HENRY'S QUEST FOR AN ANNULMENT

5

HENRY'S BIBLICAL ARGUMENTS FOR AN ANNULMENT

Catholic Jurisdiction over Divorce and Annulment
Regardless of the exact mix of Henry's motivations for wanting to end his marriage to Catherine, the dissolution of his marriage would prove exceedingly difficult to achieve; indeed, in the manner initially envisioned by Henry it would ultimately be impossible. The English Church was Catholic, and Henry VIII was a devout, practising Catholic. At that time, even for the King of England, only one recognised path to marital dissolution existed. All marriages in England were under the exclusive jurisdiction of the Roman Catholic Church. Henry would have to seek the termination of his marriage by obtaining a formal Church decree of *annulment*.

The terms 'divorce' and 'annulment' describe two technically distinct legal actions used by the Church to terminate a marriage. Divorce is a legal termination of an initially valid marriage because of some particular situations that arose or were disclosed after the wedding. In the sixteenth century, the Catholic Church generally did not permit divorce except for some limited exceptions for post-wedding developments such as insanity, impotence, or inability to consummate.[1]

But the Church did recognise another group of highly technical procedures for dissolution of an apparently existing marriage that had never been valid – even if the marriage had continued for long time or had produced children. The primary route to a Church-sanctioned dissolution of such an invalid marriage was to obtain a decree of annulment from the Church under Catholic canon law. The term 'canon law' refers to the group of religious laws that govern members of a religion. For Catholicism, these are embodied in the religious law codes and procedures adopted under the authority of the pope and his delegates.

A decree of annulment would determine that there had been some pre-existing, serious impediment to the legality of the original marriage. If the original marriage was found to have been illegal and therefore void, the parties had never actually been married. Thus, an annulment recognised that each party continued to have the status of an unmarried person, including the ability to enter into marriage with another person. (See Appendix B for additional details about the canon law governing annulments at the time of Henry's marriage to Catherine of Aragon.)

By the sixteenth century, annulments were not uncommon, at least for royalty and nobility who had the wealth to pursue such a remedy. The upper classes often had the influence and power to induce a favourable ruling by the Church. It should therefore be no surprise to us that Henry VIII and his advisors would have been confident that the Catholic Church would in due course grant the annulment he sought. What may be surprising to us, however, as it seems it was to King Henry, is that the combination of personal and political circumstances at that particular point in time would lead to a seemingly unbreakable pattern: the powerful monarch of England would suffer repeated frustration and failure with each new strategy, argument, and manipulation that he and his supporters attempted against Rome. Throughout what would become Henry's fruitless six-year quest for annulment from the Church, Pope Clement VII would deftly parry each new royal strategy with a series of stubborn, clever counter-moves. Clement artfully combined tactics of debate, delegation, and delay to serve what was his natural tendency of indecisiveness.

We have noted that, from the outset, Henry insisted that his representatives use the name 'the King's Great Matter' when referring to his pursuit of an annulment. This was the king's futile attempt to keep the matter secret from his subjects, who seemed to have adored Catherine from the time of her arrival in England a quarter of a century earlier. This hope for secrecy would be only the first of many unfulfilled expectations held by Henry in the annulment matter. Despite the king's attempts at privacy, his Great Matter promptly became a notorious topic of sordid gossip throughout western Europe. All seemed to be watching as what began as a technical legal matter turned into a furious dispute between the Catholic King Henry VIII and Pope Clement VII over an elusive issue of Catholic law.[2]

Although Henry obviously had sufficient wealth, power, and influence to expect that the Church would grant his annulment, he still had to be careful how he publicly expressed his reasons for wanting to terminate his marriage to Catherine. Henry's actions must not lead to domestic civil unrest. Queen Catherine continued to be very popular with Henry's English subjects. The marriage had continued for almost two decades, and – unlike Henry – the people appreciated how Catherine had struggled through many tragic pregnancies in her attempt to provide England with heirs to its throne. In addition, although Catherine was a daughter of the Spanish royal family and an aunt of the Holy Roman Emperor, she had never intrigued with foreign powers to weaken England. Catherine had earned the people's affection and loyalty by demonstrating her loyalty to England. Henry therefore needed to express to his subjects a motive that would justify, or even require, ending the marriage despite Catherine's opposition.[3]

Moreover, Henry's subjects weren't the only ones who had to be shown good reasons for the annulment. The Protestant Reformation was gaining strength throughout Europe in large part due to Martin Luther's complaints that the Catholic Church prized money over morality. Before granting Henry's annulment, Pope Clement VII would need to be convinced that he could do so without giving the world further reason to believe that the Church valued financial and military support from someone like Henry more than it valued the sanctity of marriage.

Henry's Basic Public Argument: The Leviticus Prohibitions
As previously mentioned, from the beginning of his active pursuit of the annulment in 1527, the king adopted a consistent and superficially respectable public position claiming that his principal motivation was a matter of obedience to God's law. Henry insisted that, through his careful recent examination of the Bible, he had reluctantly concluded

that his conscience could not allow him to continue in a marriage that he was now convinced was illegal and void. His purported marriage to the widow of his deceased brother, Arthur, violated the divine laws expressed in the Leviticus Prohibitions.

> Lev. 18:16: Thou shalt not uncover the nakedness of thy brother's wife: because it is the nakedness of thy brother.
> Lev. 20:21: He that marrieth his brother's wife, doth an unlawful thing: he hath uncovered his brother's nakedness. They shall be without children.[4]

At least at the beginning, the king's reliance upon the Leviticus Prohibitions seemed to be a very clever strategy. His argument was simple enough to be understood by the English commoners and serious enough so that it could not be ignored out of hand by Pope Clement. It also helped that the pope would not have to get into awkward issues such as whether Henry's petition was motivated by dynastic ambitions or lust for his mistress. Instead, Henry could claim that his actions were dictated by his moral scruples that did not permit him to ignore the clear law of God. Leviticus expressly prohibits a man from marrying – more specifically, from engaging in sexual intercourse with – his brother's wife. The Bible refers to this act euphemistically as 'uncovering [her] nakedness'.

King Henry properly asserted that this biblical prohibition barred marriage to the widow of a deceased brother, and not just to the current wife of a living brother. This was the prevailing interpretation under the law of the Catholic Church at that time and continues as such today.[5]

What Was the Source of Henry's Doubts as to whether His Marriage Was Barred by Leviticus?
From the start of the Great Matter, Henry's claim as to his motivation to seek an annulment was that he had recently become concerned about the legality of his marriage to Catherine due to his studying Leviticus. Initially, this claim was not made by Henry himself, but through Cardinal Wolsey, his Lord Chancellor and closest advisor. At the close of 1527, Wolsey sent several detailed instructions to Gregory Casale, England's ambassador to the Vatican, on how the matter should be privately presented to Pope Clement. Wolsey

explained that Henry's scruples arose as a result of his study of the Bible:

> I have told you already how the King, partly by his assiduous study and learning, and partly by conference with theologians, has found his conscience somewhat burthened with his present marriage ... [5 December 1527]
>
> You shall represent to him [Clement] how much this affair concerns the King's conscience, the prosperity of his kingdom, and the security of his succession. [6 December 1527][6]

Similarly, the English ambassadors to the Holy Roman Emperor Charles V were instructed at that time to relate the following to the emperor, referring to the specific punishment for violation of Lev. 18:16 that is expressed in Lev. 20:21:

> ... that whereas the King for some years past had noticed in reading the Bible the severe penalty inflicted by God on those who married the relicts [widows] of their brothers, he began to be troubled in his conscience, and to regard the sudden deaths of his male children as a Divine judgment.[7]

Even if the stories about Henry's conscience were true, the question would remain: did the king's troubled conscience arise from his recent Bible study, or were those doubts first suggested to him by others? The historical record is not definitive.

The picture that Henry attempted to paint – a loving husband's contentment in a two-decade marriage interrupted by theological scruples that had been awakened by recent Bible studies – is difficult to believe. The theological issue concerning the incest laws of Leviticus was a central element of Pope Julius's dispensation for Henry and Catherine's marriage, which took place when he was eighteen years old and well acquainted with theological issues. It is unlikely that it would take him another eighteen years to feel the first pangs of conscience about the validity of his marriage under Leviticus. [8]

Over the centuries, Thomas Wolsey has evoked a range of praise and blame for his part in the Great Matter. It is possible that, as some have asserted, Wolsey could have been the source of Henry's initial and basic theological argument. As the king's principal advisor, Wolsey had both ready access to Henry, together with the ability to convince him that claiming a troubled conscience was the best public justification for his insistence on ending his marriage. Or, Wolsey could have engineered this suggestion indirectly, perhaps by having Henry's personal confessor, John Longland, plant the seeds of doubt while ministering to the king.[9]

We know that Catherine accused Wolsey of having been the source of Henry's theological conviction that their marriage was not lawful. She claimed that Wolsey had been motivated by anger against her for her previous accusations that he had abused his position of influence over the king in an attempt by him to usurp royal powers. In addition, she asserted that Wolsey was acting from personal bitterness over the role played by Catherine's nephew, Holy Roman Emperor Charles V, in frustrating Wolsey's previous attempt to be named pope.[10]

In analysing who might have first devised the king's argument from Leviticus, we must in fairness acknowledge that Henry VIII was intelligent and well educated, including in matters of theology. It is at least possible that, regardless of his actual beliefs, King Henry by himself initially came up with using theological grounds for challenging the validity of his marriage.[11]

All that we know for certain is that the king's moral scruples over the Leviticus Prohibitions were consistently asserted by and on behalf of Henry throughout his six-year quest for the annulment, although with some variations in some secondary details.[12] It is probable that Henry and Wolsey together, or perhaps Henry alone, came up with this rationale as a basis for Henry's petition for an annulment.

Of course, Henry's unwavering public reliance upon the Leviticus Prohibitions to justify the annulment does not prove that he was truly as troubled by the Bible as he claimed to be. His position could have demonstrated more rationalisation than motivation. Henry may have urged the argument based upon the Leviticus Prohibitions merely because that was the rationale most likely to induce Pope Clement to annul the marriage.

Previous Dispensation of Leviticus by the Bull of Pope Julius II
The Church recognised several specific grounds for annulment, including *lack of consummation* due to illness, physical abnormalities,

or the husband's impotence; a somewhat flexible requirement of *public honesty*, the appearance of decency and morality in the marriage; *consanguinity*, where the parties were related too closely by blood; and *affinity*, where the parties were related too closely through prior marriages between their families. Henry's arguments based upon the Leviticus Prohibitions addressed the last category, affinity – the rule that certain in-law relationships between a prospective bride and groom arising from prior family marriages prohibited the proposed marriage because it would be incestuous.

But before Henry could argue the theological merits of his assertion that his marriage to his sister-in-law Catherine had always been impermissible under the rules concerning affinity, he first had to get around what turned out to have been an extremely damaging procedural step taken before his marriage to Catherine. As previously mentioned, royal and noble families often had histories of ancestral intermarriages. It was therefore common, before most aristocratic marriages were begun, to obtain a Church decree of dispensation excusing the parties from what might otherwise be an *impediment* (violation of a prohibition) under the incest rules governing affinity or consanguinity.

Soon after Arthur's death, Henry VII and Ferdinand II had obtained from Pope Julius II exactly such a decree of dispensation, in a formal papal document called a Bull, so named because of the lead seal – *bulla* – used by the pope for such special documents. In Julius's Bull, dated 26 December 1503, the pope granted dispensation from the impediment of affinity incest for the prospective marriage between Henry and Catherine. Any potential moral objections concerning violation of the Leviticus Prohibitions should have been resolved by that papal dispensation more than five years before the young widow Catherine married her brother-in-law.[13] Now, after almost two decades of Henry's marriage in reliance upon that dispensation, what more could Henry VIII say in support of his claim for annulment? The answer to that question is that Henry could – and did – have much more to say. Six years more, in fact.

Henry's Arguments against Julius's Bull of Dispensation

In 1527, trying to convince the reigning pope, Clement VII, to overturn Pope Julius's 1503 dispensation was not, on its face, an impossible task for Henry. Pope Clement had the papal authority to reverse the earlier pope's ruling, since Julius's dispensation was not subject to the Catholic doctrine of Papal Infallibility, which applied only in rare cases when a pope intended to declare permanent, universal Catholic doctrine.[14]

However, although Pope Clement technically had the power to reverse Julius's dispensation, he understandably had reservations about the institutional propriety of failing to give deference to a recent public ruling by a predecessor pope. If Henry hoped to terminate his marriage to Catherine quickly, he had to find arguments against Julius's dispensation that were persuasive enough to overcome Clement's widely recognised tendency to procrastinate in order to avoid having to make any controversial decision.[15]

Henry and his advocates started out with a lengthy list of technical objections to the form and wording of Pope Julius's ruling. The king claimed that Julius's Bull failed to include certain required formal language; that it misstated facts, such as an alleged risk of war between Spain and England; that two of the petitioning parties, Queen Isabella of Spain and King Henry VII of England, had died before Henry's marriage; and that Henry had been a minor at the time of the Bull.

But although these technical objections would occasionally resurface during the years of Henry's dispute with Clement, they were never sufficiently weighty to move the pope to take action. Even considered in combination, Henry's legal quibbles could not be expected to push Pope Clement to take the very grave step of overturning a recent papal ruling, especially since Henry's Great Matter had become so closely followed throughout the Catholic and Protestant worlds.[16]

Instead, Clement made a clever counter to Henry's arguments about the technical irregularities in Julius's dispensation. If Henry were sincerely troubled by deficiencies in the wording of Julius's Bull, Clement offered to satisfy the king's moral scruples on these points by issuing a new Bull that would retroactively amend and correct any technical shortcomings of the prior dispensation.[17]

In reality, Clement's cure would have secured the opposite of what Henry was truly pursuing. Henry wanted his marriage to Catherine to be annulled, not legitimised. To achieve his goal, he needed a stronger, more substantive argument. He was, after all, disputing with the pope and the Church. He needed a theological contention that did not get bogged down in the petty details of a technical legal attack on Julius's factual findings and wording.

Henry's Natural Law Arguments

Henry promptly found his new core argument. As his Great Matter continued, he increasingly shifted the emphasis of his position away from the technical complaints so that he could focus upon the theological basis for his petition. He asserted that the Leviticus Prohibitions against marriage between persons who were too closely related, in his case by affinity, were not mere enactments of *positive law* – man-made rules that could be amended or revoked in the courts. The Leviticus laws against incest were expressions of *natural law* – universal and timeless moral law sourced in the divine, and thus binding upon all humanity forever.

The prohibitions against violations of natural law were of a higher order than other biblical commandments. Natural laws, which Henry now claimed included the Leviticus Prohibitions against incest, were universal rules of God that existed independently of recognition, acceptance, or interpretation by mankind. If the Leviticus Prohibitions were recitations of natural law, they could not be modified by positive law rulings such as a pope's attempt to grant dispensations.[18]

For more than a thousand years before Henry made these arguments, the Catholic Church had debated whether the Leviticus Prohibitions were expressions of natural law or positive law. Henry claimed that the early Church Fathers and subsequent popes had agreed that the biblical rules against incest were statements of natural law. But while papal acceptance of the natural law doctrine may have reflected a common Catholic position, the issue was far from settled.

For example, at the end of the sixth century, Pope Gregory I (Saint Gregory the Great, r. 590–604) ruled that he could to some extent excuse new converts to Christianity for some past violations of the Leviticus Prohibitions, specifically including having married a deceased brother's widow. This position was incompatible with the Leviticus Prohibitions having the force of universal, natural law. Gregory was saying that the Church had the power to modify, interpret, and excuse some affinity incest violations. Pope Gregory's ruling is analysed in further detail below in Chapter 8.

Even worse for Henry, the practice of papal dispensation of serious impediments to marriage was not merely ancient or infrequent.

Several of the recent medieval popes had issued dispensations in prominent cases sustaining Gregory's position that a pope could excuse even clear violations of the Leviticus Prohibitions.

However, papal responses to requests for such dispensations had not been consistent. Some conservative popes and theologians had strongly insisted that Leviticus incest prohibitions indeed constituted natural law and could not be dispensed. Therefore, despite lack of uniformity in prior papal dispensation rulings, Henry could make at least a respectable argument that the Leviticus Prohibitions were expressions of natural law and could not be dispensed by any pope.

In 1527, Henry and his advisors might have concluded that a single, simple argument regarding natural law could be more easily understood by Henry's subjects than offering them a confusing menu of legal arguments. Especially in light of widespread English dissatisfaction with the ecclesiastical authority of Rome, it might be enough for Henry to appeal to the people of his realm by simply pointing out that God had amply provided proof that Henry's marriage to Catherine constituted affinity incest as a matter of divine, natural law. Leviticus 20:21 recited God's specific punishment for marrying a brother's widow – that they shall be childless – and none of Henry's male children had survived beyond two months. In Henry's eyes, the whole point of a king having children was to provide an acceptable male heir to the throne. The utility of English royal daughters in that era was presumed to be limited to becoming objects of political marriages. Seen in this light, the failures of so many of Catherine's pregnancies, and especially her failure to produce a surviving male heir, might be seen by Henry to confirm that he and Catherine had been living in sin.[19]

The king and his supporters may also have believed that a natural law argument would be simpler to express to Clement in their attempt to keep the pontiff focused on reaching a decision. But this would have been a miscalculation. Clement neatly sidestepped this challenge by claiming that he had to rely upon his cardinals on such weighty issues because he was ignorant of the canon law.[20]

Moreover, the threats and pressures of the growing Protestant Reformation had already fully focused Clement upon his awesome responsibility to defend and preserve the Catholic Church at this critical time. Henry was asking Clement to do more than reverse a ruling by a particular prior pope in a particular case. Henry was asking Clement to adopt a natural law theory that would bar all future popes from dispensing marriage impediments in any Leviticus incest matter. It is difficult to imagine Pope Clement, who shrank from reaching decisions on even mildly controversial matters, agreeing to declare a permanent limitation on a significant dispensation power of the papacy.[21]

The Pope's Counter-argument from Deuteronomy

Fortunately for Pope Clement, he did not have to make any sophisticated analysis of the Catholic canon law position on natural law to enable him to oppose King Henry's arguments against Julius's Bull. Clement had a simpler counter-argument. Henry was asserting that Pope Julius's dispensation was void because the affinity incest rules of Leviticus were absolute, and therefore beyond the power of any pope to dispense. However, Clement could simply point out that Henry's position must first overcome a very basic but extremely difficult problem for the king: God's Bible did not end with its third book, the Book of Leviticus.

The fifth book of the Bible, the Book of Deuteronomy, deals specifically with the Levitical incest situation presented by Henry's marriage to Catherine – a man's marriage to the widow of his deceased brother. This is called *levirate* marriage, from the Hebrew *levir*, brother-in-law. Deuteronomy 25:5–10 not only expressly permits levirate marriage, but declares it an obligation of the surviving brother in certain circumstances.

> Deut. 25:5: When brethren dwell together, and one of them dieth without children, the wife of the deceased shall not marry to another: but his brother shall take her, and raise up seed for his brother:
> Deut. 25:6: And the first son he shall have of her he shall call by his [*the deceased* brother's] name, that his name be not abolished out of Israel.
> Deut. 25:7: But if he will not take his brother's wife, who by law belongeth to him, the woman shall go to the gate of the city, and call upon the ancients, and say: My husband's brother refuseth to raise up his brother's name in Israel: and will not take me to wife.

Deut. 25:8: And they shall cause him to be sent for forthwith, and shall ask him. If he answer: I will not take her to wife:
Deut. 25:9: The woman shall come to him before the ancients, and shall take off his shoe from his foot, and spit in his face, and say: So shall it be done to the man that will not build up his brother's house:
Deut. 25:10: And his name shall be called in Israel, the house of the unshod.[22]

The general rule in Deuteronomy is that if a brother dies without having had children, his surviving brother must marry the widow to 'raise up seed' (create descendants) for the deceased brother, so that the name and family line of the brother who died without children will not be extinguished.

However, this general law carries with it its own escape clause. The surviving brother is given the right to refuse to marry his widowed sister-in-law, provided they undergo a specific public ceremony. This ceremony, called *halitzah*, includes her removing his sandal, an action by which she publicly shames him for his refusal to fulfil the obligation to marry her.

While the Catholic Church had adopted much of the Hebrew Bible as the Christian Old Testament, the Church went on to determine which biblical provisions it regarded as binding upon Catholics, and which provisions were merely historical vestiges of specific Jewish tribal observances that no longer applied to Christians. Henry and his supporters argued that, while the Church had adopted and even expanded upon the Leviticus Prohibitions, Catholics had never considered themselves bound by the Deuteronomy obligations of levirate marriage. Henry's opponents countered by pointing to some Church precedents for recognising levirate marriage as an exception to Leviticus.[23]

Clement and his supporters did not have to insist that the Deuteronomy obligations required Henry to marry Catherine. Henry's opponents needed only to argue that the mere existence of the levirate marriage provisions in Deuteronomy made it impossible for Henry to argue that the Leviticus Provisions were natural law that could not be modified by the pope. In Deuteronomy, God's own Bible contained a pointed modification to the affinity incest rules.

This Leviticus/Deuteronomy clash set the stage for the later, final dispute when Henry and Clement returned to arguing over these apparently inconsistent provisions of the Hebrew Bible. Later, in Part IV, below, we will examine in detail how the Leviticus/Deuteronomy dispute presented such a challenge to both parties that it drove this Catholic King of England and, to a much lesser extent, this pope of the entire Roman Catholic world to seek help from the rabbis of Italy to support their respective positions.

6

HENRY'S LEGAL STRATEGIES

The struggle between King Henry VIII and Pope Clement over Henry's request for an annulment would be interesting enough if it had merely been an intense debate over interpreting the Bible. During 1527 and continuing for the following five or six years, however, even the parties and their advisors came to understand – as modern historians now likewise understand – that the argument was driven by more than issues of biblical interpretation. Those issues were the surface manifestations of the critical underlying controversy between Henry and Clement. It was this dispute that would determine the balance of political power between the developing new English monarchy and the long-established authority of the pope. Indeed, calculating the balance of power presents an even more complex challenge if we add into the equation the other two major participating western powers, King Francis I of France and the Holy Roman Emperor Charles V.

As the overall situation rapidly evolved, Henry and his advisors had to develop a series of legal strategies in their attempt to overcome Clement's initial reluctance to grant the annulment. These legal strategies began simply but grew in complexity and audacity over time. Unfortunately for the English, each new legal manoeuvre by Henry was somehow either parried by the wily pope or frustrated by the changing fortunes of unstable political developments in western Europe.

Henry's First Legal Strategy: Have Cardinal Wolsey Grant the Annulment as the Pope's Legate in England

The king began with the aim of resolving his Great Matter swiftly and secretly. In 1527, Henry's first strategy – which presumably was planned by Cardinal Wolsey to satisfy what he finally understood to be the king's determination to end his marriage – was to take advantage of Wolsey's unique position in the Church. Ordinarily, the highest-ranking cleric of the Catholic Church in England would be the Archbishop of Canterbury. That position had been held for almost twenty-five years by William Warham, then aged seventy-seven. In 1515, however, Thomas Wolsey, Henry's new Lord Chancellor, was made a cardinal, thereby outranking Archbishop Warham in the ecclesiastical hierarchy.

Moreover, by the time of the Great Matter, Cardinal Wolsey's most significant status in the Catholic Church was not just that he was a cardinal, but that he had also previously been appointed by a series of popes as the papal legate for England.[1] In that special capacity, Wolsey had specific authority to serve as the pope's personal representative in England to decide important ecclesiastical matters, including presiding over and deciding trials regarding marital impediments. Wolsey therefore tried to exercise his special jurisdiction to terminate Henry's marriage promptly and privately. On 17 May 1527, Wolsey convened a secret ecclesiastical trial at his residence in Westminster to hear the evidence and decide the question of whether Henry and Catherine were validly married according to canon law. Although Henry personally appeared at the trial, Catherine did not attend. It appears that she was not made directly aware of the trial for some time, at least until after it had begun without her.

Following the established legal procedure for such cases, the Westminster trial was initiated by Wolsey to investigate and rule upon what he claimed was an anonymous accusation that Henry might be cohabiting with Catherine outside of a legal marriage relationship. Procedurally, therefore, Henry was the accused defendant, not the petitioner.

A canon lawyer for the court, Dr Richard Wolman, serving as the equivalent of a prosecuting attorney, formally detailed the arguments against the validity of the marriage. Because of the reversed procedure, these positions were actually Henry's arguments for the annulment. Wolman's accusations included attacking the effectiveness of Pope Julius's Bull of dispensation because of its asserted misstatements of fact and various technical omissions. Wolman also claimed that affinity incest was a violation of unmodifiable natural law which was therefore not subject to papal dispensation.[2]

This should have been enough for Wolsey to be, or appear to be, convinced, and declare the marriage void. Instead, in a sudden surprise move, Wolsey suspended the trial on 31 May 1527, asserting that the complex and important theological issues that had been raised required consultation with other leaders of the clergy in England.[3]

It appears that Wolsey's abrupt closing of the trial before announcing a judgment was not simply due to theological uncertainties, but was the direct result of political wars then raging on the Italian peninsula. The nation of Italy did not yet exist. The land was divided into many city-states, which offered inviting targets for conquest by foreign armies. The land of Italy had therefore become, literally, a battleground between the western world's two most powerful monarchs. On one side was the Holy Roman Emperor Charles V leading armies of the Hapsburg alliance, which included Spain. This imperial army and its allies were opposed by King Francis I of France, who led the principal army fighting for the League of Cognac. The League also included the armies of some of the stronger Italian city-states such as Venice, Milan, and Florence, and was assisted by non-military pledges of financial contributions from England and the Vatican.

The armies of these opposing alliances also included mercenary troops. Unfortunately, Charles appears to have forgotten that mercenary armies do not fight for national honour or political principles, but simply for money and booty. When Charles neglected to pay his army, some of his troops mutinied and determined to obtain their wages by looting the riches of Rome.

In the last few days of May 1527, London finally received the news of the Sack of Rome that had occurred on the 6th at the hands of mutinous imperial soldiers. According to the report, which by then was three weeks out of date, Pope Clement had to flee his Vatican residence and took refuge with his cardinals in the nearby Castel Sant'Angelo, surrounded and besieged by Charles's troops.

Charles V was the nephew of Catherine of Aragon. Having Pope Clement under the physical control of the queen's close relative and natural ally changed the entire outlook for Henry's Great Matter. The quick and easy solution expected at Westminster had suddenly evaporated. It was this that had impelled Wolsey to abruptly adjourn the Westminster trial on 31 May 1527 without reaching judgment.[4]

Henry's Second Legal Strategy: Have Cardinal Wolsey Appointed as Deputy Pope with the Power to Decide the Annulment Petition

An agile and crafty international diplomat, Wolsey promptly found within the military debacle in Rome the seeds of a new strategy for Henry. So long as the war with the emperor deprived Clement of his personal freedom, the Church would need someone to wield the pope's authority throughout the rest of the Catholic world. Wolsey already served in a similar but geographically limited role as the pope's legate in England, and he had also been a principal contender to become pope in 1523 when Clement was elected instead at the end of a lengthy and highly political conclave. Wolsey could therefor reasonably conclude that he was the most likely cardinal to become the captive Pope Clement's emergency deputy for administration of the Catholic Church outside of Italy. Wolsey immediately started implementing the political steps needed to secure that appointment. If Clement were to cede all papal authority to Wolsey during the Italian war emergency, the cardinal would be able to grant Henry's petition for annulment quickly, without Clement having an opportunity to participate in the decision.

However, before Wolsey could obtain significant political support among the other cardinals in his pursuit of becoming Clement's deputy pope, the political situation in Italy changed again. Charles V concluded that it could be politically unwise to continue to keep Clement a virtual prisoner in Rome, and so permitted him to escape from the Castel Sant'Angelo and flee to the old papal palace in Orvieto, in central Italy. The emperor allowed Clement and many of his administrative cardinals to reside there and to continue performing most of their official duties. This arrangement did not fully free the pope from the emperor's influence or the implicit threat from his military forces, but as a first step it was sufficient to quickly resolve the emergency for the Church. The political strategy for obtaining the annulment by having Wolsey designated as the pope's emergency deputy had failed almost before it could begin.[5]

Henry's Third Legal Strategy: Use Henry's Importance to the Church to Influence Clement to Grant the Annulment

The relationships among the various parties in the war against Emperor Charles in Italy were complex and often in a state of flux.

Alliances were frequently broken. Parties switched sides. Troops sometimes refused to fight, changed loyalties, or attacked or retreated without permission from their military leaders. Clement, lacking an army of his own, was especially sensitive to the shifting fortunes of the war. He depended entirely upon the military efforts of others. This situation significantly complicated Henry's next strategy for obtaining the annulment.

Now that Clement had fallen under the influence of Charles, due to the emperor's actual or threatened military control of Rome and Orvieto, Henry and Wolsey had to face the enormous problem presented by the family loyalty Charles felt towards his aunt Catherine. England's only hope was to try to keep the relationship between Clement and Charles on something of a middle course. The imperial-papal relationship must not totally deteriorate to the point of Charles threatening or using physical force or captivity to make Clement refuse to grant the annulment, but neither should that relationship be allowed to improve so much that Clement would voluntarily side with Charles against Henry.[6]

Henry and Wolsey therefore agreed upon a third legal strategy to obtain an annulment from Clement despite the influence of the emperor. They would craft a direct petition to Clement requesting the annulment, using some of the arguments raised in the Westminster trial. But first Wolsey would go to France to try to negotiate with King Francis I in this matter. Although France was England's historic enemy, the two nations were now formally allied with the Vatican in the League of Cognac. Moreover, the French possessed something that England would greatly need if Henry's petition had a chance of being favourably received by the pope. France had several cardinals at the Vatican who were very influential with the pope, and who also were very responsive to instruction from King Francis. Henry sent Wolsey to France to negotiate for the crucial support of King Francis and his Vatican cardinals in the annulment matter.

The Personal Risks to Wolsey

So focussed was Wolsey on trying to develop a new relationship between Henry and Francis that he failed to realise he was making a huge personal mistake. Wolsey was taking for granted his own position of exclusive and enduring political influence over his king. By late 1527, however, Henry's relationship with Anne Boleyn had progressed. Henry now treated her as his principal partner in planning how to obtain the annulment so that they could marry. Moreover, Anne had developed direct relationships with some members of the king's inner circle who could envision their own advancement if Anne continued to grow in political influence – but only if Wolsey could be dislodged from his powerful role as the shadow king of England.

Thus, while Wolsey was in France, Anne Boleyn took advantage of his absence to consolidate and wield her ever-increasing influence over Henry. Her initial project was to eliminate Wolsey's power over the king. Anne apparently convinced Henry that they had no further need to rely upon Wolsey's position as cardinal and papal legate in the Church. They also should no longer require Wolsey's diplomatic contacts, international intelligence operatives and personal negotiating skills as Lord Chancellor of England. Anne and Henry believed that they could prepare the appropriate documents and convince Clement to sign them. Whatever technical assistance the king and his queen-to-be might need could instead be furnished by the faction of influential nobles who were ready to support Anne.

If she could accomplish this change, Anne would not only eliminate the chief rival for her influence and power over the king, but she would also revenge what she still saw as Wolsey's interference in her previous love relationship with Henry Percy. By getting in the middle of this classic war between Catherine the wife and Anne the mistress, poor Wolsey had somehow managed to earn the distrust, animosity, and long-smouldering hatred of both women.

Secretary Knight's Mission
As a result of Anne's scheme, without consulting or advising Wolsey, who was still on his mission in France, Henry sent his personal secretary William Knight to deliver a petition for annulment directly to the pope.[7]

By the time Knight reached Italy in early December 1527, Charles had allowed Clement to leave Rome, so Knight followed the pope to Orvieto to present Henry's petition. There Knight would eventually learn that Clement could not ignore the implicit threat to the Vatican and to the pope himself caused by the imperial army's continued controlling presence in much of Italy. Clement would neither immediately grant Henry's request nor refuse it outright.

The pope insisted that his cardinals must first revise Henry's draft language into an acceptable form. The resulting document, however, was more than simply altered in its technical language. It was trickier – a document that superficially appeared positive, but which in fact would not deliver the annulment that Henry sought. Clement signed the revised document on 23 December 1527. Secretary Knight failed to understand that the papal Bull he triumphantly brought back to England at the beginning of 1528 was not what he had been sent to acquire. Knight had obtained only a dispensation for Henry and Anne to marry *upon the condition* that Henry's marriage to Catherine was determined to be unlawful.[8]

The Failure of Knight's Dispensation

The revisions made to the draft dispensation that Knight had brought to Rome were justified by the pope and his cardinals as being mere matters of form. Henry, Anne, and Knight accepted the pope's explanation at face value. If they had possessed more direct experience in dealing with the Vatican, Knight and his masters might have recognised the pope's explanation as just a diplomatically worded excuse to obscure Clement's favourite strategy for disputes: procrastination.

Before Knight returned to England with Clement's modified dispensation, Cardinal Wolsey realised that – especially if Knight's optimism somehow turned out to be justified – he was in immediate danger. The cardinal could lose his personal control of the Great Matter and perhaps also his overall position as Henry's chief advisor. Wolsey abruptly returned from his diplomatic mission in France to be in London when Knight arrived. As a consequence, he was one of the first to see Clement's dispensation, and he was the first to grasp how useless the conditional document was for achieving Henry's goals.[9]

In fact, Knight's ill-fated mission had worsened Henry's position. The king had always publicly asserted that he was seeking the annulment out of conscience-stricken concern for having violated the divine prohibition against affinity in-law incest. But in the course of the negotiations with the pope, Knight had foolishly disclosed that Henry was not simply driven by moral scruples but also by his infatuation with, and determination to marry, Anne Boleyn.[10]

For Wolsey personally, this political disaster had a bright side. With the failure of Knight's mission, Henry and Anne would surely recognise how difficult and delicate a task it was to obtain the annulment – and, more importantly, how indispensable Wolsey was to their success.

Henry's Fourth Legal Strategy: Convince Clement to Authorise Wolsey to Try the Matter in England and Make a Final Ruling
The Path to a Decretal Commission

If Clement could not be pushed into personally granting the annulment, Henry and Wolsey would somehow have to arrange for the matter to be decided by another method. They needed to move the venue for the decision from Rome to London. Their previous attempt to accomplish this – the secret Westminster trial – had failed. This time, their strategy would not be to attempt to have Wolsey decide in secret. Instead, England would first apply political pressure on Clement to formally delegate to Wolsey the specific authority to preside over a public trial in England. That trial would determine the effectiveness of Pope Julius's original dispensation for Henry's marriage to Catherine, and would decide whether the marriage was valid or void. Most importantly, Wolsey's decision must be final and without appeal or recall to Rome.

In normal civil or ecclesiastical trials, the first step is to determine the facts. Then, based upon those facts, the court determines the applicable law and decides the outcome. But canon law recognised a procedure for reversing this typical order of trial. In such a reverse procedure, known as a *decretal commission*, the pope in Rome would initially issue a decree defining and ruling upon the applicable law, but conditional upon the determination of specific facts. Then the pope would grant a decretal commission to a special legate to determine whether those required facts existed. This allowed trial of the facts to occur in a foreign venue where the best testimony and evidence could be found, rather than requiring the parties and witnesses to come to Rome. If the facts determined by the legatee satisfied the conditions in the pope's decree, then the pope's decree automatically became final without further action from Rome.[11]

For this decretal commission procedure to work for Henry, Pope Clement had to be convinced to select Wolsey to preside over the trial that would determine the facts of the case. Under Wolsey's detailed directions, the task of convincing the pope to issue him a decretal commission was assigned to one of Henry's agents in Italy – Gregory Casale, Henry's ambassador to the Vatican. Casale was joined by Stephen Gardiner, Wolsey's secretary and later Bishop of Winchester, and Edward Fox, also Wolsey's secretary and later Bishop of Hereford. Despite Clement's stubborn refusals and postponements, Henry's agents persevered tirelessly through countless meetings, arguments, drafts, and side conferences with powerful cardinals. They soon encountered several detours on the path to a decretal commission.

Henry Should First Marry Anne and Then Litigate

The negotiations were long and difficult for both sides. Clement and his cardinals tried everything to avoid having to make a final decision. In mid-January 1528 they even tried to convince the English that the requested decretal commission would not be Henry's best chance for an ultimately favourable final ruling by the Church, claiming instead that Henry should simply take the initiative and marry Anne Boleyn, based upon his conviction that the marriage to Catherine was void. Then there could be a trial in England by Wolsey or another legate to confirm the new marriage. When that approval of the marriage was inevitably appealed to the pope by Catherine, the case would not involve Henry's violation of any prior rulings of the pope. Clement would be dealing with an accomplished fact and not a request for permission, and supposedly could then sustain the new marriage without being blamed by the emperor or the Spanish.[12]

However, to assure Tudor succession to the throne of England, Henry determined that he could not accept the risk of Clement ultimately failing to legitimise any immediate marriage to Anne, which would also fail to legitimise what the king hoped would be the prompt production of a male heir after marrying her.[13]

The pope's suggestion that Henry marry Anne before seeking Church confirmation of the invalidity of his marriage to Catherine may seem surprising, but it would not by itself constitute bigamy. If the end result of that strategy were indeed to be the pope's annulment of Henry's marriage to Catherine, such a subsequent ruling would establish that Henry had never been married to Catherine. Thus, in the eyes of the Church, Anne would be Henry's first and, up to that point, only legal wife.

Henry Could Take Anne as a Second Wife

If the Vatican's suggestion that Henry marry Anne Boleyn before obtaining the annulment seems surprising, we should note that over the next few years Henry and Clement actively tried to negotiate for a much more bizarre solution to Henry's marital problems – the possibility that Clement could allow Henry to have two wives concurrently, following the example of the Hebrew Bible Patriarchs. In November 1528, the king instructed his agents in Rome to 'inquire whether the Pope will dispense with [the King] to h[ave *duas*] *uxores* [two wives], making the children of the second marriage legitimate as well as those of the first; w[hereof] some great reasons and precedents, especially of the Old Testament, appear'.[14]

Two years later, in September 1530, it was Clement's turn to propose the two-wives solution. The English ambassador to the Vatican, Gregory Casale, reported to Henry:

> A few days since the Pope secretly proposed to me the following condition; – that your Majesty might be allowed to have two wives.[15]

By that point in the extended negotiations, however, Henry's agents were wary of the pope's proposal. Clement likewise expressed that he had his own concerns with allowing two wives. In September 1530, Girolamo Ghinucci, Bishop of Worcester, then helping the king, reported to Henry his discussion with the pope:

> The Pope, however, continued to speak of the King's having two wives, and found several difficulties, especially that the Emperor would never consent to it on account of the prejudice which would ensue to the Princess [Mary, Catherine's daughter and the emperor's cousin, who was at that time Henry's only legitimate child]. ... From what he said about the Emperor, [Ghinucci] does not feel sure that he would grant such a dispensation, even if the King would be content with it.[16]

By the end of October 1530, Clement finally told Henry's new envoy, William Benet, that after receiving the advice of his cardinals, the pope would not dispense the impediment of bigamy:

> Shortly after Benet's coming there, the Pope spoke to him of a dispensation for two wives, but so doubtfully, that Benet suspects

he spoke it for two purposes [to get Henry to acknowledge that the pope can dispense such marriage impediments, and to placate the king and defer the case] ... Benet asked the Pope whether he was resolved that he could dispense in that case. He said 'No;' but he had been told by a great doctor he might, for the avoidance of a greater scandal; but he would advise further with his Council. Lately he has said plainly, that he cannot do it.[17]

Thus, despite lengthy negotiations, neither of these unusual suggestions turned out to be a viable alternative to Henry's demand for an annulment.[18] Henry would not agree to marry Anne Boleyn immediately and depend afterwards upon the Church to confirm that his marriage to Queen Catherine had been illegal and void. On the other hand, Clement would not agree to dispense the impediment of bigamy to allow Henry to have two wives concurrently.[19]

The Compromise Commission

The only immediately visible path to King Henry's goal was for his envoys to redouble their efforts to obtain a decretal commission. However, this initially produced very problematic documents. Clement firmly refused to grant a full decretal commission, and the English envoys had to settle for documents they hoped would provide a level of certainty functionally equivalent to a decretal commission. On 13 April 1528, the pope signed and sealed a joint commission to Wolsey and Cardinal Lorenzo Campeggio to try the matter in England and issue a final, non-appealable judgment. Although this was only a general commission, it used strong language of finality and was enhanced by two accompanying documents signed by the pope. The first was a new dispensation signed in advance for Henry to marry Anne Boleyn upon securing the final judgment. The second, whose delivery was delayed for some months, was Clement's private written guaranty (a *pollicitation*, or solemn personal promise) that he would not intercede in the trial by revoking the commission or by accepting an appeal of the judgment decreed in England.[20]

Initially, the king and his counsellors were satisfied. They thought that, while not perfect, these three documents together would at last allow the legate trial to commence. However, just as happened with Secretary Knight's earlier failed papal dispensation document, the period of initial satisfaction with these documents was brief. Despite the language of finality expressed in Clement's documents, Wolsey and the king's other canon law experts soon had serious misgivings. This commission did not grant a papal dispensation automatically upon determination of the facts in England. And although it stated that the judgment by the special legates in England would be binding, there were technical loopholes whereby Clement could change his mind. Wolsey sent more instructions and more agents to do what they must in order to obtain a true decretal commission.[21]

The Secret Decretal Commission

Finally, the unrelenting exertions of the king's team of envoys seem to have simply worn down the beleaguered pope. In June 1528, Clement signed and issued a decretal commission for final determination of the annulment matter in a legatine trial in England.[22] However, once again Henry and Wolsey would soon learn that they had not quite secured their hoped-for total victory. To avoid the appearance of partiality in the trial, Clement would only grant the decretal commission if it once again ran jointly to two legatees. Cardinal Wolsey was one, but he would have to officiate together with a cardinal from Rome. At Wolsey's suggestion, Clement again selected Cardinal Lorenzo Campeggio, the nominal Bishop of Salisbury.

Campeggio's bishopric did not require clerical services or even residence in England, but it did entitle him to significant annual income in exchange for being available to help England in Vatican matters. The selection of Campeggio turned out to be another huge miscalculation by the English. Wolsey apparently presumed that Campeggio's economic self-interest – to be sweetened, if necessary, by an offer of additional income as the next Bishop of Durham – would ensure that he would be a reliable supporter of Henry's cause.[23]

In the end, Campeggio showed that his loyalty was neither to King Henry nor to Emperor Charles. Cardinal Campeggio was a Vatican insider. He was loyal only to Pope Clement. Clement relied upon Campeggio's obedience to assure that Henry would not, at least for the time being, force him to rule on the annulment. For Clement, the entire project of the new legate trial was only another exercise in the fine art of delay. He did not want to confront Henry with a flat denial of the petition, which could risk immediately pushing England out of the Roman Catholic Church. At the same time, Clement did not want to enrage Charles by granting the annulment, which could risk pushing the emperor into intensifying his military conquest of the Vatican and the Vatican States.

Wolsey's negotiating acumen was no match for Clement's evasive dexterity. The pope signed a new decretal commission, but only with the strict instructions that it must be physically retained by Campeggio alone, and Henry and Wolsey could see it only once. The document could not be copied, and its existence was forbidden to be revealed to anyone else, including Henry's Privy Council.[24]

Clement's rigorous demand for secrecy about the commission was not even Henry's worst problem. The pope harboured a bigger secret – one that neither Henry nor Wolsey suspected. He had given secret instructions to Campeggio that countermanded the terms of his written commission, telling him that his primary duty in England would be to delay the proceedings as long as possible, and that he must do whatever was necessary to stop the matter from going to final judgment.[25]

Cardinal Campeggio

Cardinal Campeggio turned out to be the ideal papal agent to ensure delay. He suffered from severe gout, so his journey from Rome to London was laborious, taking an especially long time, including recuperation after his arrival in London. Once he was able to begin his duties, Campeggio did all he could to avoid or at least delay the matter. First, he tried to get Henry and Catherine to somehow reconcile. That would have achieved Catherine's greatest hope, but of course Henry would not consider it.

Then, Campeggio and Wolsey tried to convince Catherine to avoid a public dispute by retiring to a convent, which would thereby end the marriage with dignity and goodwill.[26] This would have pleased the king, but for Catherine it was simply one of many opportunities for her to declare her resolute, immovable position that she was and always would remain Henry's legal wife and queen.[27]

The Blackfriars Trial

When Campeggio's preliminary delaying tactics were exhausted, the legatine trial finally opened in London at the end of May 1529 in the great hall at Blackfriars, a former monastery building of the Order of Dominican Friars, whose uniforms included black cloaks. It

Henry's Legal Strategies

was a unique event in English history – the reigning king and queen summoned to appear at a public trial concerning the legitimacy of their long marriage.

Catherine had previously informed the court that she objected on the grounds that the trial was unfair and the judges and witnesses were biased. She declared that she was therefore petitioning the pope for removal of the case (*advocation*) to Rome where she could be properly represented and impartially judged. Not surprisingly, Wolsey and Campeggio ruled against her objections and ordered the case to proceed and the parties to appear.

On the first day of regular proceedings, 31 May, a swarm of ordinary Londoners turned out to line the approaches to Blackfriars. Their cheers for Catherine as she walked to the trial clearly showed which party they supported. Catherine appeared at the trial only on that first day of regular hearings, but it was an intensely dramatic and memorable day. She was not accompanied by canon lawyers, but by four English bishops, including her chief clerical supporter, John Fisher, Bishop of Rochester. As the legal proceedings began, Henry was seated in a chair of honour surveying his team of canon lawyers and the panel of distinguished leaders of the English Church, almost all of whom he could count on to be obedient to his wishes.

When called by the clerk to confirm her presence, Catherine instead walked across the hearing room, knelt before the king, and gave an impassioned speech, pleading with him to end the proceedings and continue with their marriage. She recounted her unwavering love and loyalty to him over their two decades of marriage, and how she had persevered despite her many tragic pregnancies. Tellingly, while Catherine was kneeling in the courtroom before a surprised Henry, she swore that her prior marriage to Henry's brother Arthur had never been consummated. She insisted that she had been a virgin when she married Henry, and that he knew this was true. The public observers must have been shocked when the queen spoke openly of such matters. Henry made no immediate response in her presence.[28]

Finally, in what must have marked the end of a stunned silence in the hearing room, Catherine rose and walked out, deaf to the court clerk's repeated shouts for her to return. Henry recovered his astonishment in time to make an improvised response in the courtroom. He falsely insisted upon his continued contentment with her, and expressed his deep regret that his conscience would not allow him to continue in a marriage if it were found to be prohibited by God.[29] For her part, Catherine refused thereafter to personally appear at any trial of the matter in England.

In the several years subsequent to the Blackfriars trial, Henry continued to argue that Catherine's prior marriage to Arthur had been consummated. However, he never denied under oath that she had been a virgin at their marriage, even when the pope confirmed that Catherine was willing to have that fact determined in whatever way Henry would be willing to swear to under oath.[30]

In publicly denying that Arthur had consummated her first marriage, Catherine directly attacked one of the crucial factual issues essential to Henry's position. Affinity incest with a brother's widow was not established merely by the fact that the widow and the deceased had been formally married, but required that sexual relations with the deceased brother had occurred. The Leviticus Prohibitions would only be applicable if Catherine's marriage of five months to Arthur had been consummated.[31]

Catherine's refusal to return to the Blackfriars trial would have been legally sufficient for a default judgment to be rendered in favour of Henry. However, the king was also using the trial to make his case to the world, and especially to his own subjects. He needed his eventual marriage to Anne Boleyn to be respected. More importantly, he needed the hoped-for male child of that coming marriage to become the recognised heir to the throne. Therefore, the Blackfriars trial continued without the queen. Henry's advocates presented witnesses and arguments to support the annulment. Catherine left her defence in the hands of the able Bishop John Fisher, who bravely offered passionate arguments against the king's position.[32]

In the end, Cardinal Campeggio followed his secret instructions from the pope that he must block the Blackfriars trial from going to judgment. On Friday 23 July 1529, the Blackfriars trial reconvened with the expectation of hearing the court's final judgment. Instead, Cardinal Campeggio abruptly adjourned the trial without announcing a verdict. He claimed that the recess was necessary to observe Rome's Papal Court summer vacation, and he apparently added that the matter was sufficiently important that he required consultation with the pope to reach a judgment.[33]

The Spanish Brief

At the time Campeggio forced the adjournment of the Blackfriars trial in 1529, the dispute had become even more complicated when it was discovered that Julian had issued not just one formal dispensation, in the form of a Bull, but also a second, less formal dispensation, in a document called a Brief (a *Breve*).

A Bull was the most formal and typically most authoritative public ruling of a pontiff that decided a specific individual matter, executed with the pope's distinctive lead seal. Authenticated copies would be available to the party or parties involved in the particular matter. Papal Bulls would also be registered in the Vatican Library's permanent records and could have significant precedential value in the development of the canon law of the Catholic Church.

A papal Brief likewise expressed a ruling on a specific matter. As the name implies, however, in contrast with a Bull, a Brief could be a shorter, more informal document in the form of a private letter from the pope. Therefore, a Brief need not include all of the traditional language of a formal Bull. It could omit or summarise some of the introductory language or some of the detailed factual recitals that would be expected in a Bull. Physically, the originals of a Bull and a Brief were readily distinguishable. While a Bull was executed with the pope's special lead seal, a Brief was executed with a red wax seal of the Fisherman, a reference to the Catholic tradition that the first pope of the Catholic Church was St Peter, who had originally been a Jewish fisherman named Simon. Papal Briefs had their own registry in the Vatican, but because Briefs were in the form of private and sometimes less formal correspondence, the practice of registering them may have been less consistent.[34]

Thus, when Catherine's appeal against the proceedings finally reached Rome, it was accompanied by a copy of the Brief, commonly called the Spanish Brief, a papal document that had only recently been found in Spain. It purported to be a contemporaneous private legal summary by Pope Julius II of his 1503 public dispensation Bull.

In both the original Bull and the newly discovered Brief, Pope Julius had expressly permitted Henry to marry Catherine. However, the Spanish Brief altered the recital of factual circumstances in two crucial ways. First, the Brief seemed to help Catherine's cause by curing several of the technical objections that Henry had raised when he had recently attacked Julius's Bull of dispensation.[35] For example, the English attacked the Bull because it falsely stated that the requested dispensation was motivated by the desire to further peace and friendship between Spain and England at a time when there was no threat of war or dispute between the nations.[36] The Spanish Brief described its motivations in almost identical terms, but with the important additional qualification, 'and certain other causes', thereby removing from relevance the factual issue of the state of relations between the two nations.[37]

Second, in a somewhat more subtle manner, the Spanish Brief potentially might help Henry's cause regarding the issue of whether Arthur and Catherine had consummated their marriage. The original Bull, in Latin, stated that the couple 'did perhaps [*forsan*] consummate' their marriage. This equivocal word, 'perhaps', in the Bull left open the possibility that there had been no physical consummation. Without consummation, the Leviticus Prohibitions would not apply to bar Henry's marriage to Catherine, which would destroy Henry's central argument for annulment. However, the Spanish Brief changed the phrase, this time in Henry's favour, by deleting the troublesome word *forsan* [perhaps]. As a result, Julius's Brief declared flatly that Arthur and Catherine 'did consummate' their marriage.[38] (For a detailed analysis of the canon law and theological aspects of the issues of consummation and public honesty in the Great Matter, see Appendix B.)

The immediate English response to this newly discovered Brief failed to appreciate the potential gift to Henry's case. Instead, Henry's advisors reflexively attacked the entire Spanish Brief as being a forgery. Given the Brief had been allegedly lost without a trace for more than a quarter of a century, its discovery in Spain just in time for the Blackfriars trial seemed too convenient to be coincidental.

Henry's advisors had raised technical objections to aspects of the Bull throughout the Blackfriars trial, and they now tried to convince Clement VII that the Spanish Brief was a forgery. They cited a variety of issues regarding the provenance, physical appearance, and wording of the Brief: being dated 26 December 1503, the same date as the Bull; not following the special protocol for dating Briefs; being signed in different handwriting than the text of the document; not being written by Julius's usual administrator; the calligraphy not in well-formed Italic; several unusual abbreviations; several misspelled names of the parties; the absence of various standard and customary clauses; several erasures and mis-aligned words; the parchment did not appear to be twenty-five years old; the red wax seal appeared to be raised in the middle, as if it were covering another seal; and that such an important document was neither entered in the Vatican registry, nor found in the official papers and archives of England or Spain, but was only uncovered by family members among the papers of former Spanish ambassador Dr Roderigo De Puebla.[39]

The deep distrust was mutual. Spain was at that time within the Hapsburg imperial domain of Holy Roman Emperor Charles V, who also ruled Spain directly as King Charles I of Spain. Charles, Catherine's nephew and strongest supporter, insisted that the Brief was authentic, but that the original could not be handed over to the English for fear of it being hidden, altered, or destroyed by them.[40]

Even before Campeggio's suspension of the Blackfriars trial, Clement found that he could no longer ignore Charles V's insistence that the annulment matter must be determined in Rome, not in England. Clement seized upon the last-minute discovery of the Spanish Brief, together with Catherine's pending appeal, as new developments important enough to require him to hear the matter in the Vatican, contrary to his secret personal pledge to the English that he would never do so. Clement asserted that only he as pope could disavow Julius's original Bull. Further, such a final ruling would require Clement to have both parties appear before him in Rome to present their arguments before the pope and the Rota, a special ecclesiastical court of Vatican cardinals that heard marriage and family law disputes.[41]

On 21 April 1529, Clement continued to assure Henry that

> ... [he has] not been able to satisfy the King's wishes as expressed by [Henry's ambassadors], although he has sought to do so night and day, and taken the best lawyers to his counsel. Would be glad if he could do what the King desires. Cannot declare the Brief of Julius false without hearing both sides, considering his position and responsibility to God.[42]

However, while Clement was giving his personal assurances to Henry that he wanted to grant the king's request, Henry was receiving sharply contrary warnings from his agents in Rome. The envoys' letters cautioned that both Pope Clement and Cardinal Campeggio were actually in league with the emperor on this issue and would not do anything to help Henry. Regardless of what the two men might say, it seemed hopeless to expect the pope to grant the annulment in Rome without Henry presenting some new and more compelling arguments.[43]

7

HENRY'S CHRISTIAN THEOLOGICAL STRATEGY

With the premature shutdown of the Blackfriars Trial, the only positive development for Henry at this low point in 1529 was that Clement's removal of the case to the jurisdiction of the Vatican at least guaranteed further delays. Previously Henry had chafed at Clement's postponements. Now the king welcomed the additional time to come up with some new strategy. He had to accept that the matter would now inevitably get bogged down in the cumbersome procedural formalities and the crowded calendar of the ecclesiastical court system in Rome. Especially in light of how the Spanish Brief had undercut many of the king's technical attacks against Julius's dispensation, Henry recognised that he would need this extra time to open a new front in his assault upon his marriage to Catherine. But what more could he say to convince Pope Clement?

Thomas Cranmer's Strategy

As sometimes happens in human affairs, the answer to what should be done at this crucial juncture did not come from tedious and lengthy legal or theological analysis by Henry and his advisors. The answer came from a chance encounter with a highly unlikely source.[1] With the collapse of the Blackfriars trial and Clement's advocation of the case for hearing in Rome, there seemed nothing further that could be accomplished by Henry's principal envoys to the Vatican, Stephen Gardiner and Edward Fox. Henry therefore recalled Gardiner and

Fox to England. When they arrived, London had been temporarily abandoned by the king and his royal court, who had fled the ravages of that summer's seasonal plague, probably the English sweating sickness, to seek shelter in the healthier countryside. By the time the two envoys joined up with the court, the king was in Waltham, where Gardiner and Fox were assigned to lodge with the Cressey family. As it happened, Cambridge University had also closed to avoid the plague, and Thomas Cranmer, a young but prominent Doctor of Divinity on the Cambridge faculty, was also living with the Cressey family while tutoring their two sons, who had been his university students.

Gardiner and Fox, both Cambridge men, were pleased to find Cranmer at their lodging, and invited him to dine with them. At dinner, they discussed the king's case and the recent breakoff of their negotiations with the pope. When they asked him for his ideas on the matter, Cranmer suggested that they stop their direct assault against the procedural complexities and delays of the ecclesiastical courts in Rome. Instead, Cranmer proposed that they could obtain quicker and more compelling support by putting the basic issue – can a man marry his brother's widow – to the faculties of theology and law of the great Catholic universities of Europe, starting with Cambridge and Oxford. Cranmer felt confident that, recognising this as an issue of reading the Holy Word, King Henry would soon be able to secure uniform rulings in his favour by the universities. The pope would have to acknowledge the force of theological conclusions reached by such renowned academics. This would avoid the interminable delay, uncertainty, and inconvenience that would otherwise result from continuing to seek an answer through the court system.

Henry returned to Greenwich the next day, and promptly summoned Gardiner and Fox to discuss how to convince the pope to grant the annulment. When Henry learned of Cranmer's suggestion of obtaining university faculty opinions that would enable him to avoid a trial in Rome, he sent for Cranmer.[2]

As soon as Cranmer appeared and explained his suggestion, Henry ordered him to help effectuate the plan. Cranmer was immediately to write a book on the matter, citing the Scriptures, the views of the Church fathers, and rulings of the Church councils. Cranmer also included his own opinion that the pope had no power to dispense a natural law of God given in the Bible, such as the Leviticus

Prohibitions. Henry was so pleased with Cranmer's book that he sent the cleric to Rome to present it personally to Pope Clement.

The king wasted no time in beginning to implement Cranmer's broader strategy, sending a network of agents to search for helpful evidence at Europe's great universities and libraries. His representatives were directed to find and copy the ancient writings of the Church Fathers showing that, despite Pope Julius's attempted dispensation, Henry's marriage to Catherine was void and must be annulled. Then, Henry's agents were to use these materials to obtain from the law and theology faculties, under seal of the universities, formal determinations that the marriage must be annulled. They were also to obtain letters from individual theologians.

Thus, by the end of 1529, Henry essentially abandoned his earlier technical and legal attacks against the wording of Pope Julius's 1503 Bull granting dispensation. He could see that Thomas Cranmer was correct. Further attempts to obtain a favourable ruling in the ecclesiastical court system would only lead to endless delay. Henry's goal was to make Anne Boleyn his wife and queen, and hopefully the source of a legitimate and recognised male heir to the throne. The past twenty years had taught Henry how chancy the production of a male heir could be. Despite many pregnancies, Catherine and Henry had only produced one surviving child, their daughter, Princess Mary. Further delay could be the equivalent of total failure in Henry's Great Matter.

The Theological Issues Underlying Cranmer's Strategy

The essence of Cranmer's strategy was to give up the legal dispute and shift to a theological attack. His plan would also greatly simplify the specific theological issues for which Henry required support from ancient Church authorities and contemporary Catholic theologians. Although the expected issues were sometimes expressed in a longer list of overlapping logical propositions, the core of Henry's theological arguments consisted of only two conclusions necessary to invalidate the marriage: first, that the Leviticus Prohibitions expressed in Lev. 18:16 and its companion verse Lev. 20:21 unconditionally prohibit a man from marrying his brother's widow; and second, that these prohibitions express divine, eternal, and natural law, beyond the power of a pope to dispense.

On a surface reading, it would seem that Leviticus does expressly determine that Henry's marriage to Catherine was void, just as Henry now claimed. But on closer reading, the Leviticus Prohibitions raise several complex and interrelated issues of interpretation, including how to reconcile the Leviticus Prohibitions with the obligation of levirate marriage mandated by Deut. 25:5–10; whether the Leviticus Prohibitions still apply if the wife's first marriage was never consummated; and of course, whether the pope has the power to dispense the marriage impediment of affinity incest in the case of a widowed sister-in-law.

In light of these significant and unsettled questions of interpretation, Cranmer seems to have been overly optimistic in suggesting that Henry's pursuit of the annulment would be faster and more likely to be victorious if the dispute were changed from a formal legal trial to a theological argument based upon the opinions of Catholic clerics and universities.

Obtaining the Opinion from Cambridge University

At Cranmer's suggestion, the quest for faculty support started with England's two major universities, Cambridge and Oxford. We might expect that these two faculties, being subject to reward or punishment from their absolute monarch, would not offer significant challenge to the king's request for opinions supporting his position that his marriage to Catherine was void. In fact, however, of all the universities in Europe, these two were among the most troublesome for Henry. It took enormous pressure, connivance, and outright fraud for Stephen Gardiner and Edward Fox to have the English faculties vote for Henry's position. The two Cambridge men began with their alma mater, where they had strong faculty contacts and influence.

Stephen Gardiner, writing for himself and Edward Fox, composed a detailed report from Cambridge to the king in a famous letter dated February 1530, while the Cambridge faculty members were still determining their response.[3] Gardiner explained that he and Fox had received the cooperation of the university vice chancellor, Dr William Buckmaster, and others. But Gardiner complained that their efforts to secure clear-cut faculty support for the king's position had been more than matched by the efforts of their opponents, who believed the marriage was valid. Two hundred faculty members assembled on a Sunday afternoon and argued the issue back and forth. When night came, it was apparent that a majority of the faculty would not support the king. The group refused to authorise Buckmaster to decide the matter on behalf of the university, and he could do nothing but adjourn the assembly until formal voting on the following Monday afternoon.

At the Monday meeting, Buckmaster proposed that the matter be referred to a subcommittee to decide the university's response. This proposal to refer was initially voted down, and a second vote was evenly divided. Then Henry's supporters convinced some opposing members, who were perhaps fearful of the consequences of going on record as opposing the king's request, to leave the meeting. But even that manoeuvre was not sufficient to give Henry's side a clear majority of the remaining faculty voters. Further negotiations forced Henry's supporters to increase the subcommittee's vote required for approval of the king's request from a simple majority to a 'two parts' [two-thirds] majority.

The king's supporters employed an additional tactic to lessen the burden of having to obtain a two-thirds vote of the subcommittee. They arranged for more than half of the subcommittee to consist of men who were already committed to the king's cause. Gardiner sent his letter to the king at this point of the process with an attached list of the twenty-nine subcommittee members, identifying the sixteen who could already be counted upon to vote for Henry. Gardiner assured Henry that they should be able to obtain the few more votes needed to approve the king's proposal:

> Your highness may perceive by the notes, that we be already sure of as many as be requisite, wanting only three; and we have good hope of four; of which four if we get two, and obtain of another to be absent, it is sufficient for our purpose.[4]

However, despite all of their advantages and stratagems, Henry's agents still lacked full control over the outcome. The issue deeply polarised both the university faculty and the students and residents of Cambridge generally.

Vice Chancellor Buckmaster later reported to Dr John Edmunds, master of Peterhouse College at Cambridge, detailing Henry's royal displeasure with the university's final determination.[5] However, Henry's angry reaction did not acknowledge that his problems with the university's position were at least in part caused by how the king had personally expressed his wishes. In his earlier letter of

16 February 1529 to the Cambridge faculty requesting the university's opinion on the proposed annulment, he had reduced the complex theological issues to a single simple proposition. Henry misleadingly referred to other support, which at that point he still only hoped to obtain from various sources, as if it had already been received. The king stated that he had received many written opinions from a great number of 'the greatest clerks [clerics] of Cristendom' in England and the Continent as to 'the chief and principal point in our cause ... to take the wife of a brother who died without children is forbidden by divine and natural law'.[6]

Henry was angered at Cambridge University's response, both for what it omitted and what it had inserted. The university had expressed its verdict: 'To take the wife of a brother who died childless, who had been known by her former husband through sexual intercourse, is forbidden by divine and natural law for us Christians today.'[7]

The Issue of Papal Power to Dispense

Henry now saw that his request to the faculty had oversimplified the matter. Cambridge University's favourable determination of what he had identified as 'the chief and principal point in our cause' – that the Leviticus Prohibitions were statements of natural law – was important but not sufficient. The king's cause also required the answer to an implied second question: can the pope dispense from a divine, natural law? The answer to this second question was conspicuously absent from the Cambridge determination. Buckmaster assured the king that they could never have obtained sufficient Cambridge faculty support if they had required an express limitation on the power of the pope to dispense. However, Henry made it clear that this would not be the end of the matter for Cambridge. As Buckmaster reported to Dr Edmunds:

> I assure you, he [the king] was scarce contented with Mr. Secretary [Stephen Gardiner, secretary to Wolsey], and Mr. Provost [Edward Fox, Provost of King's College, Cambridge] that this was not also determined, *An papa possit dispensare, etc.* [Can a pope dispense, etc.?] I made the best, and confirmed the same that they had shewed his grace before, and how it would never have been so obtained. Then he opened his mind, saying, that he would have it determined at after Easter, and of the same we counselled a while.

I pray you therefore study for us, for our business is not yet at an end, *An papa possit dispensare cum jure divino, etc.* [Can a pope dispense with divine law, etc.?][8]

The Condition of Consummation

The faculty's failure to determine that the pope lacked the power to dispense for a marriage that violated the Leviticus Prohibitions was only the first of two issues in the Cambridge determination that angered Henry. The Cambridge faculty had also inserted an additional condition to their decision: that the widow had been carnally known by her previous husband. This requirement held major theological significance for the academics because it related to the underlying rationale for the Leviticus Prohibitions regarding affinity in-law incest. By their prior act of marital intercourse, the deceased husband and his wife had become one flesh.[9] If Catherine's marriage to Arthur had not been physically consummated, she had never become one flesh with Arthur. She therefore would not have acquired any relationship to Henry that would make his subsequent spousal relations with her incestuous.

This requirement of consummation of the original marriage may have been good theology, but it caused the university's opinion to depend upon a factual issue for which, after Henry and Catherine's twenty years of marriage, neither of the parties could marshal inarguable proof. England still remembered the conflicting rumours and gossip swirling around this very question of consummation when Arthur had died aged fifteen after only five months of marriage. Some of the royal court had observed that Arthur had been sickly and frail throughout his brief marriage, lending credence to speculation that there had been no consummation. Others insisted that he had been in fine health until a sudden illness just before his death, and that he and Catherine had slept together on various nights. Still others acknowledged that he had appeared somewhat weak and tired since the wedding, but attributed that to his excessive physical efforts in the nuptial bed.[10]

Making things more confusing, the English and Spanish positions on the question of consummation had fluctuated over the years, embracing whatever story seemed most beneficial for each party at the time. Immediately after Arthur's death, the real issue wasn't consummation but rather the more urgent possibility of pregnancy.

His grieving widow's return to London from Wales was a very slow journey because she was carried in a draped carriage, although she was known to be an excellent horse rider. This suggested that the ladies of her court perhaps thought that she might be pregnant. The same concern for Catherine's possible pregnancy may have motivated her father-in-law, King Henry VII, to wait several months before formally designating his surviving son Henry as Prince of Wales and heir apparent. If Catherine had given birth to Arthur's son after Arthur's death, it would be that son, not Arthur's younger brother, who would become the Prince of Wales as the next successor to the throne.[11]

On the morning after the wedding, Arthur had told his gentlemen companions in his court that he had, indeed, enjoyed the pleasant labours of a bridegroom: 'Willoughby, bring me a cup of ale, for I have been this night in the midst of Spain.'[12] Some thought that this may have been no more than unreliable adolescent boasting.

We should remember that Henry married Catherine when he was only a few years older than Arthur had been at Arthur's wedding. Therefore, it is ironic that Henry likewise spoke to his companions about his own bridegroom experiences with Catherine. The difference was that Henry's boast was that Catherine had been a virgin when they married. However, he later disavowed that claim when it became relevant to his annulment efforts. Henry dismissed his earlier inconsistent statements as merely a jest – the same sort of young man's braggadocio that some had imputed to Arthur.[13]

On her part, Catherine's parents and their envoys likewise made a parallel reversal of some initial Spanish assertions that the marriage with Arthur had been consummated. Immediately after Arthur's death, Ferdinand and Isabella recognised that, to avoid bad financial consequences, Spain had to manoeuvre Henry VII into having Prince Henry marry Catherine under the same terms as the earlier marriage agreement.[14] In analysing this plan, the Spanish monarchs initially admitted that they were not certain whether the marriage to Arthur had been consummated.[15]

They were soon assured by Doña Elvira Manuel, Catherine's chief attendant, that the young bride had remained a virgin.[16] Ferdinand and Isabella thus became personally convinced that Catherine had not consummated her marriage to Arthur. However, the complexities of the new marital negotiations carried on by King Ferdinand for his widowed daughter's proposed marriage to Prince Henry caused Ferdinand to disregard his beliefs and agree to the equivocal language – 'perhaps consummated' – that had found its way into Pope Julius's 26 December 1503 Bull of dispensation for Henry and Catherine to marry.[17]

It is important to note that Catherine herself never allowed Spain's considerations of state interests or national finances to cause her to waver from what she insisted was the truth of this issue, namely that she and Arthur had merely shared the same bed on seven occasions during their brief marriage.[18] Moreover, in the decade of life remaining to her from the outset of Henry's first attempt in 1527 to obtain an annulment until her death in 1536, Catherine repeatedly and solemnly swore that she had come to Henry as a virgin bride.[19] In the 1529 Blackfriars trial she had challenged Henry to contradict her under oath on this point, and she agreed to be governed by whatever Henry would swear to regarding her intact virginity when they married.[20] Henry never countered under oath Catherine's denial of consummation with Arthur. This did not, however, stop him from continuing throughout the dispute to deny, when not under oath, that she had come to him as a virgin, despite his previous boasts to his friends.

Reactions at Cambridge

Henry and his advisors apparently expected that the questions they were asking Cambridge University to answer might, at worst, engender some scholarly theological debates. They were not prepared for the actual response of Cambridge to be so much more heated, to the point of physical fighting and civil riot. In a letter to Dr Edmunds, Vice Chancellor Buckmaster describes the explosive response to the university's final determination in favour of the king. First there was a physical fight between a servant of Stephen Gardiner and a parson of St Nicholas' Hostel, a lodging house for Cambridge students.[21] The servant was injured, and when Buckmaster sent the parson to jail for a breach of the peace, there was a great public outcry. Buckmaster described the event to Edmunds:

> All the world almost crieth out of Cambridge for this act, and specially on me, but I must bear it as well as I may. ...[T]hat night [of the arrest] there was such a jetting [violently throwing

objects] in Cambridge as ye never heard of, with such boyng [booing?] and crying even against our college, that all Cambridge might perceive it was in despite of me.[22]

By the time the story of the Cambridge disorders reached Eustace Chapuys, Holy Roman Emperor Charles V's ambassador to England, the body count seems to have multiplied to 'six or seven of them being left dead on the spot'.[23] But Chapuys acknowledges that he had only indirect reports of the incident. (The arrival of Chapuys and the central role he played in our understanding of the King's Great Matter is discussed in greater detail below in Chapter 11.)

In retrospect, it appears that Henry and his supporters were surprised by the Cambridge response because they had failed to understand the deep political/theological schism within the university faculty at that time. By 1530, Catholicism in Europe was in the grip of a growing struggle for its survival due to the threat of the Protestant Reformation. Since Martin Luther had ignited the flame a decade earlier, partisan religious fervour had been running high in both groups of believers.

Indeed, for several years leading up to this point in the struggle to end his marriage, Henry had already repeatedly made it clear to Pope Clement that if he could not obtain his annulment within the Church, he would be forced to obtain relief elsewhere, by joining the Reformation or by taking other steps to withdraw England from the authority of the Holy See.[24]

The Roman Catholic Church's concern with the European movement towards reform was obvious to Henry and his advisors. But Henry apparently did not understand that a part of the Cambridge faculty was already on the front lines of agitating for some sort of Protestant-inspired reformation of the Catholic Church in England. This liberal faction, led by Thomas Cranmer, and promoted by fiery pulpit orators such as Hugh Latimer, induced an angry reaction from religiously conservative members of the Cambridge faculty.

The conservatives at Cambridge naturally favoured Catherine, a sincere, traditional Catholic. They distrusted Anne Boleyn who, with her family, appeared to be very open to Lutheran ideas. They also feared that Henry's arguments with Clement over annulment threatened the supremacy of the pope. Therefore, conservative Cambridge faculty members strongly opposed aiding Henry's quest for annulment.

When confronted by this bitterly divided faculty, Henry's supporters resorted to trickery and fraud so that they could claim that Cambridge University agreed that the royal marriage was void.[25]

Obtaining the Opinion from Oxford University

Having secured the Cambridge determination, Henry promptly attempted to obtain a comparable approval from Oxford. He tried to use similar techniques and ended up with many of the same problems. The Oxford University determination was similarly open to attack and controversy as to its authenticity. Once again, the king's emissaries were met with riots, but here the public demonstrations were primarily from the women of the town. Catherine was always popular with the English people, but especially with the women of England. As had been the case in his previous reports about Cambridge, Imperial ambassador Chapuys seems to take some satisfaction in relaying to Charles V the news – and gossip – of the riots, this time at Oxford:

> The bishop of Lincoln [Bishop John Longland] and an Italian Cordelier [a Franciscan friar], who went recently to Oxonia [Oxford], to obtain for the King the sceau [seal] of that university, were driven away by the women of the place and pelted with large stones. The King, in order to punish this act of violence and prevent any more serious outbreak, also to intimidate the doctors of that university who dispute his opinion, has sent thither the duke of Sufforcq [Suffolk], and the treasurer of the Household, charging them that where they could not meet the argumentations of the contrary party with reason, they should pay them with ready money. The Duke has committed the said women to prison, and is eagerly following up the King's commission in order to obtain the seal by bribes or threats, as it may be.[26]

In Cambridge, Buckmaster also heard early reports about the Oxford riots, and expressed his concerns for the safety of Edward Fox, Provost of King's College, Cambridge, who had been sent to Oxford in an effort to replicate the Cambridge voting results: 'I am informed, that Oxford hath now elect certain persons to determine the king's question. I hear say also, that Mr. Provost [Edward Fox] was there in great jeopardy.'[27]

The Oxford voting procedure closely followed the pattern in Cambridge, including similar fierce opposition between the religious conservatives and the reformers on the faculty, together with delegation of the faculty's determination to a smaller committee with the authority to speak under seal of the university. There are inconsistent reports of some details of the vote, but it appears that the final vote in favour of the king's request was barely carried by a slim majority.[28] One of the alternate versions reports that, out of fear of the king's disfavour, eight men met secretly in the night, broke into the chapel where university seals were kept, and affixed the seal to a forged determination favourable to Henry.[29]

Although Oxford determined on 8 April 1530 that Henry's marriage to Catherine was void, the verdict could not have fully pleased the king. Following the wording of the Cambridge determination of 9 March 1530, the Oxford determination also included the unwelcome condition that Henry's marriage to Catherine was void only if Catherine's prior marriage had in fact been physically consummated. This similarity in wording was not a coincidence, and we must assume that the partisan factions of the faculties in each of the two great English universities were in close contact with their respective counterparts.

Henry had hoped for more. He had conveniently mischaracterised the substance of the Cambridge determination when he wrote to Oxford in an attempt to prod them into providing a prompt and helpful determination. In his third letter to Oxford, dated 17 March 1530, soliciting the university's support for the annulment, Henry simply deleted the inconvenient conditional clause requiring consummation when he described the Cambridge determination:[30]

> ... our university of Cambridge hath ... sent unto us their answer under their common seal, plainly determining, There is a prohibition of divine and natural law that a brother may not take as his wife the widow of a brother even if he died childless.[31]

Despite Henry's efforts to sneak the consummation condition clause off the table, the Oxford opinion managed to insert it. Many of the opinions solicited from other European universities and theologians would likewise incorporate the express condition that the first marriage must have been consummated.

Henry's Quest to Obtain Opinions from Continental Universities and Theologians

Many continental European faculties were similarly highly resistant to deciding the theological issue in favour of Henry. As Henry's agents had done in England, his foreign envoys subjected many of these other European university faculties to bribery, rigged voting, and even the theft of the university seal or voting records in an attempt to control the voting or to enable an outright forgery of the university's opinion. In France, Henry's agents succeeded only after King Francis I intervened and influenced the vote as part of his efforts to reach an alliance with Henry against Charles V. Some of the other major universities in France and Italy also provided determinations supporting Henry, including Orleans, Bourges, Toulouse, Bologna, and Padua. Confirming opinions by some individual Catholic theologians were also obtained.

However, these faculty and individual opinions supporting Henry were significantly weakened in authority by evidence of the widespread bribery and other improper means used to obtain them, and nobody was more effective in recording these shortcomings and shortcuts than Chapuys, the Imperial ambassador.

Bribery, Intimidation, and Fraud

Chapuys used his information network to offer helpful predictions and practical advice to the emperor. On 16 March 1530, while the king's efforts to obtain support from Cambridge and Oxford were close to success, Chapuys warned Charles of what might happen in Henry's next major attempt, at the Sorbonne University of Paris.

> There can be no doubt, as I have already informed Your Majesty, that the King, by fair means or foul, will at last wring consent from the English universities, *but there still remains that of Paris, which is said to have the privilege of* [enjoy a privileged relationship with] *the Apostolic See, and to be in great difficulty as to its decision; the fear is that the king of France, in fulfilment of the promise made here by his ambassador, will by* 'fas aut nephas' [right or wrong (methods)] *induce that university also to give her* [opinion under] *seal, and by threats or promises through those already on their side gain over many more, oblige*

> *their opponents to absent themselves, and then bring about a unanimous decision in favour of this king* [Henry]. [Italics in the original.][32]

The general accuracy of Chapuys's prediction has been confirmed by many subsequent accounts of the corrupt voting proceedings in Paris and other French universities during 1530. In the words of H. A. L. Fisher, one of the first major Tudor historians of the twentieth century and still one of the most useful, 'The influence of Francis I was solicited and exerted to promote Henry's cause with the French divines, and in the course of the summer favourable opinions were duly obtained from the doctors of Paris, Orleans, Angers, Bourges, and Toulouse.'[33]

The accounts of Paris initially present a puzzle. How is it that King Francis I of France would go to such extreme measures to assist the King of England when they had been such bitter enemies over the centuries? The answer is found in France's most recent significant military defeat. The armies of Emperor Charles V and King Francis I had for years been battling each other for land and influence in the Italian peninsula and on the Continent, and France had lost heavily. The enormity of its defeat was marked by the capture of King Francis by imperial troops in the Battle of Pavia in 1525. Under the subsequent peace treaty, Francis was eventually released, but two of his sons had to temporarily replace him in captivity as Charles's hostages to ensure that France would honour the terms of the treaty.

By July 1530, Charles finally agreed to release Francis's sons, at which point the French king began to seek revenge for his humiliating defeat. As a first step, Francis immediately directed his agents to force the Sorbonne theology faculty to determine in favour of Henry VIII. Regardless of the actual beliefs of the faculty, the university must determine that the Leviticus Prohibitions were divine, natural law, and could not be dispensed by the pope. Today we would explain France's help to its traditional arch-enemy England with the adage, 'The enemy of my enemy is my friend.' The sixteenth-century historian Nicholas Harpsfield expressed it similarly:

> It is also here to be considered that the French King was mortal enemy to the Emperor, and joined with the King of England to further the new marriage [to Anne Boleyn] to the uttermost of his power.[34]

Henry's Christian Theological Strategy

Harpsfield was an English Catholic writer who was strongly critical of Henry VIII's actions, and so should be read with some reservations. He does, however, offer an often-quoted story about England's outright bribery to obtain academic opinions supporting Henry. Harpsfield claims to have heard this story from a primary, or at least a well-informed secondary, source:

> This I am sure that I have heard a doctor and countryman of our own that said he was joined in commission beyond the seas with others about these affairs, report that he full well knew that mules were well laden with English angels [gold coins] that flew far and wide among the learned men of Fraunce and Italic.[35]

In addition to Chapuys in England, another Imperial ambassador was also in a position to report to Charles about developments in Henry's dispute with the pope. Miguel Mai was Charles's ambassador to the Vatican during this period, and on 27 June 1530 he wrote to the emperor about the high amounts of English bribes there and suggested that Catherine's supporters could obtain better results with more modest bribes of their own. The entry in the official records of England summarises Mai's communication:

> The English are still procuring votes by money in Italy, thinking that Italian opinions will gain more credit as being neutral [not English or French]. Thinks 1,000 ducats ought to be spent for the service of the Queen [Catherine of Aragon], as we can do more with 1,000 than they with 25,000. Has already written to suggest this to her Highness.[36]

Later, on 11 September 1530, Mai wrote to Charles that the English were bribing higher-ranking clerics by promising Church positions that would pay substantial annual incomes:

> [H]e had heard that cardinal Trani, who is not a lawyer nor of much authority, had been offered 10,000 ducats of rent to favor the king of England's cause.[37]

Other sources similarly confirmed that the English were purchasing favourable academic opinions to convince the pope. On 23 May 1530,

Charles was sent a discouraging report from Paris written by Dr Pedro Garay, a Spanish envoy attempting to help members of the Sorbonne faculty to oppose the underhanded English attempts to obtain support for Henry:

> I may inform you how they [the faculty of theology] annulled the signatures (*como me quitaron las firmas*) which I had obtained in the Queen's [Catherine's] favor. Until now I have not been able to recover them, with all the efforts used by your ambassadors. The other side [Henry's agents] have gained, by money, threats, and importunity, with the favor in which they are held, thirty-five signatures or more; among which are four or five even of those who had signed for the Queen. Fears they will gain a vote in the name of the whole faculty for the king of England.[38]

Also in May 1530, Rodrigo Niño, the Imperial ambassador in Venice, reported to Charles that he had convinced the Signory, the governing body of Venice, to try to protect the authority of the Holy See by blocking the English attempts to bribe the professors at Padua:

> Of six professors, five answered that they would obey the command of the Signory, notwithstanding that they had been spoken to by the agents of the king of England and [had been] offered great rewards, and they would get out of the business with the best grace they could.[39]

Despite this imperialist intervention, the situation in Venice for Queen Catherine and her major ally, her nephew Charles V, worsened. By July 1530, Ambassador Niño warned Charles:

> Hears the king of England's agents have obtained more than 150 signatures. Wonders they are not 100,000; for those that they cannot obtain by promises [of financial rewards] they do by threats, and all their proceedings are secret. ... They told him also that he knew it was the intention of the king of England, when he had got the opinions of the learned, if the Pope [Clement] refused to annul (*dar por ninguna*) the dispensation [by Pope Julius authorising Henry to marry Catherine], to marry in fact

the lady he meant to marry [Anne Boleyn], and put the Queen [Catherine] in a castle where no one should see her.[40]

Niño also wrote to Charles in July 1530 that the English ambassador admitted that Henry's agents in Italy had sought 'the opinions of friars who could not read' and that they also had withheld the opinions 'of the many learned men who had given a contrary opinion'.[41] This was confirmed by Ambassador Mai:

> The bishop of London [Stokesley] has got eleven friars at Padua, not very well qualified either by learning or religion, to give an opinion, in the name of the university, that the Pope could not dispense in the matter of the king of England.[42]

Indeed, the Bishop of London appears to have been so busy bribing Italian clerics to issue favourable opinions for Henry that he sounds somewhat surprised that he could obtain any without having to pay for them. In his 23 September 1530 letter to Henry, Stokesley tells the king:

> The theologians of Bologna are so well affected to the King they will take no reward, *'sed quod a Spiritu Sancto gratis acceperunt, gratis et libenter impertiunt'* [but the Holy Spirit received, freely and willingly impart].[43]

It has been noted by many of the other contemporaneous observers and modern commentators that both sides resorted to some measure of bribery, political pressure, and fraud in seeking favourable opinions from university faculties and Christian theologians. However, England seems to have been the initiator and most persistent and widespread practitioner of these stratagems.

The Role of Richard Croke
The best evidence of England's bribery and fraud in procuring the European university faculties' purported support for Henry's case can be found in the extensive correspondence from Henry's chief agent in that procurement process. Professor Richard Croke, a Cambridge scholar in Greek language and history,[44] was well suited to the initial part of his task – to gain access to Vatican or other private libraries

and obtain copies of ancient theological writings of the Church Fathers and early popes that might support Henry's case. But the second part of his assignment was to obtain supporting opinions from universities and individual clerics in Italy. This second role seems to have presented some pragmatic challenges not familiar to a Cambridge professor of Classics.

In his correspondence, Croke shamelessly makes no attempt to disguise the level of bribery and trickery that he orchestrated in Italy. Indeed, the most central recurring theme in Croke's reports during 1530 is money. Among his largest expenses were the funds used to pay for university faculty determinations and individual opinions in favour of the king's case.

As an example, on 1 July 1530, Croke wrote to Henry recounting his successful efforts in obtaining a favourable opinion under university seal from the faculty at Padua. Croke not only admits that he had to spend 100 crowns to obtain that opinion, but he goes on to complain that he could have achieved much more if only he had been provided with sufficient funds to purchase further support.[45]

Even if we look only at correspondence from or to Richard Croke quoted or summarised in England's official records collected in *Letters and Papers* for 1530, we can find almost thirty references in that single year to payments used to procure opinions and subscriptions in support of Henry's case.[46]

8

WHY HENRY'S CHRISTIAN SOURCES FAILED

After the collapse of the Blackfriars trial in 1529, Henry hoped to convince the pope that he must grant the annulment based upon the rulings of ancient and contemporary Christian authorities. However, the royal envoys were never able to produce sufficiently convincing Catholic interpretations of the Leviticus Prohibitions as natural law beyond the power of papal dispensation. The problem was that the Leviticus Prohibitions against affinity incest appeared to conflict with the Deuteronomy obligations of levirate marriage. Not only did the two biblical provisions themselves appear inconsistent with one another, but the interpretations among the Church fathers as well as contemporary Christian theologians were also often inconsistent.

The Opposition Cites Levirate Marriage Examples in the Bible
The opposition responded in kind to counter the king's new theological strategy. Henry's opponents were able to point to several situations in the Old Testament (the Catholic version of the Hebrew Bible) and the New Testament where, without suffering divine disapproval or punishment, prominent biblical characters had married in situations that were, or came close to being, levirate marriages in apparent violation of the Leviticus Prohibitions.

Judah and Tamar
The first levirate marriage story, in Genesis 38:6–30, tells the saga of Judah and his daughter-in-law Tamar. According to the biblical

timeline, this occurs before the giving of both the Levitical laws, Lev. 18:16, 20:21, and the levirate marriage obligations in Deuteronomy, Deut. 25:5–10. Nevertheless, the story offers strong support for God's insistence upon the moral obligations underlying levirate marriage.[1]

Judah's second son, Onan, refuses to fulfil the duty of impregnating Tamar, the widow of his older brother, Er. God deems Onan's refusal as wicked and takes his life. At the close of the story, Judah acknowledges that he had been wrong to withhold his remaining son, Shelah, from performing the levirate duties to Tamar.

The problem for Henry is clear: if God is squarely behind the obligations of levirate marriage later proclaimed in Deuteronomy, then the Leviticus Prohibitions cannot constitute immutable natural and divine law.[2]

Ruth and Boaz

Later in the Hebrew Bible, the Book of Ruth deals with a quasi-levirate marriage situation describing many elements closely similar to those recited in Deuteronomy. After their respective husbands die, Naomi discourages her Moabite daughters-in-law, Orpah and Ruth, from accompanying Naomi back to her homeland in Bethlehem. She urges them to stay and remarry in Moab. Naomi explains that she is too old to remarry, and even if she could, and could bear other sons, it would take too long before those infants would grow old enough to marry Orpah and Ruth.[3]

Orpah complies and returns to Moab, but Ruth insists on accompanying her mother-in-law to Bethlehem. The story ends when Boaz, a kinsman of Ruth's deceased husband, wishes to marry her. The Bible describes how Boaz must first arrange for a closer redeeming kinsman to refuse the priority for performing the duty of marrying Ruth. The description of this refusal includes many of the unique *halitzah* ceremonial requirements of Deuteronomy, including Ruth removing the sandal of the closer redeeming kinsman in the presence of the elders at the gate.[4]

The Grandfathers of Jesus

For Christian interpreters, the New Testament similarly presents an illustrious example of God's apparent acceptance of levirate marriage. St Joseph, husband of Jesus' mother, Mary, is given two genealogies in the Gospels of Matthew and Luke, which name two different fathers of Joseph, Heli and Jacob. Each named father of Joseph is a son of Joseph's grandfather called 'Matthan' in Matthew or 'Matthat' in Luke. Joseph's two fathers are therefore taken to be brothers. An early explanation for this situation was that the two brothers named as fathers of Joseph married the same woman. After the death of Heli without children, his brother Jacob married Heli's widow, who gave birth to Joseph. Thus, Jacob was Joseph's biological father, but just as under the Jewish levirate marriage tradition, Joseph was legally treated as the descendant and heir of Heli, Jacob's deceased brother.[5]

Henry's Response to the Challenges of Deuteronomy
Henry Denies that His Marriage to Catherine Qualified under Deuteronomy

Henry's supporters tried to shake off the threat posed by these significant biblical exemplars of levirate-type marriage. Henry had previously attempted to raise technical arguments to show that his marriage to Catherine could not come under the Deuteronomy requirements for levirate marriage. Henry could convincingly show that his motivation in marrying Catherine was to establish his own line of descendants who would become heirs to his crown, and not to produce an heir of his deceased brother, Arthur.

At this juncture, however, attempting again to raise such a technical argument would miss the point. The question was no longer a legal issue of whether Henry's particular marriage could be deemed to satisfy the Deuteronomy requirements for levirate marriage, and might therefore threaten to exempt him from the Leviticus Prohibitions. By 1530, Henry had turned to theological arguments. The central issue was now simply whether Deuteronomy's levirate marriage provisions remained in effect for Christians, showing that there could be some exceptions to the Leviticus Prohibitions. It made no difference whether Henry's own marriage did or did not fall within the Deuteronomy provisions. Henry had to overcome the dispensation of Pope Julius II.

The problem for the king was that the Catholic Church was 1,500 years old. During that long existence, it had produced and preserved a record on the Deuteronomy/Leviticus debate that included inconsistent theological opinions, and even inconsistent formal rulings by popes and councils. Because there were enough opinions and decisions to support either side of the argument, both King Henry and Pope Clement could support their positions by selectively relying upon helpful Church precedents. The answer remained stubbornly ambiguous. It appears that, on the issue of levirate marriage, Church history offered Henry's side only modest theoretical support for the Leviticus Prohibitions to control, while Clement and the opposition could point to more impressive confirmation that the obligations of Deuteronomy were still theologically relevant for Catholics. The pope remained unmoved by the Christian authorities offered by the king.

Henry had to find a different way to attack Deut. 25:5–10 if he wanted to convince Clement that the Leviticus Prohibitions against affinity incest constituted indispensable natural law. This theological issue of biblical interpretation became the final battleground for Henry's assault upon his marriage.

Henry's Proof from Lev. 20:21

Of course, Henry could still point to his original proof – the argument that he had used at the beginning of the Great Matter, three years previously, when he began to explain the origin of his scruples concerning his marriage to Catherine. It is not clear how sincere that argument had been at that time, but by 1530 the king seemed to have convinced at least himself that his cause was unquestionably just. According to Henry, the biblical proof that justified his scruples is found in the second of the Leviticus verses mentioning the specific prohibition of sexual access to your brother's wife. Lev. 20:21 not only repeats the initial prohibition of Lev. 18:16, but also expresses the particular divine punishment for its violation – the offending couple shall remain childless (*Aririm yihiu*: 'They shall be without children' in the Douay–Rheims Bible of 1609).[6]

In 1527, Henry had claimed that his conscience was deeply troubled because, in almost two decades of marriage, Catherine had failed to provide him with a male heir to his throne. He saw this as the divine punishment promised in Lev. 20:21. This confirmed to him that, in God's eyes, Henry's marriage to his brother's widow constituted impermissible affinity incest despite Pope Julius's dispensation, and despite the levirate marriage provisions in Deuteronomy.

In 1530, Henry continued to spin his interesting story based upon this explanation. Unfortunately, while the king was deeply disappointed by the facts of his marriage, those facts did not fit very well with the wording of the punishment specified in Lev. 20:21. The

Bible's punishment states that the couple will be 'childless'. However, Catherine had at least seven pregnancies during those two decades of her marriage to Henry, and several of those occasions resulted in live births. In 1511, Catherine gave birth to a son who survived for fifty-two days. Another son was born in 1513, but died very soon after birth. By 1527, when Henry first asserted that his marriage was childless, Princess Mary, born in 1516, had already survived early childhood. Indeed, she would survive until age forty-two, and during the last five years of her life she would reign as Queen Mary I of England.

Henry's argument from Lev. 20:21 might have been accepted by some of his subjects, but it was not sufficiently convincing to sway the pope. The argument relied upon retranslating the biblical language to change 'without children' to say 'without sons', or perhaps 'without [surviving] heirs'. Henry did receive some early support for such a translation from Robert Wakefield, one of England's earliest Christian Hebraists,[7] who was willing to argue that the translation of Lev. 20:21 appearing in the Vulgate, which had served as the authoritative Latin translation of the Bible for the prior millennium, was in error.

According to Wakefield, the Hebrew text of this Leviticus verse declares as punishment that the offending couple will be without 'sons' rather than without 'children'. The linguistic foundation for Wakefield's position is simply wrong as a matter of Hebrew biblical grammar.[8] Moreover, even if correct, it would be irrelevant to Henry's situation because Catherine had previously provided her husband with a son and heir who survived for almost two months. Worse, Wakefield's critics noted that he had earlier taken a contrary position, and only changed his opinion after Henry started to pay him for doing so.[9]

Wakefield's creative translation of the biblical verse was forcefully opposed by John Fisher, Bishop of Rochester. Fisher noted that the Vulgate had been authoritative for many centuries. Surely God would not have left his children without appropriate guidance for so long. Therefore, only the pope could change such long-accepted interpretation. Fisher's opposition was joined by several of the most respected Catholic theologians of that time.[10]

Do the Levirate Marriage Provisions of Deut. 25:5–10 Apply for Christians?
To gain traction for his arguments against Deuteronomy, Henry had to move beyond his argument based upon Lev. 20:21. He had to show

Clement that the Deuteronomy provisions requiring levirate marriage did not apply for Christians. He asserted that Deut. 25:5–10 was only a historical recital of an ancient Jewish ritual, and that those biblical verses constituted recollection, not legislation. Moreover, the New Testament did not formally approve those Deuteronomy provisions, and Jesus had never expressly confirmed them. Therefore, Henry argued, the existence of the historical recital in Deuteronomy did not diminish the absolute force of the Leviticus Prohibitions for Christians.[11]

Catherine's Supporters Cite Prior Rulings by Popes Permitting Violations of Leviticus Prohibitions

Some of Henry's major supporters in England, including Thomas Cranmer and Edward Lee, later Archbishop of York, had stated that levirate marriage had never applied to Christians.[12] But the king could garner only disappointingly meagre additional support on this point from independent clerics or major universities in continental Europe. Once again, some inconvenient facts interfered with Henry's hopes.

Pope Gregory I (r. 590–604)

The sixteenth century was far from the first time that the Church had grappled with the question of whether the Leviticus Prohibitions applied to Christians. As previously mentioned, the first major papal ruling on the issue was issued by Pope Gregory I at the end of the sixth century. Coincidentally, Gregory's ruling also happened to be directed to the Catholic Church in England – specifically to the first Catholic Archbishop of Canterbury, Augustine of Canterbury (served 597–604 and later canonised as St Augustine of Canterbury).

Pope Gregory had sent Augustine to England to convert the Anglo-Saxon pagans. Augustine asked Gregory to instruct him regarding those new Catholics who, prior to conversion, had married an in-law within the degrees of Leviticus affinity. Pope Gregory determined that the Leviticus Prohibitions prohibited marriage within 'three or four generations', expressly including marriage to a deceased brother's wife. However, in the interests of encouraging conversions, Gregory determined that new Catholics who had contracted such marriages before conversion need only 'be admonished that they [henceforth] abstain from each other', but that they were neither disqualified from conversion nor deprived of the sacrament of communion.[13]

Gregory did not declare the in-law marriages void, and he did not require the offending parties to divorce. His response to Augustine distinguishes between sinning through ignorance before conversion, which can be treated with leniency, and knowingly sinning after conversion, having been instructed concerning the laws.[14]

Beyond the specific facts upon which Gregory ruled, his assertion of a pope's ability to treat some transgressions with leniency, including the Leviticus Prohibitions, presents a powerful rebuttal to Henry VIII's core argument that Julius II had lacked the power to dispense any violation of the Leviticus Prohibitions.[15]

Pope Innocent III (r. 1198–1216)

This ancient ruling of Pope Gregory I was confirmed and expanded at the outset of the thirteenth century by Pope Innocent III, who likewise favoured liberal rules to facilitate conversion, as well as reducing the forbidden degrees of relationship for all Catholics for purposes of the Leviticus Prohibitions.[16] In 1201, the pagan converts being considered were not in the British Isles but in the Baltics. However, like the pagans who had been considered earlier by Gregory, the pagan tribes of Livonia observed the custom of marrying the widow of a deceased brother. In his 19 April 1201 decretal letter, *Deus Qui Ecclesiam*, to the Bishop of Livonia, Innocent III ruled that the pagan converts

> may continue in marriages contracted with the widows of brothers if they contracted this marriage in order to raise a seed in the name of the deceased according to the Mosaic law when a brother dies childless, provided they do not enter into such a forbidden relationship any more after they adopted the Christian faith ... [Pope Innocent III goes on to state that:] following in the footsteps of Pope Gregory, [Innocent makes] the following dispensation, that, until the people are more firmly rooted in the Faith, they may contract marriages in the fourth and subsequent generations.[17]

Pope Innocent had dealt Henry's position a double blow: not only did the Deuteronomy provisions about levirate marriage continue to have some relevance for Christians in derogation of the Leviticus

Prohibitions, but since Innocent expressly granted 'dispensation' for some transgressions of Leviticus rules, it follows that Leviticus marital laws were not matters of indispensable natural law.[18]

Other Instances of Medieval Papal Dispensations from the Leviticus Prohibitions

Henry's opponents also pointed to other relatively recent instances in the fifteenth and sixteenth centuries where medieval popes granted dispensations for marriages despite the Levitical laws against affinity incest, including Pope Martin V (r. 1417–1431), as approved by the Council of Constance, and Pope Alexander VI (r. 1492–1503).[19]

By coincidence, several of the recent papal dispensations regarding these general topic areas had direct connections with the parties involved in Henry's attempt to obtain an annulment. Queen Catherine's sister, Princess Isabella of Aragon, had been the first wife of King Manuel I of Portugal. She gave birth to a son named Miguel, who died in infancy, and she thereafter died in 1498. Alexander VI then allowed King Manuel to marry his sister-in-law, Princess Maria of Aragon, another sister of Catherine. Although Lev. 18:18 technically prohibits marrying a wife's sister only during that first wife's lifetime, the affinity relationship apparently seemed close enough to the kind of conduct barred by the group of Leviticus Prohibitions that papal dispensation had been requested and granted.[20]

Even Henry VIII had a personal connection with a consequential papal dispensation of the Leviticus Prohibitions – the very thing that Henry now claimed could not be granted. The Tudor line had been established by Henry's father, Henry VII, whose legal claim to inherit the throne came through Henry VIII's paternal grandmother, Margaret Beaufort. Margaret Beaufort's claim came through her grandfather John Beaufort, the grandson of King Edward III and the legitimised son of John of Gaunt. Despite the Leviticus Prohibitions, John Beaufort had received a dispensation to marry his uncle's widow, Margaret Holland, who bore him six children including Margaret Beaufort's father, the first duke of Somerset.[21]

Even worse, it certainly did not help Henry VIII's dispute with Pope Clement VII that the most recent papal dispensations in somewhat related situations had been issued by Clement himself: he had allowed at least two noblemen to marry the sister of a previous wife.[22]

Why Henry's Christian Sources Failed

While none of these later precedents appears to have expressly relied upon Deuteronomy, they made the salient point that a succession of relatively recent papal rulings amply demonstrated that the Leviticus Prohibitions were subject to papal dispensation. If Henry wanted to make a winning argument from theology, he would have to look elsewhere to find convincing support for his right to an annulment.

PART IV

HENRY TURNS TO THE RABBIS

9

HENRY TURNS TO JEWISH LAW

It was at the outset of 1530 that Henry's already unprecedented campaign to end his marriage took an even stranger turn. The argument with Pope Clement had narrowed down to a single crucial question of biblical interpretation: despite the existence of the levirate marriage provisions in Deuteronomy, did the Leviticus Prohibitions create an indispensable bar to Henry's marriage to Catherine? If the ancient, medieval, and contemporary Catholic opinions on this question failed to convince Clement, where could Henry find higher authorities to support his theological arguments to the pope?[1]

Origin of the Strategy to Seek Jewish Support
It is not entirely clear who deserves credit for devising Henry's final strategy of obtaining helpful interpretations of Jewish law from rabbis in Italy. It is possible that when Thomas Cranmer initially suggested seeking theological authorities to convince Pope Clement, he may have also mentioned that, in addition to consulting Christian sources, Henry should obtain rabbinic opinions about Jewish law and current practices.

However, the initial instructions given to Richard Croke, describing Croke's duties in Italy, apparently referred only to searching for ancient Christian documents, which was within the area of Croke's scholarly expertise, and obtaining contemporary Catholic opinions. The additional orders, to seek helpful early or current Jewish interpretations of the Leviticus/Deuteronomy conflict, were given to Croke in subsequent instructions by John Stokesley, Bishop of London, who had been sent to join Henry's envoys in Italy. Some historians conclude that the concept of gathering the theological views of the Jews was not simply passed along by Stokesley, but that he may have initiated the idea.[2]

Even if we cannot be certain who came up with the idea of seeking Jewish opinions, it is not difficult to imagine the thought process that led to this strategy. In the Great Matter, the most unique aspect of the dispute concerning biblical interpretations was that the issues were centred on the apparent conflict between the affinity incest provisions in the Book of Leviticus and the levirate marriage provisions in the Book of Deuteronomy. These are both books of the Hebrew Bible, which had been incorporated, with some variations, as the Old Testament portion of the Catholic Bible. By 1530, the Jews possessed access to a rich, long history of interpretation of the Hebrew Bible, beginning before the Common Era, which had been recorded in their Talmud and later works of rabbinic commentary. Moreover, in 1530, Jewish communities continued to exist in some Christian and Muslim lands, and rabbinic academies had been established in some of these communities. These Jewish communities also had local community rabbinic courts or individual rabbis who regularly determined how to apply the laws of the Hebrew Bible to current situations.

Jews and Christians alike agreed that God had initially given Leviticus and Deuteronomy to the Jews, who still read them in the original Hebrew language. If there existed any possible source of biblical interpretation regarding the apparent Leviticus/Deuteronomy conflict that could be presented to the pope as more authoritative than even the Church's own mixed rulings and interpretations, perhaps it could be found in the traditional and contemporary laws and community practices of the Jews.

Early Hope of Support from the Rabbis

At the end of 1529, before hearing from the Jews, it appeared that Deuteronomy might be an insurmountable theological barrier to Henry's right to an annulment. Then, on 18 January 1530, one of Henry's agents received news of what Henry may have regarded as an extremely providential development. Richard Croke, Henry's busiest representative in Italy, told Bishop Stokesley that he had obtained and was sending over definitive rabbinic opinions on Jewish law and practice. These opinions would show that, at least since the fall of Jerusalem in 70 CE, Jews no longer observed the levirate marriage provisions of Deuteronomy. Moreover, the Jews had always interpreted the Deuteronomy rules as being subject to the Leviticus affinity incest prohibitions, and in any event, they had always regarded levirate marriage as an option, not an obligation:

> The Jews tell him [Croke] that the law of Deuteronomy has never been kept since the fall of Jerusalem, and, what Stokesley was very desirous to have confirmed, that it is not intended to be kept, except where it is allowed by the Levitical law, and they do not consider it obligatory except where causes and circumstances expressly urge it, and not even then is it absolutely obligatory. They say that it was always an alternative, either to marry the brother's widow, *'vel pati discalciationem'* ['or suffer removal of the shoe' – referring to the shaming ceremony of *halitzah* specified in Deut. 25:8–10 for a brother who is obligated to perform levirate marriage but refuses to do so. Cf. Ruth 4:7–10]. Has letters on this point from two Jews, – one a physician and a rabbi, and the other a convert to Christianity.[3]

The physician/rabbi referred to by Croke was Elijah Menahem Halfan, whose support for Henry's case will be detailed below. The convert to Christianity refers to Mark Raphael, who became Henry's most important and longest-serving authority on Jewish law and practice for the dispute. His unique activities will also be discussed in detail below.

When Henry's search for Jewish authorities began, Stephen Gardner and Edward Fox were no longer his principal envoys in Italy. Moreover, by 1530, Henry had also lost confidence in, and ceased any significant contact with, his former chief advisor, Cardinal Wolsey. Stripped of his power and wealth, the cardinal would die at the end of 1530 on the road to the Tower, where he would have likely faced execution.

Therefore, for critical tasks in Italy, Henry now personally supervised and primarily relied upon Richard Croke, aided by England's two major resident representatives in Italy, Girolamo Ghinucci, Bishop of Worcester, and Gregory Casale, Henry's ambassador to the Vatican.

Bishop Stokesley also remained in Italy to help obtain university opinions.

Henry Is Reassured by Richard Croke

It is not clear if Henry was aware that Croke's style on this mission was to make overly optimistic promises to deliver favourable opinions and votes. The king had several reasons for believing Croke's repeated assurances that he would soon receive the crucial supporting opinions of Jewish law and practice.

For one thing, Henry was ready to receive – and believe – good news because by this time he had fully convinced himself of the righteousness of his cause. He believed he was, essentially, the absolute monarch of England and thus did not feel that he needed any outside confirmation of his judgment in the matter. Nevertheless, it must have been pleasing for him to hear that ancient and modern Jews shared his conclusions about Leviticus triumphing over Deuteronomy in this conflict. After three years of painful disappointment, Henry was more than ready to finally receive some good news, especially news that heralded the imminent and favourable end of his Great Matter.

Perhaps most importantly, Henry could readily believe whatever was reported to him about the Jews, since he knew essentially nothing about the Jewish people or their religion, history, or culture. After all, Henry was the Catholic king of a Catholic England without Jews.

An England without Jews

As detailed in Chapter 1, since 1290 – which was 240 years before Henry sought help from the rabbis of Italy – and continuing until about 1657, Jews were barred from the Kingdom of England.[4] Although there were a few individual exceptions to this in the first half of the sixteenth century, there was no significant, openly identifiable Jewish community in England then – no Anglo-Jewish academies existed that could decide, and there were no Anglo-Jewish rabbis who could openly opine or instruct.[5]

Moreover, Jewish scholarly works of biblical interpretation were not yet easily accessible for study by Christians in England. This makes all the more noteworthy Henry's ultimate reliance upon Jewish authorities to try to convince the pope.[6] Extraordinarily, despite his personal isolation from Judaism, Henry's final strategy to win annulment by Clement was to search in Italy for evidence of rabbinic opinions and Jewish communal practices.

This in no way implies that Henry wanted his marriage to Catherine to end by means of a formal divorce decree from a rabbi or a rabbinic court.[7] The king didn't care in the slightest whether the termination of his marriage to Catherine would be recognised by the wider Jewish community. This is because, during the time that he was attempting to convince the pope to end his marriage to Catherine, Henry saw himself as continuing to be what he had been for his entire life up to then – a devout Roman Catholic.

Henry attended mass several times a day, read the Catholic Bible in Latin, composed Church music, and led the royal court in celebrating the crowded calendar of Church holidays. He had even earned for himself and his successors the title of Defender of the Faith from a grateful Pope Leo X in 1521 for writing a strong defence to Martin Luther's theological attacks against Catholicism.[8] It is fair to say that the whole point of Henry enduring his ultimately unsuccessful six-year struggle to have Pope Clement VII issue a formal decree of annulment was not the king's determination simply to end his marriage to Catherine. Henry hoped, at least for most of those six years, to end that marriage within the laws and procedures of the Roman Catholic Church.

Therefore, it is especially ironic that issues of Jewish theology and Jewish practice became the basis of what would become this very Catholic king's final attempt to convince the pope to annul his marriage. Henry VIII's last-ditch reliance upon Jewish law certainly presents a fascinating historical anomaly. Perhaps it also provides us with a new marker of the depth of Henry's unflagging determination to marry Ann Boleyn.

The Talmud and Early Rabbinic Interpretations of Levirate Marriage

As we have seen, when Henry sent new English agents to Italy to find ancient Church documents and opinions that would convince Clement to grant the annulment, he chose as his primary envoy Richard Croke, an academic classicist who could readily read early documents written in old style Latin or Greek. Croke's assignment was almost immediately broadened to include obtaining Jewish authorities on the Deuteronomy/Leviticus conflict. However, any original ancient Jewish books or documents on this issue would not be written in formal Latin or Greek, but rather in Hebrew or Aramaic languages. There is no evidence that Croke or Henry's other agents in Italy were fluent in these tongues.[9]

Thus, Croke's search for Jewish authorities was restricted to securing opinions from contemporaneous rabbis and scholars in the Jewish communities located throughout Catholic Italy. Since he lacked easy access to those communities, he needed help to locate rabbis who might be helpful. To arrange for such contacts, Croke had to rely heavily on former Jews who had converted to Catholicism, and a few Catholic clerics who were early Hebraists – Christian scholars who learned to read and translate Hebrew and Aramaic documents so that they could better understand the Hebrew Bible and the Jewish religion.[10]

Thanks to the early development in Italy of Hebrew language printing using moveable type with Hebrew fonts, a significant number of authoritative books of Jewish law and commentary on the law had been printed in Hebrew and were available in Italy by 1530.[11] However, like the Hebrew Bible itself, these books require informed interpretation to help the reader comprehend normative Jewish beliefs and practices. Croke and the other English envoys in Italy do not seem to have been aware that such books were available, and in any event, Henry's representatives would have been unable to read and interpret books printed in Hebrew and Aramaic.

Without being able to study Jewish books of interpretation, Henry and his English agents in Italy lacked the critical ability to understand and evaluate the bias, context, nuance, and even the basic accuracy or inaccuracy of the oral and written reports of Jewish law, custom, and current practice that Croke and the others managed to obtain from some local rabbis and converts. In particular, the English envoys lacked functional access to the two Jewish works that then, and still today, contain the most important detailed discussions of levirate marriage – the Babylonian Talmud and Maimonides's *Mishneh Torah*.

The Babylonian Talmud

The most significant early Jewish commentary and interpretation regarding the Deuteronomy levirate marriage provisions is found in the Babylonian Talmud (the 'Bavli'). The Bavli is a compilation of hundreds of years of rabbinic oral commentary on the Torah by a series of rabbis who lived and studied in Babylonia for many centuries after the destruction of the First Temple in Jerusalem in 586 BCE.[12] The final form of the Bavli was completed around the year 600 CE.

If Henry's agents had obtained – and, of course, if they could have read – copies of the Talmud available in Italy in 1530, they would have seen that an entire section (a *tractate*) called *Yevamot* ('sisters-in-law') is devoted to the topic of levirate marriage.

Much of Yevamot records the rabbis' attempts to explore the laws of levirate marriage by subjecting almost every word of the six verses of Deuteronomy 25:5–10 to deep analysis of increasingly complex hypothetical situations, each requiring more inventive answers. What are the rules if two brothers marry two sisters? What if six brothers are born, marry and die in a particular order?[13] Especially as formulated for a culture that recognised polygamy, the hypothetical variations in these intellectual mind games involving multiple spouses are almost dizzying to follow.[14]

The rabbis of Yevamot offer a further challenge to readers by considering in detail whether and how to apply the rules of levirate marriage to special situations of sexual intercourse such as rape, infidelity, minor widows, minor brothers-in-law, ritual disqualification for marriage to a priest, levirate betrothal without physical consummation, and physical consummation without levirate betrothal.

In addition to directly examining how the levirate marriage law would apply to various situations, Yevamot also applies the Talmudic technique of attempting to explore the law of one matter by citing analogies from other matters that are sometimes entirely factually unrelated. The arguments of various rabbis in the Talmud about the laws of levirate marriage turn for support to rules relating to such amazingly diverse topics as fringes on a prayer shawl; the time set for reading the Megillah Scroll of Esther on the holiday of Purim; cutting oneself in mourning; disputes between the House of Hillel and the House of Shammai; the force of local custom to change application of a general law; ritual impurity; the status of illegitimate children (*mamzerim*); the status of converts to Judaism; specifications for plumbing connections required for ritual baths (*mikvot*); and the construction of olive barrels.

Thanks to printers such as the Soncino family in Soncino in modern-day Italy, and especially Daniel Bomberg in Venice, printed copies of the Bavli in Hebrew and Aramaic were available in 1530 to Henry's agents in Italy. However, an England without Jews and without established Christian Hebraists simply lacked the resources and time that would be necessary to learn from the substantial but deeply complex discussions of levirate marriage in the Talmud.

Maimonides and *Mishneh Torah*

Although the Talmud can be forbiddingly complex without extensive prior learning, it was not the only authoritative source of traditional Jewish interpretation of the biblical laws of levirate marriage available in early sixteenth-century Italy. Indeed, the most important alternative authority – and one of the first works of rabbinic commentary to be printed in Hebrew – had been written as a direct response to the complexity of the Talmud. This book was *Mishneh Torah* (the Torah 'repeated', or 'restated') by Rabbi Moses Maimonides – Rabbi Moshe Ben Maimon (1135–1204) – often called by his acronym, *Rambam*.

Maimonides

Maimonides was born in Cordoba, now part of Spain but then a Muslim territory, in 1135. The family had to leave Cordoba in 1147, moving about to avoid persecution by the militant Almohad invaders. The family moved to Fez, Morocco, in 1159. After brief periods of living in Palestine and Alexandria, they eventually settled in Fustat (today, Old Cairo) in Egypt in 1167. There, after a few years, Maimonides began writing *Mishneh Torah*, which he completed about a decade later, in 1180.

Maimonides was a man of remarkable achievements. One of Judaism's greatest philosophers, theologians, and authors, he was also a renowned physician to the Jewish community of Fustat, as well as appointed court physician to El Fadil, vizier to Sultan Saladin in the royal palace in Cairo.[15] He became the acknowledged leader and religious judge of the local Jewish community as well as the rabbinic authority for many Jewish communities throughout the world. He read the Torah as informed by, rather than in opposition to, the classical system of Aristotelian philosophy and logic.

Maimonides recognised that the typical Jew of his era lacked the time and training needed to properly master the convoluted discourses of the Talmud. Moreover, since Maimonides was writing in the twelfth century, before the era of the printing press, the average Jew had no practical access to the precious handwritten copies of the Talmud and early rabbinic commentaries. Therefore, Maimonides wanted to enable even the simplest, poorest Jew to understand what was commanded by Jewish law, requiring access only to the Torah itself and to his *Mishneh Torah*. Accordingly, he reordered the topics of the Talmud into a more logical presentation and offered a comprehensive but compressed code of Jewish biblical law. By enumerating and briefly explicating all of the 613 commandments of the Torah, Maimonides was able to make his code of Jewish law easier to access, understand, and remember.

Somewhat ironically, this lofty goal of universal access was misunderstood by some in the Jewish community when the book was written. Many Jews thought that Maimonides was attempting to interfere with the continuing grand project of traditional Talmudic study and post-Talmudic commentary when he failed to include the recorded interpretations by some two thousand revered rabbis of Jewish antiquity.[16] Instead, Maimonides essentially presented only his conclusory statements of the laws of Torah.[17] Therefore, some Jewish factions in that early era rejected *Mishneh Torah*, believing it to be anti-Talmudic. However, in a second turn, later generations came to revere both Maimonides and his *Mishneh Torah*, which explains why it became one of the first rabbinic books printed in Hebrew characters by the new Jewish publishing houses of the late fifteenth and early sixteenth centuries.[18]

Mishneh Torah and Levirate Marriage

Even if Richard Croke and Henry's other agents in Italy had obtained one of the printed copies of *Mishneh Torah* available in Italy in 1530 – and presuming that they had been able to read it – King Henry would likely not have been pleased with the mixed results found in this resource. At first, he might have been pleased that it confirms the negative commandment of Lev. 18:16, as stated by Maimonides: 'Not to have sexual relations with one's brother's wife, as it is written thou shalt not uncover the nakedness of thy brother's wife [Negative commandment #344].'[19]

However, *Mishneh Torah* also provides a very extensive discussion of other rules of marriage. Therefore, if Henry had sought to use parts of Maimonides' Code to prove his case, the pope could in turn have relied upon other parts of the same book to oppose the king. The Vatican cardinals would have been able to point out several specific Jewish laws recited by Maimonides that would have been very damaging to Henry's position.

The primary problem for Henry would have been the extensive discussion in *Mishneh Torah* of the Deuteronomy obligations of levirate marriage. As previously noted, by 1530, the core of Henry's position was his reliance upon the theory of natural law – that the Leviticus Prohibitions against affinity in-law incest were absolute and indispensable divine law, applicable to all peoples regardless of their specific religions. To be consistent with this, Henry also argued that the obligations of levirate marriage in Deuteronomy were nothing more than a historical recital of ancient Hebrew tribal customs. Levirate marriage may have once been binding upon Jews, but it was never formally adopted by the Christian Bible. Henry tried to convince Pope Clement that, as a matter of logic, levirate marriage simply could not coexist with Catholicism's long history of express adoption and active implementation of the laws recited in the Leviticus Prohibitions.

Unfortunately for Henry, *Mishneh Torah* would have demolished that position, at least as a matter of Jewish law. The book begins with a preface that enumerates each of the 613 laws that declare commandments (*mitzvot*) of the Torah – 248 positive commandments and 365 negative commandments. Maimonides makes clear that the laws of levirate marriage in Deut. 25:5–10 contain three of the Torah's 613 commandments.[20] Thus, under Jewish law as codified by Maimonides, the divine laws of Deuteronomy continue very much alive. They were not repealed by the Leviticus Prohibitions.

Mishneh Torah *and* Halitzah

Similarly, according to *Mishneh Torah*, the *halitzah* ceremony detailed in Deut. 25:9, whereby the surviving brother can refuse to marry his widowed sister-in-law, does not render the entire group of levirate marriage commandments void. Maimonides takes the position that, although *halitzah* is also a divine commandment, the basic levirate marriage obligation provisions of Deuteronomy are to be preferred over the Deuteronomy exception for *halitzah* release: 'The commandment to contract levirate marriage has precedence over the commandment to perform *halitzah*.'[21]

Mishneh Torah *and the Leviticus/Deuteronomy Conflict*

Maimonides also explains how Jewish law resolves the apparent conflict between the Deuteronomy obligation of levirate marriage and the Leviticus Prohibitions against affinity incest. Traditional Jewish law reads all of the Torah commandments as having been decreed by God at Sinai, and therefore as having equal, divine authority, regardless of the order in which they appear in the Torah. The Deuteronomy provisions appearing later in the Torah cannot be read to repeal, or to be repealed by, the negative commandment in Leviticus prohibiting sexual relations with a brother's wife. When a positive commandment appears to be in conflict with a negative commandment, the rabbis must search for a way to interpret the provisions in a manner that would uphold both provisions. If that cannot be done, however, Maimonides states that 'wherever you find a positive and a negative commandment together [in conflict regarding the same action], the positive commandment supersedes the negative commandment'.[22] This is a restatement of the same principle in the Talmud:

> Any place where you find a positive *mitzvah* [commandment] and a prohibition that clash with one another, if you can find some way to fulfill both, that is preferable; and if that is not possible, the positive *mitzvah* will come and override the prohibition.[23]

Thus, under Jewish law, if a brother has died without issue, the positive commandment under Deuteronomy requiring Levirate marriage applies, subject to the *halitzah* release, while in all other cases of a living or deceased brother, the prohibition against marrying a brother's wife applies.

Even more problematic for Henry would be the analysis in *Mishneh Torah* concerning Lev. 18:18, which forbids having sexual relations with two sisters during their joint lifetimes. Maimonides agrees with the Talmud that this Leviticus provision is a very strong prohibition. Thus, even if Henry secured an effective annulment of his marriage to Catherine, if Jewish law applied, his previous sexual relationship with

Anne Boleyn's sister, Mary Boleyn, would prohibit him from marrying Anne while Mary was alive. (As it happened, Mary outlived Anne by seven years.)[24] Maimonides would not be an authority that Henry would want to discuss.

Note that Henry had been sufficiently concerned about this issue to have previously asked Clement to grant dispensation for his intended marriage to Anne despite the existence of any situation such as his prior relationship with Mary. As a matter of logic, that previous request would have made it difficult for Henry to later cite the Talmud or *Mishneh Torah* in his dispute with Clement. Henry's basic assertion would have to be that, according to the rabbis and Maimonides, Pope Julius II had lacked the power to dispense a violation of the Lev. 18:16 law against uncovering the nakedness of his brother's widow. However, Henry himself had requested that Clement grant dispensation of his violation of the parallel law of Lev. 18:18 prohibiting marrying (having sexual relations with) two sisters during their joint lifetimes.

Thus, on the basis of this entire analysis, it appears that even if Henry or his agents had been able to obtain and study the Talmud and *Mishneh Torah*, it would have simply been too risky for the king's cause to attempt to use either of these books to support the king's petition for annulment.

How the Rabbis Were Supposed to Help Henry VIII

Without access to the Talmud or *Mishneh Torah*, and perhaps even unaware of them, Henry nevertheless pursued his strategy of searching for arguments from Jewish law. He doggedly continued trying to find something in the Jewish interpretation of the law that might show that the levirate marriage provisions of Deuteronomy did not weaken his central theological position. The king had to somehow convince Pope Clement that the Leviticus Prohibitions constituted recitals of absolute and indispensable natural law.

Henry should not be personally faulted for persevering in this somewhat odd and ultimately unsuccessful final strategy in his quest for the annulment. Reports to London from Croke and the other agents in Italy generally took weeks to arrive. Henry had little choice but to rely heavily upon his envoys, because timely conversation with anyone knowledgeable about Jewish law and practice was impossible. In an England without Jews, Henry had no rabbis to consult.

It is therefore not surprising that Henry accepted the reports, written in Croke's typical overly optimistic style, promising definitive rabbinic support for Henry's case. Knowing little about the daily goings-on in Italy, and almost nothing about Jews, a desperate Henry could imagine that in Italy, anything was possible.

10

HENRY'S RABBIS

Many historians require only a condemnatory sentence or two to dismiss Henry's entire 1530 enterprise of obtaining rabbinic opinions that he hoped would convince Clement to grant the annulment. Some of those commentators observe that the rabbis of the Italian ghettos were so destitute that Croke needed only to offer the smallest imaginable bribes to get them to say whatever he needed. But such summary condemnations ignore the complex story of what Henry and Croke managed to achieve – and what they failed to achieve – in their resort to Jewish law and custom to prop up Henry's natural law arguments.[1]

Francesco Giorgi

The individual who proved to be the key to Croke's access to contemporary rabbinic opinions supporting Henry was not a rabbi. He was not even Jewish. Francesco Giorgi (1466–1540), sometimes referred to in Croke's correspondence as Father Francis, was a friar of the Franciscan Order. He was a renowned Christian theologian and an early Christian Hebraist and Cabalist in Venice.[2]

Francesco Giorgi's life was far from that of the typical image of a cloistered mendicant brother. He was a member of an influential family, and was well connected with the Venetian governing class. When Croke arrived in Italy at the end of 1529, Giorgi had recently published his monumental work on Christian Cabalism, *De Harmonia Mundi* (The Harmony of the World), 1525. He was recognised internationally for his theological quest for universal ecumenical concordance.³

The relationship between the new Christian Cabalism and its counterpart, ancient Jewish Kabbalah, is complex. Both terms refer to an organised system of mystical beliefs and activities of Christianity and Judaism respectively. Both share the ultimate goal of knowing and experiencing the essence of God. However, the relationship between these two mystical belief systems is not a reciprocal one.

Jewish Kabbalah is the older of the two, claiming origination in the second-century thought of Rabbi Shimon bar Yochai. The most significant written work of Kabbalah is the *Zohar* (Splendor or Radiance), a mystical commentary on the Torah. It was published in thirteenth-century Spain by Moses de Leon, a Jewish writer who claimed he had found a manuscript that had been written in the second century by Rabbi Shimon. Most modern scholars have concluded that de Leon was the original author, although some current believers insist that the book was indeed written by Rabbi Shimon, or perhaps that his concepts had been orally transmitted through a millennium-long chain of disciples until compiled by de Leon in the *Zohar*.

The Jewish mystical tradition of Kabbalah became of great interest in the development of the parallel movement of Christian mysticism. For Italian Cabalists, this interest intensified at the end of the fifteenth century, when some of the Jews fleeing from the Inquisitions in Spain and Portugal brought with them to the Italian peninsula the Jewish Kabbalah tradition, including copies of the *Zohar* and related mystical works.⁴

Francesco Giorgi is an example of one of the most scholarly of the early Christian Cabalists. He learned Aramaic, Hebrew, and other ancient languages so that he could study the Hebrew Bible and rabbinic literature, in particular the *Zohar* and other Jewish Kabbalistic writings.

The Christian Cabalist movement did not read the *Zohar* in order to Judaise Christianity; it was the reverse. Giorgi and his fellow Cabalists were certain that their examination of Kabbalah would serve as their instrument for the Christianisation of Judaism. The Cabalists read the Bible through the lenses of Neoplatonism and multiple humanistic disciplines such as numerology, mathematics, astronomy, astrology, cosmology, music, and architecture. They were determined to find in the symbolism of Jewish Kabbalah such strong justifications and proofs for Christian belief in the divinity and messianic role of Jesus that the Jews would surely accept Christianity. To this end, the Christian Cabalists searched for corresponding expressions of universal harmonies in the mystical systems of Christianity and Judaism, redefining and appropriating many of the basic symbols of Jewish Kabbalah such as its core belief in the ten *Sefirot*, the divine emanations or qualities of God.[5]

Richard Croke was fortunate that Father Francis Giorgi was one of the most distinguished Italian theologians of the era. But even more valuable for Croke, Giorgi was also a rare instance of an important Italian Christian theologian who supported Henry VIII's quest for an annulment. He wielded great influence over the Franciscan friars as well as the members of other religious orders, many of whom lacked his intellectual abilities. This made him an almost indispensable ally, through whom Croke could secure from individual Catholic clerics and university faculties opinions in favour of Henry's theological arguments in the Great Matter.

In Croke's letter to Henry dated 18 February 1530, Croke acknowledges Giorgi's unique importance to the task and expresses surprise that he refused to accept payments for his efforts and accomplishments to help the king. It can be noted, however, that Giorgi apparently had no qualms about personally distributing English money to pay others for helpful opinions. Consistent with his other letters to the king, Croke also felt compelled to squeeze in a complaint to Henry about the incompetence or perhaps disloyalty of England's resident ambassador to Venice, John (*Giambattista*) Casale:

> Sends the writings of Francis Georgius, the chief theologian here, in the opinion of all, and well skilled in Hebrew, fortified by the subscriptions of four preachers and lecturers on theology. Hopes to obtain subscriptions from all the theologians in Padua, Venice, and other parts of Italy, – such is Georgius' authority with all the Orders. ... Though he [Giorgi] has done everything for Croke, could not prevail upon him or his nephew to take a penny in compensation. Has paid him 50 gold pieces, at the desire of the bishop of Worcester [Ghinucci], to engage doctors of law ([ju]ris) and theology for the King, of which he will give Croke account. If a stranger [Croke], concealing his name and country, has done so much in a month, what could not the ambassador [John Casale] have done in three years, if he had liked.[6]

Francesco Giorgi did more than help Croke to obtain written opinions from university faculties and individual clerics supporting Henry's arguments on the annulment generally and on the Deuteronomy issue in particular. More crucially, Giorgi was the gateway to securing access to two important rabbis in Italy who would uphold Henry's final theological arguments.

Elijah Menahem Halfan

Giorgi apparently personally obtained one of the first and most prominent Italian rabbis to support Henry's position. Rabbi Elijah Menahem Halfan was, among other things, a notable Jewish Kabbalist in Venice. Halfan was a well-known rabbi, physician and descendant of an illustrious family of Jewish scholars.[7]

Not uncommon for the Jewish families living in the Italian peninsula at the time, Halfan had been born there to a family that had emigrated from Provence, France over 100 years earlier. Provence was within the western European area settled by the Ashkenazi, the German-European branch of Diaspora Jews.

Francesco Giorgi was promptly able to induce Elijah Menahem Halfan to help Croke because in many ways Halfan and Giorgi resembled twin brothers, one Jewish and one Christian, who led parallel and connected lives. Both were descendants of prominent families. Both were among the leading Kabbalists/Cabalists in Venice. Both enjoyed extensive contacts with members of the other's religious community. Giorgi had become a very proficient Hebraist, while Halfan was a popular teacher to Christian humanists who were eager to learn the Hebrew language and Jewish Bible interpretation. Both men were advocates of ecumenical intellectual exchange.[8]

Richard Croke was delighted to receive the opinion of a rabbi of Halfan's stature, which stated that, under Jewish interpretation and practice, the existence of Deut. 25:5–10 did not interfere with the invalidation of Henry's marriage under Lev. 18:16. As was his style, in his reports to the king and to John Stokesley, Croke treated finding this unique source as his personal accomplishment.

Henry had initially sent John Stokesley, Bishop of London, to serve as England's ambassador to Bologna for the meeting there between Pope Clement VII and Holy Roman Emperor Charles V, and Stokesley had remained in 1530 as Henry's highest-ranking agent in Italy for managing his Great Matter. In a letter to Stokesley dated 18 January 1530, Croke assures the bishop that he has already obtained the proofs that they had been seeking from learned Italian rabbis.[9] Croke refers to letters from 'a physician and a rabbi' [Elijah Halfan] and from 'a convert to Christianity' [former rabbi Mark Raphael]. Halfan and Mark Raphael were not only the first, but as we shall see, they were the two most significant of the Italian rabbinic supporters for Henry's attack on the Deuteronomy provisions regarding levirate marriage.[10]

In his letter dated 18 February 1530, introduced above, Professor Croke sent essentially the same triumphant report direct to his former pupil, King Henry, but with some additional details:

> [Croke is sending to the king] ... some writings by learned Hebrews in his favor; by which, what Stokesley wished, is proved indisputably; viz., that the Levitical law has always been holy and intact, and never abolished nor weakened; on the other hand, the law of Deuteronomy was never in force except when the conditions therein expressed were present, and when it is allowed by the Levitical law; and that it was never observed, even by the Jews themselves, after the destruction of Jerusalem, except in matters concerning inheritance. From this it is inferred that this must necessarily be, in my judgment at least, closely related to that which is in the end of the Book of Numbers broadly against the daughters of Zelophehad from God, which [practice of marrying otherwise forbidden relatives], as I received proof from Marcus Raphael, is allowed [for Christians] only in the line of the Savior. Raphael, who is now converted to Christ, was at one time a chief rabbi.[11]

In his letter to the king, Richard Croke was quick to claim victory for producing evidence proving that the Leviticus Prohibitions took priority over the levirate marriage provisions of Deuteronomy. However, it seems that he was not quick enough to become the first to make this claim. That priority belongs to one of the king's several other resident agents charged with assisting Croke and Stokesley in Italy – Girolamo Ghinucci, the absentee Bishop of Worcester.[12]

Ghinucci appears to have obtained a copy of a letter, presumably Halfan's, and promptly sent it to Henry on 7 February 1530, giving the impression that he had been the one responsible for obtaining it, rather than Croke and Giorgi. Ghinucci says only that he secured

Henry's Rabbis

the letter 'through a friend', and that he does not read Hebrew but a friend tells him that the letter confirms that, according to Jewish law, the Deuteronomy obligations of levirate marriage have ended for the Jews, and that Leviticus remains in effect to prohibit marrying the widow of a childless brother:

> ... Sends also by him the judgment of a Hebrew, which he has obtained through a friend. Does not understand it, as it is written in H[ebrew], but a friend tells him ... the rule of Deuteronomy has ended; it was no longer permitted to marry the childless widow of his childless dead brother despite Leviticus.[13]

Subsequent records in the *Letters and Papers* archives for 1530 indicate that, during the first half of the year, Halfan, sometimes referred to as Helias or Helyas, continued to solicit opinions from other rabbis and continued to refine and add to his own opinions. Copies of Halfan's opinions circulated among Henry and his agents in Italy.[14]

On 2 March 1530, Croke wrote to Ghinucci that Halfan had written a new opinion that levirate marriage in Deuteronomy only applied if used for the purpose of creating heirs for inheritance, as a corollary to God's command that ownership of land initially allocated to the ancient Jewish tribes remain within those original tribes:

> ... Sends a new writing by Helias, plainly affirming that the [Deuteronomy] precept was given for the purpose of raising offspring for the inheritance, and therefore *correlaria* [correlates] to what is written in Num. 27th and last chapters about the daughters of Salphaad [Zelophehad].[15]

On 11 March 1530, Croke wrote again to the king, sending more copies of Mark Raphael's opinions relating to the New Testament's recognition of levirate marriage being limited to the grandfathers of Jesus, and writings by Halfan on the Jews' limitation of levirate marriage to inheritance situations. Croke refers to other writings by Halfan, here called Helias, and notes two other important rabbis who agree with Halfan:

> Sends duplicates of Hebrew writings by Mark Raphael, who is paid a salary by the Venetian government, two writings by

Helias, a Hebrew, doctor in arts and medicine, in which the former proves that Deuteronomy refers to the genealogy of the Saviour, and the latter to inheritance, and is only observed by the Hebrews under certain conditions. ... Those who have subscribed Helias' writings are Benedict, a German, of great weight among the Jews for his years and learning, and Calo, a doctor of arts and medicine, whose books will be sent to the King.[16] ... Sent a fortnight ago new writings of Helias and Marc Raphael, translated into Latin by father Francis; of which one is to prove that the King's marriage is impious, and ought to be dissolved, and the other affirms that the Rabbis consider that Deuteronomy refers to inheritance. Sends some extracts made by father Francis from the Chaldaic commentaries that the Levitical prohibitions are part of the law of nature. ... Venice, 11 March.[17]

But Halfan's critical efforts for Henry were short-lived. Pope Clement, urged on by Emperor Charles V, used the Vatican's substantial influence throughout the Italian peninsula to enforce countermeasures against the English campaign of obtaining opinions from both Jews and Catholics. By mid-1530, Rabbi Halfan's stature in the Italian Jewish community was no longer sufficient to attract other rabbis who would dare to support his views even at the prices the English were willing to pay. On 9 June 1530, less than five months since Croke's triumphal first letter to Stokesley about the Jews, he was singing a very different tune:

Jacobus [Rabbi Jacob Mantino, discussed below] and other Jews who came lately from Bologna report the Pope's displeasure, and that Helyas [Halfan], w[hose] opinion so many subscribed gladly and without stop, cannot now get one to subscribe .... Venice, 9 June.[18]

It appears that during the summer of 1530, Halfan not only found it impossible to obtain additional confirming opinions from rabbis of the Jewish communities in Italy, but he also stopped presenting further versions of his own opinions. Perhaps this was not only due to the pope's displeasure with the solicitation of clerical opinions.

Halfan's withdrawal might have been a consequence of the tide of theological opinion in Italy turning against Henry's position. It had become apparent that a majority of Catholic and Jewish theologians did not support Henry.[19]

Although Halfan was paid by the English, he was not just another poor rabbi of the ghetto. Halfan was a successful, well-connected physician, as well as a leading rabbi of Renaissance Italy. We should not expect that bribes would be enough to buy his unlimited cooperation and loyalty to Henry's cause.

Therefore, perhaps the more interesting question to ask here is not why Halfan stopped his active support of Henry's case in mid-1530, but rather, why he had even begun that cooperation and support at the start of the year. To answer this question requires examination of another leading rabbi in Italy who became involved in Henry's Great Matter.

Jacob Mantino

We have remarked on the unusual pairing of Rabbi Elijah Halfan with Father Francesco Giorgi. However, stranger still is the fact that Halfan's life at this point had been essentially taken over by his fierce struggles with a nemesis. Halfan's relentless adversary was Jacob Mantino, also a renowned physician and rabbi. Indeed, in 1530, Halfan and Mantino were regarded by both Jews and Christians as perhaps the two greatest rabbis active in Italy.[20]

Mantino possessed an important advantage in this rabbinic rivalry with Halfan. While both men were highly regarded by the Jewish communities in Italy, Rabbi Mantino also enjoyed unparalleled access to, and admiration from, the very highest levels of leadership of the Church and civil authorities throughout Italy. In the years following his opposition to Halfan on the issues of the annulment, Mantino's reputation continued to flourish in Italy in several capacities – as a doctor who became personal physician to Clement's successor, Pope Paul III; as translator of Hebrew and Arabic works, especially Avicenna's *Canon of Medicine* and the philosophical works of Averroes; and as one of the leading rabbis in Rome and Venice. It is a marker of the esteem in which he was held by the leaders of Venice that even when Jews were being forced into segregation and inferior social status, the Venetian Council of Ten granted Mantino a rare exemption from the humiliation of wearing the yellow pointed hat required at that time of all Jews in Venice.[21]

In 1530, Mantino's most significant contact within the leadership in Italy was with Pope Clement. It was at Clement's request that he served as judge of the disputation at Bologna between opposing parties on the question of whether Deuteronomy or Leviticus applied to the royal marriage of Henry and Catherine. Mantino held in favour of the pope's view, declaring that the marriage was legitimate.[22]

Richard Croke met Mantino under confusing and deceptive circumstances. Croke describes two meetings in his letters to Bishop Ghinucci dated 25 January 1530 and 29 January 1530. In the first letter he reports being introduced to Mantino while visiting at Francesco Giorgi's house. Mantino came in and said that he had just met with the English ambassador to Venice, Prothonotary John Casale, brother of England's ambassador to the Vatican, Gregory Casale. Mantino had been interrogated by John Casale about the divorce matter, and in particular about the Leviticus/Deuteronomy conflict. At this point, Croke inserted himself into the conversation. He posed as an adversary of the position taken by Henry VIII, in an attempt to test whether Mantino was for or against the king:

> While in the chamber of Father Francis, Jacob Mantineus, a Jewish doctor, came in, saying that he had just come from the English ambassador, who asked him many questions about the affair of the king of England, and the laws of Leviticus and Deuteronomy, concerning which he [Mantino] had disputed by the Pope's order at Bologna. And immediately begun those discussions to which I listened attentively, and in the meantime I started to speak in the opposite direction to the King…[23]

The letter goes on to make clear that this first meeting was so early in Croke's mission to Italy that he was still concealing his identity as Henry's agent in order to foster cooperation from Jewish rabbis and Christian clerics, including Giorgi, his most important contact. At this point, Giorgi still knew Croke only as John of Flanders, who was trying to solve a personal inheritance matter. Therefore, when Mantino asked Giorgi who Croke was, Giorgi introduced him as a scholar from Flanders, and Croke said he knew nothing about Henry VIII or English matters:

Father Francis told Mantineus, in answer to his inquiries, that Croke was a native of Flanders; and the latter asked Croke if he knew the learned young German who was with the king of England. Denied all knowledge of England.[24]

Until his identity became known, perhaps because of disclosures by the Casale brothers, Croke persisted in his deceptions so that he could encourage Giorgi and others to help. Croke was rightly concerned that Christians and Jews would be reluctant to furnish favourable opinions out of fear that the pope might be very displeased with any clerics who advanced Henry's arguments for the annulment.[25]

A few days later, Croke's second letter to Ghinucci, dated 29 January 1350, describes what appears to have been his second meeting with, or at least about, Mantino, this time at John Casale's house. Croke's report to Ghinucci about the second meeting does not clearly describe Mantino's role or statements, and instead focuses on what Croke considers John Casale's disloyalty and betrayal.[26]

In this second letter, Croke expresses his suspicions that Mantino did not truly sympathise with the king's cause. Croke's suspicions about Mantino's position were certainly correct. Mantino was not a supporter of Henry's case, and Clement had not been foolish to select him to officiate at the debate in Bologna. The judgment in that disputation acknowledged the traditional Jewish recognition, under appropriate circumstances, of levirate marriage as a valid exception to the Leviticus Prohibitions.[27]

It is difficult for us in retrospect to assess Mantino's motives for supporting the pope's opposition to the annulment. Mantino could have been simply expressing his theological conclusions on the issue. As previously noted, it seems that most of the intellectual leaders of both Catholic and Jewish theology in Italy opposed Henry's arguments for annulment.[28]

Mantino is also known for his deep concerns for the welfare of the Jews in Italy. When he returned to Venice and attempted to dissuade Jews from expressing support for Henry's case, he did not present theological arguments, but rather voiced pragmatic concerns. Mantino warned his co-religionists that the pope's displeasure over public support for England's position could lead to punishments or loss of privileges for the entire Jewish community.[29]

Halfan versus *Mantino*

It may be surprising to learn the real basis for these two leading rabbi-physicians of Italy, Elijah Halfan and Jacob Mantino, being on opposite sides of the dispute over the annulment. It seems that these rabbis' circumstances were not as similar as they first appeared to be. Mantino may have seen himself as someone who was, or was close to becoming, a Jewish insider at the centre of power of the Church. The Hebrew Bible and Jewish history celebrate several significant Jewish heroes who were able to serve and attempt to protect their Jewish communities by standing at the right hand of a king, including Joseph, Mordechai, Daniel, Maimonides, and Isaac Abarbanel. Perhaps Jacob Mantino felt compelled by his concerns for the Jewish community to side with the pope so that he could stay in favour with the Vatican and the government of Venice.

Mantino was an existential pragmatist, striving to protect and improve the position of the Jewish community. In contrast, Halfan was a Kabbalist, focused more on preparing the Jewish community to anticipate and bring about the coming of the messianic era. Although Halfan was also well received as a scholar and teacher by some humanist intellectuals in the Catholic Church hierarchy, he never achieved the recognition and influence in the non-Jewish world that Mantino did.

It turns out that the mutual enmity between these two renowned rabbis was much more than a simple instance of professional rivalry. Halfan and Mantino had become archenemies as a direct result of what is generally regarded as an unlikely footnote in history, one of the strangest events at the intersection of the Jewish and Catholic worlds in Italy during the entire sixteenth century. Despite all of Halfan's and Mantino's similarities as members and leaders of the same Jewish minority suffering severe discrimination in Italy, by 1530 they had become bitter opponents because of their different views of the Messiah.

Their antagonistic dispute had nothing to do with Jesus, the Christian Messiah. In the sixteenth century, as now, Jesus as Messiah was the theological concept at the core of both the Catholic Church and the Protestant Reformation. However, Jews do not believe that Jesus was the Messiah promised in the Hebrew Bible. Instead, since the beginning of the Common Era, various groups of Jews experienced repeated episodes of intense belief in some contemporaneous Jewish messianic figure, only to be followed at some point by deep disappointment when their hoped-for Messiah failed to bring about the messianic era.[30]

At the turn of the sixteenth century, only a few decades before Henry's agents sought support in Italy, Venice had become the centre of the most recent Jewish messianic movement of the period. Asher Lemlein, born in Germany, came to Venice to study the mystic teachings of the Kabbalah brought to that city by the Jews who had fled persecution and banishment in Spain and Portugal. With his intense, inspirational preaching, Lemlein convinced many Jews in Venice and in the broader Jewish world that he was the prophet Elijah, sent by God to lead the Jewish people to return to and reclaim the Promised Land. Many believed that he was not merely the forerunner of the Messiah, but that he would ultimately reveal himself to be the Messiah. Lemlein's movement coincided with widespread rabbinic computations that the Messiah would make his appearance in the first years of the sixteenth century. But as soon as all those promises and expectations totally failed, the Lemlein messianic phenomenon ended almost as suddenly as it had begun.[31]

The year 1530 marked only a quarter of a century since the Lemlein fiasco. It would be rational to expect that the Jews of Venice would not have had time enough to forget the lessons of the Lemlein movement. But very little about Jewish messianic movements has been rational. The Jews of Venice forgot those lessons, the Jews of Italy and Europe forgot, and many of the Christian leaders of Church and state in the Italian peninsula and the rest of Europe forgot. Instead, a new wave of extreme credulity was soon triggered when not just one, but two new Jewish messianic figures arrived at the same time in Italy – David Reuveni and Shlomo Molkho.[32]

David Reuveni

David Reuveni's background has been the subject of unresolved historical analysis and dispute for 500 years. He claimed to be from Arabia, and his fantastic story, as he told it, was that he was the general of a huge army of descendants of some of the Lost Tribes of Israel. His older brother, Joseph, ruled as king of those tribes somewhere in Arabia. For historians, David Reuveni's documented story begins in 1523, when he was perhaps forty years old. At that time, the Jewish community in Egypt ransomed him from Arab captivity.[33]

Reuveni travelled to the Holy Land, where his messianic career began with telling his story to a growing group of followers. He also claimed credit for some miracles there. Reuveni announced that he was the general whose Jewish army would recapture the Land of Israel. This would fulfil a biblical pre-condition to the beginning of the messianic era. However, as had been the case with Asher Lemlein, many of Reuveni's ardent followers presumed that this declaration was simple modesty meant to temporarily mask his true identity as the Messiah.

In 1524, he went to Italy on what he said was a divinely inspired mission to convince the pope to call for Christian troops to ally with the 300,000 Jewish soldiers supposedly somewhere in Arabia awaiting his return. They would then launch a final Christian–Jewish crusade that would retake the Holy Land from the Ottoman Sultan Suleiman I (Suleiman the Magnificent) and the Muslim Turks.

Reuveni first went to Venice, where the strongest Jewish community on the peninsula resided. He quickly won new and influential believers, who expressed their support with gifts of fine clothing and a retinue of mounted servants. This enabled Reuveni to make a flamboyant grand entrance into Rome. The spectacle of his arrival became the news of the day, and in turn enabled him to obtain a personal audience with the recently elected pope – our unfortunate Clement VII. Clement could not then have even imagined what troubles would soon be inflicted upon his reign by what would become his epic struggle with Henry VIII.

Reuveni's story, which had already won him support from several high-ranking Jews in Venice, now found further acceptance and support from Clement. The pope did not directly command an army, but he knew which secular leader could best provide modern weapons, ships, and troops necessary for the new joint crusade. Therefore, after Clement's typical delay to fully consider the matter, he gave Reuveni letters of safe passage to Portugal, to meet there with King John III.

Reuveni arrived in Portugal in 1525, during the time of the horrific Inquisition that had forced Portugal's Jews to either flee the country or convert to Catholicism. For many of the Jews who had stayed as *conversos*, their forced conversions did not stop their secret religious practices and identification as Jews. When they saw David Reuveni making his triumphant entry into Lisbon, where he was received by the king as an honoured guest and given promises of royal support for the new Holy War, many *conversos* presumed that they could now openly return to their Judaism. This certainly wasn't what the pope or the Portuguese king hoped to obtain from David Reuveni. King John III abruptly withdrew his offers of ships and arms, and Reuveni had to flee the kingdom.[34]

Shlomo Molkho

Of all the Portuguese *conversos* who were inspired by Reuveni's visit to reconvert to Judaism, unquestionably the most momentous reconversion was that of Diogo Pires, a secretary for the king's council and member of the royal court. Unlike many of his fellow *conversos*, Pires did not merely dream of openly practising as a Jew. He did not simply ponder following Reuveni into the promised messianic era. Diogo Pires accepted that Reuveni was the general who would bring the Jews back to Jerusalem where it had been promised the Messiah would appear. But Pires received his own divine vision – that he, not Reuveni, was the Messiah chosen by God to initiate the messianic era for the Jews and for all of humanity.

Diogo Pires circumcised himself and changed his name to one that was more suitable to a Jewish Messiah: Shlomo (Solomon) Molkho (from the Hebrew *melech* – king). He, too, fled separately, traveling from Portugal through Europe in 1525, studying and preaching as he visited Jewish communities in Europe, all the while developing a reputation for his inspirational teachings. A growing number of his fervent admirers came to believe that Molkho was, as he claimed, the Messiah. His followers became so vocal when he visited Salonika that the leaders of that Jewish community feared reprisals from the Muslim Turkish government. In 1529, the Jewish community forced Molkho to leave Salonika, and he went on to Italy.

Molkho continued his messianic enterprise in Ancona, on the Adriatic coast of central Italy. There he enlarged his group of enthusiastic Jewish and Christian followers. He then proceeded to Rome. Rather than strive for the kind of triumphant, regal entrance that had opened the gates of the Vatican to David Reuveni a few years earlier, Molkho carefully staged the opposite first impression. Seeking to match one of the traditional descriptions of the coming of the Messiah, he set aside his usual fine silk outfits in favour of dirty rags and sat with the poor and sick at the city gates for thirty days. Only then did he begin preaching in Rome, including making several predictions of a coming flood, earthquake, and comet. As each of these prophecies came true, Molkho won over his most important supporter – Pope Clement.[35]

The Halfan–Mantino Dispute over Shlomo Molkho

Regardless of Clement's readiness to believe in Molkho, the reaction in the Jewish communities of Italy to the new Messiah was sharply divided among rabbinic leaders as well as among members of the broader Jewish community. Some Jews ecstatically accepted Molkho as the Messiah, especially when his public prophecies started to be fulfilled in 1530.

In general, belief in the coming of the Messiah was recognised as a formal tenet of faith for all Jews. But many Kabbalists and other followers of mystical Judaism went beyond formal recitals of faith. They believed that their personal behaviour could advance the coming of the messianic era. Therefore, it is not surprising to find that Elijah Halfan, Kabbalist and teacher of Jewish mysticism, was squarely within the camp of Molkho supporters. Halfan soon assumed an unofficial position as Molkho's chief rabbinic supporter in Italy. He was even responsible for receiving and holding letters that had been sent to Venice for Messiah Molkho.

Unlike Halfan, Mantino was not one of the rabbinic leaders in Italy who was a proponent of mystical Kabbalism. The supreme value for Mantino's rabbinic leadership was his pragmatic concern for the protection and advancement of the Jewish community. He would naturally feel driven to labour against what he felt was the existential threat to the Jewish community that might result from any public Jewish support for Molkho.

For Mantino, the risk for the Jews was not merely the result of some academic theological dispute between the Italian Christian belief in Jesus as the Messiah versus the Italian Jewish community's widespread acceptance of Molkho as the Messiah. The problem was the Inquisition.

That murderous institution, the Inquisition, acted within Italy as in other lands as a semi-autonomous entity of the Catholic Church. Technically, the Inquisition did not have jurisdiction over Jews or other non-Catholics except in instances of blasphemy or other acts directed against Catholicism. However, once someone had been born into a Catholic family and baptised in the Catholic Church, which was the case with Shlomo Molkho, the Inquisition acquired lifelong jurisdiction to examine and punish that individual for the capital offence of Judaising – engaging in Jewish religious practices in violation of Church rules. The same situation applied to individuals who had been born Jewish but had personally converted to Catholicism.

Moreover, it would not be difficult for the Inquisition to find evidence of blasphemy in the mystical preaching of Molkho. This in turn would extend the jurisdiction of the Inquisition to any Jews who showed support for even an implicit denial of Jesus as the Messiah. In the eyes of the Church, not only Molkho but also his *converso* and Jewish supporters could be subject to death by the Inquisition.

Mantino enjoyed unique contacts with Catholic humanist intellectuals, as well as the highest-level authorities in the Vatican and the secular states of Italy. He felt a profound moral obligation to use his relationships with Catholic Italy to stop the Molkho phenomenon before it resulted in tragic retribution against the Jews. With a level of fervour that matched, if not surpassed, the dedication shown by Halfan, Mantino undertook his own crusade – a campaign to stop Molkho.

Mantino left Venice to follow Molkho to Rome. However, once Molkho received the support of the gullible Clement, Mantino had little chance of mobilising the rest of the Church hierarchy to resolve the problem of this new Messiah. Therefore, Mantino turned to an almost unthinkable ally for help. He informed the Inquisition of Molkho's history of impassioned preaching that had incited Jews, *conversos*, and Christians to believe that he was the Messiah. This extreme path indicates the depth of Mantino's concern for the dangers facing the Jewish community from Molkho's growing messianic impact.

With the information provided by Mantino, the Inquisition in Rome found Molkho guilty of the most serious offences. The Messiah was sentenced to join a group of blasphemers and Judaisers to be burned at the stake in the Vatican. However, no one, not even Mantino, could have imagined the fantastic consequence of the Inquisition's verdict. Despite the pope's personal support for Molkho, he apparently could not bring himself to publicly override the Inquisition. For once in his reign, however, instead of trying to resort to his favourite tactic of delay, the ordinarily cautious pontiff took immediate and astounding action. He secretly brought Molkho into the papal living quarters in the Vatican and hid him there. To keep this a secret and to allow the planned group execution to proceed with the correct body count, Clement substituted another hapless Vatican prisoner for the convicted Molkho.[36]

This life-and-death conflict over the Jewish Messiah Shlomo Molkho locked Elias Halfan and Jacob Mantino into their deep and permanent enmity. The mere fact of Mantino's opposition to Henry's petition for annulment may be sufficient to explain why Halfan became one of Henry's foremost rabbinic supporters in Italy. Indeed, their clash over the English king's Great Matter was essentially an extension of their dispute over the messianic claims of Shlomo Molkho.[37]

Henry's orders to his English agents in Italy to secure support from rabbis and members of the Jewish community in Italy had overlooked a major problem: his envoys understood little or nothing about Jews and Judaism. This lack of the most basic information about Jewish history and current practices included ignorance of how the heated conflict over the messianic claims of Shlomo Molkho – and not the authority of Jewish law and practice – may have been what drove Halfan to support the king's position.

11

HENRY'S SEARCH FOR ADDITIONAL RABBINIC SUPPORT

As the year 1530 progressed, Henry's initial plan to convince Clement to grant the annulment failed to develop in the way he had hoped. The most distinguished of the contemporary Catholic theologians opposed Henry's demand for annulment. This opposition seemed to push him into even greater reliance upon his final strategy of obtaining rabbinic support for what he saw as the issue that could obtain victory – that under Jewish law, the levirate marriage provisions of Deuteronomy were no longer in effect. Henry ordered that the search for Jewish opinions be intensified:

> The tenor of the King's letters and instructions sent to me [*Croke*], in the King's name, by my lord of Worcester [*Ghinucci*]
>
> ... The sayings of the Jews about Deuteronomy and Leviticus, and whatever else can be found anywhere to aid the cause, must be sent with the greatest diligence to his Majesty.[1]

Collecting Opinions from the Rabbis in Italy

The English had previously been confronted with difficulties in England and on the Continent when the king's agents could not find solid support from university faculties. In those situations, Henry's men had swiftly improvised techniques to overcome those difficulties, including threats, intimidation, selective or fraudulent reporting of the faculty vote outcomes, soliciting unlearned and suggestible clerics, and, above all, bribery. Those shameful techniques would be repeated in Italy, as admitted in Croke's summary of Ghinucci's instructions:

> [i.] It will be expedient to hire as many Italian doctors as possible to defend the King's cause against opponents. ... Attempts must be made to gain as many as possible to his Majesty's side, by help of friar Francis George, so that he may conquer by numbers as well as by justice and truth.
> ii. From a letter of the bishop of Worcester, dated 'ex Bon]onia, 31 March [1530]'.

> What I wrote about learned theologians, who you say are rare in Italy has been provided for by the King, who does not wish so much to obtain excellent ones, as all.[2]

If great university faculties and individual Catholic theologians were willing to sell their votes and opinions, how much easier must it have been to purchase the opinions of poor and struggling rabbis living as part of an oppressed minority in the Venice ghetto or in the ghettos or fringes of other communities in Italy? It follows that, just as with the English efforts to obtain favourable opinions from Catholic clerics regardless of whether the signatories were learned or even literate, Croke and his fellow agents were also able to purchase a number of favourable opinions as well as clerical and translation help from Jews in Italy, which is repeatedly documented in England's official records for 1530.[3]

It is noteworthy that the efforts in 1530 by Croke, Ghinucci, the Casale brothers, and Stokesley to obtain rabbinic support for Henry's case have been ignored by so many recent historians. Professor Scarisbrick at least includes Hebrew scholars and rabbis together with the many Christian sources in his list of clerics and others who were pursued and paid by the English.[4]

However, it is especially distressing that the most memorable phrase in twentieth-century histories about Henry's search for rabbinic opinions is harshly and unjustifiably antagonistic to the Jewish participation. In 1906, H. A. L. Fisher's otherwise fine *History of England (1485–1547)* compressed Henry's entire 1530 strategy of obtaining Jewish authorities into the gratuitously hateful phrase, 'Needy rabbis were fished out of their ghettos to opine against Deuteronomy at a minimum charge of twenty-four crowns.'[5]

The English Response to Negative Opinions

At this point, we should again bear in mind the special circumstances affecting the reliability of the historical record of these almost 500-year-old events. We have already noted that the English envoys were relatively clueless about Jewish beliefs and customs in general, and especially about the rabbis they were soliciting. Unlike the Catholic Church, there was no formal hierarchal rabbinic structure of authority in Italy. Individual rabbis and Jewish scholars expressed their individual opinions. It was therefore inevitable that the efforts of the English agents to find support for the king would also produce some refusals by rabbis to write in support of Henry, and perhaps also result in some opinions unfavourable to Henry's case. The English relied upon two tactics to minimise these problems.

First, the problem of negative opinions by individual rabbis or Christian clerics in Italy was sufficiently significant to trigger a refinement in the English procedures for bribery. In April of 1530, Bishop Ghinucci somewhat delicately suggested to all of the English agents in Italy the appropriate procedure for purchasing only opinions favourable to King Henry:

> The tenor of the King's letters and instructions sent to me [*Croke*], in the King's name, by my lord of Worcester [*Ghinucci*]
>
> [I]t is thought better first to find out the opinion of the persons to be engaged, and then to treat with them by name [disclose that the opinion is being sought by Henry VIII], propose a reward, and promise gratitude, which his Majesty will, without doubt, perform....[6]

Secondly, for their formal applications for faculty votes at the European universities, the English had already developed a notorious technique for dealing with authorities, opinions, and documents unfavourable to Henry's arguments – such contrary views were simply never acknowledged or mentioned again, either to Pope Clement or to the ecclesiastical courts. The only mention by the English of adverse opinions occurred when the king's representatives brazenly misrepresented those opinions as being favourable to Henry. Presumably, the English would try to extend their established non-disclosure tactic to any rabbinic opinions adverse to Henry's position that they obtained.

The English practice of ignoring negative responses does not mean that Clement was unaware that the English were resorting to bribery and fraud, as well as omitting or misrepresenting authorities that were actually favourable to the pope's position. On 30 July 1530, England's parliamentary leaders, including members of the nobility and senior Church figures, sent to the pope a plea that he grant the annulment. When he finally responded to this declaration on 27 September 1530, Clement expressly identified one of the reasons why he was not convinced to issue the annulment decree – he could not accept the English practice of citing university and individual opinions that did not include discussion of Christian or Jewish precedents, or that outright misrepresented some of the purported conclusions:

> ... you say that sentence [of annulment] ought to be given by us, though no body entreated it, nay, tho' some oppos'd it in this case, which has been adjudg'd just by all the learned in England, France and Italy, and by the decrees of so many universities... [but that would be] contrary to the opinion [against the divorce] of several doctors (which you urge also on your behalf) and those very learned and grave men, and who confirm their judgment both by the laws of God, and by arguments taken not only from the Latins, but likewise deriv'd from the Jewish law... As for the opinion of learned men, and the decrees of universities which you mention, few of them have come to our notice, shewn us not in proper form by your ambassadors, nor in the name of the king exhibited, and those were but bare opinions of those men, alleging no reasons for their determinations, nor supporting them by any authority from Scripture, or the canons, which herein ought only to prevail.[7]

When Clement later received from the English a book of university and clerical opinions in support of the annulment, Dr Pedro Ortiz, the emperor's representative to the Vatican, confirmed the pope's previous assessment:

> The opinions of the said universities [Orleans, Paris, Angers, Bourges, Padua, and Toulouse, which were favorable to Henry] were concocted in haste, without knowledge of the subject, and without honesty. They were procured by bribes, which deprive

Fig. 1: KING HENRY VIII. J. S. Brewer, *The Reign of Henry VIII*, vol. I, 1884, frontispiece, engraving by William Thomas Fry. Courtesy of the Getty Research Institute, via Archive.org.

Fig. 2: CATHERINE OF ARAGON. Cornelis Martinus Vermeulen, engraving, 1697, detail. Courtesy of Rijksmuseum. See Image Note for Fig. 2 – Catherine of Aragon.

Left: Fig. 3: KING HENRY VII, WITH ELIZABETH OF YORK. George Vertue (1648–1756), engraving. Courtesy of Yale Center for British Art.

Below: Fig. 4: KING FERDINAND AND QUEEN ISABELLA OF SPAIN. William H. Prescott, *History of Ferdinand and Isabella*, 1837, frontispiece. Courtesy of University of California Library via Archive.org. See Image Note for Fig. 4 – Reading the Ferdinand and Isabella Portraits.

Fig. 5: ANNE BOLEYN. Achille Devéria, lithograph, 1832, detail. Courtesy of Paris Musees.

Fig. 6: THOMAS WOLSEY. William H. S. Aubrey, *The National and Domestic History of England*, 2:284, 1867. Courtesy of British Library.

Fig. 7: HENRY VIII'S ARMOUR AT AGES 53 AND 36. Right panel: 1527 (Henry age 36). Left panel: 1544 (Henry age 53). Courtesy of Metropolitan Museum of Art. See Image Note for Fig. 7 – Henry VIII's Armour.

Fig. 8: POPE CLEMENT VII. Sebastiano del Piombo, 1531. Courtesy of Getty Museum via Useum.org.

Fig. 9: POPE JULIUS II. Gustav Schauer, photo reproduction of a print after a portrait of Pope Julius II by Raphael, *c*. 1851 – in or before 1861. Courtesy of Rijksmuseum.

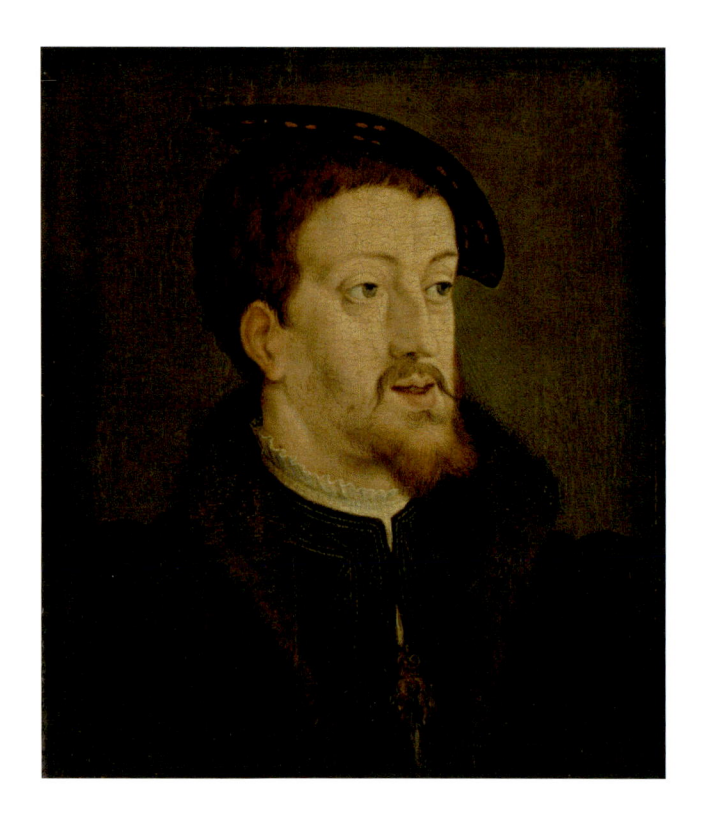

Fig. 10: EMPEROR CHARLES V. Jan Cornelisz Vermeyen (manner of), *c.* 1530. Courtesy of Rijksmuseum.

Fig. 11: CASTEL SANT'ANGELO, ROME. Adapted from a picture postcard created 1900–1910, anon. Courtesy of Rijksmuseum.

Fig. 12: SCENE FROM SHAKESPEARE'S *KING HENRY VIII*, Act 3, Scene 1. Edward J. Potbury, engraving and etching, 1825–1840. Courtesy of Metropolitan Museum of Art. See Image Note for Fig. 12 – Scene from Shakespeare.

Fig. 13: TRIAL OF THE MARRIAGE OF HENRY VIII. Robert Smirke RA, artist, and Albert Henry Payne, engraver, in William H. S. Aubrey, *The National and Domestic History of England*, 2:485, 1867. Courtesy of the British Library via Flickr.com. See Image Note for Fig. 13 – Trial of the Marriage of Henry VIII.

Fig. 14: JOHN FISHER. Jacobus Houbraken, engraver, after an image by Holbein, *c.* 1745. Courtesy of Yale Center for British Art. See Image Note for Fig. 14 – John Fisher.

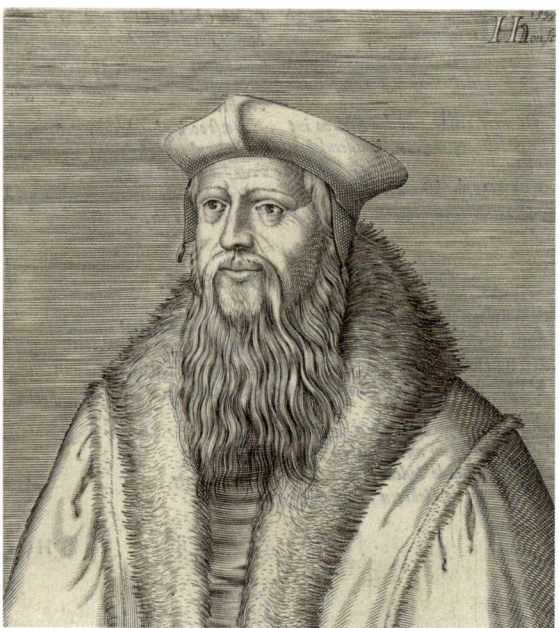

Fig. 15: THOMAS CRANMER. Hendrick Hondius (studio of), engraving, 1599 (detail). Courtesy of Rijksmuseum. See Image Note for Fig. 15 – Thomas Cranmer.

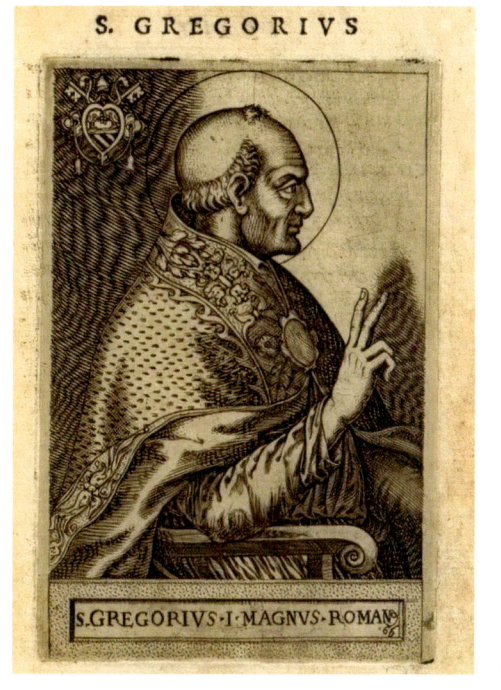

Fig. 16: POPE SAINT GREGORY I AND POPE INNOCENT III. Giovanni Battista Cavalieri, *Images of the Catholic Popes (Pontificum Romanorum effigies)*, 1591, pp. 66, 179. Courtesy of National Central Library of Rome, via Archive.org. See Image Note for Fig. 16 – Gregory I and Innocent III.

Fig. 17: SIGNATURE LINE OF RABBI JACOB RAPHAEL RESPONSUM. Detail from British Library document at Arundel ms 151 ff190–191v f190r, 1530. Courtesy of the British Library. See full document at Figs 26–28, and see new English translation at Appendix C.

Fig. 18: THOMAS CROMWELL. Jacobus Houbraken, engraving, 1739. Courtesy of Yale Center for British Art. See Image Note for Fig. 18 – Thomas Cromwell.

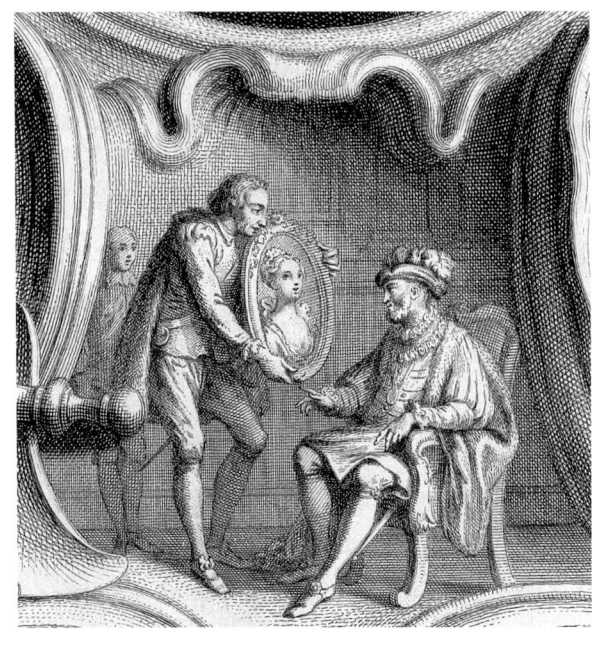

Fig. 19: THOMAS CROMWELL (detail from Fig. 18).

Fig. 20: JANE SEYMOUR. Wenceslaus Hollar, etching, after a portrait by Holbein, 1648. Courtesy of Metropolitan Museum of Art.

Fig. 21: KING EDWARD VI AS A CHILD. Hans Holbein, 1538. Courtesy of National Gallery of Art, Washington, via Useum.org

Fig. 22: LADY JANE GREY. William H. S. Aubrey, *The National and Domestic History of England*, 1867. Courtesy of the British Library via Flickr.com.

Fig. 23: QUEEN MARY I. Francis Delaram, engraving, 1600–1627. Courtesy of Metropolitan Museum of Art.

Fig. 24: QUEEN ELIZABETH I. Crispin van de Passe I, engraving, 1550–1559. Courtesy of National Gallery of Art, Washington.

Fig. 25: MARY QUEEN OF SCOTS. Robert Strange, hand-coloured etching and engraving, mid-eighteenth century, detail. Courtesy of Metropolitan Museum of Art.

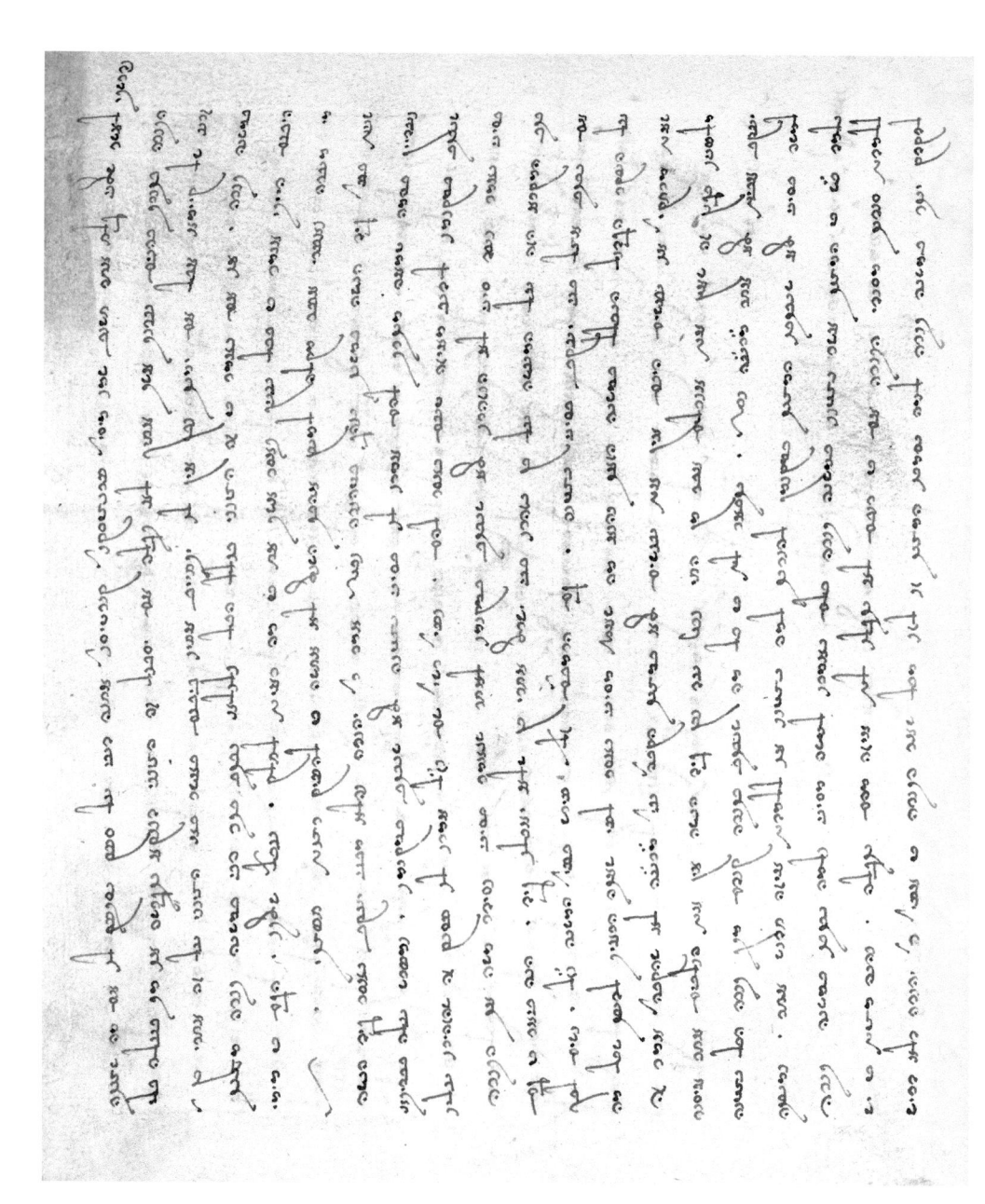

Fig. 26: RABBI JACOB RAPHAEL RESPONSUM – PART 1. Image of the top half of the first page of the responsum of Rabbi Jacob Raphael, 1530, rotated 90 degrees counterclockwise. Courtesy of the British Library. See Image Note for Figs. 26, 27, and 28 – Rabbi Jacob Raphael Responsum.

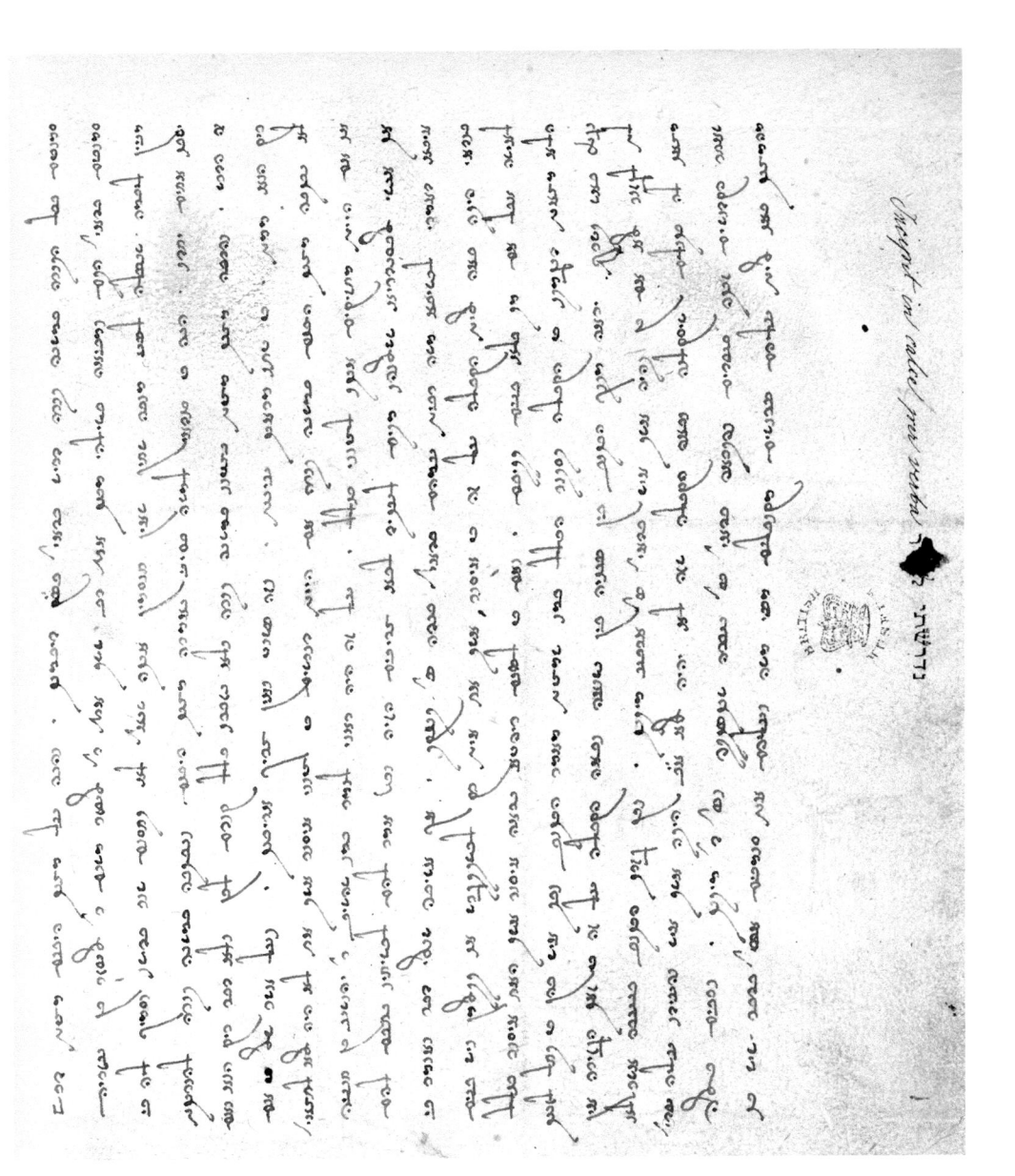

Fig. 27: RABBI JACOB RAPHAEL RESPONSUM – PART 2. Image of the bottom half of the first page of the responsum of Rabbi Jacob Raphael, 1530, rotated 90 degrees counterclockwise. Courtesy of the British Library. See Image Note for Figs. 26, 27, and 28 – Rabbi Jacob Raphael Responsum.

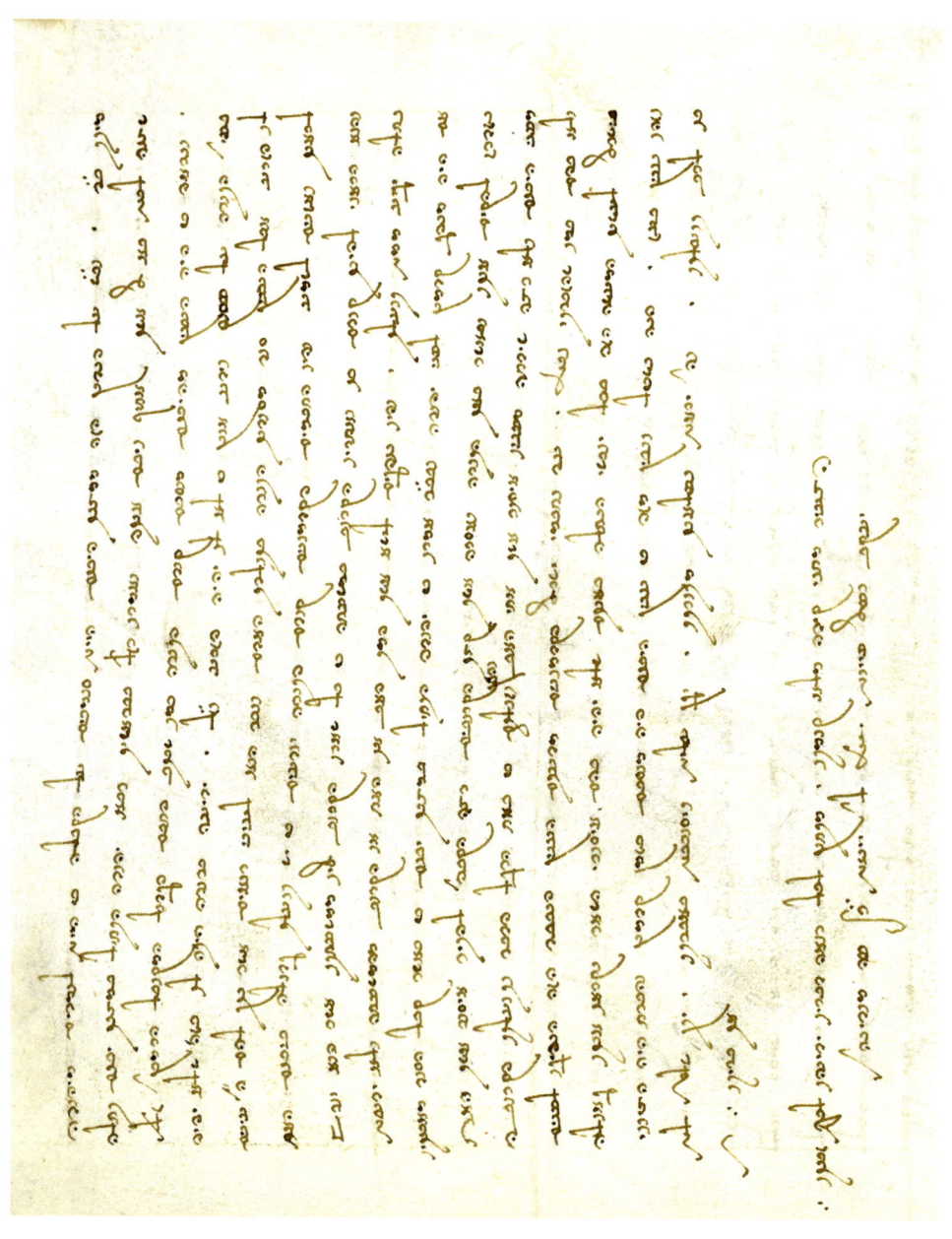

Fig. 28: RABBI JACOB RAPHAEL RESPONSUM – PART 3. Image of the second page of the responsum of Rabbi Jacob Raphael, 1530, rotated 90 degrees counterclockwise. Courtesy of the British Library. See Image Note for Figs. 26, 27, and 28 – Rabbi Jacob Raphael Responsum.

them of all value. Besides, some of these alleged opinions of the universities had no more votes in their favor than those of two or three doctors. Where a great majority was in favor of the King of England, as, for instance, at the university of Paris, the best and most learned men were in favor of the Queen. The reason thereof is that good men cannot be corrupted with bribes.

The author of the book [that was presented to the pope] in favor of the king of England quotes many authorities, which are decidedly against him.[8]

Rabbi Jacob Raphael Peglione of Modena

Because the English were attempting to manipulate, distort, and control the record of authorities, it is all the more fascinating that today we can read a formal rabbinic opinion, called a *t'shuvah* in Hebrew, or a responsum in English, by Rabbi Jacob Raphael, dated 30 January 1530. Although the opinion had been solicited by Henry's agents, it decided the Deuteronomy/Leviticus conflict adversely to Henry.[9]

The original of this document, preserved in the British Library, is beautifully calligraphed on parchment in an ornate, decorative Judeo-Italic semi-cursive script. It is not clear how the document reached England to be preserved until today, but presumably it was dutifully sent to Henry, who had asked that all results of the quest for supporting opinions be promptly sent to him.[10]

The responsum of Rabbi Jacob Raphael follows the general format for rabbinic determinations of that time, but somewhat modified to state only the writer's interpretation of how Jewish law would be applied to the situation. It does not purport to include a ruling binding on the parties involved, since the responsum was not directed to a member of the Jewish community. The following summary of Rabbi Jacob Raphael's responsum offers a taste of the unique form of rabbinic logic often expressed in such documents in that era.

The responsum opens with an explanation of why the rabbi is interpreting the point of law he is about to discuss. He states that he has been requested by the Catholic priest Francesco Curtiso (also known as Francesco Curtis, or da Corte) to provide his opinion on the matter of the Leviticus/Deuteronomy conflict, referring to these books of the Torah by their early names: *Torah HaKohanim* (the Priestly Torah, now called Leviticus) and *Mishneh Torah* (the Repetition of Torah, now called Deuteronomy).

Curtis was active on behalf of Bishop Ghinucci in obtaining various rabbinic opinions supporting Henry's case.[11] The specific question Jacob Raphael was asked by Curtis was whether under Jewish law, except perhaps for the levirate marriage provisions in Deuteronomy, the commandment stated in Lev. 18:16, 'Thou shalt not uncover the nakedness of thy brother's wife', was an absolute prohibition against marrying one's sister-in-law.

The rabbi begins his response by examining the rabbinic commentaries concerning the biblical prohibition against Jews eating the sciatic nerve of a kosher animal. Jacob Raphael discusses at some length the commentaries in the Talmud and subsequent writings of Rashi and Maimonides on this commandment. On the surface, at least, an extensive discussion of one of the many rules of kosher eating (*kashrut*) seems an unlikely starting point for an analysis of in-law incest. However, the rabbi makes an important foundational point: the discussions of these commentators on the rule against eating the sciatic nerve establish that under Jewish law all of the Torah commandments (*mitzvot* [plural]; *mitzvah* [singular]) derive their binding authority from having been revealed to Moses at Sinai, regardless of where in the Torah they are expressed.

Thus, although the levirate marriage obligations in Deuteronomy appear later in the Torah than the Leviticus Prohibitions, both commandments were revealed at Sinai. *Mitzvot* mentioned in Leviticus have no automatic priority over commandments mentioned later in Deuteronomy. Commandments are mentioned in different particular locations of the Torah narrative simply to help teach us how to interpret them, or to teach us some other lesson.

According to Jewish tradition, since the entire Torah was revealed at Sinai, no two Torah commandments, such as the Leviticus Prohibitions and the Deuteronomy levirate marriage obligations, can be considered inconsistent. If at all possible, any two Torah commandments must be interpreted and applied so that both can be observed.

Rabbi Jacob Raphael acknowledges that the question asked by Curtis – if the levirate marriage provisions did not appear in Deuteronomy, would the Leviticus Prohibitions be absolute laws? – is a contrary-to-fact hypothetical and thus does not require the rabbi to answer. He nevertheless agrees to respond. First, he points to the rabbinic modifications softening the death penalty specified in the Torah for a priest's daughter who becomes a prostitute, or for any unmarried girl who is not a virgin. These instances of rabbinic reductions of express Torah punishments establish that the oral law (interpretations of the laws by the rabbis through the ages) can modify even seemingly universal, absolute commandments written in the Torah.

The rabbi finally concludes, citing the commentary of Nachmanides, that even in the absence of the express levirate marriage provisions of Deuteronomy, Jews would have developed an oral tradition of the obligation of levirate marriage, because the Torah shows that this was an ancient practice, as evidenced by the story of Judah and Tamar in the Book of Genesis, and the story of Ruth and Boaz in the Book of Ruth.

The responsum closes not with a ruling in Henry's particular case, but with Jacob Raphael diplomatically expressing his hope that these authorities convincingly show that, under Jewish law, the Deuteronomy provisions commanding levirate marriage are the Torah codification of a salutary ancient practice that continues as a divine exception to the Leviticus Prohibitions.

The 30 January 1530 responsum of Rabbi Jacob Raphael is a remarkable document, all the more so because the ink-on-parchment original is still held as one of the treasured manuscripts preserved for public access in the British Library, despite the fact that Jacob Raphael concluded that Jewish law undercut Henry's natural law argument for the annulment.[12]

Because of the absence of other evidence, it is not clear to what extent Jacob Raphael was aware that the inquiry of Francesco Curtis was being made on behalf of Henry. By early 1530, however, Henry's campaign for annulment, including its focus on the Leviticus/Deuteronomy conflict, was not a secret in Italy or the rest of Europe. We can presume that the rabbi was aware that the opinion he was providing would not be welcomed because it was being solicited by the English. This presents another aspect of the document's uniqueness. At a time when the English were paying generously for favourable opinions from university faculties and individual clerics, Rabbi Jacob Raphael displayed intellectual honesty and a significant measure of personal bravery when he provided this meticulously reasoned opinion concerning Jewish law adverse to Henry on the central issue of the king's position.[13] (For a new English translation of Jacob Raphael's responsum, see Appendix C.)

Henry's Final Rabbi, Mark Raphael

Henry and his advisors hoped that Jewish law and practice would demonstrate the inviolability of the Leviticus Prohibitions despite the Deuteronomy obligations of levirate marriage. However, the attempts of Henry's agents to implement this final strategy offered only partially helpful results. Opinions of Jewish law regarding the Great Matter continued to be divided. Certainly, some opinions favourable to Henry were produced from notable and influential Jewish scholars. However, while Henry had Rabbi Elijah Halfan, a recognised rabbinic scholar who supported him, Pope Clement had Rabbi Jacob Mantino, perhaps more renowned, who opposed the king. And while Henry had his Francesco Giorgi, the leading Catholic Hebraist who cooperated with the search for Jewish authorities favouring the annulment, Clement's opposition was supported by Rabbi Jacob Rafael of Modena, who penned his erudite opinion that, according to Jewish law, levirate marriage was an exception to the Leviticus Prohibitions – an exception which significantly weakened Henry's natural law argument for the divorce.

Despite this diversity of opinion, by the end of that fateful year of 1530, Henry seemed to rely even more upon theological arguments from Jewish authorities. Unfortunately for the king, this was not because his agents were finally securing more or stronger Jewish testimony. Rather, it was because Henry's other arguments had already failed to convince Clement or his cardinals. Henry's reliance upon Jewish law increased because it was one of the few arguments that Henry had not yet been forced to abandon.[14]

As the year ended, Jewish theological and legal authority from Italy became physically embodied for Henry in a most unusual vessel. In January 1531, Mark Raphael, who had been identified by Croke as a former chief rabbi who had recently converted to Christianity, arrived in London to become the king's chief advisor on Jewish law.[15] If he can be counted as a rabbi despite his being at least in the process of converting to Catholicism, then Raphael was one of Croke's two earliest and most important rabbinic authorities, together with Elijah Halfan, to actively and publicly support Henry in the annulment dispute.[16] Once Halfan's efforts dried up in the middle of 1530, Raphael became, by default, Henry's most significant rabbinic supporter on questions of Jewish law and practice.

By that time, Henry had assumed firm personal control of his theological dispute with Clement. The resolution of the Leviticus/Deuteronomy conflict had become the most prominent of their battlegrounds. In late 1530, the king therefore concluded that he needed immediate access to Raphael so that he could avoid the delays and uncertainties of having to depend upon receiving written opinions from Italy. To accomplish this, the king summoned Raphael to London to enable direct discussions about what would have seemed in England to be ancient Judaism's puzzling theological concepts.

Imperial Ambassador Eustace Chapuys

It may sometimes happen that two entirely independent historical events occur simultaneously. The result of this fortuitous timing can be that these events inform and alter each other in significant ways. Thanks to one such historical coincidence, we know many of the details of Mark Raphael's career in London. Just before his arrival, a new Imperial ambassador to England arrived on behalf of Charles V. This man, Eustace Chapuys, proved to be an intelligent, articulate, and skilled diplomat.

From the time of his arrival, Chapuys immersed himself in the King's Great Matter. He cultivated an efficient network of insider informants, and he analysed the political implications of each development with great skill. Best of all, he reported all of these facts, evaluations, and predictions to the emperor in frequent and richly detailed diplomatic reports. The correspondence from Chapuys to Charles provides us with a unique window through which to view Henry, Catherine, Anne, Parliament, and the English Church at that time. Many of Chapuys's reports were based upon his personal contacts with Henry, with whom he established an increasingly candid relationship of mutual respect despite their fundamental disagreement over the annulment.

Before we rely too much upon Chapuys's reports concerning Raphael, we should note that the ambassador was far from being a disinterested observer. He soon became Catherine's principal confidant and supporter in England. When we review the historical record of his reports during Catherine's lifetime, it becomes clear that his deep sympathies for the queen's position were more than a strategic effort to ingratiate himself with his employer, Catherine's nephew Charles V. From the record, it seems clear that Chapuys's compassion for Catherine's plight was heartfelt and genuine. He certainly did not hide his bias. His diplomatic reports could not disguise his deep antagonism towards Anne Boleyn. Indeed, he could not bring himself to refer to her by name, or to her position as Henry's wife or queen even after she formally attained those titles. In the Chapuys reports, Anne was never more than 'the Lady', and in his later reports, even that reference often became 'the Concubine'.[17]

Mark Raphael in England

In 1530, London was not the only location where Emperor Charles maintained an important resident ambassador who was charged, in part, with monitoring the King's Great Matter and acting where possible to frustrate Henry's quest for an annulment. Like Chapuys in England, Miguel Mai, the Imperial ambassador to the Vatican, was very sympathetic towards Catherine. When he learned that Raphael was to be sent to London to assist the king's case, he tried to block the journey, having the routes out of Italy closely watched by agents with orders to seize him. Despite these efforts, Raphael was successfully smuggled out of Italy and arrived in London in January 1531, when he was promptly summoned to meet with King Henry.[18]

If Ambassador Mai felt badly about having failed to stop Raphael from escaping to England, he must have been cheered by Ambassador Chapuys's reports to the emperor about Raphael's initial two meetings with the king. The first meeting was simply a formal royal welcome, but the second meeting was supposed to be a working session, and it had not gone well. Henry at last had his personal resident rabbi, and he expected to hear some sophisticated Judaic theological proof that he could finally use to convince the pope to grant the annulment. The king was looking for strong evidence that, under the laws of the Jews, the Leviticus Prohibitions against in-law incest absolutely and indispensably barred his marriage to Catherine. Further, he no doubt expected some confirmation of the earlier reports he had received that the special language in Deuteronomy concerning levirate marriage in no way applied to create an exception to the Leviticus Prohibitions even for contemporary Jews, let alone for Catholics.

However, Raphael, a recent convert to the Church, apparently had not yet developed a keen appreciation of what contemporaneous Catholics would consider fundamental marital law standards for civilised society. Raphael told the king that if he was looking at Jewish law and custom for a way to marry Anne Boleyn, he could ignore the niceties of theology by simply emulating the Patriarchs of Genesis and taking Anne as his second wife.[19]

As a New Christian, former rabbi Mark Raphael may have been thinking in terms of Hebrew Bible patriarchal polygamy, but all Henry heard was 'bigamy'. This was not the first time that the king had considered – and ultimately rejected – such a suggestion, including during several years of prior negotiations with Pope Clement, as discussed previously. But by now Henry was forcefully clear in his response. He expressed Christian outrage at the suggestion, and flatly refused even to contemplate marrying Anne Boleyn without first receiving an annulment of his marriage to Catherine.

Chapuys seems to have taken some pleasure in sending to the emperor a graphic – and antisemitic – description of Henry's indignation at Raphael's opinion that Jewish law permitted the king to take a second wife:

> ... which opinion the King has found so extravagant and absurd that he has openly declared to the Jew himself that this will not do, and that he must devise some other means of getting him out of the difficulty, for that he would never adopt, indeed would rather die than resort to such expedient, as it would be an infamous and blameable act for him to have two wives at the same time. ... So that the said Jew who pretends to have been baptised some time ago, would now under the cloak of charity, spread his Judaizing doctrines.[20]

In another version of that same report, Chapuys elaborates further in his attack on the converted 'Jew'.[21] In the ambassador's view, the consequences of Raphael's initial meetings with the king demonstrated a lack of any sincere theological principles, Jewish or Christian, on the part of a mercenary former rabbi who was ready to deliver whatever opinion might please Henry:

> The Jewish law also permits him to take another wife, so that the said Jew, who says he has been some time ago baptised, under colour of charity *'vouldroit semer telle dragee indaignee'* [wants to sow such disgraceful dredgings].[22]

Putting aside the question of whether Anne Boleyn would ever be satisfied with such an ambiguous – or perhaps simply bigamous – relationship, we should remember that Henry sought a solution that would also maximise the likelihood of the nation's acceptance of his hoped-for son as the next king of England. The question was not only whether Raphael's proposal would actually constitute bigamy, but also whether it might be seen by the people as bigamy.

Whatever the mix of motivations for Henry's displeasure at Raphael's initial recommendation, the king abruptly sent his new advisor away from the palace, ordering him to return only when he could produce an acceptable argument from Jewish law that would require applying the Leviticus Prohibitions to the marriage with Catherine of Aragon.

Henry apparently expressed himself sufficiently clearly to direct Raphael back onto the appropriate path. He fell back upon simply repeating one of the basic arguments from Jewish law that he and others had already made to support Henry's case: levirate marriage under Deuteronomy only applied if the surviving brother's intention was to produce issue that would be attributed to the deceased brother for inheritance purposes, which clearly had not been Henry's intent when he married Catherine.[23]

In the absence of full qualification for a levirate marriage under Jewish law, marriage to a sister-in-law would indeed be a violation of the Leviticus Prohibitions. Lev.20:21 declared that God's punishment would be that the union would not produce issue. Henry had argued that his marriage to Catherine had been punished in this manner when the marriage failed to produce a male heir capable of succeeding to the throne. Chapuys told Charles V that these were also the elements of Raphael's subsequent advice:

> The Jew called hither, finding his first opinion not accepted, has forged another equally illfounded, and says it is indeed lawful to marry a brother's widow, provided it is done with the will and intention to raise issue for the deceased brother; but without such intention the marriage is unlawful, and that God has reproved such unions by the mouth of Moses, so that issue shall not proceed of them, or shall not live long; and that it has been seen that the male children the King had of the Queen scarcely lived at all; from which he inferred that the King had

not the said intention, and consequently that the marriage is unlawful.[24]

According to this second argument proposed by Raphael, Henry had not married Catherine with the requisite intention to qualify under the Deuteronomy provisions permitting levirate marriage. This was proved by the fact that he and Catherine had suffered God's specific punishment for violating the Leviticus Prohibitions – that the couple would be childless – as recited in Lev. 20:21. Former rabbi Mark Raphael apparently had no theological qualms interpreting 'childless' (*aririm*) as used in Israel's ancient Torah to include Henry's sixteenth-century royal desire for male issue who survived for a long time, perhaps long enough to succeed to the crown without challenge.[25]

Whatever the theological merits of Raphael's revised Jewish law justification for the annulment, his opinion obtained special force when it was expressed in an England without Jews. There was almost no one in the kingdom who could speak with authority to dispute his purportedly authentic interpretation of Jewish law. That was enough for Henry. Mark Raphael became a member of the royal court, available for further assignments and conversations with Henry, and in general being retained in readiness as a sort of ultimate weapon that might win the king's final annulment battle against the pope.

There were many layers and levels to Henry's royal court, and it is not clear which personal benefits Raphael got to enjoy. We know that some of his living expenses were paid, and he may have been allowed to sit at table in the palace with many other minor functionaries for at least some meals. Presumably he found in London that he had much time, little to do, few if any acquaintances, and insufficient income. He therefore supplemented his income for a time by going into business as an importer.[26]

Raphael had already amply demonstrated his survival instincts. He had gone from being a so-called chief rabbi to a converted Catholic. He had enjoyed a regular stipend from the Venetian government[27] and had, or claimed to have had, meetings with Emperor Charles V. He was brought to England by King Henry, and he was able to recover from a cool start to say what was necessary to satisfy the English monarch and to become a member of the royal court. He then went into business to supplement his income. It is therefore not surprising that, even while in the special service of the King of England, this perpetual survivor kept his options open. He was already making plans for a future relationship with a new centre of power. By April 1531, Chapuys could tell Charles V that Raphael had signalled his hope to switch loyalties once again, this time to serve the emperor:

> The Jew whom the King sent for from Italy has sent several times to me to justify himself, saying he has done better service than is supposed, and expects at his return to kiss your Majesty's hands; of whom, in passing, you may learn some particulars.[28]

Mark Raphael in France

We don't know exactly how long Mark Raphael continued actively to serve King Henry, or the nature of any further contributions by him to the king's final attempts to obtain the annulment from the pope. However, we do know that Henry was prepared to rely upon Raphael as late as October 1532, at his second grand meeting with King Francis I in France. The two kings had previously held their historic Field of Cloth of Gold meeting in France, near the then-English territory of Calais, over two and a half weeks in June 1520. That earlier meeting, marked by an opulent tournament, was intended to celebrate the new treaty of alliance between the historic enemies, England and France.

After twelve subsequent years of shifting political loyalties, alliances, wars, and peace treaties throughout Europe, the two nations again wanted to commemorate their friendly relationship. No longer youthful, however, neither of the kings was still eager for personal participation in the rigors and risks of jousting tournaments and wrestling matches. And neither country was interested in spending its treasure on another extravagant spectacle to impress the other. Instead of the weeks of showpiece tournament competition in 1520, an evening of dancing with the ladies would suffice for 1532:

> The French king supped with the king of England; and after supper the lady marques of Pembroke [Anne Boleyn], lady Mary, lady Darby, lady Fitzwater, lady Rocheford [Anne's sister-in-law Jane], lady Lisley, and lady Wallop, came in masked, and danced with the French king and lords. The King then took off their visors, and they danced with French gentlemen for an hour.[29]

There was no clear advance agenda for this second royal meeting. Speculation about what matters of business might become part of this social occasion included the possibility of a new peace treaty, a formal adjudication of Henry's Great Matter by the French cardinals, or perhaps even the wedding of Henry VIII to Anne Boleyn. It turned out that none of these rumoured events came to pass at the 1532 meeting.

Henry had tried to prepare for all possible eventualities. Just prior to the conference, he elevated Anne Boleyn to high nobility by bestowing upon her the title of Marchioness of Pembroke, together with extensive related grants of lands and incomes. She thereby became an appropriate companion to accompany him to the meeting of the kings in France. She was treated there as Henry's de facto queen even though there had yet been no annulment or new marriage, and Catherine was still alive. For Anne Boleyn, who had served in Paris in her youth as one of Queen Claude's young ladies-in-waiting, this triumphal return at Henry's side must have brought her great gratification.[30]

Henry also prepared for possible discussion of the annulment issue at the meeting by bringing along his expert on Jewish law, Mark Raphael, as reported by Chapuys:

> The King is taking with him a legion of doctors and monks who are in his favor about the divorce, and among them the three Cordeliers [Franciscan Friars] whom the French king sent from Brittany, and the Jews he summoned from Venice. There will probably be some conference about the divorce, and perhaps the King wishes it to be discussed before the French Council and Cardinals, and decided by them. If the Cardinals are so rash or ill advised as to do this, the King will not fail to complete his folly.[31]

As already noted, however, no substantive discussions about the Great Matter occurred during the 1532 meeting, so Raphael's services were not actively utilised in France. After Raphael's return to England, with the exception of a few payments recorded as being made to him, he seems to have essentially disappeared from the historical record.

Mark Raphael had managed to become the only 'Jew', as he was repeatedly described by Ambassador Chapuys, in Henry's royal court during this period, although this is a somewhat ironic description for a former rabbi who had converted to Catholicism. In any case, he did not advance the King's Great Matter with new and convincing insights into Jewish law and customs that would resolve the Leviticus/Deuteronomy conflict. This court Jew was no Joseph or Mordechai. In the end, Mark Raphael's greatest distinction was only to have been the last significant rabbinic supporter for the king's cause before Henry abandoned his final strategy of relying upon Jewish authorities and rabbinic opinions to convince Pope Clement to grant the annulment.

12

WHY JEWISH LAW FAILED TO HELP HENRY

In retrospect, of course, we know that Henry's final strategy was a failure. But why it failed is not obvious. It turns out that Henry's reliance upon rabbinic opinion proved insufficient due to multiple factors.

Exclusion of Jews from England
Several of the specific reasons for the failure of Henry's rabbinic strategy shared the same underlying root cause – the exclusion of Jews from England for the prior 240 years. Compared to Italy, only a few of the educated scholars and clergy of England had taken even basic instruction in biblical Hebrew. However, even those scholars shared with the rest of the English clergy and intellectuals the severe disadvantage of not knowing anything about matters such as the traditional Jewish interpretations of the Bible, the current organisation of worldwide Judaism, or the religious practices in contemporary Jewish communities.[1]

The resulting lack of England's awareness of Jews and Judaism meant that essentially no one in England – and certainly not the king, his principal advisors, or his agents in Italy – could fully understand and evaluate what they were being told about Jewish law and practice. The consequence of this was a huge misunderstanding about the purported Jewish support for Henry's petition for annulment.

Differences between Catholic and Jewish Administrative Systems

One factor contributing to this misunderstanding by the English was that the Catholic and Jewish institutional systems of administration were – and essentially continue today to be – fundamentally different from one another.

In the hierarchal structure of the Roman Catholic Church, the pope has supreme and absolute power. A pope can promulgate universal rulings on central issues of Catholic life. In contrast, after the first century CE, Diaspora Judaism has featured almost the opposite of a hierarchal administrative structure. Diaspora Judaism lacks any locus of centralised authority that is universally recognised by all Jews.

Henry and his envoys failed to appreciate that Jews in Italy operated under a system that permitted – and in many ways seemed to welcome – continuing disagreement on many important issues of theological interpretation. Instead of universal Jewish agreement on such issues, some particular group of Jews might resolve a particular issue by recognising the authority of a historical or contemporary rabbinic leader of their local community. With further migration, members of such a community would carry their interpretations to new geographical locations.

Two Judaisms

Henry's envoys to Italy failed to recognise that many of the religious beliefs and practices among the Jews and rabbis whom they encountered in Italy differed from one another based upon the family origins of the particular Jew. The English appear to have been unaware of the theological and cultural distinctions between the two major streams of Judaism that had resulted from the exile of ancient Jews from the Holy Land – Ashkenazi and Sephardi Jews.[2]

Because of the primitive conditions of travel and communication during much of the Common Era up to the sixteenth century, the Jewish Diaspora resulted at times in a partial isolation of Jewish communities from one another. This naturally caused each individual Jewish community to increase its reliance upon its local rabbis for religious leadership. Moreover, especially in times of suppression, hostility, and isolation that were periodically imposed by local governments and peoples, various Jewish communities naturally adjusted to their new cultural and physical environments through partial assimilation of local secular life in order to survive. The

Ashkenazi Jews – those families living in Germany, and later in Poland, Russia, and many parts of western Europe – acculturated to different conditions as compared to the Sephardi Jews, who had obtained refuge for hundreds of years in Spain and Portugal.

The distinction between the Ashkenazi and Sephardi groups was manifested in part by their acceptance of different rabbinic books and opinions as authoritative.

With regard to marital laws of the sort relevant to Henry VIII's situation, these Jewish communal differences became acute around the turn of the eleventh century with the promulgation of the ban attributed to Rabbi Gershom (c. 960–1028), prohibiting the biblical patriarchal practice of polygamy. This prohibition against multiple wives was directed to and accepted by Ashkenazi Jews only. Indeed, polygamy was not banned for Sephardi and Mizrahi Jews (those in the Muslim world) until the Chief Rabbis of the State of Israel did so in 1950.[3]

It seems very doubtful that Henry or his agents understood the implications of this major difference between Ashkenazi and Sephardi Jews regarding polygamy. But the distinction became an extremely significant factor in the rabbinic responses to King Henry's search for opinions asserting that under Jewish law the Deuteronomy rules for levirate marriage did not weaken the absolute Leviticus Prohibitions against marrying a brother's widow.

Jews in general had little difficulty in granting respect and obedience to both the Deuteronomy and the Leviticus provisions. For Jews, Leviticus prohibited marrying a brother's widow unless the very limited conditions of Deuteronomy applied: the deceased brother must have died without having produced children, and the surviving brother's levirate marriage to the widow must be intended by him to produce a child who would be treated as a child of the deceased brother.[4]

As we have noted, however, the Deuteronomy provisions themselves also include an express alternative to the levirate marriage obligation. Deut. 25:7–10 gives the surviving brother the option of *halitzah* – a public ceremony which includes the widow removing her brother-in-law's sandal from his foot.[5] The rabbis and elders of the various Jewish communities from time to time could be very influential as to whether, in their particular community, the surviving brother should marry his widowed sister-in-law or should release her so that she could marry whomever she wished. Local rabbinic and community pressure could prioritise either performing levirate marriage or granting both parties the release of *halitzah*.

This local preference was greatly affected by whether the Ashkenazi or the Sephardi rule regarding polygamy applied at that particular time and place. Since the eleventh century, it was difficult for Ashkenazi communities to favour levirate marriage, because that left no satisfactory answer when the surviving brother was already married and the ban against polygamy would be applicable. To avoid those difficulties, it was simpler for Ashkenazi communities to favour the *halitzah* release ceremony in all cases. For Sephardi communities, however, and especially for Mizrahi Jews, some of whose traditions were derived from surrounding Muslim cultures where polygamy was common, there was no polygamy-related discomfort in favouring levirate marriage.

This was the major issue obscured by the elation of Richard Croke and the optimism of King Henry in early 1530 when Croke obtained the help of two high-profile rabbis, Rabbi Elias Halfan and former rabbi Mark Raphael. Those rabbis gave assurances that, since the time of the destruction of the Second Temple by the Romans in 70 CE, Jews had abandoned the practice of levirate marriage:

> [Croke is sending to the King] some writings by learned Hebrews in his favor [Elias Halfan and Mark Raphael], by which, what Stokesley wished, is proved indisputably; viz., that the Levitical law has always been holy and intact, and never abolished nor weakened; on the other hand, the law of Deuteronomy was never in force except when the conditions therein expressed were present, and when it is allowed by the Levitical law; and that it was never observed, even by the Jews themselves, after the destruction of Jerusalem, except in matters concerning inheritance.[6]

These assurances by Henry's two most significant rabbinic supporters that Jews had abandoned levirate marriage grossly oversimplified complex Jewish theology and history. The supportive statements were generally correct only after the tenth century, and only for Ashkenazi communities. However, both Croke and the king lacked the background necessary for understanding that such statements were certainly not true for all Jewish communities in the sixteenth century, especially Sephardi and Mizrahi communities.[7]

Other Limitations of Henry's Arguments from Jewish Law

If the English had understood more about the law, history, theology, and practice of Judaism, Henry might have been able to recognise some of the other significant factors that undermined much of the specific rabbinic support produced by Richard Croke. For example, when we consider Henry's two major rabbinic supporters found by Professor Croke, we have seen that Rabbi Elias Halfan may have sided with the king primarily as an extension of his devotion to Kabbalism and his bitter animosity towards Rabbi Jacob Mantino. We have also seen that Croke's other so-called rabbinic expert, Mark Raphael, may have been an unreliable reporter who was primarily looking to promote his personal status.

Perhaps there is another, more cynical explanation for Croke's and Henry's apparent lack of concern for the motivations, sincerity, and correctness of the rabbinic opinions supporting his annulment. Perhaps it was not only that the prior banishment of the Jews from England meant that the English lacked the knowledge to understand and evaluate the rabbinic opinions they sought. It could simply be that Henry was unconcerned with the soundness of the Jewish authorities because his goal was to obtain opinions – any opinions, whether they were right or wrong – that might possibly convince Clement.[8]

The End of the Final Strategy – the Wedding in Rome

As with many of Henry's prior failed strategies to convince Clement, Henry once again clung too long to his unrealistic hopes that rabbinic support would soon solve his problems. For example, the king retained Mark Raphael in his service until at least 1532, long after his services were employed. The particular event that would eventually kill off Henry's rabbinic opinion strategy – although no one seems to have recognised its full significance at the time – had in fact occurred earlier, in that critical year of 1530.

The event marking the final failure of the king's last strategy was not due to clever editing by Clement's cardinals of the draft decrees presented by the English. Henry was not defeated by forceful counter-arguments urged by Charles V and his Imperial ambassadors, nor was he deterred by any scholarly opinion bravely written in Queen Catherine's defence by Bishop John Fisher. Even Pope Clement's seemingly inexhaustible ability to postpone taking definitive action had not been enough to force Henry to give up. No book, argument or court ruling landed the killing blow. Henry's final Jewish law strategy for a royal annulment was ended, quite appropriately, by an event that was the exact opposite of an annulment. It was a wedding.

However, the wedding in question was not the one that Anne Boleyn had been fiercely insisting upon for the previous three or four years. It was an otherwise ordinary ceremony in the Jewish community of Rome, with a singular distinction – it was a levirate marriage. A Jewish man married his childless deceased brother's widow in a public ceremony attended by the leaders and members of the local Jewish community. Henry's rabbis had previously assured him that the Jews had abandoned the practice of levirate marriage fifteen centuries earlier. Yet, suddenly, here was seemingly inarguable proof that the practice was still in force. Ambassador Mai was quite pleased to report the event to Charles V on 2 October 1530:

> Your Majesty will be glad to hear that here this very year, among the Roman Jews, one has been compelled to marry the widow of his brother, who had died without children, a thing which not only is not prohibited, as we maintain, but is actually enjoined by Jewish law.[9]

What could Henry argue after this? He could try to distinguish his situation because he was a Catholic whose seemingly comparable marriage to his brother's widow was not subject to Jewish law or practices. Or he could argue that the bridegroom in Rome must have acted from the required motive of providing children who would be attributed to his childless deceased brother, while Henry had married Catherine with the intent to provide successors for himself. Nevertheless, if the Deuteronomy levirate marriage obligations were being observed and celebrated in the contemporary Jewish community in Rome, it was almost impossible that any amount of theological analysis could convince Pope Clement that the Jews no longer acknowledged any exceptions to a supposedly absolute rule of the Leviticus Prohibitions.

Why Jewish Law Failed to Help Henry

There is one further observation that several historians have since noted, but it was not one that Henry could have put forth with profit: the timing of the Roman wedding ceremony seemed too convenient to be purely coincidental. It would not be surprising if that suspicion were accurate. However, it would not have been useful for Henry to mention such a suspicion to the pope. Even if it could be proved that the levirate marriage ceremony in Rome had been staged by Henry's opponents, then surely the persons who had been able to arrange and pay for such a tactic would have been agents of Clement himself, or his ally Charles V.[10]

PART V

THE GREAT MATTER ENDS

13

HENRY'S FINAL TACTICS

If these developments during 1530 had occurred earlier, at the outset of King Henry's quest for an annulment, he might have had time to rethink the problem and perhaps come up with a new line of attack. By 1531, however, even he could see that it would be futile to revisit strategies that had already proved ineffective to overcome the perpetual procrastination by the pope and the scheduling delays endemic in Rome's ecclesiastical court system. Two additional factors were also pushing the king to abandon his entire 1530 enterprise, once so promising, of seeking Catholic and Jewish theological arguments to convince the pope.

First, the king's failed strategies had already greatly delayed his marriage to Anne Boleyn. Given the strength of his passion, he was perhaps unwilling to wait any longer for full and regular sexual access to her. His ability to produce a legitimate male heir for undisputed succession to the throne also might not survive further delays.

Second, these years of frustrating arguments between London and Rome had already achieved a significant benefit for Henry. In the course of the dispute, Pope Clement had revealed a major weakness of the Holy See. The shifting fortunes of international power, especially the military successes of the Holy Roman Empire in Italy, meant that Clement was no longer a strong and independent political leader in the mould of some of his predecessor popes. Moreover, the growing threat from the nascent Reformation in western Europe meant that Clement had to do everything reasonably possible to keep England within the Roman Catholic Church. Against this political backdrop, the pope was left with only one weapon that might still force Henry's submission – the power to excommunicate.

The Threat of Excommunication

The problem for Clement was that threatening excommunication to force Henry's compliance could work only on two levels, either the religious or the military. It might have some religious force to the extent that Henry was concerned about the state of his soul and the consequences for eternity in the afterlife, or else it might be effective through military power if the pope could obtain temporal enforcement of his decree by summoning all Catholic nations to wage war upon England until Henry relented.[1]

Those threats might have held some weight four or five years earlier. By now, however, Henry had thoroughly convinced himself of the righteousness of his theological position. He was not concerned with the eternal state of his soul. He was certain that God agreed with him. Likewise, international invasion was no longer an effective threat. During the prior years, Henry had been busy consolidating his domestic and international powers and alliances.

As we know from subsequent events, Parliament and the English people would ultimately agree to have Henry replace the pope with the ruling monarch of England as head of the Catholic Church in England. This in turn would enable Henry to confiscate and control the English lands and assets of the Church. The resulting wealth would further strengthen the royal treasury and consolidate the king's domestic influence by funding opportunities for expanded patronage and alliances with the English nobility.[2]

On the international scene, moreover, there was no longer any military leader willing to invade England. France and England had transformed their historical mutual enmity into an alliance marked by acts of reciprocal cooperation. The only other significant military power in Europe was the imperial army of Charles V. However, at this crucial time, the emperor could not allow any military diversion to distract him from fending off the Ottoman forces who were actively threatening Hungary, Austria, and the eastern border of the Hapsburg empire.

In light of all this, 1531 marked the end of any realistic negotiations to try to convince the pope to annul the marriage. Although Henry made no formal declaration of his change in strategy, it took him only a little time to pivot to simple pragmatism. Before breaking with the Roman Catholic Church, he made one last attempt to use the basic tactic that had served the English so well in obtaining university faculty votes and clerical opinions – bribery. For this last time, he tried to bribe the pope directly. In July 1531, Henry instructed his envoy Benet on what to say to Clement to get the annulment proceedings transferred to London:

> If you can obtain his promise in writing, send it to us; and if he deny it, urge it again, or offer him a sum of money in secret.[3]

The attempted bribery failed. Henry's only back-up plan was to make it completely clear to Clement that he was not at all concerned with excommunication – especially now that the pope lacked any military means by which to enforce it. In mid-1531, Henry told the papal nuncio:

> I shall never consent to his [Pope Clement] being the judge in that affair [the annulment]. Even if His Holiness should do his worst by excommunicating me, and so forth, &c., I shall not mind it, for I care not a fig for all his excommunications. Let him follow his own at Rome, I will do here what I think best.[4]

Confiscation of Church Property

Henry's recognition that the Church was too weak to interfere with England's domestic affairs was confirmed when he saw that the emperor, without apparent concern for the wishes of the pope, was willing to give up ownership of Church property in some of the German lands in the hope of forestalling the spread of the Reformation. In July 1531, the king remarked on how the pope's acquiescence was instructive for all the remaining rulers of Catholic countries, including his own England:

> We learn from Flanders that the Emperor is going into Germany, and has determined to treat with the princes of Germany upon the question of the Faith; and as he will doubtless look chiefly to his own reputation, he will probably grant the princes all that can be allowed without prejudice to orthodoxy. He will, therefore, probably allow the laity to appropriate the possessions of the

Church, which is a matter that does not touch the foundations of the Faith; and what an example this will afford to others it is easy to see.[5]

Controlling Parliament through Thomas Cromwell

As a final factor, Henry would soon no longer feel the loss of the diplomatic skills of his former Lord Chancellor and chief advisor, Thomas Wolsey. The cardinal and papal legate died at the end of 1530 after falling out of royal favour in 1529. By 1534, Henry would be emboldened and enabled by his new principal minister, Thomas Cromwell, to chart a new course. Cromwell, who had previously been Wolsey's assistant, was a master politician and manipulator of Parliament and his vision for the centralisation of national power and wealth in the monarchy fit perfectly with Henry's desires. Relying upon Cromwell's political and legal skills, Henry was able to obtain a series of parliamentary laws enhancing the king's new position as head of the English Church. This legislation barred any appeal to, or censure from, the Vatican in matters of religion in England. At the same time, the new laws stifled domestic opposition to Henry's consolidation of Church and Crown.

This parliamentary legislation allowed Henry to achieve two major goals from a single tactic. First, Henry could arrange for the annulment denied him by Pope Clement and force its acceptance by the English. Second, he could consolidate his royal power by personal control over – or outright confiscation of – the property and wealth of the Holy See in England. Regardless of what the English Reformation might eventually mean theologically to the people of England, these beginnings would certainly serve their king's immediate personal goals.[6]

The Wedding in England

We have seen how, towards the end of 1530, the public celebration of a levirate marriage by Rome's Jewish community ultimately crushed Henry's hopes to use Jewish theological arguments to convince Clement to annul the marriage to Catherine. It is therefore fitting that it would be yet another wedding celebration, this time in England in early 1533, that would make Clement's steadfast opposition to the annulment irrelevant.

Henry's Final Tactics

Henry and Anne announced that they had been privately and secretly married on 25 January 1533.[7] Their daughter, Princess Elizabeth, who would ultimately reign as Queen Elizabeth I, the last Tudor monarch, was born on 7 September 1533. Of course, it is easy to conclude that this secret wedding was, much like that earlier wedding in Rome's Jewish community, simply too conveniently timed to be believed. But whether or not it actually occurred on the date claimed, it is difficult to accept that Princess Elizabeth's early September 1533 birth was fully legitimate.

There is a reasonable alternative scenario to the story of the secret 25 January 1533 wedding. By the first half of 1532, Henry had given up on expecting the pope to grant the annulment. Instead, he determined to remove the English Church from membership in the Roman Catholic Church. The King of England would become the head of the Church in England in place of the pope, who would be demoted for English purposes to the title of Bishop of Rome.[8] Anne, in turn, became convinced that Henry would soon secure complete ecclesiastical power in England, and that the annulment of his marriage to Catherine of Aragon was imminent. It appears that Henry and Anne therefore finally began – or perhaps resumed – their full sexual relationship around the time of their return trip from the late October 1532 conference with King Francis I in France.[9]

We know that a few days before or after the beginning of 1533, Anne told others that she was pregnant.[10] We can presume that this pregnancy drove the couple to marry promptly, or perhaps it merely pushed them to fabricate a story of a secret marriage.[11] Either way, in the event that Anne was carrying a male child, they had to be able to plausibly argue against any later opposition to their son's right to succession. Their hoped-for son must not be illegitimate.

If the secret marriage – or at least the story about the secret marriage – was the king's strategy to smooth the way for succession to the Tudor crown, it did not work out as he planned. Even in the early sixteenth century, people could count to nine. This was an era when aristocrats, royalty, and even Church officials commonly engaged in extramarital sexual liaisons and longer-term sexual relationships. It was also a time with almost no medical knowledge about obstetrics. The infant mortality rate for premature births was very high. As a result, people living five hundred years ago were probably quite used to counting the time elapsed between a wedding and a birth in which the infant survived. They understood the implications when the elapsed time for the birth of a healthy, normal-sized baby was – as it was for the Princess Elizabeth – no more than seven and a half months rather than nine months after the wedding.

Why Did Anne Finally Agree to Sexual Relations without Marriage?

If we think back to the very beginning of Henry's pursuit of Anne, we recall that his love letters confirm that Anne had at least initially refused him full sexual access until she had become his legal wife and his recognised queen. However, at the end of 1532 and the beginning of 1533, Anne was still neither wife nor queen. Catherine of Aragon was alive, and there had been no divorce or annulment. There was still no formal basis for Anne to be crowned queen without a legal marriage to Henry. Although it is generally accepted that Anne became pregnant sometime during this period, it is not clear what caused her to change her previous determination to withhold full sexual activities.

It is possible that Anne and Henry had engaged in sexual relations earlier in their relationship, but that is not very likely. For Anne, that activity would have risked the loss of her bargaining strength for advancing to the throne. Henry's past relationships with Elizabeth Blount and Anne's sister, Mary, must have demonstrated to her that he did not marry mistresses who became pregnant – he discarded them.

Henry, too, would have had reservations about sexual intercourse with Anne up to this time. An earlier pregnancy probably would have cost any hope of Pope Clement granting the annulment of the marriage to Catherine. Moreover, even if such an earlier pregnancy produced a boy, Henry already had Fitzroy, his acknowledged illegitimate son whom he had elevated to the nobility. Another illegitimate son would not solve the king's continuing concerns for succession to his throne.

Assuming that the late 1532 or early 1533 sexual relations between Henry and Anne did constitute a new level of intimacy for them, there were two major factors that could have combined to convince Anne to move on with their relationship – the death of William Warham, Archbishop of Canterbury, on 22 August 1532, and Henry's elevation of Anne to become the Marchioness of Pembroke on 1 September 1532.

The Death of William Warham

The primary seat of Church authority in England became vacant on 22 August 1532 with the death of William Warham, Archbishop of Canterbury, then eighty-two years old. As he had gotten older, Warham had become increasingly independent in his decisions. He had a long history of important service to both Henry VIII and his father, Henry VII, but he refused to join most of the rest of the English clergy in acquiescing to Henry's takeover of the ecclesiastical powers of the pope, or the reduction of his own powers as Archbishop of Canterbury.[12] Indeed, along with John Fisher, Bishop of Rochester, Warham had been one of the few important voices in the English clergy to risk speaking out as a champion for Queen Catherine.

The timing of Warham's death was very fortunate for the king, who now had a clear path to select a vastly different sort of churchman for the role. The king needed an Archbishop of Canterbury for the new English Church who would use that office to grant the annulment, legitimate Henry's marriage to Anne, crown Anne as queen, and, assuming that Anne was carrying their son, as Henry had been assured by astrologers, establish the succession to the throne.

At the 1531 Convocation of Canterbury, the king had forced the English clergy to acknowledge that he was the Supreme Head of the Church in England. A year on, Warham's death had removed the last significant obstacle impeding Henry from exercising his new powers as he wished. Anne now apparently had no further concerns that Henry might not be able to achieve all of their goals. At last, Henry had begun openly engaging in a flurry of actions with the clergy and with Parliament so that he could satisfy Anne's preconditions to full sexual access. She was indeed finally about to become his wife and queen.

Anne's Elevation to the Nobility

Henry promptly began planning to arrange for a new Archbishop of Canterbury who would formally confirm his marriage to Anne. He also began planning for two very significant public events for Anne – her participation as Henry's companion at the forthcoming meeting at Calais with King Francis I, and her elaborate coronation in London.

However, Anne's qualification for these pending events – the formal confirmation of their marriage, the meeting at Calais, and her coronation – shared a basic problem. Although descended from the Howard, Butler, and Boleyn lines, Anne was not a high-ranking member of the titled nobility, and she did not already own, in her own right, any substantial property or income. Thus, she lacked the social class status that would typically be expected of a noble woman to serve as Henry's consort at a meeting with the King of France, or to be Henry's bride or queen. The solution was for Henry to anticipate these pending events by first granting substantial property and income to Anne, as well as giving her a title that would transform her into a member of the high aristocracy.[13]

Even before Warham's death, Henry had begun planning for the proposed autumn 1532 meeting with Francis I in Calais to celebrate the new alliance between their two nations. He was also starting to plan for Anne's coronation.[14] But the most important preparation for these events occurred ten days after the death of Warham. On 1 September 1532, Anne was formally elevated to become the Marchioness of Pembroke. This was not only marked by an elaborate, prescribed formal ceremony, but was also accompanied by the transfers to her of a lifetime annuity and the rents of a large group of Crown interests in manors, lands, and leases.[15]

Now that Anne was a member of the aristocracy, Henry manoeuvred to have Francis I invite the newly minted marchioness to come to the conference. Chapuys observed that Henry was so besotted with Anne that he would have brought her to France even without an invitation:

> ... the French king wishes ... to ask the King to bring the new Marchioness with him. ... Francis has probably made this request, knowing that it would please the King and the lady, and that the King would bring her without being asked, as he cannot leave her for an hour.[16]

Thomas Cranmer Becomes Archbishop of Canterbury

With all of this happening at the end of 1532, both Henry and Anne seem to have become quite confident that they could overcome any obstacles to their wedding and Anne's coronation. However, the question of royal succession remained. When Anne realised at the beginning of 1533 that she was pregnant, she and Henry both desperately hoped that the child Anne was carrying would be a boy. If that were the outcome, the king wanted to do all he could to ensure full public support for his new son's future succession to the

Henry's Final Tactics

throne – and he saw one last opportunity to obtain Clement's aid in furthering this final goal.

In January 1533, Henry recalled Thomas Cranmer from the Continent, where he had been continuing his assignment to present theological arguments to the emperor and the Vatican. Immediately upon Cranmer's return to England, Henry nominated him to succeed Warham as Archbishop of Canterbury. The king must have felt certain that he could rely on Cranmer to follow his new instructions as faithfully as he had previously done in writing opinions and making arguments to support the annulment.

It is surprising that Clement acceded to Henry's wishes in naming Cranmer as Archbishop of Canterbury. Perhaps the pope's decision demonstrates the imbalance of bargaining power between him and Henry at this point in time. By agreeing, Pope Clement could have been making one final but futile concession in the hopes of avoiding England's looming break with Rome. Despite being warned of the dangers of appointing Cranmer, Clement once again retreated to a strategy of procrastination rather than outright refusal, which would risk what the pope apparently feared most at this point – immediately and irrevocably pushing England out of the Roman Catholic Church. Ambassador Chapuys warned the emperor of the likely consequences for his aunt if the pope approved Cranmer's appointment:

> Dr. Cremmer, late ambassador with your Majesty, had not been here a week, before the King, to the great astonishment of everybody, promoted him to the archbishopric of Canterbury. ... Besides, the King has advanced the money for the expedition of the Bulls [Clement's formal appointment of Cranmer], so as to have no delay. It is suspected that the object of this haste is, that the Archbishop, as Legate of the kingdom, may authorise the new marriage in this Parliament, judging this divorce necessary.[17]

In order to strengthen his bargaining position, Henry applied enormous economic pressure on Clement by having Parliament reduce by 90 per cent the *annates* – the first year's profits of Church appointments – that traditionally were paid to the pope. A year before, Henry had overridden Parliament and sent full annates to Rome. But it was obvious, and apparently had already been privately expressed to

Clement, that the king would not continue this generosity if he failed to promptly confirm Cranmer's appointment:

> In spite of the prohibition of the last Parliament that only the tenth part of the previous sums should be paid as annates to Rome, the King has ordered the entire payment as usual. Many think there is some secret intelligence between the King and the Pope.[18]

In light of England's economic threats to the Vatican, Clement may have felt that he had no choice but to let Henry pick the next Archbishop of Canterbury, even if he clearly saw that this could be the final step enabling Henry to obtain the annulment and the ultimate breach between London and Rome. These concerns were promptly fulfilled as soon as the papal bull confirming Cranmer's appointment arrived in England.

Prior to swearing loyalty to the pope as part of his formal induction as Archbishop of Canterbury, Cranmer attempted to absolve himself by taking a secret oath. He declared in advance that any promises of obedience to the Holy See that would require him to act contrary to the laws of England and of the English Church would be void.[19]

In short, Archbishop Cranmer was ready to use the authority of his new office to implement Henry's wishes. On 23 May 1533, after brief hearings on the matter, Cranmer annulled Henry's marriage to Catherine. Five days later, Cranmer ruled that Henry's previous private wedding to Anne Boleyn was valid and effective. Finally, on 1 June 1533, Archbishop Cranmer crowned Anne as Queen of England at a formal public ceremony at Westminster.

After six years of pursuing his Great Matter, Henry VIII finally received his annulment – except that, even as the powerful King of England, he had not been able to obtain the annulment from the pope as he had wished.

14

WHY HENRY'S QUEST FAILED

We have examined Henry's final strategy in his quest to obtain an annulment. When Christian theology arguments did not convince the pope, the king sought opinions from the rabbis of Italy as to Jewish law and practice. We have also examined why that particular strategy failed. But Henry's strategy of relying upon Jewish interpretations of Leviticus and Deuteronomy was only the last in a long list of attempts to convince the pope throughout years of arguments. Now one final question demands an answer regarding not only his last strategy of using Jewish law, but encompassing all of Henry's arguments for annulment: why did the King's Great Matter fail?

Henry Had Ample Motivation
Henry was obviously very highly motivated to obtain the annulment from the pope. His passionate early love letters to Anne Boleyn appear to be the sincere responses of an infatuated lover rather than merely the calculated posturing of a powerful man pursuing his next sexual conquest.

Henry's other major motivation – his anxiety about establishing an unquestioned Tudor succession to his throne – was a justified concern, especially because his father had won the throne for the Tudors more by military conquest than traditional claim of superior lineage.

Further, Henry cared much about his domestic and international reputation as an exceptional man and an unrivalled monarch. He soon learned that he was unable to keep his quest for annulment secret from England and the world, and once his plans became public knowledge, he became even more stubborn in pursuit of his goals. He convinced himself that he was in the right, and he could not accept a public failure in such an important matter.

In light of all these strong motivations, why was Henry unable to win the cooperation of Pope Clement? The inevitable conclusion is that the king happened to fight his battle at the wrong time. He failed to understand – or, more likely, would not let himself acknowledge – that the issues that really mattered at that point of time were neither legal nor theological. Henry's quest for annulment had the misfortune of being caught up in a unique tangle of political circumstances. The results for Henry might have been quite different if his Great Matter had occurred a decade before or after his years of struggles in 1527–1533. Instead, his mission at the time he undertook it was doomed by an extraordinary convergence of international political forces whose combined power he could not overcome.

Ascendancy of Holy Roman Emperor Charles V
Perhaps the most significant single factor blocking Henry's attempt to annul his marriage to Catherine of Aragon was the growing power of Charles V, the Holy Roman Emperor. Charles was a Hapsburg whose fierce sense of family honour and loyalty in this matter was not subject to negotiation. To Henry's great misfortune, Charles was Catherine's nephew. In that relationship, the emperor instantly became Catherine's most powerful international defender and supporter.

The imperial military victories in Italy meant that throughout the remainder of Henry's six-year attempt to have Clement annul his marriage to Catherine, the pope was either physically controlled by Charles or under implicit threat of imprisonment by him. Clement was never completely free to ignore the possibility of imperial military support for Catherine, with the result that by the end of 1529 the pope and the emperor were more unified than ever. Clement agreed to a major conference with Charles in Bologna, at which he performed the ceremonial coronation of Charles as Holy Roman Emperor. By 1530, Clement had learned that he could peaceably co-exist with Charles so long as the Church did not entirely abandon Catherine.[1]

The Protestant Reformation

In contrast to his growing rapprochement with the Holy Roman Empire, Clement could not presume that the Church would be able to coexist with the burgeoning Protestant Reformation.

In 1517, only a decade before the start of Henry's pursuit of the annulment, the beginnings of the Protestant Reformation had been sparked by Martin Luther's issuing his 95 Theses. That manifesto proposed some key theological reforms of Church doctrine. It also listed Luther's complaints against various unjust practices in the Roman Catholic Church. One of the major injustices on Luther's list regarded the Church selling indulgences – forgiveness of sins with the promise of eternal salvation of the soul – to provide wealth for Church leaders, as well as to provide funds for costly Church operations such as the construction of St Peter's Basilica.[2]

It would have been obvious to Clement that granting Henry's public request for a decree of annulment would vindicate Luther's complaints that the Church favoured wealthy supporters.

Henry tried to capitalise on Clement's fears and weakness by repeatedly threatening to take England out of the Roman Catholic Church. However, he failed to appreciate that the pope simply could not find an acceptable response to England's threat. If Henry was not merely bluffing, then Clement's refusal to grant the annulment could cost the Church the loyalty and membership of one of the great Catholic nations. On the other hand, if Clement gave in and granted the annulment, such a capitulation might contribute to the triumph of the Protestant Reformation and the very death of Roman Catholicism. Clement dealt with this quandary in his usual manner, continually promising Henry whatever was necessary, but putting off taking any definitive action. While Clement could live with further delay, Henry could not. Along with the urgings of Anne Boleyn, it was her eventual pregnancy at the end of 1532 that finally forced Henry to follow through on his threat to marry Anne without receiving an annulment from the pope.[3]

Duelling Queens: The Relative Popularity of Catherine and Anne

Marriage to Anne Boleyn gave Henry a chance to produce a male heir. But even if Anne were carrying a son, that alone might not necessarily achieve the second of Henry's two major goals – peaceable succession for the Tudor dynasty. Royal succession turned upon acceptance by the English people, and if the English people's ultimate acceptance were to be predicted by the relative popularity of Catherine and Anne in 1533, then Henry would have had good cause to worry. In many ways, Henry's duelling queens could not have presented a greater contrast in character and popularity.

Catherine of Aragon had been warmly accepted by Henry's subjects from the day she arrived in England in 1501 as a young and beautiful foreign princess. When Arthur Tudor died five months after their wedding, it seemed that all in England were ready to cheer again for a planned second royal wedding, this time to the boy who would become the next King of England, Prince Henry Tudor. Sadly, when that marriage came, the resulting public joy gradually returned to sorrow as Catherine went through at least seven pregnancies during her first decade as Henry's wife and England's queen. Catherine gave birth to only one child who survived beyond a month or two – Princess Mary Tudor. Especially the women of the land could understand and sympathise with Catherine's suffering and bravery throughout her repeated family tragedies.[4]

Catherine earned great popularity for her staunch loyalty and personal dignity during the initial two decades of her marriage to Henry. Thereafter, that popularity continued to grow with Catherine's public expression of her unchanging noble character in the face of Henry's ruthless efforts to have their marriage annulled. She was unswerving in her insistence that she remained and would always remain Henry's wife and queen.[5]

The contrasts in the public reactions to Catherine of Aragon and to Anne Boleyn were glaring. In the people's eyes, almost all points of comparison favoured Catherine. She was a royal princess, daughter of Ferdinand and Isabella. In contrast, Anne Boleyn's great-grandfather had established the Boleyn family wealth from commercial success in London's mercantile trade.

Upon Catherine's arrival in England and wedding to Prince Arthur, she had been acclaimed for her beauty. Anne, however, did not model the then-conventional image of beauty. She was described as short, with dark hair, having some sort of minor deformity on one finger and showing some disfiguring warts or moles on the skin of her neck and chest.

Of course, when young Anne caught Henry's eye at court, she was probably about nineteen years old. Queen Catherine was forty-two. The queen's multiple pregnancies over the prior eighteen years had taken a great toll on her general health and her former beauty. For what appears to have been the majority of the English people, their queen's natural loss of beauty was seen more as evidence of her service and devotion to the realm than as a demerit in comparison with Anne Boleyn.

Anne Boleyn did have some supporters. Among Henry's nobles and court advisors there were a few who joined with the Boleyns in an informal faction to support Anne's cause. Some of these insiders supported Anne because they assessed her influence over Henry as likely to make her the winner, the next queen. Some supported her because they shared a common enemy. Anne's initial political fight was to undermine, dislodge, and finally vanquish Cardinal Wolsey. He had been Henry's intimate friend and chief advisor, but some in the king's inner circle saw him as unworthy of that position, or at least they felt that he was an impediment to their own, more merited rise to power.

More broadly, however, the decision of Henry's subjects to support either Anne or Catherine was based primarily upon religion, not politics. There were a few conservative churchmen and statesmen, such as John Fisher, William Warham, Sir Thomas More, and Thomas Abel, who felt compelled by their consciences to defy Anne and Henry. These men supported Catherine in order to remain true to their Catholic beliefs and maintain their loyalty to the pope.

On her side, Anne was able to find support from some liberal churchmen and academics because she and the Boleyns were seen as favouring the Protestant Reformation. For much of the general public, however, England was still a Catholic nation, and Catherine had amply shown that she was a devout and sincere Catholic. Since many ordinary English subjects at that time feared the Reformation, the issue of religion became another major factor in the people's love for Catherine and their rejection of Anne Boleyn.

Dueling Monarchs: The Relative Popularity of Queen Catherine and King Henry

It wasn't only Catherine and Anne who competed for public popularity. In some ways, Henry also found himself in a popularity contest with his first wife. From its beginning, the King's Great Matter had taken the form of a legal battle between the spouses over Henry's claim that they had been living together for two decades without being legally married under the law and in the eyes of God. This adversarial legal format practically invited the public to become partisans of one or the other of the contestants. The public's judgment was clear.

Henry consistently claimed that his quest for annulment was motivated by conscience – his marriage to Catherine had never been legal because it violated the Leviticus Prohibitions. Much of the public supported Catherine against the king because of the injustice of what was commonly perceived to be Henry's true motivation for seeking an annulment – Henry's lust for the younger and, by that time, prettier Anne.

How Timing Contributed to Henry's Failure

As we look back on Henry's many unsuccessful strategies and manoeuvres during his six-year campaign to obtain the annulment, there is a sense that extraordinarily bad timing played a significant role in his overall failure.

At the very outset of the King's Great Matter, Henry tried to achieve the annulment by taking advantage of Cardinal Wolsey's special ecclesiastical authority as the papal legate. However, Wolsey suspended the secret Westminster Trial when news reached London that mutinous imperial troops had sacked Rome.

At the other end of the contest, the most dramatic example of bad timing for Henry was the sudden performance of a levirate marriage ceremony in the Jewish community of Rome in 1530. Whether that dramatic event was staged or truly coincidental, it furnished an inescapable demonstration that the Jews still recognised the obligations of levirate marriage. The Jewish wedding in Rome destroyed Henry's final strategy for trying to convince the pope that the Leviticus Prohibitions overruled Deuteronomy's levirate marriage obligations.

The end of Henry's Great Matter was likewise dictated by another insurmountable timing issue. Anne became pregnant around the end of 1532. Because the coming birth might produce Henry's longed-for son, it was critical for Henry and Anne to marry immediately so that they could deflect any potential issues of illegitimacy concerning the next heir to the Tudor crown. The timing of the expected birthdate left Henry with no alternative. He could no longer wait for Clement to grant an annulment.

Final Consequences

This time-driven resolution of the conflict in 1533 was not quite the final chapter in the story of Henry's Great Matter. Clement went along with Henry's appointment of Thomas Cranmer as Archbishop of Canterbury, a risky concession that represented the pope's last desperate attempt to keep England within the Roman Catholic Church – a goal that was not to be realised.

During the balance of his reign, Henry presided over additional church reforms, such as adopting English-language Bibles and prayer books. These steps would ultimately lead to the full-scale English Reformation. Despite the English Church thereafter undergoing some alternating periods of Protestantism and Catholicism during the remainder of the Tudor dynasty's reign, England ultimately became a Protestant nation under the Church of England.

But the resolution of Henry's Great Matter also produced some surprises. Anne Bolen never gave birth to a son. The child born to her in 1533 was a daughter, Elizabeth, who eventually ruled England as Queen Elizabeth I (r. 1538–1603). Elizabeth would be the last of the Tudor dynasty and one of England's greatest and most popular monarchs. However, her reign had to await the completion of the reigns of two intervening Tudor monarchs. Upon Henry VIII's death in 1547, his rule was followed by the six-year regency of Edward VI, his son with his third wife, Jane Seymour. When Edward died in 1553 while still a minor, the regency was followed by a unique nine days when his Tudor cousin Lady Jane Grey was designated heir by the influential nobility at the palace. Due to the insistence of the people, however, Princess Mary Tudor, the daughter of Henry VIII and Catherine of Aragon, became Edward's formal successor to the throne. Mary reigned for five years until her death in 1558.[6]

The twenty-five years between Elizabeth's birth and her succession to the throne upon Mary's death contained for England an incredibly complex and varied series of royal events, including divorces, marriages, births, deaths, executions, armed insurrections, civil war, succession disputes, and usurpations of royal power. However, throughout the entire balance of the Tudor years after Henry VIII obtained his annulment from Catherine, Jews continued to be formally excluded from England.

The role of Henry's rabbis in sixteenth-century English affairs had ended.

Afterword

HENRY CRAFTS THE TUDOR DYNASTY

The core of this book has focused upon King Henry VIII's six-year quest to make Anne Boleyn his wife and queen, including the surprising role of Jewish law and Henry's rabbinic advisors in that struggle. The story told here is history, not fiction. It attempts to be as true as possible to the human lives and events it relates. But since human lives and events tend to be complex and somewhat messy, this has been a complex and somewhat messy story as well. We've seen some individuals acting from mixed or undisclosed motivations. Unexpected external events and coincidences have frustrated even the reasonable expectations of some of the participants, while bringing unlikely victories to others. Depending upon your judgments of the morality of various major and secondary actors in this drama, virtue seems not to have always been rewarded and wickedness not always punished, at least in the short term.

If this book had been a work of fiction, however, its central tale might well have begun with much the same storyline: a king's eye, and soon his heart, are captured by the allure and intelligence of a young lady in the royal court. Facing seemingly overwhelming obstacles, the king plunges his kingdom, the Catholic Church, and much of Europe into fierce controversy and turmoil to achieve his goals. At the end of six years of challenge and frustration, the king succeeds in making the lady his wife and queen.

But here is where fiction and history would diverge. If this story were fiction, many authors would be tempted to gloss over the enormity of the wicked actions and personal tragedies littering Henry and Anne's path to their marriage – the isolation and suffering of Catherine of Aragon and her daughter Mary; the devastating downfall of Cardinal Wolsey; and the ultimate executions of some very brave and principled people, including Henry's advisor and Lord Chancellor Thomas More, and Catherine's loyal defenders Bishop John Fisher and chaplain Thomas Able.

Moreover, if this were a work of fiction, some authors could not resist transforming the story into a simple tale of royal romance. Despite all of the tragic consequences for so many of the other characters, fiction could picture the couple living happily ever after. In reality, however, Henry's six years of pursuing Anne Boleyn resulted in only three years of marriage for them. The end was marked by a shockingly obscene trial of the new queen on charges of treason and adultery with five men. The foregone conclusion was swift and terrible – the immediate execution of all five of the alleged partners in adultery, followed a few days later by Anne's beheading. That brief marriage and its consequences for the succession to the Tudor dynasty fall beyond our targeted six years, but nevertheless deserve the following brief mention to illuminate some ultimate consequences of the King's Great Matter.

Anne's Marriage: 1533–1536

Princess Elizabeth was born on 7 September 1533. We have noted that the timing of the birth – just seven and a half months after the claimed secret marriage of Henry and Anne on 25 January 1533 – raised suspicions about Elizabeth's legitimacy. But three years after her birth, there arose a second and much graver basis for public doubt about her right to take the throne. The roots of this issue are deep.

Previously, Anne had secured her position as Henry's closest companion and chief influencer by eliminating or constraining her three principal challengers: Cardinal Wolsey lost his power and position at the end of 1529 and died under arrest on journey to the Tower at the close of 1530; Queen Catharine was supplanted by Anne at the palace and exiled to isolation away from London; and young Princess Mary was made unwelcome at the palace and kept separated from her mother. By these harsh means, Anne became Henry's unchallenged chief advisor.

Unfortunately, as a consequence of having achieved her new position of power, Anne ceased to work so diligently to show her deference to the king and keep him happy. As early as April 1531, Chapuys reported that Anne was already harshly and openly manipulating royal family matters. Henry was beginning to chafe at this unaccustomed domestic turmoil. Anne had become a demanding partner. Chapuys reported that her sharp presumption with King Henry even made Henry nostalgic for his earlier, calmer relationship with the dutiful and ever-caring Catherine:

> The Princess [Mary] has not yet quite recovered from her stomach attack, but it is not serious. She wrote lately to the King that no medicine could do her so much good as seeing him and the Queen, and desired his licence to visit them both at Greenwich. This has been refused her, to gratify the lady [Anne], who hates her as much as [she hates] the Queen Catherine, or more so, chiefly because she sees the King has some affection for her. Of late when the King praised her in the lady's presence the latter was very angry, and began to vituperate the Princess very strangely. She becomes more arrogant every day, using words and authority towards the King, of which he has several times complained to the duke of Norfolk, saying that she was not like the Queen [Catherine], who had never in her life used ill words to him.[1]

More ominously, once they were married, Queen Anne Boleyn failed in the worst way possible for Henry, and therefore for herself: she failed to provide a male heir to succeed the king. Her first pregnancy resulted in the birth of a daughter, Princess Elizabeth. From what happened next, we can gauge how much both Henry and Anne felt it was crucial for them to produce a healthy son.

Within only a few months after giving birth to Elizabeth, Anne was pregnant again. Word of this reached Rome before the end of January 1534. By late February, the king told Chapuys that he thought he would soon be having a son. Sometime in 1534, the king ordered his goldsmith to make an elaborate, bejewelled silver cradle. And by late April, an observer reported from the palace at Greenwich: 'The King and Queen are merry and in good health. The Queen hath a goodly belly, praying our Lord to send us a prince.'[2]

However, Anne's birthing of a son and heir in 1534 was not to be. She suffered a miscarriage in July 1534. Since Chapuys had stayed in London while the king and his court were on their summer progress, he did not report the event until September. By that time, he could include news about how Henry and Anne were reacting. The news was not good for Anne. Henry had resumed his attentions to an unnamed lady of the court. When Anne attempted to send that lady away, Chapuys confirms that the king spoke very severely to Anne:

Since the King began to doubt whether his lady [Anne] was *enccinte* [*encinta*, pregnant] or not, he has renewed and increased the love he formerly had for a very beautiful damsel of the Court; and because the said lady ... wished to drive her away, the King has been very angry, telling his said lady ... that she had good reason to be content with what he had done for her, which he would not do now if the thing were to begin, and that she should consider from what she had come, and several other things.[3]

It took a little more time after her 1534 miscarriage, but by the beginning of 1536, Anne could once again be optimistic regarding her future. She was pregnant again, and hoped that she might literally be carrying the solution to all of her problems with Henry. The year opened with the death of Catherine of Aragon on 7 January 1536. It seems that only death could end the continuous conflict between these two women who both claimed the titles of Henry's wife and queen.[4]

The controversy had proved extremely uncomfortable for Henry and Anne, especially since Catherine had continued to enjoy the affection and loyalty of so many in England. Now, the death of Catherine finally resolved many of the potential issues that previously confronted the king and his new queen. They made little effort to try to hide their relief. There was no mourning at court. Henry and Anne appeared at festivities the next night wearing joyful yellow costumes: 'On the following day, which was Sunday, the King dressed entirely in yellow from head to foot, with the single exception of a white feather in his cap.'[5]

Henry and Anne's undisguised joy at Catherine's death did not last long, however. According to Chapuys's informants, Anne's happiness was immediately mixed with fear when she began to appreciate that she was now reliving Catherine's life. She wept when she realised that she was at risk of experiencing the great unhappiness Catherine had suffered when she had been displaced by Anne:

> ... the King's concubine [Anne], though she showed great joy at the news of the good Queen's death, and gave a good present to the messenger who brought her the intelligence, had, nevertheless, cried and lamented ... herself on the occasion, fearing lest she herself might be brought to the same end as her.[6]

Perhaps the worst aspect of this new situation for Anne was that she must have already heard the rumours circulating about Henry's new infatuation with Jane Seymour, a young lady of the court who was now in precisely the position Anne had been a decade earlier. Jane had caught the king's eye, and he was already paying special attention to her:

> [The general opinion was that Anne was feeling] ... the fear of the King treating her as he treated his late Queen – which is not unlikely, considering his behaviour towards a damsel of the Court, named Miss Seymour, to whom he has latterly [lately] made very valuable presents...[7]

Three weeks after Catherine's death, on the day of her funeral, 29 January 1536, Anne suffered another miscarriage. This was a double tragedy, since the foetus was three and a half months old and male. Thus, Anne not only lost their son, but she thereby lost her last opportunity to keep her marriage, her crown, and, as it soon turned out, her head:

> On that very day [29 January 1536] the good queen [Catherine] of England's burial took place...
>
> On the same day that the Queen was buried this King's concubine [Anne] miscarried of a child, who had the appearance of a [male] about three months and a half old, at which miscarriage the King has certainly shown great disappointment and sorrow. The concubine herself has since attempted to throw all the blame on the duke of Norfolk, whom she hates, pretending that her mishap was entirely owing to the shock she received when, six days before, he [the Duke] came to announce

to her the King's fall from his horse. But the King knows very well that it was not that, for his accident was announced to her in a manner not to create alarm; besides which, when she heard of it, she seemed quite indifferent to it.[8]

All of this explains why, in 1536, after only three years of marriage to Anne, Henry resolved upon a straightforward remedy for both of the problems she presented to him – her feisty lack of deference and submission, and her inability to provide him with a clear successor to the throne. Henry's solution was to end their marriage so that he could wed Jane Seymour. At this point, Henry was ready to exchange Anne's intelligence and strength for Jane's quiet compliance and obedience. And while these matters were obviously not predictable, Henry hoped that Jane might prove herself more able to produce a male child. This was a bizarre repeat of Henry's Great Matter. When that began, he had been married to Catherine but desired Anne; now he was married to Anne but desired Jane.

This time, however, Henry had the benefit of his recent experience in terminating a marriage. He no longer had to endure the arduous and ineffective exercise of petitioning the pope in Rome for an annulment, having already solved that problem in order to marry Anne. Now it was Henry, and not the pope, who was the supreme leader of the English Church. And by now, with the help of his new principal minister, Thomas Cromwell, Henry had further consolidated his power over Parliament and the clergy.

At his master's bidding, Cromwell swiftly employed his legal skills to develop the charges and testimony that would permit Queen Anne to be tried and convicted by a jury of her peers. The charges are now generally regarded as specious. The chief accusation was adultery with five men, including her brother, George. Anne and the five men were found guilty. The men were executed on 17 May 1536, and on that same day, Anne's marriage was hastily annulled by Thomas Cranmer, Archbishop of Canterbury. Two days later, Anne was beheaded at the Tower of London.[9] The following day, Henry and Jane Seymour were betrothed. They married in a private ceremony ten days later.[10]

As we might expect, the public trials of such scandalous and salacious charges ignited a second wave of speculation about Elizabeth's birth, at least among those politically opposed to Henry. Once Anne was convicted and executed on multiple charges of adultery and treason, it was not difficult for political enemies of Henry – and, later, enemies of Elizabeth – to whisper that Elizabeth might not be Henry's biological child.

How easy for the public to imagine that Anne, understanding how crucial it was to Henry to produce an heir, had actually instigated those adulterous affairs of which she was accused. Perhaps they were not love matches, but simply pragmatic means of becoming pregnant at a time when Henry may have been unable to father a child. Thus, as young Elizabeth grew older, she regularly suffered accusations of illegitimacy from those who did not want to see her become her father's successor to the throne.

In one of those many strange parallels that seem to populate the Tudor universe, Elizabeth's older half-sister, Princess Mary, was already in a comparable situation. Mary had become retroactively illegitimate when Henry had Archbishop Cranmer annul his marriage to her mother, Catherine of Aragon.

Henry VIII eventually recognised the problem he had caused when he had forced Parliament to determine that both his daughters were illegitimate. Deciding that he must do all that he could to protect the Tudor succession, he ultimately made Parliament undo the series of statutes he had obtained that would have excluded his daughters from possible succession. Instead, Parliament delegated the determination of succession to Henry. The king then specified under his will that, if no legitimate male heir of his was available to succeed to the throne, the next successors would be his daughter Mary and her issue, and after them Elizabeth and her issue.[11]

The Great Ironies within the King's Great Matter

Henry VIII's Great Matter drove him to take several momentous steps in the history of his kingdom. He discarded Catherine of Aragon, his wife of two decades. He consolidated the power of the monarchy. He disputed mightily with Pope Clement VII and Emperor Charles V for six years. He was able to end the struggle of those six years only by making the English Church independent of the Roman Catholic Church, eventually leading to the full English Reformation.

All these achievements in the Great Matter resulted from two principal motivations: Henry's infatuation with Anne Boleyn and his concern that the Tudor succession would be imperilled if he did not leave a legitimate male heir. However, these two motivations produced the two greatest ironies marking his Great Matter. Henry's love for Anne Boleyn turned into anguish and execution only a few years after they finally married, while Henry's great concerns about leaving only female successors to his throne turned out to be entirely misplaced.

When Henry died in 1547, he left an unquestionably legitimate male heir who succeeded to the throne as King Edward VI. Edward was the nine-year-old son of Henry and his third wife, Jane Seymour, who died two weeks after Edward's birth. When Henry and Jane had married, both of Henry's previous wives, Catherine of Aragon and Anne Boleyn, had already died, removing any serious question about Edward's entitlement to the throne under England's traditional rules for legitimate succession.

It was not until King Edward's death, six years after the passing of his father, that Henry's concerns about the acceptability of English royal succession by a female heir would be tested. He would not have been displeased. The English people first welcomed Henry's daughter Mary, and upon her death they cheered his younger daughter Elizabeth, as Tudor monarchs of the realm.

Conclusion

WHO WAS HENRY VIII?

This book has been an attempt to unravel the tangled threads of history and examine the unique six years of Henry VIII's quest to end his first marriage, including his remarkable attempt to rely upon Jewish authorities to support his demand for a Catholic annulment. This has not only been a search for events and facts. It has been a search for the motivations, intentions, and often hidden connections behind the facts.

The Character of the King
Now there remains, as for every work of history, a final question. What was the essence of our protagonist? What was Henry VIII's true character, at least as displayed in the limited period under examination? This is a question that each of us might answer differently, depending upon our perceptions of the Great Matter. As a backdrop for final judgment, we should note the following four summary assessments voiced by significant twentieth-century historians.

The first evaluation is from H. A. L. Fisher's *Political History of England*, covering the reigns of the first two Tudor kings, Henry VII and Henry VIII. This important work, published at the outset of the twentieth century, helped to usher in the modern period of Tudor historiography. Because it is a political history and includes the entire reign of Henry VIII, Fisher's evaluation is seen through a unique lens. The Great Matter is briefly covered, but more as a prelude to what Henry went on to accomplish in remaking the government, courts, religion, and national character of England. The ugly defects of the king's character are acknowledged, but seem to be discounted in Fisher's fulsome praise for Henry's political mastery:

> Henry at least understood his own age. Gross, cruel, crafty, hypocritical, avaricious, he was nevertheless a great ruler of men. His grasp of affairs was firm and comprehensive; his devotion to public duty was, at least after Wolsey's fall, constant and sustained by a high and kingly sense of his own virtues and responsibilities. ...Despite violent oscillations of mood he saw the large objects of policy with a certain steadfast intensity, the preservation of the dynasty, the unity of the state, the subjection of Scotland.[1]

Published a half-century later, G. R. Elton's *England under the Tudors* is another classic modern history of Tudor England. Elton accepts the king's claims of being motivated by scruples of conscience, tracing the many important achievements of the King's Great Matter to Henry's unshakeable belief in the urgings of his conscience:

> ... Henry did not argue the matter out: he was convinced in his conscience that his marriage to Catherine had been a great sin. Henry's conscience is, indeed, the clue to the whole affair. Extreme and uncompromising egoist that he was, he possessed to perfection that most dangerous weapon – a complete conviction of his own rightness. ...Therein lay his strength: it was this unshakable conviction into which all the arguments of policy and passion had been transformed by the forces of his self-centred nature that carried him through the setbacks of six tiresome years, through the break with Rome and the creation of a new polity, through the vast and profound revolution which grew out of Catherine's childlessness and Anne's winning ways.[2]

In another mid-twentieth-century biographical history of the period, *Catherine of Aragon*, historian Garret Mattingly tries to capture the paradoxical complexity of Henry's character – a character that was not understood even by Henry's most prolific contemporaneous chronicler, Imperial ambassador Eustace Chapuys:

After a while, Chapuys could predict, within limits, what Henry would do or say next, but the inwardness of that majestic childishness, that absurd mixture of naïveté and cunning, boldness and poltroonery, vindictive cruelty and wayward almost irresistible charm always eluded him.[3]

The most recent literary analysis of Henry VIII's character and psychological makeup is found in John Guy and Julia Fox's 2023 work, *Hunting the Falcon*:

Over-indulged by a doting mother and over-protected by an autocratic father, Henry grew into a narcissist who saw exercising control as his birthright, a man who never accepted blame for his own actions and always looked for scapegoats. A stickler for obedience and a stranger to remorse or guilt, he confronted any challenge to his authority with a wall of anger, his fear and insecurity so effectively buried that he did not even acknowledge they existed.[4]

Of these four views, Mattingly's approach best recognizes a dynamic, complex, and conflicted character. This comes closest to satisfying me. However, all four of these modern summary evaluations of Henry's character suggest an explanation for today's widespread and seemingly endless fascination with the Tudors in general, and Henry VIII's Great Matter in particular. Despite our modern access to a broad range of primary historical sources – or perhaps precisely because of the plenitude and range of those materials – we feel enormously challenged by any attempt to agree upon the character and ethics of the principal participants in this matter.

Having lived with Henry VIII almost daily for this past decade, I was initially troubled when I saw my own judgments of his character vacillating as I observed more extremes of his behaviours, large and small, displayed in his role as the major actor in this drama. I now appreciate that those increasingly extreme and inconsistent behaviours should not simply be seen as presenting a difficulty in assessing Henry's character – they define his character.

I do not believe that I can answer whether Henry VIII was predominantly good or evil. That question suggests it could be meaningful to weigh morality. That might perhaps work for most of us – ordinary individuals whose missteps are minor and whose virtues are limited.[5] However, a different moral accounting should apply to persons like King Henry VIII. Simply put, I believe that his complex life contains more than the maximum permissible measure of intentional evil. In my moral calculus, such a cruel and murderous life cannot be redeemed, no matter how many instances of positive political service to England can be pointed out by Henry's supporters.

Who Was the True Hero of Henry VIII's Great Matter?

Based upon everything that we have learned about the critical six years of mid-1527 through mid-1533, it is difficult to determine who, if anyone, should be considered to be the hero of Henry's Great Matter. There are too many fundamental, unanswerable questions about each of the main actors in this story. The resulting differences among widely divergent public opinions about almost all of the characters involved seem irreconcilable.

We have just discussed some differences in possible views about Henry. Was King Henry a greedy monster consumed by his passions, or was he a master of statecraft? Was his character strong or weak? Was he motivated by lust, greed, and egoism, or were his goals primarily public welfare and the protection of the state religion? I have shared my opinion that Henry VIII was indeed all of those things at various moments in his life, but that the extremity of his lifetime of bad acts cannot be outweighed by any number of actions by his better self.

Comparable inconsistencies are presented by other principal actors in this drama. Was Anne Boleyn a manipulative, evil enchantress, or was she a victim of misunderstanding and gross injustice? Was Pope Clement a weak and indecisive prevaricator, or was he a wily opponent who managed, even when stripped of temporal power, to do everything possible to protect the Catholic Church against England's schemes? Was Cardinal Wolsey a consummate and loyal political advisor who was unjustly dismissed, or was he a power-hungry, self-seeking opportunist?

I believe that the answer to all of these questions is that at various times each of these major participants exhibited several disparate sides of their characters. I cannot regard any of these central figures as a heroic character.

As in most major events, the King's Great Matter also had its share of minor participants and observers. In their limited roles, but in the face of extreme personal risk, some of these individuals did speak and act with bravery in the service of high moral standards – the very definition of heroic character. Any negative judgments about this historical episode should not ignore principled, compassionate actors and truth-tellers such as William Warham, John Fisher, Thomas More, Thomas Able, Rabbi Jacob Mantino, and Rabbi Jacob Raphael.

However, as for the major actors in this remarkable drama, I have come to believe that only Catherine of Aragon presents a relatively consistent heroic character. She somehow managed to respond to an almost unthinkable amount of adversity by continuing to be loyal to her Church, loyal to her conscience, loyal to England, and loyal to her marriage. Her decisions were driven by deeply held principles. Some of her actions, or her decisions not to act, may have been strategically disadvantageous to her. She would not be considered the winner of this conflict in any conventional sense. Nevertheless, Catherine remained unwavering in her dedication to the highest principles as she saw them, and she was willing to bear the often grave personal consequences of her actions with unfailing dignity, courage, and resolve.

Henry VIII created the King's Great Matter. But there would have been no Great Matter without Catherine of Aragon's steadfast character and bravery. For that, we Tudor enthusiasts certainly owe her our admiration and gratitude.

Appendix A

Summaries of Henry VIII's Love Letters to Anne Boleyn

The following are summaries of each of Henry VIII's seventeen love letters written to Anne Boleyn in 1527–28.[1]

Letter I, before July 1527
Henry begins the series of letters by declaring his devotion, using the language of classical chivalry to describe courtly love – Anne is his idealised Mistress and friend, and Henry is her loyal Servant and friend. The Mistress/Servant theme is repeated in Letters II, IV, V, X, XI, and XII.

The term 'mistress' is not used here in the modern sense of the female partner in a continuing physical sexual relationship between a man and a woman who are not married to each other. Despite what Henry may have been expecting or trying to make happen, using the language of idealised courtly love did not by itself imply that there was, or would necessarily ever come to be, physical love. However, when this language is used by a king, and directed to the younger sister of his previous long-time sexual mistress, the words carry a different set of implications.

Letter II, before July 1527
Henry expresses his pain and disappointment that Anne is apparently refusing to return to court. He seems to turn from first expressing his despair to next threatening Anne that if she doesn't want to be with him, he will have to accept the situation and gradually recover from his affections for her.

Letter IV, before July 1527

Henry seems tormented by uncertainty as to whether his love is reciprocated. His torment is intensified by ambiguities in Anne's prior letter, and his dismay has been fuelled by Anne's refusal to commit herself. He complains of his suffering from not knowing her intentions, and notes that he has been 'stricken with the dart of love' for over a year. He promises Anne exclusivity and fidelity, but with a not-so-subtle mention that there are others 'that are in competition with you'. He pointedly offers to continue his relationship on the express condition that Anne act as 'a true, loyal mistress and friend' and 'give up your body and heart to me'. After a year, Henry has finally begun working to move the relationship beyond idealised courtly love to a frankly physical love.

Letter X, before July 1527

Henry complains that Anne has not fulfilled her promise to answer his previous correspondence, perhaps Letter IV, which sought a declaration of intent. But although he seems disappointed, he continues using the terms of courtly love, 'Mistress' and 'Servant'. He sends her a buck from the hunt to serve as a remembrance of him, and closes romantically, referring to himself as 'your servant, who often wishes you were in your brother's place'. Anne's brother, George Boleyn, was one of the king's personal attendants at the palace.

Letter VIII, before July 1527

This brief letter indicates that Anne has returned to London from the Boleyn family castle at Hever but has declined to stay in the residence that Henry had arranged for her. She apparently preferred one that she had chosen. Henry's tone seems a little cool and formal, and may show some disappointment or even irritation at her display of independence. If that is what Henry was indicating, Anne's downfall less than a decade later suggests that she failed to perceive and take to heart this revelation of another aspect of Henry's nature. The letter ends with a coded phrase that seems not yet to have been fully deciphered with universal acceptance: 'B.N.R.I. de R.O.M.V.E.Z.'

Letter V, early January 1528

In this romantic letter, Henry acknowledges Anne's New Year gift of a diamond with a maiden on a ship, with her accompanying letter, which has never been found, but which together apparently signified her promise of ultimate submission to his wooing. His letter suggests, however, that Anne has not yet submitted to full sexual relations, a matter which remains paramount in his concerns. He assures her that 'henceforth my heart will be dedicated to you alone, and wishing greatly that my body was so too', and that he prays to God daily for that resolution. As in the later Letter XI, Henry's signature surrounds his assertion that he seeks Anne exclusively: 'H seeks A.B. no other **Rex**.'

Letter XIV, 11 February 1528

The new year has brought a definite change in the relationship. This is a short, hurried, almost businesslike letter introducing Anne to Stephen Gardiner and Edward Fox, Henry's envoys who are stopping briefly on their way to the Continent to advance the Great Matter. Anne is still Henry's 'darling' and 'mine own sweetheart', but Henry seems sure enough of her commitment to him that he begins to treat her as his partner in his pursuit of the divorce. He closes with a new confident note of mutuality in their relationship: 'Written with the hand of him which desireth as much to be yours as you do to have him.'

Letter IX, 15 June 1528

In this romantic letter, Anne is Henry's 'good sweetheart', his 'darling', and 'my own darling'. He is very unhappy with her absence, and anxious to hear that she remains in good health. He has moved away from London because the seasonal return to England of the sweating sickness, a major concern also noted in Letters III, XII, and XIII. And as he also does in Letters X and VI, Henry tells Anne about his deer hunting. By this time, their relationship has progressed from the courtly to the bawdy, and Henry makes an extremely lewd joke about the deer's flesh that he is sending to her. The nineteenth-century historian James O. Halliwell considered the joke so vulgar and indecent that he refused to include it in his 1848 edition of the love letters.[2]

Summaries of Henry VIII's Love Letters to Anne Boleyn

Letter III, 20 June 1528

Henry is relieved to have heard that Anne continues in good health. The sweating sickness, also a topic of his concern in Letters IX, XII, and XIII, caught up with his household at Waltham, and several of his attendants were ill but have recovered. He encourages her to remain optimistic, as few women have caught the illness in the current epidemic, and overall there have been few deaths. He wishes she were in his arms. This is one of several letters (see also Letters V, X, XI, and XII) where Henry embellishes his signature with a declaration of his feelings. Here he declares the permanence of his love by embedding his signature in the word 'Unchangeable': 'Un **H Rex** changeable.'

Letter XII, 23 June 1528

Henry shows deep concern for Anne when she becomes ill with the sweating sickness, although he also reveals his self-concern by continuing to keep his distance. He sends her one of his royal physicians to help her recover. Again, Anne is his 'mistress' and he is her 'loyal and most assured servant'. Here, her initials are inserted in the middle of his initials in the signature: '**H. A.B. R.**'

Letter XIII, 7 July 1528

This is the last of Henry's letters referring to the sweating sickness plague, which appears to be easing. He mentions several more of his household members who had been stricken but have recovered. The bulk of the letter is Henry's attempt to explain how it happened that Anne's efforts to obtain a valuable clerical appointment for her sister Mary's sister-in-law were frustrated by Cardinal Wolsey. This episode was to become the basis for not only some additional ill will between Anne and Wolsey, but also a rare rebuke of the cardinal from Henry, resulting in Wolsey's abject apology. The letter includes Henry's use of romantic language, addressing Anne as 'mine own darling', and closing in French with 'Of yours alone'. Henry expresses his disappointment but he understands that Anne still feels safer from the plague by staying longer at Hever rather than immediately joining him.

Letter XI, 21 July 1528
Henry writes as a very impatient and frustrated lover, declaring, 'I am so looking forward to the approach of the time for which I have waited so long...' But he is also confident that his love is reciprocated and that they will soon experience 'entire fulfilment'. Henry even asks Anne to have her father, Thomas Boleyn, bring her back to court two days earlier than planned.[3] As in Letter XI, Henry's signature surrounds his assertion that he seeks only Anne: 'H seeks A.B. no other **Rex**.'

Letter XV, 21 July 1528
Although this brief letter is framed with romantic phrases, it simply explains why Henry is sending George Boleyn to privately tell his sister the substance of his message. He complains that their supposedly secret communications seem instantly known to everyone in London.

Letter XVI, July 1528
This is the most famous, and perhaps the most scandalous, of Henry's love letters. Anne has very recently left the palace, and already Henry complains that he is suffering great loneliness (*elengeness*). He is somewhat comforted because he is now coming, or is about to come, to her. He is also comforted by his labours in writing his book, *A Glasse of the Truthe*, in which he declares his arguments for his annulment. He wrote the book in English, rather than Latin, so that it could convince not only Pope Clement but also Henry's ordinary subjects.

Then Henry makes a daringly explicit reference to anticipating an evening embracing Anne and kissing her pretty breasts: '... wishing myself (especially an evening) in my sweetheart's arms, whose pretty dukkys [breasts] I trust shortly to cusse [kiss]'. This indicates that by mid-1528 they were spending time together in bed, with Anne at least semi-naked, and they were engaging in intimate sexual contact, although not necessarily full sexual intercourse.[4]

Letter VII, 20 August 1528
Henry states that, through Wolsey's efforts, he has arranged lodgings in London for Anne. Placing Anne in a separate residence at this time may have been a show of propriety as the papal legate, Cardinal Campeggio, was due to visit for the divorce trial. Henry also assures Anne that all that can be done is being done regarding their 'other affairs' (pursuing the divorce).

Summaries of Henry VIII's Love Letters to Anne Boleyn

Letter VI, 16 September 1528
Henry announces the imminent arrival of Cardinal Campeggio to preside with Wolsey at the Blackfriars trial, which is to decide the legitimacy of Henry's marriage to Catherine of Aragon. Henry anticipates a prompt and favourable result, using language suggesting that he has not yet been granted full sexual intercourse with Anne: 'I trust, within a while after, to enjoy that which I have so longed for, to God's pleasure and our both comforts.'

Letter XVII, 8 October 1528
As an update to his prior Letter VI, Henry advises Anne that Campeggio has finally arrived in London. The king explains that Campeggio will be a little delayed in moving the Great Matter to its conclusion because of his 'unfeigned sickness' (he suffered greatly from gout). But Henry expresses great confidence that the Blackfriars trial will soon result in the annulment, and he denies rumours that Campeggio is 'imperial' (biased in Catherine's favour because of the influence of her nephew, Holy Roman Emperor Charles V).

Appendix B

Canon Law Governing Annulments: Consummation and Public Honesty

Why Did It Take So Long to Resolve the Great Matter?
Many of us today are quite familiar with some features of Henry VIII and his reign. However, the popular plays, films, television dramas, and historical novels swirling around this memorable figure of history tend to produce in us the impression that he was a powerful but immoral autocratic ruler who could and would do whatever he thought was necessary to get what he desired. With this impression, and of course knowing something of the outcome regarding his marriage to Catherine of Aragon, modern readers may wonder why King Henry allowed his annulment negotiations with the pope to drag on for six years. Henry began his smitten courtship of Anne Boleyn in 1527. However, it wasn't until 1533 that Henry finally exercised his royal and political powers in England to take drastic independent action to invalidate his marriage to Catherine. The explanation for this surprisingly long delay requires understanding the respective roles and positions of the Catholic Church and the great Catholic nations of Europe regarding the governance of marital issues in the early sixteenth century.

Jurisdiction of the Catholic Church over Marriage
In 1527, when Henry began his campaign to have his marriage to Catherine dissolved, the Catholic Church occupied a position of enormous power in Europe. Although Pope Clement VII had no army of his own, the pontiff was constantly negotiating and renegotiating military and political alliances with the great national powers of that

Canon Law Governing Annulments: Consummation and Public Honesty

time: the Holy Roman Empire, France, England, Spain, and various city-states of the Italian peninsula.

England in 1527 continued as a Roman Catholic nation, with a highly developed and wealthy hierarchy of Catholic Church administrators and institutions. In England, as in much of the western world, the Roman Catholic Church retained its traditional powers of authority over particular matters of ecclesiastical law – legal matters relating to the Christian Church or its clergy.[1]

At the outset of Henry VIII's reign, matrimonial matters, together with other formal matters such as baptism or the ordination and elevation of clergy, remained outside the aegis of England's Crown and Parliament. Marriage was regarded to be not a matter of civil law, but a sacrament that remained under the supreme jurisdiction of the pope. As a result, in England prior to the resolution of Henry's Great Matter, legal issues regarding marriage, and termination or dissolution thereof, were governed solely by *canon law* – the ecclesiastical laws promulgated, interpreted, and administered by the pope and his councils and delegates. There was no alternative or supplemental English civil court jurisdiction in such cases, and neither Parliament nor the king held any reserved powers to act in these matters. Thus, despite King Henry's sovereign powers, when it came to the legality of any marriage or dissolution of marriage in Catholic England, it was the Church that had the sole and final power to adjudicate and determine such issues.

Ordinarily, marital law termination cases – to the extent that the parties were wealthy enough to undertake the process – were decided by the bishop of the local diocese, who considered the arguments submitted by canon law experts. But there could be appeals, or in special cases a direct submission for final decision, made to the pope and the *Rota*, the papal court of expert cardinals in Rome who advised the pope on marital law cases. In addition, in some situations, the pope could delegate the power to hear and determine some marital law cases to one or more legates who could conduct the hearing where the parties lived.

Canon Law Governing Marriage and Dissolution of Marriage

The canon law applying to marriage and termination of marriage was extremely complex. This book sometimes refers to Henry VIII's 'divorce', the term that was commonly used to describe Henry's goal.

However, in the early sixteenth century, as now, for most existing valid marriages, the Roman Catholic Church did not typically grant a 'divorce' in its technical sense of terminating a marriage based upon circumstances that arose or were revealed after that marriage began. The Church recognised only a few unusual circumstances occurring after the wedding that would justify a divorce, including insanity, the husband's impotence, either party taking religious orders with a vow of chastity, and a few other situations.[2]

Nevertheless, the Catholic Church had long understood that it needed to find some other way to accommodate the human condition. The Church therefore recognised the similar but distinct legal concept of a decree of nullity, or *annulment*. An annulment is a determination that there had been no effective marriage in the first place. Such a decree finds that there was a flaw in the original marriage that was so significant that the purported marriage was void, as if it had never taken place. Since the consequence of an annulment decree was that there had never been a marriage, both parties became free to enter into new marriages.

Because of the expense and complexity of the procedure to obtain a decree of annulment, this option was, as a practical matter, utilised only by royalty, nobility and the wealthy. That certainly presented no hindrance to Henry. He could rationally expect that, as the monarch of one of the world's most important Catholic kingdoms, he could, with some inconvenience and perhaps a little delay, use the annulment procedure to dissolve his marriage to Catherine of Aragon and marry Anne Boleyn.

It wasn't too difficult for Henry and his advisors to find – somewhere deep in the tangled, technical rules of the Roman Catholic canon law governing marriage – recognition of several factual situations that they could claim supported the king's petition for annulment. Henry and his representatives attempted to rely upon several of these claims at various times during the dispute.

Henry's Claims of Fraud and Technical Objections to Pope Julius's Bull of Dispensation

Pope Clement was reluctant to annul Henry and Catherine's marriage. Their fathers had obtained a Bull of dispensation from Pope Julius II, bearing the date 26 December 1503, granting permission for Henry and Catherine to marry despite the fact that Catherine had

Canon Law Governing Annulments: Consummation and Public Honesty

previously been married to Henry's older brother, Prince Arthur.[3] In the absence of Pope Julius's dispensation, Catherine's prior marriage to Arthur would ordinarily cause canon law to prohibit Henry from marrying his brother's widow in 1509, and Henry would be entitled to the decree of annulment which he was seeking in 1527. It was therefore obvious that Henry must somehow overcome Pope Julius's Bull of dispensation if he were to qualify for an annulment.

Henry's clerics and canon law specialists made one of their first attacks against the Bull of dispensation by focusing upon over a dozen technical issues and factual recitals in the pope's Bull that they asserted invalidated the dispensation and justified an annulment. The most prominent of these technical objections included the following.[4]

- Prince Henry was a minor and could not legally have sought, authorised, or been a party to the request for dispensation, or to any engagement or marriage pursuant to the dispensation. And because the Bull was silent as to Prince Henry's age, it was also invalid because it should be presumed fraudulently procured through the parties' failure to provide that fact.
- Even if the Bull had been potentially valid, Prince Henry subsequently made a formal protestation upon attaining puberty, whereby he renounced the dispensation and denied any intention to marry Catherine.[5]
- The Bull recited that the proposed marriage between Prince Henry and Princess Catherine was primarily required to preserve peace between Spain and England. However, contrary to what the parties had apparently told Pope Julius, no state of war or conflict existed or was threatened at that time between the two nations. and the dispensed marriage was not necessary to avoid hostilities between the Catholic nations of England and Spain.
- King Henry VII of England and Queen Isabella of Spain, two of the parties to whom the Bull of dispensation had been directed, died before the marriage of Henry VIII and Catherine. Their deaths should be deemed to have terminated the dispensation.

Henry hoped that, by proving any of these technical or fraud allegations regarding the Bull, he would be free to pursue his direct argument that the Book of Leviticus prohibited his marriage to

Catherine. However, a major surprise awaited Henry, and apparently everyone else involved in the King's Great Matter. At the end of the Blackfriars trial, Henry's factual and technical legal arguments were instantly undercut by recitals made in a newly discovered document, which purported to be a Brief – a private summary by Pope Julius of his Bull of dispensation. The Brief (*Breve*), often referred to as the 'Spanish Brief', had been discovered in Spain among a private collection of diplomatic papers. The original came into the possession of Charles V, who sent a copy to his aunt Catherine of Aragon in 1529, during the final year of the legatee trial of the annulment matter at Blackfriars. Catherine and her advisors upended that trial, which was suspended without reaching a verdict, when she finally provided copies to King Henry, Cardinals Wolsey and Campeggio, and Pope Clement VII.[6]

Pope Julius's Spanish Brief of Dispensation, and Henry's Claim It Was a Forgery

The Spanish Brief corrected many of the major technical legal issues that had been raised by Henry during the early years of the Great Matter. Indeed, Henry and his representatives immediately concluded that the Spanish Brief was so convenient for Catherine's interests that it must be a recent forgery rather than an authentic dispensation written by Pope Julius a quarter of a century earlier.

However, Henry's advisors soon learned that it would not be easy to convince others that the Spanish Brief was a forgery. Emperor Charles asserted that he feared the English would destroy or alter the original Brief if they could obtain it. Therefore, only a few of Henry's envoys received even so much as highly limited access to quickly view the physical condition of the original Brief.[7] The English attack on its authenticity had to be based upon their notes and recollections of that hasty viewing and the wording of the notarised copies that were provided to London and Rome.[8]

Henry finally had to abandon his various technical legal arguments attacking the Bull and the Brief because they were not strong and clear enough to convince either the pope or his own subjects. Henry could not afford to win a formal annulment in a manner that would create public doubt regarding the legitimacy of the male children he hoped to father with Anne Boleyn. He had to ensure the future peaceful succession of Tudor children to the throne. Therefore, Henry pivoted to restricting his final arguments to two substantive elements of his petition for annulment: first, that Arthur's marriage to Catherine had been consummated, so that, in the absence of an effective dispensation by Pope Julius, Henry would be entitled to an annulment on the grounds of affinity in-law incest; second, that even if Henry failed to establish that Arthur consummated his marriage to Catherine, the dispensation by Pope Julius would not excuse the impediment of public honesty, and Henry would be entitled to annulment on that ground.

Arthur's Failure to Consummate His Marriage

Henry had to respond to Catherine's opposition to the annulment that she based upon one of the canon law's most important substantive grounds for denying the validity of any marriage – the absence of consummation, including a husband's impotence. Obviously, Catherine was not referring to her marriage to Henry, which had produced at least seven pregnancies including three live births. What Catherine strongly and consistently maintained was that her prior five-month marriage to Henry's older brother, Arthur, had never been consummated, and that she had been a virgin when she subsequently married Henry. Catherine's assertion of Arthur's failure to consummate, if she could prove it, could completely undermine Henry's ultimate central argument in the Great Matter, namely that he was entitled to an annulment because Leviticus absolutely banned marrying a brother's widow. The key to Catherine's argument could be found in the wording of Leviticus:

> 18:16: Do not uncover the nakedness [*lo t'galei ervat*] of your brother's wife; it is the nakedness of your brother.

To *uncover the nakedness* is a biblical euphemism for sexual intercourse.[9] Leviticus prohibited marrying a brother's widow because once a man's sister-in-law had consummated her marriage with the man's brother, that brother and his wife had become one flesh for purposes of affinity incest, a status that continued even after that prior marriage had been terminated by divorce or the death of the first husband.[10] Thus, the failure to consummate – in this case, Arthur's alleged failure to consummate his marriage to Catherine – could mean that Catherine and Henry had indeed been free to marry each other after Arthur's death without any difficulties under Leviticus 18:16, and had no need of a papal dispensation to legitimate their marriage. This would be a major loss of Henry's primary basis for claiming an annulment.

Unfortunately for Catherine, her attempt to block Henry's petition for annulment by asserting that Arthur had not consummated his marriage to her faced an almost insuperable obstacle. Her brief marriage to Arthur had occurred a quarter of a century before Henry began his Great Matter. After such a long time since Arthur's death, and especially with regard to intimate details of the several times Catherine and Arthur spent the night secluded in bed together – she admitted to seven such occasions – Catherine lacked convincing factual evidence for her claim that Arthur had never consummated their marriage.

One fact that Catherine could claim to be at least consistent with failure to consummate would be that Arthur died from severe illness only five months after their wedding. Both Arthur and Catherine had become ill, perhaps from the English sweating sickness, after Henry VII sent the Prince of Wales and his bride to Ludlow that winter, in the cold, damp frontier region known as the Welsh Marches. However, evidence of Arthur's illness, especially if it had suddenly appeared at the end of their marriage, was clearly insufficient to prove an inability to have consummated that marriage.[11]

Another fact that Catherine could allege to have caused Arthur's failure to consummate could have been Arthur's youth. He was only fifteen years old during his marriage. Henry's later trial evidence on this issue included testimony from various noblemen that they had been able to physically consummate their own marriages at ages even younger than Arthur's. Again, even if Catherine's representatives could have countered with evidence that some bridegrooms at that age may lack the physical ability to consummate a marriage, such evidence would fall far short of proof that Arthur failed to consummate his marriage to Catherine.[12]

Catherine faced several other difficulties in trying to convince Pope Clement of Arthur's failure to consummate. Immediately after Arthur's death, Catherine's parents, Ferdinand and Isabella, were uncertain about whether the marriage had been consummated.[13] Eventually, they were convinced by Catherine's chief attendant, Doña Elvira Manuel, that their daughter was still a virgin.[14]

Nevertheless, Henry VIII could be optimistic in his argument that Catherine's first marriage to Arthur had been consummated. Many of the most important official documents regarding Henry's marriage to Catherine confirmed the fact, or at least the possibility.

The 23 June 1503 marriage treaty between England and Spain for the marriage of Prince Henry Tudor to the recently widowed Catherine of Aragon recited that Catherine and Arthur's marriage had been solemnised in Church 'and afterwards consummated'.[15]

In a letter dated 23 August 1503, referring to that clause in the marriage treaty, Ferdinand instructed his ambassador to the Vatican, Francisco de Rojas, that the truth was that Arthur had not consummated his marriage to Catherine. Despite this fact, Spain had to agree to have the language in the Bull state that Arthur had consummated his marriage. Ferdinand explained that the English were picky, and Henry VII's lawyers were concerned that, if all factual alternatives were not covered, the English people might some day raise problems of legitimacy and right to succession of the anticipated descendants of Princess Catherine and Prince Henry. '[T]he dispensation of the Pope must be in perfect keeping with the said clause of the treaty,' Ferdinand insisted, referring to the clause stating that Catherine's first marriage had been consummated.[16]

Pope Julius's Bull of dispensation, dated 26 December 1503, goes further than the earlier agreement between the Spanish and the English that the dispensation should conform to the marriage treaty and state that Catherine's marriage to Arthur had been consummated. Instead, the Bull recited that Catherine and Arthur 'did perhaps [*forsan*] consummate [their marriage] by carnal knowledge' [*illudque carnali copula forsan consummavissetis*]'.[17] The reason why the Bull included the extra qualifying word 'perhaps' is not clear. In 1503, Julius was a new pope, and he may have depended more on his assisting cardinals for highly technical wording in such matters.

Julius's Spanish Brief, also dated 26 December 1503 but discovered decades later, did not say 'perhaps consummated', but unequivocally recited that the marriage 'had been consummated'.[18]

The Imperial ambassador to London at that time, Eustace Chapuys, was a firm supporter of Catherine. He noted that, because decades had passed since the end of Arthur's marriage, it was unlikely that either Henry or Catherine could present conclusive evidence of the presence or absence of consummation. In such a situation, the ecclesiastical courts might resort to a legal presumption that Arthur had consummated his marriage.[19]

Public Honesty

Thus, in order for Henry to argue that the dispensation by Pope Julius was not effective to overcome the absolute Leviticus Prohibition of affinity incest where the prior marriage had been consummated, Henry would have to establish that Arthur had consummated his marriage to Catherine. However, even if it were determined that Arthur had failed to consummate, Henry could still argue that another substantial basis for annulment recognised in canon law was the doctrine requiring *public honesty* – the appearance of decency and morality in a marriage. This requirement somewhat softened the rules limiting annulments so that the outcome could take into account the public's reaction to the appearance of a situation. Based upon this rule, Henry could argue that, regardless of the technicalities, if the overall public reaction to his marriage to his brother's widow was that it seemed to violate the Leviticus commands, such an appearance of immorality could be sufficient for an annulment.

In this case, Pope Julius's 1503 Bull of dispensation harboured an obscure and highly technical legal issue. Ordinarily, a papal dispensation to marry despite the possible impediment of affinity incest under Lev. 18:16 would be effective, by implication, to also dispense the lesser and related impediment of public honesty regarding the community's perception of such a violation. If Catherine were successful in establishing that her marriage to Arthur had never been consummated, so that Lev. 18:16 did not apply, Henry could argue that such a determination would render the dispensation expressed in the Bull of 1530 ineffective. As a result, there would have been no implied dispensation of the impediment of public honesty.

On this basis, if there had been no consummation, Henry could assert that it would still seem to people that Henry's marriage to his brother's widow was immoral, and that Julius had not dispensed that impediment of public honesty. Indeed, we might conclude that the Church may have promulgated the impediment of public honesty for just such a situation as this – the likely inability of the public to understand the niceties of such a convoluted legal situation.

It has been argued by some commentators that Henry and his legal advisors were unaware of this highly technical but potentially winning argument based upon the impediment of public honesty. However, we know that Henry expressly threatened Catherine with his argument based upon public honesty when he finally decided to forego disputing the factual question of whether Arthur's marriage had been consummated.[20]

Moreover, that was not the first time that the English royal advisors, and presumably Henry VIII after his father died in 1509, had focused upon the issue of public honesty. The 23 June 1503 marriage treaty for Princess Catherine of Aragon and Prince Henry Tudor had stated that Henry VII and Ferdinand and Isabella, on behalf of their respective children, shall cause to be obtained a Bull of dispensation sealed by the pope's lead seal, permitting Henry and Catherine to marry 'notwithstanding the hindrance of Public Honesty and Justice' by the fact that Catherine had contracted to marry Prince Arthur.[21]

The impediment of public honesty is not expressed in the Bible, however, but was only an ecclesiastical prohibition adopted by the Church. Henry and his advisors may have been discouraged by this because Clement might feel more comfortable in retroactively dispensing a non-biblical impediment. Henry's 'public honesty' argument could be easily negated if the pope were willing to cure the defect.[22]

As with some of his other potential arguments, Henry felt that he had to abandon the public honesty issue because its complex technicalities rendered it incomprehensible to his English commoner subjects. Convincing his subjects that the hoped-for male heir or heirs of his marriage to Anne Boleyn were unquestionably legitimate was crucial for Henry's goal of assuring the peaceful succession of the Tudor dynasty.

Appendix C
Responsum of Rabbi Jacob Raphael

Responsum by Jacob Raphael Pegiano
Translated, with explanatory endnotes, by Gabriel Wasserman
[All biblical quotations from the 1917 JPS translation of the Hebrew Bible]

I have been consulted by a certain important priest, named Messer Francesco Curtiso, that I should tell my opinion about a question that he had: when the Torah commands in Leviticus [18:16]: *Thou shalt not uncover the nakedness of thy brother's wife*, does this commandment cover only situations where she has been divorced, or her husband has died and left living progeny, whereas, [on the other hand], if her husband dies without progeny, his brother would be obligated in levirate marriage, as is later commanded in Deuteronomy? Or, rather, does the commandment [in Leviticus] cover all cases, such that if the commandment of levirate marriage were not written later, in Deuteronomy, I would say that one's brother's wife is always forbidden, for why would there be a reason to distinguish? This is his question.

Although my waters are waters of a cave, and my ashes are burnt ash,[1] nonetheless, out of love for the questioner, I shall not remain silent, for I would like to do what he wants.

The Mishna states in the chapter 'The Sciatic Nerve' in the mishna beginning 'It is relevant in a kosher animal' [Tractate Ḥullin 7:6]: 'Rabbi Judah said: Was not the sciatic nerve forbidden to the children of Jacob, at a point when non-kosher species were still permitted to them? They [the other rabbis] replied to him: [The commandment] was repeated [to the Israelite Nation] at Sinai [by which point the distinction between kosher and non-kosher species already existed], but it was written only in its place [i.e., the Torah mentions the prohibition of the sciatic nerve only in Genesis].' And in a *baraitha*[2] it explains that [the verse about the sciatic nerve] was written in its place [in Genesis] so that we would know why it was forbidden to them.

And Rashi explains there:[3] 'They said to [Rabbi Judah]: this verse, in which [the Israelites] are instructed to avoid it, was said at Sinai. Until Sinai, they were not yet instructed to avoid it. But [the verse] was written in its place [in the story], after it was said at Sinai; when Moses wrote out the Torah, he wrote this verse in the story: therefore, the Israelites were later instructed not to eat the sciatic nerve.' Thus, he explains that even though it is written [in the story of] Jacob's children, [in fact the Israelites] were commanded about it in Sinai.

Maimonides, too, explains in his commentary on the Mishna: 'Set your mind on the great principle that is stated in this Mishna, namely that it says that [this commandment] was commanded at Sinai. For you are taught here that everything that we avoid or do today is only because God commanded so through the agency of our teacher Moses, peace be upon him – not that God said so to other prophets preceding him. For example, our avoidance of eating a limb from a living animal, [...] and so also the sciatic nerve: we do not follow the prohibition due to our father Jacob, but rather by force of the commandment [given to] our teacher Moses, peace be upon him ....' It is thus clarified for us that everything that is written in the Torah before [the story of] the giving of the Torah was all commanded to Moses in Sinai, but the commandments were written in their place [in the stories], in order to teach why they were commanded, or in order to teach something else.

From this we can derive, all the more so, that the commandments that are instructed in Deuteronomy were already stated to Moses at Sinai. Why were they written [only] in Deuteronomy? In order to teach us particular secrets of the Torah; although most of them have not been revealed to us, some have indeed been revealed. Indeed, we find that we need to take particular care about examining the juxtaposition of commandments in Deuteronomy, for even Rabbi Judah, who did not give any heed to the juxtaposition of commandments elsewhere in the Torah, did pay attention to it in Deuteronomy, as stated in the first chapter of Yevamoth.[4]

Now, regarding the commandment of levirate marriage, we find that [the rabbis] expound upon the juxtaposition of commandments, as stated there [in the first chapter of Yevamoth], and it is cited also at the end of Tractate Makkoth:[5] 'Rabbi Shesheth said in the name of R. Eleazar ben Azariah: How do we know that if a woman liable for levirate marriage has fallen in the lot of a [brother-in-law] afflicted with skin-disease, we may not muzzle her [i.e., prevent her from voicing opposition to the marriage]? As it is written: *Thou shalt not muzzle the ox when he treadeth out the corn* [Deuteronomy 25:4], and juxtaposed to it is: *If brethren dwell together* [Deuteronomy 25:5, the opening words of the passage about levirate marriage].' Now, the rule of levirate marriage was definitely stated to Moses at Sinai, but it was written in Deuteronomy in order to teach us this teaching.

We find that many commandments are stated only in Deuteronomy, and not stated at all earlier; therefore, this is not an empty matter, and if it is empty, it is from us,[6] for our eyes are too shut to see.[7] This is clear, and we do not need to elaborate on it.

Now, [the priest] asked: If the commandment of levirate marriage had not been written in Deuteronomy, would we have derived that the prohibition against a brother's wife was meant only in some situations, or would we have held it as a universal rule? The proper response to this is what Rabbi Joshua ben Hananiah responded to the Alexandrians, who asked him: 'In the future, [when the dead are resurrected], will the dead need to be sprinkled [with the ashes of the Red Heifer in order to become purified from corpse-contamination]?' He responded to them: 'When they are resurrected, we'll investigate this matter for them.' Others say: 'When our teacher Moses comes with them.' This is in Nidda, in the chapter 'A young girl'.⁸

But [nonetheless], I will respond to my questioner, and say: yes, indeed [if the rule had not been written in Deuteronomy], we would have had an oral tradition teaching us that the prohibition on a brother's wife applies only in a situation where she is divorced, or where she is widowed but her husband already has children; but if he dies without children, she should perform levirate marriage. And even though according to the easiest reading [of the text in Leviticus], the prohibition on a brother's wife seems to be a universal prohibition, we do find parallel cases where the oral tradition contradicts the [reading of a commandment as being] universal. For example, Scripture says: *And the daughter of any priest, if she profane herself by playing the harlot, she profaneth her father: she shall be burnt with fire* [Leviticus 21:9], and it seems from Scripture that this would apply whether the woman be single or married, but the oral tradition teaches us that this applies only if she is married, as stated in the chapter 'Four Methods of Death Penalty'.⁹ And similarly, Scripture declares that a girl who is found not to be a virgin is to be stoned [Deuteronomy 22:21], but the oral tradition teaches us that this is only if she is already married, and that witnesses have testified about her that after the time of her betrothal¹⁰ she has committed fornication in front of witnesses, after having been warned; this is stated in the chapter 'A Girl Who Has Been Seduced'¹¹ and the chapter 'Four Methods of Death Penalty'.¹² And there are many such commandments, where we have explanations that have reached us in oral tradition from Moses, and we rely on them, even in matters that [are so severe that they] bear the penalty of capital punishment – and all the more so in this case, regarding the commandment of levirate marriage, we would rely on the oral tradition, for we could learn from Judah, who instructed his son: *Go in unto thy brother's wife, and perform the duty of a husband's brother unto her* [Genesis 38:8]. And [the Sages], of blessed memory, said in Genesis

Rabba:[13] 'Judah was the first to begin the commandment of levirate marriage.'

So it seems that the practice of levirate marriage was conventional before the Torah, as the great scholar, the Kabbalist, Naḥmanides, of blessed memory, wrote in his commentary on the Torah, on the verse *And Onan knew that the seed would not be his* [Genesis 38:9]:

He had clear knowledge about this, that the seed would not be his. For the matter is a secret, one of the Torah's secrets about human procreation, and it is apparent to the eyes of people that can see, to whom the Lord has given eyes to see and ears to hear. The ancient sages, before the Torah, knew that there was great effect in levirate marriage of a brother, and he [the brother] is the primary individual to perform it, and after him other relatives, for the effect can come from all relatives that are in the line to inherit. So they had the practice for the dead man's wife to marry his father, or his brother, or another relative. We do not know if this practice preceded Judah, but in Genesis Rabba they say that Judah was the first to begin the commandment of levirate marriage – for he received the secret from his ancestors, and he went ahead to fulfil it. Now, when the Torah came and forbade [marriage with] the wives of certain relatives, God wanted to relax the prohibition on the brother's wife in favor of levirate marriage; but he did not want to push aside the prohibitions of the uncle's wife, or the son's wife, or other relatives, for the usual manner [of levirate marriage] was with the brother, and the effect was closer through him and not through the others, as I have mentioned. [...] And the early sages of Israel understood this noble matter, so they instituted, on their own volition, to perform this deed also with other men in line for inheritance, as long as they were not included in the incest laws; they called this 'redemption', and this is the case of Boaz.[14]

Thus, we should take the lesson, and understand from this that the practice of levirate marriage was conventional already in ancient times, and this commandment was necessary, because of its great effects.

Responsum of Rabbi Jacob Raphael

May the Lord show us wondrous things from his Torah, and protect us and cover us with his wing, and give us peace as his covenant.

[Signed:] The young one, bowing the full height of his body, supplicating all that see his words to judge them favorably – Jacob Raphael Pegiano, January 30, [5]290,[15] here, Modena.

Appendix D

The King Who Married Six Wives

The six years of Henry VIII's Great Matter encompassed many important developments for England and the western world. The matter itself also triggered reverberations that would be felt by subsequent generations down to the present, including the evolution of the roles of the English monarchy and the Parliament, England's prominence in world affairs, and the launching of the English Reformation, with its consequences for England and the Catholic Church.

In the perception of the general public for the past five centuries, however, Henry has not been able to escape a rather unflattering primary association. It seems that he will forever be remembered as the king who married six wives. Generations of English schoolchildren have remembered the fates of Henry's six wives by learning the rhyme, 'Divorced, beheaded, died; Divorced, beheaded, survived'.

While some of these six marriages shared characteristics, they were far from identical. Henry's wives deserve to be regarded individually. Although only Henry's marriage to Catherine of Aragon and his extended courtship of Anne Boleyn occurred within the six years that are the focus of this book, we should not end our examination of the Great Matter without a reminder of how each of the king's six marriages began and ended.

Catherine of Aragon

Henry married his first wife, Catherine of Aragon, on 11 June 1509, and they remained formally married for almost twenty-four years. However, the last six years of their marriage were marked by Henry's increasingly close domestic relationship with Anne Boleyn, and the correspondingly increasing hardships and isolation of Catherine. Throughout her marriage, Catherine sacrificed her health, youth, comfort, and ultimately her access to her daughter, Princess Mary, in order to maintain her loyalty to her religion and to her marriage. After Henry was able to elevate his loyal supporter Thomas Cranmer to the position of Archbishop of Canterbury, not even Cranmer's formal decree of annulment and Henry's marriage to Anne Boleyn could break Catherine's resolute insistence that she remained Henry's loving wife and queen until her death, apparently from cancer, on 7 January 1536.

Anne Boleyn

Henry's second wife, Anne Boleyn, has been perhaps the most controversial of the six wives in the eyes of the public over the past five hundred years. Initially, opinions about her character and even her appearance varied in accordance with the religious affiliation of the commentators. To some extent, those same divisions between Catholic and Protestant views continue today. However, in recent decades, there has developed a resurgence of public interest in and support for Anne Boleyn. This new level of support for Anne may have been influenced in general by new public sensitivity to historical gender discrimination issues, and in particular by the availability of new books, films, and television series that portray Anne as being more intelligent, capable, and independent than the historians of earlier centuries acknowledged. Some now consider her the most interesting of the wives. Her marriage lasted only three years and four months from 25 January 1533 to 19 May 1536 – roughly one-half the duration of Henry's courtship of her during the six-year Great Matter. Henry's clever new chief minister, Thomas Cromwell, engineered Anne's hasty trial on what most historians conclude were the false grounds of multiple adulteries and treason. Found guilty, she was beheaded.

Jane Seymour

History has not recorded much about Jane Seymour, Henry's third wife and queen. She and Henry were betrothed on 20 May 1536, one day after Anne Boleyn's execution, and married ten days later, on 30 May 1536. Jane came from a noble house, and she was able to elevate her brothers and other family members to important positions, leading to her brothers' national leadership during the eventual regency of her son, Edward VI. Henry seems to have turned his attentions to her during his marriage to Anne Boleyn not only because she was pretty, but also because she had many of the traits that he felt Anne lacked. Although Jane was not as educated and witty as Anne, Henry was comforted that she would be demure, modest, and deferential toward him – attitudes opposite to Anne's newly assertive and quarrelsome domestic behavior.

Most of all, Jane was younger, and Henry hoped that she could provide him with a son to inherit the Tudor throne. In this, she alone among Henry's six wives did not fail him. Unfortunately, after only one year and five months of marriage, Jane died on 24 October 1537, from complications of giving birth to Prince Edward. Jane was buried in the chapel at Windsor Palace, where Henry VIII would eventually be buried near her.

Anne of Cleves

Henry's marriage to his first wife, Catherine of Aragon, was not his only marriage that ended in annulment. Seven years later, Henry's marriage to his fourth wife, Anne of Cleves, was also annulled. The differences between this and Henry's first annulment could not have been greater. Indeed, many observers conclude that Henry's marriage to Anne of Cleves was the most unusual of all of Henry's six marriages. The story is complicated and fascinating.

As we recall, Henry had known Catherine well before their wedding. As a ten-year-old prince, he had been Catherine's official escort for her wedding to his older brother, Arthur, in 1501. In the seven years following Arthur's death, Henry had further occasions to see and learn more about Catherine when she appeared at court.

Unlike the situation with Catherine of Aragon, whom Henry had known for seven years before their wedding, the king had known Anne of Cleves for only seven days before they were married. Henry had previously agreed to marry the German princess on the basis of flattering reports from his representatives, the urgings of his chief minister Thomas Cromwell, and an attractive portrait sent by Henry's favourite court painter, Hans Holbein.

Anne arrived at Rochester Abbey on New Year's Eve 1539/40. There, on New Year's Day, 1540, her first meeting with Henry turned into a disaster for both of them. Henry had impulsively decided to surprise his bride at their first meeting with an entertainment of the sort he had often led at court – acting out the chivalrous tropes of courtly love, featuring himself playing the disguised lover who would win the unsuspecting Anne as his true love. Henry and several of his courtiers duly disguised themselves in cloaks and hoods to surprise his bride.

Unfortunately, Anne knew nothing about this game, didn't recognise her betrothed, and tried to ignore him and his rude companions. On discovering the truth she was embarrassed, and Henry felt humiliated. He was, moreover, deeply disappointed with Anne's appearance. Two days later, at her formal arrival at Richmond, Henry confirmed his first impression that she was far different from the beautiful, fair woman of his agents' reports and Holbein's betrothal painting. Nevertheless, Thomas Cromwell had arranged the match so that he could obtain important alliances for England. Because of this, he was able to convince a reluctant Henry to proceed with the wedding a few days later, on 6 January 1540, so that England could avoid serious adverse international repercussions.

If that was a strange beginning for Henry's fourth marriage, the next development was even more bizarre. Henry found himself so repulsed by Anne's body – he complained about her extended belly and drooping breasts – that, although the newlyweds frequently slept together, he was not stimulated and could not physically consummate the marriage.

Fortunately for the peace of Henry and his kingdom, Anne of Cleves was agreeable to having the marriage annulled. On 1 July 1540, just short of six months after their wedding, the marriage ended by consensual annulment on the grounds of non-consummation plus another technical ground. Anne received a generous allowance and elected to live in England for the rest of her life. After the annulment, Henry treated Anne as a member of his extended family at royal affairs, calling her his beloved 'sister'.

During her brief marriage, Anne of Cleves had developed a good relationship with Henry's daughter Princess Mary. She urged Henry to reconcile with Mary, which he eventually did. This might explain why, when Anne of Cleves died on 16 July 1557, during the reign of Queen Mary I, the queen arranged to have her buried in Westminster Abbey, the only wife of Henry VIII interred there. Anne of Cleves survived not only Henry, but also his five other wives.

Catherine Howard

Henry's marital problems with Anne of Cleves had been well known among his advisors. Thomas Howard, Duke of Norfolk, saw the possibilities, and had his niece Catherine Howard placed as a lady-in-waiting to Anne of Cleves. And just as had happened with Anne Boleyn and Jane Seymour, this pretty young woman caught Henry's eye. The king started giving Catherine substantial gifts. On 28 July 1540, less than a month after the annulment of his marriage to Anne of Cleves, Henry married Catherine Howard.

Very soon, stories circulated concerning Catherine's sexual exploits with men, both before she joined the court and after she became queen. In a finale reminiscent of Anne Boleyn's trial, but this time with some factual substance behind the accusations, Catherine Howard was found guilty of treason for her secret sexual activities, and beheaded on 13 February 1542, less than a year and a half after her marriage began.

Katherine Parr

Henry's marriage to his sixth wife, Katherine Parr, followed a pattern quite different from most of his previous marriages. Katherine was not a young lady-in-waiting at the court when she met the king. After she had been widowed in two prior marriages, she had become part of Princess Mary's household, which is how Henry met her. At that time, she was romantically involved with Thomas Seymour, brother of Henry's third wife, Jane Seymour. Katherine nevertheless concluded that she must accept the king's proposal of marriage. They married on 12 July 1543, when Katherine was about thirty years of age, and Henry was fifty-one. She was on good terms with Henry's three children and became involved in their lives in a positive way, even helping to influence Henry to reinstate Mary and Elizabeth in the succession to the throne. After three years and six months of their marriage, Henry died on 28 January 1547. Six months later, Katherine Parr married Thomas Seymour. She died 5 September 1548, from complications of childbirth.

Appendix E

The Tudor Succession

Henry VII (r. 1485–1509)

The Tudor dynasty was founded by Henry Tudor, who ruled as King Henry VII. He was the son of Edmund Tudor and Margaret Beaufort. During the fifteenth and early sixteenth centuries, priority for inheriting the English crown was supposed to be determined by the primogeniture rules of direct male descent from the Plantagenet King Edward III (r. 1327–1377). Under this standard, Henry Tudor's claim to the throne was far from clear. His entitlement was under the cloud of two significant objections: his royal descent from Edward III was not through the Tudor line of his father, but only through the Beaufort line of his mother; and not only was that ancestral line maternal, but it also had its source through the illegitimate birth of John Beaufort, Earl of Somerset, to Katherine Swynford when she was the mistress of the son of Edward III, John of Gaunt, Duke of Lancaster. After John of Gaunt's wife died, he married his former mistress and arranged to have their four children formally legitimised by the Catholic Church.

In that era, it was not unusual for an illegitimate child of the nobility, royalty, or even high Church officials to be retroactively legitimised by declarations of the Church or national governments. However, such formal declarations did not always eradicate questions in the minds of the public or rivals regarding qualification for inheritance, succession to noble or royal title, or eligibility for high Church office.

As a result, Henry's accession to the throne was not accomplished so much through genealogical arguments as by force of arms. He returned from relative personal safety on the Continent to lead his

Lancastrian forces against King Richard III at the battle of Bosworth Field in 1485. When Richard's forces were defeated and he was killed in that battle, Henry Tudor seized the throne of England as King Henry VII. Later, his son Henry VIII tried to provide for a peaceable and secure Tudor dynastic succession in part by executing or imprisoning anyone who might claim a superior right to the crown through descent from Edward III.

Henry VIII (r. 1509–1547)

As detailed in the Afterword, Henry VIII was the second monarch of the Tudor dynasty (r. 22 April 1509–28 January 1547), but he was determined not to be the last. Throughout at least the latter half of his almost thirty-eight-year reign, he remained focused on securing the peaceful royal succession of his Tudor heirs to the monarchy. In his last will, Henry VIII named his three children by his first three wives – and their respective descendants if any – to be his successors to the Crown. The youngest, Prince Edward, had priority as a male, to be followed by Henry's older daughter, Princess Mary, and finally Princess Elizabeth.

Henry had caused Parliament to declare formal Acts legitimising his daughters despite the annulments of his marriages to their mothers; Parliament also delegated to Henry the ability to determine the royal succession by his last will. But however strong – or heavy – the hand of a monarch, it can seldom be extended to reliably assure succession. The actual Tudor succession contained some surprises for Henry VIII's carefully crafted plan.

Edward VI (r. 1547–1553)

Unlike his half-sisters, Edward enjoyed a clear claim to royal succession: His mother, Jane Seymour, died several days after his birth. Edward was clearly the legitimate son of Henry VIII because he was born after the deaths of both of his father's prior wives, and his parents' marriage had not been subsequently annulled. Edward was a bright, serious, well-educated child, showing promise of having a character and temperament suitable for a sovereign. But most importantly, of course, as Henry's only legitimate male heir, Edward's succession would likely be popular with the people.

However, when the time came to implement Henry's plan, Edward's succession did present a very significant problem – his age. Edward was nine years old when his father died in 1547, and the boy lived for only another six years before he died aged fifteen. Since Edward VI never attained his majority, which happened at eighteen, the boy-king never ruled in his own right. Henry had tried to account in his will for his son's age by identifying nobles from among his inner circle of advisors who were to serve as the executors for the Crown during Edward's minority. During the boy's time on the throne, and as a result of the influence of his official advisors, Edward developed into a staunch Protestant, eager to further his father's reforming of the English Church. But what Henry could not control after death were the fierce political power struggles that broke out among the executors.

Henry nominated a Regency Council that he may have expected would give voice to divergent points of view and thereby provide its own internal checks and balances, much like Henry's own Privy Council of advisors. What Henry might not have understood, however, was the critical role in the workings of his government that he himself played as a strong monarch. It did not take long after Henry's death for one member of the trusted Regency Council to have his peers elevate him to become Protector of the Realm. Edward Seymour, Jane Seymour's brother and the uncle of Edward VI, was elevated to this title and became the first Duke of Somerset at the same time. Somerset managed to withstand efforts by his brother, Thomas Seymour, to overthrow him, but eventually was displaced as Protector and later suffered execution by John Dudley, who became the Duke of Northumberland. Dudley became the de facto ruler of England for the rest of Edward VI's brief lifetime.

Lady Jane Grey, the Nine Days' Queen

When the unmarried boy-king Edward VI became extremely ill, it was clear that the Duke of Northumberland was in danger. Under Henry's plan for succession, if Edward died without leaving children, the successor monarch would be Princess Mary. At age thirty-seven, Mary was a devout and resolute Catholic, like her mother, Catherine of Aragon. She would not only be free from any susceptibility to Dudley's influence, but she would likely regard him as her enemy for having influenced Edward to actively support Protestantism in England. Dudley had to improvise quickly if he hoped to avoid losing not only his political power but perhaps also his lands, his title, and even his life.

The Tudor Succession

John Dudley is commonly thought to have orchestrated an audacious plan. Many think that he convinced the dying Edward that allowing the Catholic Mary to succeed would lead to the reversal of all their father's reforms of the Church. If Mary reigned, she would forcibly return England to Roman Catholicism. It is not clear to what extent Edward figured this out himself and to what extent he was guided to this conclusion by Northumberland's influence. In any event, Edward executed a will from his sickbed that purported to change the order of succession, naming his seventeen-year-old cousin Lady Jane Grey as his successor. Although Edward would thereby be altering Henry VIII's plan of succession, the change would protect his church reforms from reversal by a new Catholic queen. Moreover, the change would preserve the Tudor dynasty, although in somewhat less direct form – Lady Jane was the granddaughter of Henry VIII's favourite sister, Mary Tudor.

Dudley is suspected of being the architect of this plan because it embodied another of those too-convenient coincidences that we have seen before in Tudor matters. Dudley had arranged for the marriage of one of his sons, Guildford Dudley, to Lady Jane Grey. This marriage assured that, when she succeeded as queen, he could continue to exercise his power over the throne through his son, the king consort. And once the new royal couple had children, the marriage would establish a joint Dudley–Tudor family dynasty.

Lady Jane Grey, the young leading lady of this dramatic plan, appears to have been rather innocent and naïve about the matter. She clearly did not actively seek the crown. Her reluctant agreement to accept it appears to be the result of the arguments of her father-in-law, Dudley, in combination with what she perceived to be her obligation to obey the wishes of her parents and her new husband.

The best thing one can say about this plot is that it almost worked – but unfortunately for Jane, it almost worked for only nine days. King Edward's death on 6 July 1553 was not publicly announced for four days. Then Jane was officially and publicly proclaimed the new queen by the Privy Council. However, there was no time for a formal coronation until her succession could be assured.

For a very brief time, success for Dudley and his new daughter-in-law appeared likely. The existing government promptly assembled numerous troops, bolstering them with Dudley's supporters. The previous heir presumptive, Princess Mary, seemed to have only token military support. However, with her small band of local supporters in the south, Mary somehow managed to elude the government forces sent to arrest her and flee to the northern part of the kingdom, where she had many influential supporters and was popular with the people.

There she received daily increases in the troops who rallied to her aid. Her new political supporters included many of the nobility who had been only reluctant allies of Dudley, and those new supporters brought their household troops to her. At the same time, many of the government soldiery either came over to her side or simply went home, unwilling to oppose Mary and her increasingly popular cause. Similarly, in defiance of government orders, the people of important towns and cities declared for Mary and refused to take up arms against her. Only a few days passed before a nervous Privy Council reversed its declaration of Lady Jane Grey's succession.

Mary was able to return after her fearful flight from arrest and threatened execution in a much different spirit. After only a few tense days, she enjoyed a triumphal march to London to claim her throne. The citizens of the towns and cities she passed through turned out as they would have for a normal coronation celebration. The Privy Council and almost all of Dudley's former allies rushed to pledge their support for Mary and to plead for their lives, until Dudley himself had to join Mary's victory procession. After her victorious entry into London, Mary was formally crowned Queen Mary I, and began a five-year reign that would end with her death in 1558.

How can we understand Mary's surprising defeat of the government's initial attempt to ignore Henry VIII's designated order of succession and crown Lady Jane Grey? It is easy to ascribe such an unlikely victory to mere chance, or to some key tactical mistakes by Dudley, such as his failure to appreciate the importance of detaining Mary before she could escape to the north, or his ignorance of the risks of allowing unsupervised dissention to be expressed in the Privy Council after he left London to personally lead his troops.

But perhaps Lady Jane Grey's chances to obtain and hold the throne were doomed from the outset by one unsurmountable factor – Mary's popularity. The people appreciated that Mary was Henry's daughter with Queen Catherine of Aragon. A substantial segment of the population appears to have viewed Mary with the same affection they previously felt for her mother.

Mary I (r. 1553–1558)

Despite her great initial popularity among her people, Mary I later became known as Bloody Mary for her executions, by burning at the stake, of hundreds of English Protestants. She continually increased the intensity of her attempts to reverse the Church reforms initiated by her father, Henry VIII, which had been strengthened during the regency of her brother, Edward VI. Mary also had a long and close connection with her cousin Charles V, the Holy Roman Emperor. The English people soon saw her, quite accurately, as subjecting what should have been her independent reign to the active influence of the emperor. And the people's fears and disapproval intensified when Mary married Charles's son and heir, Philip II of Spain.

It was readily apparent that the quality of marital affection in this royal union was exceedingly asymmetrical. Mary seems to have been deeply in love with her young husband. For his part, however, Philip managed to find excuses to spend as much time as he could on the Continent. He explained these absences by citing his obligation to attend to imperial military and political affairs. However, there were widespread public reports of his several extramarital affairs.

In an echo of the final outcome of Henry VIII's marriage to Mary's mother, Catherine of Aragon, their daughter's marriage to Philip does not appear to have developed into the deep love-match that Mary sought. Rather, for Philip, it seems to have been little more than a diplomatic manoeuvre engineered by his father to secure a permanent alliance between Spanish/imperial interests and England. Accomplishing this alliance on a lasting basis required producing a joint child of the two lines to inherit the English throne. Philip therefore dutifully returned to England several times for what were in essence very brief conjugal visits.

Mary seemed ecstatic about even the limited time spent together with Philip. Not only was she smitten with him, but she had her own reasons for desperately wanting to bear a child. The intensity of her determination on this matter is indicated by the fact that, on two separate occasions during her marriage to Philip, she went through a very public and humiliating false or phantom pregnancy (pseudocyesis), each of which lasted well beyond nine months.

It is difficult from this distance to evaluate the relative strengths of the several likely causes of Mary's strong desire for a child. Her intense wish for a pregnancy could have been due to her hope to strengthen her husband's love for her. She could have been motivated by wanting to demonstrate through her fertility that the eleven-year difference in their ages should not be a deterrent to their love bond. When she had married, Mary was thirty-eight years old, and Philip was twenty-seven. But the simplest explanation for Mary's fierce determination to give birth can be expressed in a single word: *Elizabeth*.

It is not surprising that Mary abhorred the idea that her half-sister Elizabeth, who was seventeen years younger, would succeed to the crown upon her death if she left no children. Indeed, the real surprise for us, as it appears it was at times for Elizabeth, is that the multiple reasons for Mary's antipathy towards Elizabeth somehow did not drive the queen to execute her younger half-sister.

It had been Elizabeth's impending birth that triggered Henry's final moves to marry Anne Boleyn, so it is understandable that Mary would have seen Elizabeth as the cause for so much grief and suffering for herself and her mother. Catherine had been forced out of the palace and relegated to dreary residences with only a small number of servants and limited contact with the outside world. Mary, meanwhile, had been kept from visiting her mother and forced to coexist with her younger half-sister Elizabeth, who for a time outranked her. These cruel and humiliating actions may have been formally ordered by Mary's father, Henry VIII, but Mary attributed them to the vengeful influence of Anne Boleyn.

And the steps that Henry took to be able to marry Anne had been devastating for Mary and her mother. Henry not only annulled his marriage to Catherine, but his theory for the annulment, the Leviticus Prohibitions, made Mary an illegitimate child. Moreover, the path that Henry took to accomplish the annulment and marry Anne Boleyn ended the era of Mary's beloved Roman Catholicism in England.

On a logical level, baby Elizabeth should not have been blamed for the actions of her mother. Nevertheless, Mary could never forgive Elizabeth because her mother, Anne Boleyn, had been at least the motivating factor, and to some extent the co-architect, of the misery in Mary's and Catherine's lives. Mary took the position that, unlike the virtuous Catherine, Anne was little more than a prostitute who had bewitched Henry to fall in love with her, and that Elizabeth's existence was tainted by that inheritance.

As Mary's unpopularity with Protestants escalated during her reign, she rightly saw Elizabeth as a significant threat to her throne. Despite whatever were Elizabeth's true religious convictions, however, the young heir apparent tried very hard to avoid even the appearance of encouraging or participating in any rebellions against Mary. Even without her cooperation or permission, though, Elizabeth was at least the inspiration for various Protestant-led plots that threatened Mary.

Mary's most serious concerns about Elizabeth probably involved the sincerity of the princess's claims to have returned to the Catholic faith. Mary suspected that Elizabeth was lying, and feared that Elizabeth's succession to the throne would see England once again discard Roman Catholicism and return to the path towards Protestantism. Clearly, the best way for Mary to maintain a Catholic England would be to give birth to a new heir.

But despite all of Mary's reasons for wanting to have a child who would replace Elizabeth as the heir apparent, even a sovereign queen must bow to the decrees of nature. Mary never had children, and in 1558 she died in her sickbed at the age of forty-two.

Mary's reign was a sorry one for her and for England. In just five years she managed to transform the initial overwhelming affection and support of the masses into the almost universal disappointment and enmity of her subjects. She was England's first queen to serve as monarch in her own right, but she had received little training or serious exposure to the inner workings of the royal court. Having never learned how to assert control over her Privy Council and Parliament, she was unable to rule with her father's bold leadership and political savvy.

Mary was able to impose her will on the affairs of the kingdom in essentially only two matters, both of which earned her the deep hostility of her people. The first was her marriage to Philip of Spain rather than to an Englishman of noble blood. The second was her attempt to re-establish Roman Catholicism as the sole religion of England – a goal for which she increasingly resorted to burning Protestants as heretics.

Other factors also contributed to Mary's unpopularity. She lost the support of much of the nobility, who feared that the wealth and lands they had received as a consequence of Henry's confiscation of the monasteries would be reclaimed by the pope if England embraced Roman Catholicism again. And the common people of England blamed Mary for joining with Spain in 1556 to launch an ill-fated war against France which resulted in the loss of Calais, England's last territory on the Continent. Finally, throughout her brief reign, Mary manifested signs of a growing emotional vulnerability, if not outright instability. Her self-deception was especially evident in her increasingly one-sided, blind devotion to Philip, and in her two false pregnancies.

Despite all these failings, perhaps history should also remember Mary for her most positive single achievement as queen – she somehow managed to overcome her doubts, fears, and hostility towards Elizabeth. Mary did not attempt to remove her half-sister from the line of succession by either of the tactics readily within her power. She did not seek to change the law of succession, and despite various occasions when she sent Elizabeth to the Tower of London or other closely guarded residences, she did not have her half-sister executed for heresy or treason.

Elizabeth I (r. 1558–1603)

Elizabeth had to endure Mary's anger for almost a quarter of a century, including the stress of being at risk of losing her freedom or even her life during the five years of Mary's reign as England's queen. Nevertheless, upon Mary's death in 1558, the twenty-five-year-old Elizabeth became the final Tudor to sit on the throne. The transition came without significant civil unrest or conflict. The final provision of Henry VIII's plan of succession was ushered in by the cheers of many of the common folk.

It should be noted, however, that Elizabeth's triumph was in no way inevitable. The fact that she survived Mary's reign and succeeded as queen was an almost miraculous outcome for that era of often unbridled royal power, complex political struggles, and the Crown's traditional practice of consolidating power by imprisoning, trying, and executing political or personal rivals and opponents. It is quite understandable that, on several occasions during Mary's reign, Elizabeth feared for her life.

The relationship between the half-sisters fluctuated. Elizabeth was at times sent away from court to live in relative isolation. Once, when Elizabeth was implicated in a Protestant plot, the queen had her interned at the Tower of London. Elizabeth was able to return to her residence after convincing Mary that her name was being used by the plotters entirely without her knowledge, acquiescence, or approval.

While Mary I still ruled England, Elizabeth's ability to survive her precarious situation seems to be the direct result of her superb political intuition. Elizabeth would instantly notify Mary of any event that could possibly be interpreted as evidence of her disloyalty. Before any compromising rumours had an opportunity to reach Mary's ear, the queen would have received Elizabeth's own report of what might otherwise have been seen as an alarming visit, letter, or indirect contact with potential enemies or plotters against the queen. Elizabeth disarmed any potential suspicion with her eloquent protestations of surprise and disapproval of such incidents.

The interaction between these half-sisters saw great highs and lows during Mary's reign. Sometimes, Mary seemed to elevate Elizabeth to a position appropriate for the heir apparent. On occasion, she would invite Elizabeth to accompany her in public processions and events. When that happened, Elizabeth would be granted the closest and most favoured position in the procession, and would be dressed in royal gown and jewellery. However, Mary's elevations of Elizabeth's public position never continued for too long. Elizabeth was seventeen years Mary's junior, and had a youthful beauty that contrasted very favourably with the older Mary's rather plain appearance. Perhaps the queen noticed that the crowds sometimes seemed to direct their cheers of delight not to her but towards Elizabeth. Mary's jealousy was exacerbated after her marriage, when Philip was observed giving considerable time and attention to his sister-in-law during some lengthy private talks.

Elizabeth made a good show to Mary of making a slow but steady conversion to Catholicism. She requested books and altar pieces for her private chapel, and swore to the sincerity of her spiritual transformation from the Protestant faith. Perhaps the illusion of peacefully handing the crown to a Catholic Elizabeth was simply too tempting for Mary to deny.

Mary, Queen of Scots
Strangely, a major feature of Elizabeth I's long reign seemed to echo the earlier concerns of Mary I in the perceived threat from her younger half-sister and her followers. This time, however, the threat came from Elizabeth's younger cousin Mary, Queen of Scots. In 1568, Mary, Queen of Scots lost her Scottish throne and fled south seeking Elizabeth's protection. Mary, Queen of Scots was a Catholic, and

many English Catholics supported her claim to be the proper eventual successor to the childless Elizabeth. Some of these supporters even claimed that Elizabeth was not the legitimate queen and that Mary should be wearing the crown.[1]

Elizabeth was justifiably concerned that her cousin's Catholic supporters might not be willing to wait for her natural death without issue before they had Mary succeed to the throne. Therefore, what Mary found in England was not protection, but rather two decades of confinement and relative isolation. The situation ended only when Mary was tried and found guilty of actively participating in a plot to kill her cousin and take the throne. Charged with treason, she was beheaded in 1587.

As we now know, Elizabeth's peaceful succession to the Tudor throne did not fulfil the dreams of a Roman Catholic England hoped for by Mary I, by Mary, Queen of Scots, and by their respective Catholic supporters. Elizabeth returned England to the path towards the English Reformation set by her father and brother. Elizabeth's coronation also launched a forty-five-year reign – what we now call the Elizabethan era. Many view that time as a golden age for England, marked by control of the seas, including the defeat of the Spanish Armada; expansion of trade; increase of England's global influence; domestic peace and prosperity; and development of arts and culture, including the amazing literary phenomenon of William Shakespeare.

Henry VIII's Dynasty

Today, we embrace a variety of images of Henry VIII. In the minds of many present-day enthusiasts of Tudor history, Henry VIII has become most famous for his dysfunctional married life and the ruthless manner in which he exercised his increasingly despotic powers as he discarded or executed spouses, political opponents, and former supporters who displeased him. Historians of religion, meanwhile, focus upon his launching the first steps of the English Reformation, which ultimately helped change England and the world of Christianity forever.

However, with the benefit of hindsight, we should also acknowledge that Henry VIII achieved one of his earliest and dearest goals – the extension of the initially fragile Tudor dynasty. That line continued for a total of 118 years, ending with its most glorious period, the

Elizabethan era. Beginning with the reign of his father, Henry VII, and continuing through his own rule and that of Edward, Mary, and finally Elizabeth, the entire sixteenth century became England's Tudor century, an unlikely development that should be credited in large measure to the revolutionary succession plan achieved through the resolute efforts of Henry VIII.

ACKNOWLEDGEMENTS

The history of Henry VIII's divorce from Catherine of Aragon has been repeatedly examined and re-examined by generations of historians for almost five hundred years. It is a privilege to join them. I am deeply indebted to them for sharing with the world their observations and analyses, so many of which have served as part of the foundation for this book.

The point of this book is to examine how it could be that the very Catholic Henry VIII eventually tried to rely upon rabbis and Jewish scholars to try to convince Pope Clement VII to annul his marriage to Catherine of Aragon. It has been my great delight to be able to focus upon this somewhat bizarre intersection of traditional Jewish learning and the Catholic world of the early sixteenth century.

In many ways, I feel that I have been preparing to undertake this project through a lifetime of inspiration, learning, and cordial personal relationships and support that I have received from my many rabbis and teachers of Jewish theology and Jewish history, including Rabbis Isaac Klein, Ben-Zion Bergman, Harold Schulweis, Ed Feinstein, David Neiman, Chaim Seidler-Feller, Joshuah Hoffman, Noah Farkas, and Nolan Lebovitz, together with so many other community educators who have shared their learning through online and in-person courses and programs presented by Valley Beth Shalom Synagogue; American Jewish University; Jewish Theological Seminary; Hebrew Union College; the Jewish Studies programs at UCLA, CSUN, and USC; Jeremy Brown's blog, Talmudology: Science, Medicine, and the Talmud; the MyJewishLearning.com Daf Yomi project; and

Acknowledgements

other institutions. My deepest thanks to the very special Hershleifer-Rosett Tanakh UCLA Faculty Study Group for the past fifteen years of weekly study sessions filled with fascinating insights, exchanged with unfailing mutual respect, inspiration, and genuine friendship among fellow seekers. And for the past two years, I have enjoyed a boost in developing my writing as I learned from, laughed with, and envied some wonderful episodes from my supportive classmates as we exchanged readings in our VBS-Hazak Memoir Writing Class led by Prof. Helen Dosik.

I received special helpful research assistance from the library staff and materials at the AJU/Ostrow Research Library and the Los Angeles Public Library system. My childhood friend from Buffalo, New York, and now my freeway-close Southern California neighbour, Richard Goldberg, previously taught a course on early Tudor history, and kindly lent me his mini-library of Tudor history books to work with at my house for several years.

This book relies upon quotations and information from many early historical documents, but perhaps the most significant document is the original 1530 responsum letter of Rabbi Jacob Rafael of Modena, Italy, held by the British Library. With regard to this document, I received invaluable help from Zoe Stancell, at the British Library Manuscript Reference Service, together with Ilana Tahan, British Library Lead Curator–Hebrew and Christian Orient Studies, and Jonathon Vines, British Library Image & Brand Licensing Manager.

Included as an appendix in this book is a new English translation of the Raphael responsum by Gabriel Wasserman. I greatly appreciate his friendly cooperation and scholarly expertise, which enabled me to share his new translation with my readers. I was also fortunate to receive other translation assistance from several sources: Yossi Dresner helped with a preliminary translation of the Raphael responsum. Lola Rabow prepared a translation of the 1530 Spanish letter of King Ferdinand II regarding Spain's negotiations with the Vatican. Marvin Andrade furnished additional assistance with Spanish diplomatic language translation issues. My college roommate, Bill Shapiro, a Francophile to the end, reviewed and revised some of my laboured translations of French-language journal articles.

Several friends, including Rabbi Chaim Seidler-Feller, Rabbi Joshua Hoffman, Rabbi Corrine Copnik, Michael Waterman, and Sara Har-Shalom, helped me with suggestions for potential translators.

I must confess that, based upon my very limited early training, I prepared my own translations of several Latin-language documents from the earlier records. I take personal responsibility for any errors in any of the translations relied upon or quoted in this book.

I want to especially thank several friends and family members who undertook to read and give helpful and supportive comments on early drafts of my manuscript. The final version of my manuscript was a significant improvement over my preliminary drafts largely due to the evaluations and support, and often some spot-on corrections and suggestions from my early readers, who included Michael Rabow, Prof. Helen Dosik, Prof. Maximillian Novak, Rabbi Barry Schwartz, Carol Morrison, and Lola Rabow.

I am pleased to have this opportunity to publicly acknowledge the crucial assistance I received in developing this book, as was also the case for my previous books, from the insightful literary analysis and detailed suggestions of my son, Michael Rabow. His advice led to some major structural and style improvements to my preliminary draft. I and every reader of this book owe him thanks for many developmental alterations that were made possible by his invaluable contributions.

Special thanks also to Rabbi Chaim Seidler-Feller for not only helping me arrange for a professional translator for the Raphael responsum, but also for pointing me to the fascinating but mistaken rumours of Henry VIII's alleged connection to the recently auctioned Valmadonna Trust copy of the Bomberg Talmud.

I am very grateful for all of these generous contributions to my efforts to improve my early manuscript drafts, but of course I take full responsibility for any errors or shortcomings in my implementation of those suggestions in this final version.

An author's manuscript remains a personal exercise unless it can be transformed into a published book. I want to express my deep gratitude for the kindness shown to me by Cathy Shapiro and Stephen Isaacs, who volunteered much time and effort introducing me to some of their circle of independent editor friends. I greatly benefitted from the attention and advice I received from editors Kelli Christiansen, Katleen M. Lafferty, and Kevin Cummins, each of whom considered my project, provided positive feedback, and helped me find the right path to publication.

It was my very good fortune to have had my preliminary proposal for this book accepted by Connor Stait, in his then position as

Acknowledgements

Commissioning Editor for Amberley Publishing. Connor's enthusiasm and guidance helped keep me on track to completing my final draft of the manuscript. This in turn opened the door to Amberley's production team, and in particular, my opportunity to partner with my extremely skilled, kind, and attentive editor, Alex Bennett, in the task of moving this project from manuscript to book. Alex somehow not only managed to translate my writing from American English to UK English, but also suggested how to hone some of my less-precise phrasings, all for the benefit of his real clients, the readers. I also appreciate the enthusiastic help of the very talented graphics team and Phillip Dean, Publicity Officer. I feel very fortunate to have found a home for this project at Amberley Publishing.

I am thankful for very important support I received throughout this project from many family members, friends, and readers of my previous books who, over the past decade, could never be quite sure whether it would bring me joy or pain to be asked about the progress of my book. Nevertheless, they never failed to express their sincere interest and good wishes.

Of course, nothing can match the support and personal sacrifices of my wife, Lola, who always made space for my recitals of each day's minor advances and major problems throughout the many years of my researching and writing this book. Without her understanding and acceptance of my commitment to her that I would, some day, finish this project and finally return from the sixteenth century to the twenty-first, this book would not exist.

Jerry Rabow

NOTES

Short titles have been used for citing works in the endnotes. Frequently cited works have been identified by the following abbreviations:
BT: *Babylonian Talmud.*
CSP-Spain: *Calendar of State Papers-Spain.*
CSP-Venice: *Calendar of State Papers Relating to English Affairs in the Archives of Venice.*
LP: *Letters and Papers, Foreign and Domestic, of the Reign of Henry VIII.*

Plates

Image Note for Fig. 2 – Catherine of Aragon: The 1697 engraving of Queen Catherine of Aragon at Fig. 2 includes a subtle commentary on her faith as a Catholic and her fate as a queen. The oval frame around her image has thorns, the classic symbols of pain and suffering. She was crowned queen, but hers was to be a Crown of Thorns as described in the New Testament narratives of the crucifixion of Jesus. (See the gospels of Matthew 27:29, Mark 15:17 and John 19:2, 5.)

Image Note for Fig. 4 – Reading the Ferdinand and Isabella Portraits: Published almost two hundred years ago, the images in Fig. 4 portray both monarchs of Spain in elaborate regal gowns and crowns. Ferdinand stares sternly at the viewer, gripping his sceptre of rule in his right hand, with his left hand firmly on top of a pile of presumably important documents of state. Isabella is looking above and beside the viewer, focusing on the distance, with a more pensive expression. Her hands are clasped; she holds nothing regarding affairs of state.

However, the contrasts between these images belie the monarchs' actual powers over their temporarily joined states. Unlike the English at that time, the

Notes

Spanish recognised female heirs to the throne. Isabella was the queen regnant – ruling by inheritance, not merely by marriage – of Castile, the larger and, after the discovery of the Americas, wealthier state. Ferdinand's monarchy was the smaller Aragon, which ultimately lacked similar importance in the Iberian Peninsula.

After Isabella predeceased him in 1504, Ferdinand obtained practical control over Castile by becoming regent for his and Isabella's oldest daughter, Joanna the Mad, whom he caused to be confined. When Joanna survived her father in 1516, her son Charles arranged to continue her confinement for the rest of her life while he ruled Aragon and Castile as King Charles I. In 1519 he would also become Holy Roman Emperor Charles V, the champion of his aunt Catherine of Aragon, and the unyielding opponent of Henry VIII's efforts to annul his marriage to Catherine.

Image Note for Fig. 7 – Henry VIII's Armour: The right panel of Fig. 7 shows Henry's armour garniture (having exchangeable parts for use in battle or tournament), with decorative etching designed by Holbein, 1527, when Henry was thirty-six years old. The left panel of Fig. 7 shows Henry's field armour, likely worn at the siege of Boulogne, 1544, at age fifty-three. These two sets of armour provide a visual record of the changes in Henry's size and estimated weight during his reign.

Image Note for Fig. 12 – Scene from Shakespeare: Fig. 12 depicts Cardinals Wolsey and Campeggio unsuccessfully trying to convince Catherine of Aragon to agree to the divorce.

Image Note for Fig. 13 – Trial of the Marriage of Henry VIII: Fig. 13 illustrates Catherine of Aragon pleading with Henry VIII at the Blackfriars Trial, as described by George Cavendish in *The Life of Cardinal Wolsey*. Wolsey and Campeggio are shown presiding at the trial.

Image Note for Fig. 14 – John Fisher: Fig. 14 shows an eighteenth-century engraving by Jacobus Houbraken. If you look only at the image of John Fisher shown within the virtual oval frame of this engraving, you will see Fisher in his familiar garb as Bishop of Rochester, an office he held for thirty years. However, if you also examine the vignette at the bottom of the virtual frame you will see that it is not mere decoration, but rather tells an important part of Fisher's history. Fisher was elevated to cardinal by Pope Paul III on 20 May 1535, just before his beheading on 22 June 1535 by order of Henry VIII. The imagery at the bottom of the virtual frame tells this story:

A bishop's mitre rests on the lower left side of the frame. The *putto* on the lower right side appears about to mirror the placement of the mitre with a new broad-brimmed, tasselled cardinal's hat (the *galerum rubrum*) formerly used at a cardinal's investiture ceremony. But this gesture is interrupted when attention is drawn to Fisher's severed head at the bottom left. This scene depicts the famous response reported by Henry VIII, and retold in various forms to the effect that Henry had told Pope Paul not to bother sending the cardinal's hat to England; rather, Henry said that he would send Fisher's head to the pope. Compare the versions in *Letters and Papers*, vol. 8, #876, 16 June 1535, Chapuys to Charles V, 345; *Calendar of State Papers-Spain*, vol. 5 Part 1, #174, Chapuys to the Emperor, 492–506; H. A. L. Fisher, *History*, 351; Francis Hackett, *Henry VIII*, 246; Lewis, *Life of Dr. John Fisher*, 1:xviii–xv (introduction by T. Hudson Turner), 2:178–79. Cf. Scarisbrick, *Henry VIII*, 328.

If Houbraken were creating this image today he might well have included another small image reminding us that in 1935, almost exactly four hundred years after Fisher had been appointed cardinal, he was canonised as St John Fisher in recognition of his brave defiance of Henry VIII's demand to be recognised as leader of the Catholic Church in England.

Image Note for Fig. 15 – Thomas Cranmer: Fig. 15 shows Thomas Cranmer, who was an important agent for Henry VIII in the final unsuccessful attempts to convince Pope Clement to annul Henry's marriage to Catherine of Aragon. Henry ultimately designated Cranmer as Archbishop of Canterbury so that Cranmer could annul the marriage to Catherine.

Image Note for Fig. 16 – Gregory I and Innocent III: Fig. 16 shows Pope St Gregory I (r. 590–604) and Pope Innocent III (r. 1198–1216). Their permissions and dispensations for exceptions to the Leviticus Prohibitions against marrying a brother's widow provided a major theological justification for Pope Clement's refusal to annul Henry VIII's marriage to Catherine of Aragon.

Image Note for Fig. 18 – Thomas Cromwell: Fig. 18, Houbraken's engraving of Thomas Cromwell, follows the same narrative technique that the artist used for his engraving of John Fisher at Fig. 14. An important historical event in Cromwell's life is depicted in the image of the frame at the bottom of the engraving. As shown in the enlarged detail from this engraving at Fig. 19, the historical event selected by Houbraken depicts King Henry VIII seated, while a courtier, presumably Cromwell, shows him a portrait of beautiful lady. Despite the seeming innocence of this scene, the miniature vignette is a reference to Cromwell's fate that is equally as ominous as the image of the severed head at the bottom of the Fisher engraving.

The portrait being shown to Henry is a reference to Hans Holbein's betrothal portrait of Anne of Cleves, a German princess. Cromwell had selected Anne of Cleves for a political marriage to become Henry's fourth wife and queen after the death of his third wife, Jane Seymour. When Henry first saw Anne of Cleves, a week before their scheduled wedding, he expressed shock and dismay at how much her beauty as depicted in the painting contrasted with how she appeared in person. He was repulsed by her appearance and was highly reluctant to proceed with the wedding. Cromwell convinced Henry that breaking the marriage contract would cause unacceptable political repercussions, so the wedding took place as scheduled. The marriage lasted six months. Anne of Cleves agreed to an annulment, which occurred on 12 July 1540. Thereafter, she remained in England on good terms with Henry as part of his extended royal family. However, Henry's fierce anger at Cromwell for subjecting him to such a humiliating public failure promptly resulted in Cromwell's execution on 28 July 1540, about two weeks after the annulment had become final.

Image Note for Figs. 26, 27, and 28 – Rabbi Jacob Raphael Responsum: These images show the historic two-page responsum of Rabbi Jacob Raphael of Modena in three parts, adapted from the image online in the British Library MS Viewer for the original handwritten document at Arundel ms 151 ff 190–191v f190r.

Preface

1. **Church of England:** As used herein, the term 'Church in England' refers to the national church in sixteenth-century England, which began as part of the Roman Catholic Church administered in England, as changed during the Tudor monarchy. 'Church of England' refers to the Anglican Church, which ultimately became the established state church in England as a consequence of the English Reformation movement, including the doctrinal and institutional changes that began under Henry VIII and his successor Tudor monarchs.

2. **Bias and motivations:** Readers of some of the contemporaneous and even more recent Tudor period histories cannot avoid noticing that descriptions of Henry's motivations are often correlated with the religious beliefs and loyalties of the authors. Catholic commentators tend to attack Henry for being driven by his ignoble infatuation and lust for Anne Boleyn, while Protestant commentators tend to praise the king for acting on his noble concerns for establishing a peaceful and acceptable succession to the Crown.

    Although beyond the scope of this book, Henry's demands for marital dissolution and his ultimate break with Rome also led to his appropriation of the English lands and treasure of the Roman Catholic Church. It is possible to conclude that this enormous economic and political benefit had always been a major, although undisclosed, motivation for Henry to initiate what he called his Great Matter, his quest for annulment of his marriage to Catherine of Aragon. While wealth confiscation may have attracted Henry later in the process, any analysis of the king's initial motivations for divorce should recognise that his two principal motivations at the outset were his infatuation with Anne Boleyn and his concerns for peaceful Tudor succession.

3. **Previous sources examining the role of Jewish law:** For some of the few historical commentaries that devote more significant attention to aspects of Henry's reliance upon Jewish authorities, see David S. Katz, *History*, 1–48; Brachman, 'Oxford's Hebraists'; Kaufmann, 'Opinion of Jacob Rafael'; and Adelman, 'Levirate Union'.
4. **Diaspora Judaism:** For a discussion of the Jewish Diaspora in general and particularly in England, see Chapter 12.

1 *The Jews of Early Medieval Europe*

1. **Matzo:** A tragically ironic aspect of the antisemitic Blood Libel is that according to ancient Jewish ritual, which has been observed continuously through today, matzo must be prepared from the most restricted and pure ingredients – only flour and water – in a strictly prescribed and ritually supervised process of baking, which cannot take longer than eighteen minutes in order to assure that there has been no accidental fermentation or other impurity introduced during the baking process.
2. **Reports of the Norwich Blood Libel event of 1144:** For the original inflammatory fantasy created by Brother Thomas of Norwich in 1173, see Marcus, *Jew in the Medieval World*, 121–26. For a later retelling with additional fabrications, sometimes conflicting with the earlier account, see the excerpt from Capsgrave's fifteenth-century work *Acta Sanctorum*, quoted in Jacobs, *Jews of Angevin England*, 19–21.
3. **Ritual Murder (Blood Libel) accusations:** The most prominent Blood Libel accusations following Norwich in the twelfth and thirteenth century included the 1171 accusation – without the existence of any victim – and massacre of the Jewish community of Blois, France, and the 1255 accusations regarding the alleged victim, 'Little' Hugh of Lincoln, resulting in mass trials and almost twenty executions of Jews. The most prominent modern trials included the Damascus Affair of 1840 (see Frankel, *The Damascus Affair*), and the trial of Mendel Beilis in Kiev in 1913, fictionalised in Bernard Malamud's Pulitzer Prize-winning novel, *The Fixer* (1966).
4. **English anti-Jewish attacks after Norwich:** From 1144 until the expulsion of the Jews from England in 1290, major mob attacks were made against Jewish communities in Gloucester (1158); Bury St Edmunds (1181); Bristol (1182); Winchester (1192); and London (1189). In 1190, in the aftermath of the Coronation Riot, unrest spread to Dunstable, King's Lynn, Stamford, Norwich, and York. In the thirteenth century, mob action returned to London twice, and spread to Cambridge, Canterbury, Worcester, and Lincoln. See Enc. Judaica II, 6:410 ff, s.v. 'England'.

Notes

5. **Richard the Lionheart and the Jews:** While King Richard was in the Holy Land leading the English contingent in the Third Crusade, he is said to have offered the position of serving as his personal physician to Maimonides, the great Jewish physician and rabbi. See Arbel, *Maimonides*, 139.
6. **The Coronation Riot of 3 September 1189:** See Graetz, *History of the Jews*, 3:410–11; Margolis and Marx, *History of the Jewish People*, 386–87; Grayzel, *History of the Jews*, 307.
7. **The York Massacre of March 1190:** See the contemporaneous report of William of Newburgh quoted in Marcus, *Jew in the Medieval World*, 131–36; Margolis and Marx, *History of the Jewish People*, 387–388; Grayzel, *History of the Jews*, 307; Graetz, *History of the Jews*, 3:413–15; Cooper, *The Castle of York*, 24–25; Jacobs, *Jews of Angevin England*, 385–92. For the history of the fall of Masada, see Josephus, *The Wars of the Jews*, VII, viii, 1–ix, 2.
8. **The Jews of England at the time of their expulsion:** See Abrahams, 'Condition of the Jews', in *Jewish Historical Society of England, Transactions*. 76–84.
9. **Oliver Cromwell, Menasseh ben Israel, and the readmission of the Jews to England:** See Nadler, *Menasseh ben Israel*, 159–217; Rabow, *50 Jewish Messiahs*, 85–90; Margolis and Marx, *History of the Jewish People*, 489–93. Menasseh ben Israel's 1655 petition for readmission of the Jews to England is quoted in full in Marcus, *Jew in the Medieval World*, 66–68.

2 Henry VIII's Marriage to Catherine of Aragon

1. **Tudor genealogy:** After John Beaufort's birth, his father, John of Gaunt, married Beaufort's mother, Katherine Swynford. Thereafter, the Beaufort line was declared legitimate through government pronouncement and papal decrees, the last being confirmed in the Bull of Pope Innocent VIII when Henry VII married Elizabeth of York. Such legitimisation by civil or papal decree was how such matters were handled at that time, when the fitness of a king – or a pope – was involved. Before he became Pope Clement VII, Giulio de' Medici was commonly regarded as illegitimate, but his Medici cousin who ruled as Pope Leo X issued a decree of dispensation declaring that Clement was legitimate, enabling Leo to elevate him to become cardinal.
2. **Competing claims to the throne:** Due to the frequency of domestic and international royal intermarriages, there could be many claimants to succession in the absence of direct father–son heirs. It is sometimes mentioned that Catherine of Aragon in her own right arguably could have had a closer claim to the English throne than the Tudors. See Archer, *Henry VIII*, loc. 130; Borman, *Private Lives*, loc. 125; Dan Jones, *Wars of the Roses*, 8; see also Mattingly, *Catherine of Aragon*, 15.

Henry VIII and His Rabbis

3. **Importance of the Tudor dynasty:** Perhaps as a further demonstration of the dynastic implications of the wedding, Arthur's younger brother, Prince Henry Tudor, then ten years old and the next in line for succession to the throne after him, served as the ceremonial escort for Arthur's fiancée. Young Henry's participation would have been another marker of stability for the Tudor dynasty. However, no one at the wedding festivities could have suspected how soon Prince Henry would become the central figure in the Tudor succession.

4. **English Sweating Sickness:** See Starkey, *Six Wives*, 76–77, discussing the limited evidence of the timing and nature of Arthur's illness, including the possibility of testicular cancer.

    The question of whether Arthur had been sick at the time of his wedding is more than medical curiosity. It relates to one of the primary issues we will be discussing in our examination of the subsequent annulment dispute between Henry VIII and Catherine of Aragon – whether her marriage to the fifteen-year-old Arthur had been successfully consummated.

5. **Marital relations as cause of Arthur's death:** See Starkey, *Six Wives*, 76. The same sort of public speculation about death caused by excessive labours in the royal bedroom would be widespread thirteen years later when the fifty-two-year-old King Louis XII of France died less than three months after marrying the young Princess Mary Tudor, Henry VIII's younger sister. See Starkey, *Six Wives*, 157; see also Scarisbrick, *Henry VIII*, 56.

    Twenty-five years later, two of Arthur's former personal attendants gave depositions suggesting that Arthur had been a frequent visitor to Catherine's bed during at least the early portion of their brief marriage. Sir William Thomas testified: 'As one of the Prince's privy chamber, often conducted him in his nightgown to the Princess's bedchamber door, received him in the morning, and conducted him to his own room.' LP, vol. 4, #5774, Section 5 ii, July 1529, KATHARINE OF ARAGON, 2578.

    An unnamed witness from Arthur's courtiers testified: 'Was told by Maurice Sent [St] John, who was in the Prince's service, that Arthur, after he had lain with the lady Katharine, at Shrovetide after his marriage, began to decay, and was never so lusty in body and courage until his death, which St John said was because he lay with the lady Katharine.' Ibid., Section 13, 2580.

    This latter testimony could have been referring to Arthur's sexual exertions, or perhaps merely observing that Catherine may have come down with the disease first and Arthur caught it from her.

6. **Elizabeth's hopes for additional children:** See *Antiquarian Repertory*, vol. 2, 322–323.

Notes

7. **Spain's wealth from the New World:** Spain's great wealth from its colonies in the Americas did not develop in large scale until the latter half of the sixteenth century, with the founding of the silver-mining centre at Potosi, in modern Bolivia, and the expansion of the Spanish treasure fleet needed to transport precious metals and gems to Spain and for its world trade. Even the ultimate development of New World riches did not solve all of Spain's economic concerns. The Spanish had to deal with trade competition and military engagements with France, England, and the Netherlands. Their gold was subject to the loss of some treasure ships to pirates, warfare, and storms, while the value of gold also suffered from major deflation reflecting the sudden increase in the world's supply of bullion and coin.

8. **Catherine's Finances:** Bargaining over money seems to have become a very major issue for the monarchs of both England and Spain. After Arthur's death, both Catherine's father and her father-in-law were firm: she had to continue residing in England from the time she was widowed until the time she married Prince Henry, despite her occasions of severe financial hardship. During the worst of this period, it appears that Catherine was living almost as a hostage in England to secure the ultimate implementation of the arrangements for her marriage to Prince Henry. However, Catherine refused to consider returning to Spain, where she would become an impoverished, dependent widow. Instead, she focused upon her prospects of becoming Queen of England.

9. **Minimum Age for Prince Henry to Marry under the Marriage Treaty:** See discussion in note 11, 'Henry's Renunciation', below.

10. **Bible Translations:** In the early sixteenth century, Catholics read the Bible in the Vulgate version – the Latin translation principally authored by St Jerome in the late fourth century. In the Vulgate, Lev. 18:16 reads: '*Turpitudinem uxoris fratris tui non revelabis quia turpitudo fratris tui est.*' See *Bible*, Vulgate (Latin) Version.

    The English translation used throughout this book is from the 1610 Douay-Rheims Bible, the first Catholic translation of the Bible into English, which probably provides the closest indication of how Henry and Clement would have understood the Vulgate Latin one hundred years earlier. See *Bible*, Douay-Rheims 1610 version, which states that a man shall not 'reveal' the 'turpitude' of his brother's wife; cf. *Bible*, Douay-Rheims 1609 (modern spelling and translation version), which states that a man shall not uncover the 'nakedness' of his brother's wife. The Protestant English-language King James Bible, published in 1611, translates Lev. 18:16 almost identically: 'Thou shalt not uncover the nakedness of thy brother's wife: it is thy brother's nakedness.' *Bible*, King James 1611 version.

11. **Henry's renunciation:** An English translation of Prince Henry's formal renunciation of the wedding contract appears at Herbert, *History*, 389. There has been some confusion about the timing of this renunciation ceremony. Henry VII arranged for his son to make his formal renunciation on the day before Prince Henry's fourteenth birthday. Under general canon law of the time, the minimum age for a boy to legally marry was fourteen, considered the age of puberty. However, the 1503 marriage treaty between Spain and England for Prince Henry's marriage to Catherine stated very specifically that solemnisation of the marriage in church was not to occur until Prince Henry '*quintumdecimum aetatis annum compleverit*' (has completed his fifteenth year of age). See Rymer, *Foedera*, 82–83. Possibly because this unusual phrasing was different from the general rule at that time that the minimum age for a boy to legally consent to marry was fourteen years of age, the English-language summary of this clause in the official state records erroneously states, 'The marriage is to be solemnised as soon as Prince Henry shall have completed the fourteenth year of his age' [when he reaches his fourteenth birthday, rather than when he reaches his fifteenth birthday]. *CSP-Spain*, vol. 1, #364, 23 June 1503, Treaty between Ferdinand and Isabella and Henry VII, pp. 306–308.

12. **Henry VII contemplated remarriage:** At one point, Henry VII even considered the possibility of marrying his widowed daughter-in-law Catherine of Aragon, but any possibility of that was promptly and forcefully rejected by a horrified Queen Isabella. In her letter to Ambassador De Estrada dated 11 April 1503, Isabella instructed: 'The Doctor [de Puebla] has also written to us concerning the marriage of the King of England with the Princess of Wales, our daughter, saying that it is spoken of in England. But as this would be a very evil thing, – one never before seen, and the mere mention of which offends the ears, – we would not for anything in the world that it should take place. Therefore, if anything be said to you about it, speak of it as a thing not to be endured. You must likewise say very decidedly that on no account would we allow it, or even hear it mentioned, in order that by these means the King of England may lose all hope of bringing it to pass, if he have any.' (*CSP-Spain*, vol. 1, #360, 11 April 1503, Queen Isabella of Spain to Ferdinand, Duke De Estrada, 294–305.) After Isabella's strong objections to allowing Henry VII to even contemplate marrying Catherine, the king actively considered other potential candidates for his remarriage. These included Duchess Margaret of Savoy, daughter of Holy Roman Emperor Maximilian I; Queen Dowager Joanna of Naples, Ferdinand and Isabella's niece; and Catherine's sister, Joanna the Mad, Queen of Castile, whose mental illness permitted their father Ferdinand to rule Castile in her stead

after she was widowed and Queen Isabella had died. However, Henry VII could not find a suitable bride, and eventually, with his health worsening, he gave up his hopes of remarriage. See ibid., #551, 24 October 1507 (Margaret of Savoy); ibid. #360, 11 April 1503 (Joanna of Naples); ibid. #577, Jan. 1508 (Joanna the Mad).

13. **Henry VIII reaffirms the wedding contract:** For Henry VIII's claim that reaffirmation of the marriage contract was Henry VII's deathbed wish, see *LP*, vol. 1, #84, 27 June 1509, Henry VIII to Margaret of Savoy, 45. For Henry VII originally causing Prince Henry's renunciation because of Ferdinand's delinquencies in making payments on marriage portion, see Lingard, *History*, vol. 4, Appdx note Q, 295–96.

14. **Prince Henry danced at Arthur's wedding:** At Arthur's wedding festivities, ten-year-old Prince Henry had delighted the crowd when he took off his jacket and danced. See Mattingly, *Catherine of Aragon*, 42.

15. **Catherine is queen consort, not queen regnant:** Although it was a joint coronation, Catherine did not become a *queen regnant*, a female monarch who reigned in her own right of inheritance of the throne. Catherine's mother, Isabella, had ruled as queen regnant of Castile. Up to that time, however, England had only crowned *queens consort* – women like Catherine who became queens by virtue of being married to a reigning king.

3 Henry VIII's Children

1. **Status of obstetrical medicine:** When it came to even basic issues of women's pregnancy and delivery, this was a time of extremely primitive medical science, especially with an all-male medical profession. Midwives probably knew more about obstetrics than most doctors, but those women typically did not make and maintain written records. Therefore, it is difficult to rely upon reports of the number of miscarriages and stillbirths attributed to Catherine. Descriptions at that time might not accurately distinguish between a stillbirth or a live birth of a child who survived for only a matter of minutes or hours. Even identification as male or female are only reliable for near-term deliveries. Inaccuracy or intentional avoidance of reporting might be especially likely for early miscarriages in a royal household concerned about possible political ramifications from a public announcement of another failed attempt to produce a healthy male child.

2. **Catherine's pregnancies:** See David S. Katz, *History*, 16: 'Henry's marriage to Catherine failed to produce a male heir: only the Princess Mary (b. 1516), three babies who were stillborn or died soon afterwards (two of them males), and two more (one male) who died within a few weeks of birth, apart from

a number of miscarriages.' See also Bernard, *The King's Reformation*, 3–4, offering the following specifics:

1. Stillborn girl, early 1510
2. Son, Henry, 1511, survived 52 days
3. Miscarriage, September 1513
4. Son, died very soon after birth, December 1514
5. Daughter, Mary, 1516, survived
6. Miscarriage, autumn 1517
7. Stillborn child, November 1518.

3. **Abstinence during and following pregnancy:** See Weir, *Six Wives*, 10; and see Starkey, *Six Wives*, 274.
4. **Elizabeth Blount:** See Philippa Jones, *The Other Tudors*, 77–78.
5. **Fitzroy:** The name tells all: From the Old French, *Fitz* means 'son of', and *Roy* means 'the king'. See https://en.wikipedia.org/wiki/Fitz and https://en.wikipedia.org/wiki/Fitzroy.
6. **Edward's poor health:** Edward was a sickly child but survived long enough to become King Edward VI upon Henry's death in 1547, when Edward was only nine years old. He never ruled independently as an adult because he died from lung disease in 1553, aged fifteen.
7. **Was Fitzroy murdered?** *Encyclopedia Britannica* states that Fitzroy died 'under suspicious circumstances'. See https://www.britannica.com/biography/Henry-Howard-Earl-of-Surrey [accessed 10/1/21]. For a discussion by John Simkin of the possibility that Fitzroy was murdered, see https://spartacus-educational.com/spartacus-blogURL54.htm [accessed 10-1/21]; and see references cited there.
8. **Henry's possible paternity of Mary Boleyn's children:** See Bernard, *The King's Reformation*, 4 and note 18; Friedmann, *Anne Boleyn*, Appendix B, 289; Scarisbrick, *Henry VIII*, 148 and note 2. These historians cite the one bit of second-hand testimony appearing at *LP*, vol. 8, #567, 20 April 1535, John Hale, Vicar of Isleworth, to the Council, 215. See also Starkey, *Six Wives*, 274.
9. **Henry made little provision for Mary Boleyn:** See Friedmann, *Anne Boleyn*, 29.
10. **Catherine entered menopause early:** See Starkey, *Six Wives*, 161 (around 1520). See also Scarisbrick, *Henry VIII*, 150, noting that Catherine suffered a final stillbirth in November 1518: 'This was her last pregnancy, despite the efforts of physicians brought from Spain; and by 1525 she was almost past child-bearing age.'
11. **Henry stopped sexual relations with Catherine:** See Archer, *Henry VIII*, Loc. 470 (Henry stopped in 1524); Mattingly, *Catherine of Aragon*, 235 (Henry

stopped before 1525); Scarisbrick, *Henry VIII*, 152 (Henry stopped before 1525); see also *LP*, vol. 4, Brewer, 'Introduction', p. ccxxi, n. 43 (n. 2 to original print page): '[Henry] told Symon Grynaeus, a comparative stranger, who visited England in 1531, that he had abstained from the queen's bed seven years; that is, from 1524.'

12. **Catherine's physical condition:** Herbert, *History*, 350, quoting from Wolsey's January 1528 letter of instructions to England's ambassador to Venice John Casale for presenting to Pope Clement: 'There are besides some particular reasons to be laid before his holiness in private, but not proper to commit to writing, upon which account, as well as by reason of some distempers which the queen lies under without hopes of remedy, as likewise thro' some scruples which disturb the king's conscience, insomuch that his majesty neither can nor will for the future look upon her, or live with her as his wife, be the consequence what it will.'

13. **Anne was the younger sister:** It is generally agreed that Mary was older than Anne, but even that is difficult to document. As was not unusual for that era, there appear to be no conclusive records of the Boleyn daughters' respective birthdates. Historians have proposed various dates for Anne Boleyn's birth, ranging from as early as 1501 to as late as 1507.

4 Henry VIII and Anne Boleyn

1. **Mary Boleyn's sexual experiences in France:** The report, attributed to King Francis, concerning Mary Boleyn's sexual activities with the nobility and royalty of France, has been recently challenged as a possible fabrication. See Guy and Fox, *Hunting the Falcon*, 95 at n. 23 ('Without better evidence, the question of Mary's morals must be left open.'). Cf. *LP*, X, #450, 10 March 1536, Bishop of Faenza to Prothonotary Ambrogio, 161–181.

2. **Anne learned sexual techniques in France:** See Archer, *Henry VIII*, loc. 904; Borman, *Private Lives*, 182; Weir, *Six Wives*, 154; cf. *LP*, vol. 10, #876, 15 May 1536, Trial of Anne Boleyn and Lord Rochford, 362, quoting from the indictment for her 1536 adultery trial, that Queen Anne 'procured and incited her own natural brother, Geo. Boleyn, lord Rocheford, gentleman of the privy chamber, to violate her, alluring him with her tongue in the said George's mouth, and the said George's tongue in hers'…

3. **Conflicting reports of Anne's beauty or physical defects:** Because Anne became such a controversial person, contemporaneous descriptions are neither uniform nor reliable. Her political supporters tended to report only positive attributes and anecdotes, while her political opponents generally saw everything through the most negative lens possible.

As an example, some of her detractors demonised her by reporting that she had a sixth finger on one hand. Her supporters insisted that she only had a more minor deformity – a second nail growing on the side of a finger on her right hand.

Modern medical science now recognises that both camps might have been right (not about the demonisation, obviously). The condition of polydactyly (having a sixth digit on a hand or foot) can present in several manifestations, with the extra digit having different lengths and growing from different joints. Anne may have had a condition similar to a partially duplicated fifth intermediate phalanx, rather than a fully developed sixth digit. See the illustration in Dr Jeremy Brown's blog on *Science, Medicine, and the Talmud* discussing polydactyly at *www.talmudology.com*, for his 7 September 2023 commentary on *Kiddushin* 25a.

Of course, Anne Boleyn lacked access to either modern medical science or early rabbinic discussions of her condition. However, she responded to the situation in a very pragmatic manner. Such was her sense of style that she had gowns made with extra-long sleeves that would hide her fingers, and this innovation from personal necessity went on to set a new fashion trend at court. It is noteworthy that Anne hid her finger anomaly, while later her daughter, Elizabeth, made a point of differentiating herself from her mother, repeatedly evidencing personal vanity concerning her own long fingers, which she went out of her way to display in person and to have depicted in her portraits. See Portrait of Queen Elizabeth I, the 'Drewe Portrait,' attributed to George Gower, available to view online at *https://historicalportraits.com/artists/743-attributed-to-george-gower/works/787-attributed-to-george-gower-portrait-of-queen-elizabeth-i-the-drewe-portrait-late-1580s/*, with the commentary: 'The deft modeling (with even the hint of veins) in the long and elegant hands of which Elizabeth was so proud is superb.'

4. **Anne's beauty weighed:** For a description from a relatively neutral diplomat, see the report to the senate from the Venetian ambassador to England, Carlo Capello, 7 December 1532, quoted in Lingard, *History*, vol. 4, Appdx. NOTE R, 297: 'My lady Anne is no beauty. She is tall of stature, with a sallow complexion, long neck, large mouth, and narrow chest. In fact she has nothing in her favour besides the king's great passion for her, and her eyes, which are indeed black and beautiful.'

5. **Anne Boleyn-James Butler marriage negotiations:** See *LP*, vol. 3, #1011, 6 Oct., 1520, SURREY and the COUNCIL OF IRELAND to WOLSEY, 372; ibid., #1762, November 1521, [WOLSEY to HENRY VIII], 744. The Irish inheritance matter was eventually settled in 1527 without any marriage: see

LP, vol. 4, #3937, 18 February 1528, The BUTLERS, 1751; see also Ives, *Anne Boleyn*, 43–46; Starkey, *Six Wives*, 266–67.

6. **The Anne Boleyn–Henry Percy alleged betrothal:** Percy later denied under oath that any betrothal promises had been exchanged. However, once Anne had become the king's mistress and eventually his wife, it would have been folly for Percy to admit to a private betrothal even if one had in fact occurred. Cavendish, *Life of Cardinal Wolsey*, Letter VIII from Northumberland, 464–65, quotes Percy's 1535 letter to Thomas Cromwell confirming his previous denial under oath: '…assuring you Mr. Secretary, by the said oath, and blessed body [holy communion] which I affore received, and hereafter intend to receive, that the same may be to my damnation, if ever there were any contracte or promise of marriage between her and me.' In addition to Percy, it seems that Anne was also romantically pursued by the poet Sir Thomas Wyatt, a neighbor of the Boleyn home, Hever Castle. The evidence of the exact nature of their romantic and perhaps physical relationship is not clear, as the major near-contemporaneous source on this issue requires interpreting some of Wyatt's poetry and evaluating the biased defense of both Anne Boleyn and Thomas Wyatt written by his grandson George Wyatt. See Wyatt, *Life of Anne Boleigne*, quoted in Appendix to Cavendish, *Life of Cardinal Wolsey*, 417–49; See also Ives, *Anne Boleyn*, 63–64, 83–99.

7. **Wolsey learned about Anne Boleyn only later:** Cavendish (who, it should be noted, was extremely loyal to Wolsey) states that Wolsey did not initially know about Henry's infatuation with Anne, and that Wolsey had Henry confirm at the Blackfriars trial that the cardinal had not instigated the annulment but initially opposed it. See Cavendish, *Life of Cardinal Wolsey*, 203–4, 218–19.

8. **Anne's revenge on Wolsey:** Imperial ambassador Eustace Chapuys sent the emperor very clear predictions of Anne's role in Wolsey's downfall: '…if the said Lady Anne chooses, the cardinal will be soon dismissed, and his affair settled; for she happens to be the person in all this kingdom who hates him most, and has spoken and acted the most openly against him'. (*CSP-Spain*, vol. 4 (i), (1529–1530), #135, 4 September 1529, Eustace Chapuys to the Emperor, 188–203.)

The following year, after Wolsey's arrest, Chapuys added details about Anne's involvement: '…the duke [Norfolk], the lady [Anne], and her father (Sir Thomas Boleyn), have never ceased plotting against the cardinal, especially the lady, who has wept and wailed, regretting her lost time and honour, and threatening the king that she would go away and leave him, so much so that the king had enough to do to quiet her, and though he begged and intreated her most affectionately, and even with tears in his eyes, not to forsake him, nothing would satisfy the lady short of the cardinal's arrest'. (*CSP-Spain*, vol. 4 (i), (1529–1530), #509, 27 November 1530, Eustace Chapuys to the Emperor, 816-31.) And see Cavendish, *Life of Cardinal Wolsey*, 244–245; Ives, *Anne Boleyn*, 157–9; Scarisbrick, *Henry VIII*, 234; Starkey, *Six Wives*, Chapter 52, 'Wolsey's Fall', pp. 355–367.

9. **The survival of the love letters:** The originals are held today in the Vatican Library. A dozen or so editions have been printed since the early eighteenth century, and several of these editions now appear online.

10. **Some love letters in English:** Even Henry's English-language love letters are not easy to read today. English vocabulary, grammar, and especially spelling were not yet fully standardised in early sixteenth-century England. Moreover, when writing any language with quill pen and ink on parchment, it could be difficult to avoid unintentional ink blotches. Thankfully, readers today have ready access to early English or modern English translations of the entire series of the seventeen love letters, often accompanied by helpful explanatory notes. For a listing of some of the editions most readily available in English, see Appendix A.

11. **Privacy and secrecy of love letters:** One of Henry's early love letters, number VIII, was not only written in French, but also closed with a coded eleven-character phrase that has defied deciphering to this day. See Ridley, *Love Letters*, p. 49, n. 2. But see a recent general decipher proposed in Starkey, *Six Wives*, 281, and accepted in Guy and Fox, *Hunting the Falcon*, 131.

12. **How the love letters came to the Vatican:** Some of the commonly presented theories about the preservation of Henry's love letters conclude that the original documents either were found at Hever by a paid spy working for the Catholic Church or for the Holy Roman Emperor, or perhaps were found accidentally by a Catholic sympathiser. As for the specific means of transfer to Rome, some commentators point to a curious incident involving Cardinal Campeggio, the pope's special envoy to the June 1529 Blackfriars trial of Henry's petition for an annulment from Catherine of Aragon. When Campeggio adjourned the trial and returned to Rome at the end of 1529, his luggage was closely inspected by the English border guards, which would have been unusual treatment for the pope's legatee.

It has been claimed by some that this search indicates that Henry or Wolsey suspected that Campeggio may have been carrying the love letters to Rome. On this theory, Campeggio must have outwitted the border search and either previously had the seventeen love letters smuggled out, or somehow contrived to take them with him to Rome without discovery. That may be what happened, but it seems wrong to presume that the goal of the border search was specifically to recapture the love letters. We don't know if Henry or Wolsey suspected that Anne had retained the letters.

There is a better explanation for the search: upon his earlier arrival, Campeggio had displayed to Henry and Wolsey an even more important document – a decretal commission allowing Wolsey and Campeggio to annul Henry's marriage to Catherine. This confidential commission was signed by Clement but was not to be shown to anyone other than Henry and Wolsey. It is commonly believed that the pope soon had second thoughts, and that upon his later orders, Campeggio secretly burned the commission. Presuming that Henry and Wolsey were not aware of the document's destruction, it is likely that they ordered the border search with the hopes of recovering the precious commission, rather than seeking the love letters. See *LP*, vol. 4, #6016, 22 October 1529, HENRY VIII to CAMPEGGIO, 2677; see also Lingard, *History*, vol. 4, 260, n. 3; Friedmann, *Anne Boleyn*, 53–54.

13. **Authenticity of the love letters:** See Ridley, *Love Letters*, 14.
14. **Speculations about Henry's principal motivations:** Historians have expressed a variety of conclusions as to Henry's principal motivations. Henry wanted to marry Anne: see Brandi, *Charles V*, 263–64; Friedmann, *Anne Boleyn*, 37–38; Starkey, *Six Wives*, 287. Henry wanted a male heir to succeed him: see Herbert, *History*, 346; David L. Holmes, *History*, 184. Henry acted from mixed motives: see Francis Hackett, *Henry* VIII, 180; Ridley, *Love Letters*, 11; Weir, *Six Wives*, 138.
15. **Numbering the love letters:** The original letters were undated, and the numbering assigned by the French failed to reflect a correct chronological order. Nevertheless, those numbers have been retained to avoid confusion over the identification of the respective seventeen letters, even though subsequent scholars developed alternate theories for dating many of the letters. See Ridley, *Love Letters*, 17.
16. **The love letters in a modern text:** An excellent recent translation, commentary, and analysis of dates for the letters can be found in Jasper Ridley, *Love Letters*. Ridley not only offers some corrections to prior translations, but also includes a helpful introduction and images of several of the original letters, some of the more elaborate signatures, and portraits of major individuals mentioned in the letters.
17. **Dating of the love letters:** Under most modern chronologies, some of the love letters are tentatively attributed to specific dates, but some are only able to be assigned to particular months or even only to a broader time period, such as 'before July 1527'. Dates and time periods used in this book for the letters are approximate, and have been primarily adapted from the analysis published

in 1988 in Ridley, *Love Letters*. Other historians have offered alternative chronologies.

18. **Changes in historiography standards:** What a difference a century or two can make in standards of historiography. In his 1848 edition of letters of the kings of England, James Orchard Halliwell, reflecting the moral standards of his times, deleted the final clause of Henry VIII's Letter IX (shown in italics in this text) because of its indecency, commenting in a footnote: 'A sentence is here unavoidably omitted.' Compare Halliwell, *Letters*, vol. 1, 310, n. 1 with the original text in Ridley, *Love Letters*, 51.

19. **Duckies:** The term 'dukkys' is an affectionate derivative of the word 'dugs' (the nipples or breasts of a female mammal). To his credit, the author James Orchard Halliwell did not omit the sexually explicit language from his transcription of this letter, XVI, as he did for the bawdy language in Letter IX. However, he felt compelled to share his nineteenth-century views of the moral shortcomings displayed by both Henry and Anne regarding Letter XVI: 'Making all allowances for the manners of the times, it can only exhibit Henry's profligate passion in no very creditable light; nor does it say much for Anne's sense of propriety that she could consent to receive, much less preserve, notes of such a coarse character.' Halliwell, *Letters*, p. 318, n. 1.

20. **Love letters excerpts:** For Henry's love letter excerpts in this text, dating is from Ridley, *Love Letters* and text is from Halliwell, *Letters*, vol 1, 302 ff.

21. **Henry's refined royal court:** See Burnet/Pocock, *History*, vol. 1, 36–37: 'Being thus inclined to learning, he [young Henry VIII] was much courted by all hungry scholars, who generally over Europe dedicated their books to him, with such flattering epistles, that it very much lessens him, to see how he delighted in such stuff. For if he had not taken pleasure in it, and rewarded them, it is not likely that others should have been every year writing after such ill copies. Of all things in the world flattery wrought most on him; and no sort of flattery pleased him better than to have his great learning and wisdom commended. And in this, his parliaments, his courtiers, his chaplains, foreigners and natives, all seemed to vie who should exceed most, and came to speak to him in a style which was scarce fit to be used to any creature.' See also Weir, *Children of Henry VIII*, 1: 'The magnificence of his court attracted many great and learned men.'

22. **Henry's jousting accident and leg wound:** See Scarisbrick, *Henry VIII*, 485; Chalmers and Chaloner, '500 years later', in *Journal of the Royal Society of Medicine*, 2009, 514–17.

23. **Henry's weight and body changes:** Based upon measurements of Henry's armour over the years, we know that around the time of his marriage to

Notes

Catherine, he was over 6 feet tall and had a waist of 32 inches. It is estimated that he would have weighed approximately 200 pounds. His last suit of armour indicates that his waist had swelled to at least 52 inches, and his weight at his death is estimated at 400 pounds. See Chalmers and Chaloner, '500 years later', in *Journal of the Royal Society of Medicine* 2009, 514 (weight was 15 stone in his twenties, and 28 stone at death).

24. **Henry's other mistresses:** Although some historical materials refer to Henry's relationships with specific other women, it is difficult to separate facts from rumours, or to determine which episodes were simply courtly pursuits and flirtations and which other situations may have included full sexual activity. At least one recent book is devoted to the stories of Henry's affairs with his mistresses and his supposedly resulting illegitimate children. See Philippa Jones, *The Other Tudors*.

25. **Henry's sexual performance problems:** In the 1540 consensual annulment proceedings for terminating Henry's six-month marriage to his fourth wife, Anne of Cleves, on the grounds of inability to consummate, he told his physician, Dr Butts, that he found her so unattractive, because of the hanging of her breasts and the looseness of her flesh, that he had not been able to have sexual relations with her. But Henry insisted he was not impotent, and claimed he was having two nocturnal emissions in his nightly sleep. See Strype, *Ecclesiatical Memorials* (vol. 1, part 2), 461–62.

26. **Anne Boleyn mocked Henry's impotence:** See *LP*, vol. 10, #908, 19 May 1536, Chapuys to Charles V, 378: '[Anne had told her sister-in-law that Henry] *nestoit habile en cas de soy copuler avec femme, et quil navoit ne vertu ne puissance* [was no good in bed with women, and that he had neither potency nor force].' Translation from Starkey, *Six Wives*, 580.

27. **Anne's strategy to become Henry's wife and queen:** Although Anne may have been the first woman to say 'no' to Henry VIII, she was not the last. Anne's successor as queen, Jane Seymour, also said 'no' to the king while he was still married to Anne Boleyn, even refusing to accept his gifts on the grounds that they were improper unless accompanied by an offer of marriage. Jane's appropriation of Anne's seduction technique worked; ironically it was also the trigger for Anne's execution. In many other respects, Jane succeeded in catching Henry simply by not being Anne. Lacking Anne's intelligence and experience, she offered Henry a compliant and modest partner, something he was more than ready for, after he had lived with Anne's increasingly outspoken and oppositional independence.

28. **Henry as the one who said 'no':** At some points in time, Henry may have postponed sex with Anne to avoid ruining his chances of obtaining the pope's annulment. See Bernard, *The King's Reformation*, 8.

29. **The couple may have stopped short of full sexual intercourse:** Henry and Anne enjoyed sexual intimacy, but perhaps not full sexual intercourse. See Bernard, *The King's Reformation*, 7.
30. **Tudor dynasty male lifetimes:** Henry VIII would die aged fifty-five in poor health. His father, Henry VII, died aged fifty-two, likewise in poor health. Henry VIII's older brother, Arthur, had died at fifteen. Later Tudor males would likewise suffer early deaths. The king's illegitimate son Henry Fitzroy died at seventeen, and the king's only legitimate son and heir to the throne, Edward VI, died at fifteen.
31. **Henry's motivations:** See Chapter 4, note 14, above, for examples of the range of motivations attributed to Henry.
32. **English tradition did not recognise queens regnant:** Unlike Spain, where Queen Isabella and subsequently her older daughter Joanna became rulers of Castile by inheritance, England at that time had no significant historical precedent for being ruled by a queen regnant, a female who inherited the throne in her own right. There could be no certainty as to whether Princess Mary's ultimate succession would be acceptable to Parliament, the nobility, and the people of England. Of course, as we now know, Henry would subsequently be able to change the law and tradition of England to allow her to reign as Mary I of England (r. 1553–1558), and Elizabeth I and subsequent women to likewise reign as queens regnant.
33. **The end of sexual intimacy with Catherine:** See Chapter 3, note 11, above.
34. **Contemporaneous reports that Catherine lost her beauty:** See Giustinian, *Four Years*, 1:81 ('She is rather ugly than otherwise'); cf. *CSP-Venice*, vol. 2 (1509–1519), #624, 6 June 1515, Sagudino, to Foscaki, 248. See also Giustinian, *Four Years*, 2:313 ('She is thirty-five years old, not handsome, but has a very beautiful complexion'); cf. *CSP-Venice*, vol. 2 (1509–1519), #1287, 10 September 1519, Report by Giustinian, 560; ibid., #1230, 4 June 1519 Giustinian and Surian to the Signory, 529 ('old and deformed').
35. **Later historians confirm that Catherine had lost her beauty:** See Lingard, *History*, 4:296, Note R, 'low of stature, inclining to corpulency'; Starkey, *Six Wives*, 160–61, 'She became uglier and duller ... very short ... layers of fat swelled her face and body ... nearly as wide as she was tall'; Francis Hackett, *Henry VIII*, 165, 'squat, white and dropsical'. Henry's reaction to these changes in Catherine's appearance could have been another motivation for him to seek the annulment. We know that Henry's divorce from Anne of Cleves in 1540 was caused by his physical inability to consummate that brief marriage when Henry found her physically unappealing. See Chapter 4, note 25, above.

36. **Catherine's disease, 1527:** *LP*, vol. 4, #3644, 6 December 1527, WOLSEY to SIR GREGORY CASALE, 1638; also quoted in Herbert, *History*, 350.
37. **Catherine's disease, 1528:** *LP*, vol. 4, #4977, November 1528, The POPE [Henry VIII instructions to Sir Francis Bryan and Peter Vannes, sent to the Court of Rome.], 2158.

    In note 2 to the similar document #4980, the editor of *LP* vol. 4 warns that it may not be clear whether documents such as #4980, #4977, and similar documents such as #3644 referred to in the immediately prior note above, were merely drafts or if they were copies of correspondence that was actually sent to the addressees: 'The reader must be upon his guard against supposing that any of these drafts were really sent or submitted to the persons to whom they are addressed. They are, probably, like other papers on the great question of the Divorce, devices which occurred to the King or Wolsey from time to time, and might or might not be used as occasion served.' In this instance, however, it appears that two drafts, #4977 and #3644, almost a year apart, confirm Henry's reaction to Catherine's medical condition.
38. **Reginald Pole's attack on Henry's alleged scruples:** Pole, *Unity*, 185; see also Starkey, *Six Wives*, 287.
39. **The treaty for Henry's marriage to Catherine expressly required dispensation from affinity incest:** See Rymer, *Foedera*, vol. XIII, 81 (Latin).
40. **Henry personally benefitted from confiscating monastery property:** See Weir, *Children*, 23.
41. **Henry learned that the Church would tolerate confiscation of its property:** See *LP*, vol. 5, #326, 10 July 1531, Henry VIII to Ghinucci, Benet, and Casale, 153. An excerpt from letter #326 is quoted in the text accompanied by Chapter 13, Note 5.

5 Henry's Biblical Arguments for an Annulment

1. **Divorce and annulment:** Many of the contemporaneous reports and subsequent commentaries describing Henry's efforts to terminate his marriage to Catherine disregard technical distinctions and simply refer to the matter as a divorce, regardless of the legal grounds.
2. **Henry's inability to act in secrecy and privacy:** As early as 1514, international diplomatic observers had heard the rumour of Henry's intention to terminate his marriage to Catherine and seek heirs from a new wife: 'It was also said that the King of England meant to repudiate his present wife, the daughter of the King of Spain and his brother's widow, because he is unable to have children by her, and intends to marry a daughter of the French Duke of Bourbon.' *CSP-Venice*, vol. 2, #479, 1 September 1514 [Vetor Lippomano], 188–93.

3. **Catherine's loyalty to England:** One of Catherine's most remarkable demonstrations of loyalty to England also may have involved one of her several miscarriages. Henry named Queen Catherine as regent to rule England in his place while he was abroad leading his troops against France. The Scots under King James IV could not resist trying to take advantage of this period of apparent English political instability. They invaded England from the north in 1513, meeting the English at Flodden Field. Although Catherine was pregnant, she donned armour, emulating her mother, Queen Isabella, in the Granada War, and rode at the head of troops from the south to reinforce England's northern defenders. Her example bolstered the morale of the victorious English army and the entire kingdom. However, the rigors of her exploit may have contributed to the miscarriage she subsequently suffered that year. See Starkey, *Six Wives*, 149; Mattingly, *Catherine of Aragon*, 162.

4. **Leviticus Prohibitions:** Translated from the 1610 Douay–Rheims Bible. See comment on Bible translations at Chapter 2, note 10, above.

5. **Leviticus Prohibitions apply not only to a brother's wife, but also to his widow:** Applying the Leviticus Prohibitions of Lev. 18:16 and 20:21 to a brother's widow as well as to the wife of a living brother is still the prevailing position for Christians and Jews today. However, the real challenge to Henry's position would focus on the levirate marriage obligations in Deuteronomy 25:5-10. These provisions of Deuteronomy have long been recognised as an exception to Leviticus. See Augustine of Hippo, 'Questions on Leviticus', question 61; cf. Aquinas, *Summa Theologica*, Second Part of Second Part, Question 154, Article 9. *JPS Hebrew-English Tanakh*, 249, footnote *a* to Lev. 18:16 states the theological rationale for deeming that an in-law relationship creates a permanent bar to sexual intercourse even after the death of the first husband: 'A man and his wife are one flesh (Gen. 2:24) even if he should die or divorce her.'

6. **Henry's public argument from Leviticus 18:16:** *LP*, vol. 4, #3641, 5 December 1527, Wolsey to [Sir Gregory Casale], 1634; ibid., #3644, 6 December 1527, Wolsey to Sir Gregory Casale, 1638; see also the secret instructions to Bishop Stafilio for presentation to the pope at ibid., #3767 (2), January 1528, INSTRUCTIONS for STAFILEO, 1681.

7. **Henry's public argument from Leviticus 20:21:** Instructions to the English ambassadors to present to Emperor Charles V. ibid., #5156, [January 1529], THE DIVORCE, 2265.

8. **Henry had been aware of the Leviticus issues for a long time:** Henry claimed that his conscience became troubled after his recent studies of Leviticus. However, it seems likely that, if his conscience had truly become troubled

Notes

about his marriage, such thoughts would have occurred decades earlier, when, at age eighteen, he married Catherine of Aragon in reliance upon Pope Julius's Bull of dispensation. The core of that Bull was the dispensation of this particular prohibition in Leviticus. Julius acted despite the reservations and objections of important clerics such as Archbishop of Canterbury William Warham. Although still young at that time, Henry VIII was already known to have considerable learning and interest about theology.

As early as the Spring of 1509, almost two decades before the outset of the King's Great Matter, De Fuensalida, Spain's ambassador to England, told King Ferdinand of having learned of 'certain scruples of conscience' of Henry VIII. See *CSP*, vol. 2, #8, 11 May 1509, King Ferdinand the Catholic to Gutier Gomez De Fuensalida, Knight Commander of Membrilla, and Ambassador in England, pp. 7-19.

9. **Did Wolsey originate Henry's scruples about Leviticus?** Bernard, *The King's Reformation*, 1-2, concludes that the accusation that Wolsey originated the Leviticus argument 'lacks plausibility' although Bernard acknowledges that many early commentators have blamed Wolsey, including Ambassador Mendoza, Polydore Virgil, William Roper, John Foxe, and Nicholas Harpsfield. See Bernard, *The King's Reformation*, 1-2 and notes 4-8. George Cavendish, Wolsey's devoted gentleman usher, and therefore far from a disinterested observer, recites that it was Henry who broke the news to Wolsey about his determination to obtain an annulment and marry Anne Boleyn, and that Wolsey sank to his knees and pleaded for an hour with the king not to terminate his marriage to Catherine. Cavendish also describes Wolsey's confirmation of that event in the cardinal's deathbed conversation with Sir William Kingston, Constable of the Tower of London. Cavendish, *Life of Cardinal Wolsey*, 203-4, 388-89. In addition, according to Cavendish's recital of the first full day of the Blackfriars trial, 21 June 1529, Wolsey had Henry confirm on the record that Wolsey had not initially proposed the annulment and indeed had 'been rather against me in attempting or setting forth' on the annulment matter. Cavendish, *Life of Cardinal Wolsey*, 218-19.

10. **Catherine blamed Wolsey:** See Bernard, *The King's Reformation*, 1-2.

11. **Henry VIII's early theological education:** Initially, as the second son in the royal family, young Prince Henry might have been presumed destined for a high position in the Church. His early biographer, Lord Herbert, theorised that he could have received specialised early education in theology. See Herbert, *History*, 109. But in that era, theology would have been a part of a classical childhood education in any aristocratic family. Henry succeeded his brother Arthur as heir apparent when Henry was only ten years old. Thus, as Professor Scarisbrick points out, it is unlikely that Henry's adult interests

and abilities in sophisticated ecclesiastical matters received any appreciable boost from being the 'Spare' and not the 'Heir' until he was ten years old. See Scarisbrick, *Henry VIII*, 5.

Regardless of his childhood education, when Henry became an adult, he developed great interest and competence in theological matters. In 1528, Cardinal Campeggio reported on his private discussion with Henry about the pope's power of dispensation: 'His Majesty has so diligently studied this matter, that I believe in this case he knows more than a great theologian and jurist.' *LP*, vol. 4, #4858, 17 October 1528, CAMPEGGIO to SANGA, 2101.

12. **Henry's alternate version of the origin of his argument:** At various times over the six years of the dispute, Henry also told a variation of his story as to the origin of his scruples about the validity of his marriage to Catherine. Henry's standard story was that he first realised the invalidity of his marriage in the course of his personal study of the Bible. However, he sometimes claimed that his concerns were first aroused during negotiations for the marriage of his daughter Princess Mary to French royalty. In this alternate version, it was the French ambassador, the Bishop of Tarbes Gabriel de Gramont, who raised the question of Princess Mary's legitimacy on the grounds of doubt as to the validity of Henry's marriage to Catherine. Wolsey told Henry that he had related the Tarbes story to Bishop Fisher 'thus declaring the whole matter unto him as was devised with you at York Place'. *LP*, vol. 4, #3231, 5 July 1527, WOLSEY to HENRY VIII, 1471.

   John Sherren Brewer (1809–79), an early editor of the key *Letters and Papers* calendar of documents relating to Henry VIII, accepts the phrase 'as devised with you' as showing that the Tarbes story was no more than 'a political figment arranged between the King and Wolsey, when it had become necessary to take fresh action in the matter, and find some justification for their proceedings in the face of Europe'. *LP*, vol. 4, Brewer, Introduction to Section 4, p. ccxxiii and n. 1 [n. 46 in online version]. For extensive analysis of this issue, see Lingard, *History*, 4:234, n. 6, 237, 252, 256, 290–91 [Note N]; see also Burnet, *The King's Reformation*, vol. 1, p. 76; ibid. vol 4, Appendix, 547; Cavendish, *Life of Cardinal Wolsey*, 219 [erroneously referring to the Bishop of Bayonne]; Fisher, *History*, 269; Herbert, *History*, 346; Kelly, *Trials*, 29, n. 21; Mattingly, *Catherine of Aragon*, 244.

13. **Text of Pope Julius II Bull of dispensation:** See Herbert. *History*, pp. 370–73.
14. **Papal Infallibility:** The doctrine of Papal Infallibility had early roots in Christianity. But it had a very limited scope, applying only to the rare pronouncements declared by the pontiff *ex cathedra* – as a teaching directed by the pope to all Christians and expressly defining a doctrine of

morals to be held by all in the Church. Papal Infallibility did not extend to every pronouncement of a pope. Julius's 1503 Bull of dispensation was that pope's particular ruling about applying Church law to a particular case, which included findings of facts upon which the ruling was based. Pope Clement therefore had the power to determine that the dispensation was in error, and could issue a corrective ruling. See *New Advent Catholic Encyclopedia online*, s.v. infallibility, at *http://www.newadvent. org/cathen/07790a.htm* [accessed 12 June 2023]; *Encyclopaedia Britannica online*, s.v. Papal infallibility, at *https://www.britannica.com/topic/papal-infallibility* [accessed 12 June 2023].

15. **Clement's style of delay:** See Pocock, *Records*, vol. 1, 128 (13 April 1528 letter from Gardiner and Casale to Wolsey): 'Assuring your grace that the pope's holiness although he perceiveth better and sooner all that is spoken than any other, yet to give an answer yea or nay, *nunquam vidi tarn tardum* [I have never seen anyone so slow]'. See also Starkey, *Six Wives*, 217: '[Clement] was a wily Florentine, who turned prevarication into an art form. He would talk, at inordinate length, without ever reaching a conclusion. And he knew every word, in mellifluous Italian or fluent Latin, apart from "yes" or "no".' Francis Hackett, *Henry VIII*, 186, noted that Gardiner and Fox reported: 'His holiness is *cunctator maximus* [the prince of delayers].'

16. **Henry's legal technicalities and the consummation issue:** Henry's supporters also attacked the Bull of dispensation from Julius II because the pope had not expressly dispensed for the impediment of 'Public Honesty', the appearance of immorality. Henry eventually abandoned this very complex technical argument, in part because it was tangled up with the disputed factual question of whether Catherine's marriage to Arthur had been consummated. In the bundle of papers Catherine sent to Pope Clement accompanying her appeal from the legatine trial at Blackfriars was her insistence that she had still been a virgin at her marriage to Henry. See Kelly, *Trials*, 137: 'The masterstroke was her assertion, borne witness to by the pope in his subsequent letter to the king, that she was so certain of the truth of her virginity and of Henry's knowledge of it that she would rest content with whatever statement the king himself would make upon the matter under oath.' See also ibid., 137–38 at n. 8, 139–40 at n. 11; *LP*, vol. 4, #5762, 9 July 1529, BENET, CASALE and VANNES to WOLSEY, 2566; ibid. #5994, 7 October 1529, CLEMENT VII. to HENRY VIII, 2668.

17. **Clement was willing to cure any technical problems with Julius's Bull of dispensation:** See *LP*, vol. 4, #4858, 17 October 1528, CAMPEGGIO to SANGA, 2101; Kelly, *Trials*, 139–40 at n. 11.

18. **Natural Law doctrine:** In the twentieth century, we have been exposed to modern legal theories that discount the significance of the traditional philosophy of natural law. See, e.g., Oliver Wendell Holmes, 'Natural Law', 40–44.
19. **Henry's 'proof' that the marriage was void:** Inability to produce a male heir was claimed by Henry to be the divine punishment specified in Lev. 20:21, and thus proof that his marriage to Catherine was not valid: See Starkey, *Six Wives*, 203–4.
20. **Clement claimed that he was not an expert in canon law:** See Pocock, *Records*, Letter 51, 13 April 1528, GARDINER and SIR GREGORY CASALE to WOLSEY, 1:120: 'His holiness said that this matter consisted in the knowledge of the law, whereof he is ignorant, and must needs therefore depend upon the resolution of them which be learned in that faculty, with whom he hath counselled....' (Cf. *LP*, vol. 4, #4167, 13 April 1528, GARDINER and SIR GREGORY CASALE to WOLSEY, 1837–38.) It is likely that Clement was overstating his ignorance of canon law so that he could justify his tactics of delegation and procrastination.
21. **Protecting papal authority:** Clement was unwilling to diminish papal authority to dispense. See Bernard, *The King's Reformation*, 24–5: 'Thus Henry's cases in canon law were not strong. One [the argument, that the Leviticus Prohibitions were natural law and could not be dispensed by any pope] challenged papal authority as such and thus raised complex and controversial questions... [and Henry's second argument was based on several alleged technical issues in the original dispensation].' At Cardinal Campeggio's first private meeting with the king in 1528, the cardinal proposed that the pope would resolve any moral scruples of Henry by issuing a new dispensation to cure the technical issues in the original dispensation of Julius II. Campeggio reported that Henry adamantly rejected this resolution: 'He told me plainly that he wanted nothing else than a declaration whether the marriage is valid or not, – he himself always presupposing its invalidity; and I believe that an angel descending from Heaven would be unable to persuade him otherwise.' (*LP*, vol. 4, #4858, 17 October 1528, CAMPEGGIO to SANGA, 2101.)
22. **Deut. 25:5-10:** *Bible (The Holy Bible)*, Douay-Rheims 1609/1610 (modern spelling and type font version). Some spelling and punctuation in the quoted text have been updated for convenience of the modern reader.
23. **Catholic views of levirate marriage:** See Bernard, *The King's Reformation*, 17–18; Fischer, *History*, 302; Katz, *History*, 16–23; Kelly, *Trials*, 15–16; Scarisbrick, *Henry VIII*, 164–65, 168–91.

6 Henry's Legal Strategies

1. **Papal legate**: Pope Leo X initially made Cardinal Wolsey the papal legate in England in 1518.
2. **Westminster trial**: For a detailed record of the Westminster trial, see, Kelly, *Trials*, 21–32.
3. **John Fisher supported the marriage**: England's leading theologian of that time, Bishop John Fisher, had told Wolsey that Henry's marriage to Catherine was unquestionably valid, but that in any event, the pope had the power to dispense. See *LP*, vol. 4, #3148, June 1527, BISHOP OF ROCHESTER [JOHN FISHER] to WOLSEY, 1434; Kelly, *Trials*, 29.
4. **News of Sack of Rome**: See *LP*, vol. 4, #3136, 28 May 1527, [Bishop of Bath and Wells, John] CLERK to WOLSEY, 1426; Kelly, *Trials*, 29, note 22.
5. **Wolsey as Deputy Pope**: Wolsey had arranged for Girolamo Ghinucci, Bishop of Worcester, to negotiate for an emergency commission for Wolsey to be deputy pope while Clement was under actual or threatened imprisonment by Charles V: '… by which, without informing the Pope of your [Henry's] purpose, I may delegate such judges as the Queen will not refuse; and if she does, the cognizance of the cause shall be devolved upon me, and by a clause to be inserted in the general commission no appeal be allowed from my decision to the Pope…'. *LP*, vol. 4, #3400, 5 September 1527, WOLSEY to HENRY VIII, 1538.
6. **The Clement–Charles relationship**: See Scarisbrick, *Henry* VIII, 198–202.
7. **Knight's mission**: See Scarisbrick, *Henry VIII*, 202–4.
8. **Knight's conditional dispensation**: See *LP*, vol. 4, #3686, 23 December 1527, THE DIVORCE, 1652; Scarisbrick, *Henry* VIII, 202–6. Herbert, *History*, 393–95 contains an English-language version of the document.
9. **Wording of the dispensation**: Clement's initial dispensation may have offered at least some potential benefits for Henry. By specifically authorising that, conditional upon annulment of the marriage to Catherine, Henry could marry Anne Boleyn, the wording of the dispensation would dispense some other possible impediments to marrying Anne. First, Henry had previously had sexual relations with Anne's sister, Mary Boleyn, when Mary was his mistress. This could cause his marriage to Anne to violate the Leviticus Prohibitions of sexual relations with two living sisters. (Lev. 18:18.) Second, no one knew with certainty whether Henry had also already had, or perhaps would have, sexual relations with Anne before their betrothal, which would have also constituted an illicit relationship. Third, marrying Anne would be barred if she had previously entered into a precontract to marry another. Clement undertook to dispense any precontract provided that betrothal had not been physically consummated. This particular dispensation could

have applied to the early negotiations for Anne to marry the Ormond heir James Butler, or to her later relationship with Percy. Assuming that the facts had been fully and truthfully disclosed to Clement, all of these ancillary dispensations might have been sufficient to resolve such potential impediments if the main conditional Bull became effective. A mixed Latin and English draft indicating what Henry and Wolsey were seeking can be found at *LP*, vol. 4, #3643, 6 December 1527, The DIVORCE, §1. [Copy of Bull to be submitted to Clement VII], 1637.

10. **Knight revealed Henry's intention to marry Anne Boleyn**: Knight thoughtlessly disclosed that Henry was acting with a specific new bride in mind, and identified Anne Boleyn. He thereby destroyed Henry's carefully constructed story that the king's request for an annulment was an obligation of conscience caused by his discovery that his marriage to Catherine was prohibited by God's law. See Fisher, *History*, 272; Friedmann, *Anne Boleyn*, 39; Francis Hackett, *Henry VIII*, 178.

11. **How a decretal commission worked**: See Kelly, *Trials*, 54; Bernard, *The King's Reformation*, 9–10; Katz, *History*, 17–18.

12. **Clement suggested that Henry first marry Anne and then litigate**: See *LP*, vol. 4, #3802, 13 January 1528, The DIVORCE [extract from letter of Casale], 1694; see also Herbert, *History*, 349: '*Ut statim committat causam, aliam uxorem ducat, litem sequitur...*' ['In order to commit the case at once, he should take another wife, the suit to follow'].

13. **Henry declined to first marry Anne and then litigate**: Later, Casale confirmed to Wolsey that Clement's suggestion had never been sincere: 'Their [Clement and his cardinals'] proposal that the King should first marry was only a device to get rid of responsibility.' *LP*, vol. 4, #4120, 31 March 1528, CASALE, GARDINER and FOXE to WOLSEY, 1822.

14. **Henry suggested he be allowed two wives**: *LP*, vol. 4, #4977, November 1528, The POPE [Henry's instructions to Sir Francis Bryan and Peter Vannes, sent to the Court of Rome], 2158. The same document is quoted in Herbert, *History*, 356. See also *LP*, vol. 4, #4979 [November 1528], [Peter Vannes' list of 20 major items to be handled in Rome], 2161: '6. For the King to marry two wives, with a legitimation of the issue of the second.'

15. **Clement revives the idea of allowing Henry two wives**: *LP*, vol. 4, #6627, 18 September 1530, SIR GREGORY CASALE to HENRY VIII, 2987.

16. **Clement expresses reservations about allowing two wives**: *LP*, vol. 4, Appendix #261, September [1530], [GHINUCCI to HENRY VIII], 3189.

17. **Clement decides that he will not allow Henry to marry two wives**: *LP*, vol. 4, #6705, 27 October 1530, W. BENET to HENRY VIII, 3023–24.

18. **Interpreting negotiations:** We should keep in mind that sixteenth-century international negotiations regularly involved lies, insincere promises, and deception, even when, or perhaps especially when, a king or a pope was involved. Therefore, the negotiating positions taken by Henry and Clement do not necessarily reflect their respective true concerns, intentions, or motivations.
19. **The final word on the two-wives solution:** As we shall see in Part III below, the two-wives solution later resurfaced for Henry from a different source than the Vatican. By the beginning of 1531, Henry had imported from Italy a former rabbi, Mark Raphael, to serve as his royal advisor on Jewish law. Henry planned to use Jewish law to convince Pope Clement to grant the annulment. Mark Raphael's first advice was that Jewish law would permit Henry to take Anne as a second wife, but Henry rejected the idea immediately as being unacceptable to his subjects and the rest of the world. See *LP*, vol. 5, #70, 31 January 1531, [CHAPUYS to CHARLES V], 31–32.
20. **Clement's *pollicitation*:** An English-language version of the *pollicitation*, by which Clement gives his solemn promise 'upon the word of a pope', can be found in Herbert, *History*, 352–54. Cf. *LP*, vol. 4, #4169, April 1528, CLEMENT VII, 1843. Note that surviving copies of such private, secret documents often include deletions or errors. Sometimes they can be preliminary drafts that may or may not have been delivered in that form.
21. **Henry and Wolsey seek the decretal commission:** See Bernard, *The King's Reformation*, 9–10. For detailed reports of the new negotiations, see also *LP*, vol. 4, #4120, 31 March 1528, CASALE, GARDINER and FOXE to WOLSEY, 1819–22; ibid., #4167, 13 April 1528, GARDINER and SIR GREGORY CASALE to WOLSEY, 1837–42; ibid., #4168, April 1528, GREGORY CASALE to [VANNES], 1842.
22. **Clement issues the joint decretal commission:** See Bernard, *The King's Reformation*, 9–10; see also *LP*, vol. 4, #4345, 8 June 1528, CLEMENT VII (referring to draft of joint commission), 1909; ibid., #4380: 15 June 1528, THE DIVORCE (extract from letters from Casale), 1920.
23. **Campeggio expected to receive the bishopric of Durham as a reward for helping Henry:** See *LP*, vol. 4, #5519, 5 May 1529, FRANCIS BRIAN to HENRY VIII. 2441: 'As for what you write to us, that Campeggio is your servant, and will do what he can for you, these are fair words only because he wishes to have the bishopric of Durham.'
24. **Secrecy for the decretal Bull:** See *LP*, vol. 4, #4897, 1 November 1528, WOLSEY to SIR GREGORY CASALE, 2120–21. It turned out that Clement soon repented of even these arrangements for the secret document. He promptly sent his papal nuncio Francesco Campana to England in December

1528 to give Campeggio new instructions to burn the decretal Bull. It has never been seen since. See Herbert, *History*, 363.

25. **Campeggio was ordered to avoid reaching a judgment:** Clement expected Campeggio to convince Henry to 'conform his mind to persevere in this marriage, without the publication of a judicial sentence'. *LP*, vol. 4, #4881, 28 October 1528, CAMPEGGIO to SANGA, 2111.

26. **Taking religious orders:** Campeggio and Wolsey urged Catherine to enter a religious order to avoid a trial. See *LP*, vol. 4, #4880, 28 October 1528, CAMPEGGIO to SANGA, 2111.

    If either spouse joined a religious order under a vow of chastity, he or she was considered to become 'married to Christ' after a spiritual death and rebirth, thereby ending the previous marriage. This manoeuvre was the closest the Church came to a voluntary divorce, and it had the advantage of not affecting the legitimacy of any children of the previous marriage. See ibid., #5179, January 1529, WOLSEY to KNIGHTE and BENET, 2277; see also Scarisbrick, *Henry VIII*, 214, regarding Queen Jeanne de Valois of France ending her marriage to King Louis XII by taking religious orders. But see Kelly, *Trials*, 14, n. 15, distinguishing that case. Kelly strongly questions whether joining a religious order requiring a pledge of celibacy would qualify for terminating an existing marriage, calling such an alleged ground for divorce for Henry VIII and Catherine of Aragon a 'highly dubious and revolutionary expedient'. Ibid., 232. See also *LP*, vol. 4, #5344, 3 March 1529, PETER VANNES to WOLSEY, pp. 2351–2368: 'The most learned of the advocates consulted thinks that the Pope cannot give a dispensation that the King may marry again on the Queen entering a religion. Rome, 3 March 1528.'

27. **Catherine refused to join a religious order to end the marriage:** See *LP*, vol. 4, #4875, 26 October 1528, CAMPEGGIO to SALVIATI, 2109: '[Queen Catherine, in confession to Campeggio] ... assured me that she would never do so [make a religious vow of chastity]; that she intended to live and die in the estate of matrimony, into which God had called her, and that she should always be of that opinion, and would not change it.'

28. **Catherine at the Blackfriars trial:** Catherine's appearance at Blackfriars including her plea to Henry are described in Cavendish, *Wolsey*, 213–218. Cavendish's wording was not from a formal court record or from any draft that may have been written by Catherine, but it was his later recollection as Wolsey's loyal gentleman usher who was present at the hearing. Cavendish apparently was still writing the draft of his book during the period of the marriage of Queen Mary I and Philip of Spain, 1554–1558, since he refers to 'King Philip, now our sovereign lord'. See ibid., xi, 102. Cavendish is

Notes

careful to introduce his recital of Catherine's speech with the signal 'in effect', indicating that it was not a verbatim transcript (ibid., 214). He recites her oath that she was a virgin when she married Henry as follows (ibid., 215): 'And when ye had me at the first, I take God to be my judge, I was a true maid without touch of man; and whether it be true or no, I put it to your [Henry's] conscience.'

Catherine had previously confirmed the non-consummation of her marriage with Arthur during her confession to Cardinal Campeggio when she swore that, during her during her entire brief marriage to Prince Arthur, 'she did not sleep with him more than seven nights, *et che da lui restò intacta et incorrupta, come venne dal ventre di sua madre* [and remained as intact and pure as she came from the womb of her mother]'. See *LP*, vol. 4, #4875, 26 October 1528, CAMPEGGIO to SALVIATI, 2109.

29. **Henry claimed that he would be content with Catherine but for his concerns for God's laws:** With no regard for the truth, Henry stated at the Blackfriars trial that Catherine was 'as true, as obedient, and as conformable a wife as I could in my fantasy wish or desire ... with whom I could be as well content to continue during my life, if our marriage may stand with God's laws, as with any woman alive'. Cavendish, *Life of Cardinal Wolsey*, 218-220.

30. **Clement noted that Henry would not swear to Catherine's lack of virginity:** See Kelly, *Trials*, 139-40 [quoting from Clement's letter to Henry dated October 7, 1529]: 'But if it is true, as the queen herself affirms in her mandate, that she was not known by Arthur, and you yourself know better – she is prepared to stand freely by your oath – there is no doubt that one dispensed in this case is safe in the forum of conscience.'

31. **The consummation issue:** The question of whether Catherine and Arthur's five-month marriage had been consummated became a very complex but highly significant issue in the King's Great Matter. Because the question had important relevance at different times for different issues between the English and Spanish royal interests, each side, except for Catherine herself, took some inconsistent positions over time as to whether Catherine's first marriage had or had not been consummated.

32. **Fisher's opposition to Henry:** John Fisher was later named cardinal by Pope Paul III, just before his execution by Henry – a king who did not readily suffer disloyalty. Recently, in 1935, Pope Pius XI canonised Fisher as St John Fisher, jointly with the canonisation of St Thomas More, another devout Catholic who dared to oppose Henry VIII's Reformation of the Church, also at the cost of his life.

33. **Recess of legatine trial by Campeggio before judgment:** See Kelly, *Trials*, 127–28 [quoting from the notarial court record held in the Cambridge University Library]; Cavendish, *Life of Cardinal Wolsey*, 229–31.
34. **The Vatican had a registry for Briefs:** See Blackfriars trial testimony of Cardinal Augustinus Spinola regarding the letter 'in the form of a breve' from Julius II to Henry VII dated 6 July 1504, found in the apostolic chamber 'in the book of the register of the breves of the first, second and third years of Pope Julius II'. Spinola's testimony of the contents of that letter is set forth in Herbert, *History*, 384. Compare the summary of Julius's letter of 6 July 1504 at *CSP-Spain*, vol. 1, #396, 6 July 1504, pp. 327–8.
35. **Catherine produces the Spanish Brief:** See *LP*, vol. 4, #4977, November 1528, The POPE [Instructions to Sir Francis Bryan and Peter Vannes, sent to the Court of Rome], 2155: '... there has been exhibited on the Queen's behalf an authentic copy of a Brief, of which she affirms the original to be in the Emperor's hands, passed by pope Julius and subscribed by Sigismund, then scribe or secretary apostolic, containing such words as might seem totally to remove all the faults found in the dispensation of pope Julius...'. See also ibid., #4978, 2159; ibid., #4980, 2162; Bernard, *The King's Reformation*, 10, 23.
36. **The Bull stated that the parties' motivation was a desire to continue and expand peace between Spain and England:** See Herbert, *History*, 271–2.
37. **The Brief made the factual issue of motivation irrelevant:** See Herbert, *History*, 276.
38. **Consummation language in the Bull and the Brief:** See Herbert, *History*, pp. 370, 372, quoting the words of the Bull; compare the wording of the Brief in Herbert, *History*, pp. 373, which omits '*forsan*' ['perhaps']. In a most surprising and critical typographical error, this 1870 edition of the Herbert *History* states the correct Latin clauses for the Bull and the Brief, stating '*forsan*' only in the Bull, but erroneously also includes the word 'perhaps' in the English translation of the Brief on page 376.
39. **Technical objections to the Spanish Brief:** For a sampling of documents showing England's immediate belief that the Spanish Brief was fraudulent, including many specific grounds asserted for that belief, see, in *LP*, vol. 4, the following documents: #5375, 14 March 1529; #5376, sections 2 and 33, 14 March 1529; #5440, April 1529; #5441, 6 April 1529; #5452, April 1529; #5470, 20 April 1529; #5471, 20 April 1529. England's doubts as to authenticity of the Spanish Brief were reinforced when Henry VIII's ministers were allowed only limited access to examine the original Brief.
40. **Charles protected the original Brief from fear of England's treachery:** Charles insisted that the Spanish Brief was authentic, and would not give up its

possession because he feared that the English would alter or destroy it. See, in *CSP-Spain*, vol. 3, part 2: #563, 1 October 1528; #592, 23 November 1528; #618, 25 January 1529; see also *LP*, vol. 4, #5301, 16 February 1529. It has been generally accepted for the past several centuries that the English claims of forgery, whether or not sincere, were wrong, and that the Brief is authentic. See Lingard, *History*, 4:294: 'I am inclined to believe that the breve [Brief] was genuine.'

41. **Clement recalls the trial to Rome:** See Bernard, *The King's Reformation*, 10–11.
42. **Clement claims that he wants to help Henry:** *LP*, vol. 4, #5474, 21 April 1529, CLEMENT VII to HENRY VIII, 2414-15; see also Bernard, *The King's Reformation*, 11.
43. **Henry's envoys felt that they could not convince the pope:** See *LP*, vol. 4, #5213, 26 January 1529, BRYAN to HENRY VIII, 2298; ibid., #5393, 20 March 1529, TUKE to WOLSEY, 2370; ibid., #5481, 21 April 1529, BRIAN to HENRY VIII, 2418; ibid., #5519, 5 May 1529, FRANCIS BRIAN to HENRY VIII, 2441; see also Bernard, *The King's Reformation*, 11–12.

7 Henry's Christian Theological Strategy

1. **The origin of Henry's next strategy:** The story of this very significant event, which occurred as a matter of chance, is retold in several historical works. The story is based upon the report in John Foxe's hugely popular *Book of Martyrs*, initially published in 1563. See Foxe, *Book of Martyrs*, 455–58. Although Foxe did not write in an era of modern historiography, his version of this event has been generally accepted by many historians over the centuries. One of the preeminent modern historians of the Great Matter, Professor J. J. Scarisbrick, concludes, 'There seems no reason to doubt the substantial truth of this story. It rings true...'. Scarisbrick, *Henry VIII*, 255.
2. **Cranmer's idea:** According to John Foxe, Stephen Gardiner tried to present Cranmer's idea to the king as if it had been conceived by the two envoys. But before Gardiner could accomplish this, Edward Fox disclosed to Henry the full story of the dinner meeting when Cranmer made his suggestion. See Foxe, *Book of Martyrs*, 456.
3. **Gardiner's letter from Cambridge:** See Burnet, *History of the Reformation*, 4:130 [doc. no. 32, February 1530, orig. p. 85]. While we are fortunate to have access to this eyewitness account of the Cambridge University negotiations, we should bear in mind that although this was a first-person report, it was not written by a disinterested witness. As was true for all of Henry's agents, the careers and lives of Gardiner and Fox could be upended

or destroyed if the king were to have an extremely adverse reaction to how they were discharging their assignment and what results they were achieving. Reports to Henry by his agents were undoubtedly influenced by a strong desire to please the king, and we should carefully consider them in that context.

4. **Gardiner's hopes for the faculty vote**: Ibid., 132–33 [orig. 86–87]. It is not clear to us how Gardiner was calculating the number of votes needed for a 'two parts' majority – and it also might not have been clear to him or to the Cambridge faculty at the time, because neither fractions nor decimals were commonly understood or used in Europe in the early sixteenth century. With modern mathematics, it would seem that his assurances to Henry were guilty of some serious rounding up: With 29 voting members, Gardiner's tally shows that only 16 (16/29 = 55.2%) are initially committed to Henry. To get to a two-parts majority (2/3, or 66.67%) would require 4 more positive votes (20/29 = 68.9%), or 3 more positive votes and one absence of a negative voter (19/28 = 67.9%). But Gardiner assures the king that to win the required two-parts majority they need only get 3 more votes (19/29 = 65.5%) or get 2 more positives and arrange for one absence (18/28 = 64.3%). With modern mathematics, neither alternative would reach the 66.67% minimum for approval. See Pumfrey, 'History of Fractions' (Fractions as we use them today didn't exist in Europe until the seventeenth century); see also Sanford, 'La Disme of Simon Stevin'; *Wikipedia*, s.v. Simon Stevin (Stevin wrote the first Western book on decimals, which was not published until 1585).

5. **Buckmaster describes Henry's reaction to the Cambridge determination**: See Burnet, *History*, vol. 6, Document 16, 6:28 at 6:32–35 [orig. p. 20 at pp. 23–24].

6. **Henry's initial request to Cambridge**: Ibid., 6:28.

7. **The Cambridge faculty opinion**: Ibid., 32.

8. **Can a pope dispense natural law?** Ibid., 33.

9. **Affinity incest depends upon first husband and wife becoming one flesh**: See *JPS Hebrew-English Tanakh*, footnote *a* to Lev. 18:16, referring to Gen. 2:24.

10. **Evidence as to consummation of Arthur's marriage**: Henry wanted to prove that Catherine's marriage to Arthur had been consummated. This would help establish that the Leviticus Prohibitions barred him from marrying his brother's widow. As part of the record for the Blackfriars trial, Henry's counsel presented testimony from over a dozen witnesses that Arthur and Catherine had consummated their marriage. See *LP*, vol. 4, #5774, July 1529, KATHARINE OF ARAGON, depositions, sections 1–17, 2576–81.

11. **Catherine's possible pregnancy**: See Starkey, *Six Wives*, 79.

Notes

12. 'I have been this night in the midst of Spain': *LP*, vol. 4, #5774, section 3, July 1529, KATHARINE OF ARRAGON [Deposition of Sir Antony Willoughby], 2577.
13. **Henry disavows his initial claims that Catherine came to him a virgin as being a young man's jest:** See *LP*, vol. 6, #351, 15 April 1533, CHAPUYS to CHARLES V, 164.
14. **Spain wanted to keep the benefits of the original marriage treaty by having Catherine marry Prince Henry:** See *CSP-Spain*, vol. 1, #317, 10 May 1502, Ferdinand and Isabella, Instructions given to Duke de Estrada, 267–69 [Spain to demand return of first half of marriage portion, payment of widow's dowry, and that Catherine be sent back to Spain]. But these were only Spain's first moves in the new wedding negotiations. For Spain's true bargaining position, see ibid., #322, 14 June 1502, Ferdinand and Isabella to Ferdinand Duke de Estrada, 269–71 [Their request that Catherine return was only a negotiating ploy]: '... you should speak immediately to the King of England about her coming over here, as you received directions. Do this in such a way that he may believe we are desirous of it, for in this manner the business may best be furthered.' See also ibid., #323: 'Some persons have advised the Princess of Wales not to accept what the King of England has offered her. The advice is bad. She must accept whatever she can get.'
15. **Catherine's parents initially uncertain about consummation:** See *CSP-Spain*, vol. 1, #325, 16 June 1502, Ferdinand and Isabella to Ferdinand Duke de Estrada, 269–71: 'Be careful also to get at the truth as regards the fact whether the Prince and Princess of Wales consummated the marriage, since nobody has told us about it. You must, moreover, use all the flattering persuasions you can to prevent them from concealing it from you.'
16. **Catherine's parents assured of her virginity by Doña Elvira:** The original virginity report of Doña Elvira has been lost, but it is referred to in Queen Isabella's instructions to Estrada. See ibid., #327, 12 July 1502, Queen Isabella to Ferdinand, Duke de Estrada, 272–76: '... since it is already known for a certainty that the said Princess of Wales, our daughter, remains as she was here (for so Doña Elvira has written to us), endeavour to have the said contract [for Catherine to marry Prince Henry] agreed to immediately...'.
17. **Catherine's parents nevertheless agree that there had been consummation:** See excerpt from Ferdinand's letter to Ambassador Rojas at Appendix B, note 16, below.
18. **Catherine and Arthur shared a bed seven times during their marriage:** See *LP*, vol. 4, #4875, 26 October 1528, CAMPEGGIO to SALVIATI, 2109: '[In confession to Cardinal Campeggio, Catherine affirmed that she did not sleep

with Arthur more than seven nights,] *et che da lui restò intacta et incorrupta, come venne dal ventre di sua madre.* [and remained as intact and pure as she came from the womb of her mother].'

19. **Catherine declared to the pope that she came to Henry a virgin:** See *LP*, vol. 4, #5762, 9 July 1529, BENET, CASALE and VANNES to WOLSEY, 2566.

20. **Catherine's oath of virginity:** Catherine swore that she had been a virgin when she married Henry, and challenged him to take his oath to the contrary. See Cavendish, *Life of Cardinal Wolsey*, 215: 'And when ye had me at the first, I take God to be my judge, I was a true maid without touch of man; and whether it be true or no, I put it to your conscience.' See also Kelly, *Trials*, 139–40 and n. 11 (quoting from Clement's letter in Latin to Henry of 7 October 1529, found in Augustinus Theiner, *Vetera Monumenta*, Rome, 1864, p. 566), regarding Catherine's willingness to have the question of her virginity at the time she married Henry be decided by what he would swear to: '... she is prepared to stand freely by your oath ...'.

21. **St Nicholas hostel:** On the relationship of the Cambridge hostels to the university, see Roach, 'The University of Cambridge: The Middle Ages', 150–66: 'St. Nicholas's Hostel was prominent among the houses of jurists, and had many eminent men among its members. It also seems to have had a reputation for rowdiness...'. See at footnote 151.

22. **Buckmaster describes the Cambridge riot:** Burnet, *History*, 6:34, doc. 16.

23. **Chapuys's report of the Cambridge riot:** *CSP-Spain*, vol. 4 (i), #270, 16 March 1530, Eustace Chapuys to the Emperor, 472–91.

24. **Henry's threats to remove England from the authority of the pope:** See Bernard, *The King's Reformation*, 30–35, and documents cited there. The English Reformation appears to have been more than a late and unanticipated potential development of the King's Great Matter. Bernard makes a strong case that many previous historians have overlooked the significance of Henry's early campaign of using the Reformation to threaten Clement in order to obtain a papal annulment.

25. **Henry obtained the Cambridge opinion by trickery:** See Burnet, *History of the Reformation*, 4:130 [doc. no. 32]. Gardiner admitted that he had to manipulate the faculty's vote for delegation of the decision to a smaller committee, which he was then able to fill with Henry's supporters: '[The motion for the faculty to delegate the decision to a committee] was first denied: when it was asked again, it was even on both parties, to be denied or granted; and at the last, by labour of friends to cause some to depart the house which were against it, it was obtained...'. And see ibid., 4:131, 1:151; Lingard, *History*, 4:297, NOTE S-2.

Notes

26. **The Oxford riots:** See *CSP-Spain*, vol. 4 (i), #270, 16 March 1530, Chapuys to the Emperor, 472-491. Scarisbrick adds that Bishop Longland was one of those pelted with stones by Oxford women, and that another of Henry's agents was 'similarly treated when he was caught immobilised as he relieved himself against a town wall'. Scarisbrick, *Henry VIII*, p. 256.
27. **Fox at risk in Oxford:** Burnet, *History*, 6:34-35 [doc.16].
28. **The vote at Oxford:** For the Oxford vote, see document of delegation to a committee of 33 members, 4 April 1530 quoted at Herbert, *History*, pp. 471-2; also discussed at Burnet, *History*, 1:148-49; and see Lingard, *History*, 4:297-98, NOTE S-3; but see Fisher, *History*, 301 [the Oxford committee vote split 27 to 22 in Henry's favour, indicating a slim majority of a committee of 49 members].
29. **Stealing the Oxford seal:** The burglary story comes from an extremely pro-Catholic, anti-Henry author who has been generally attacked by later historians for bias and factual unreliability. See, Sander, *Schism*, 82. The dispute over credibility was, at least for historians, quite lively. Sander's burglary story received some support by Oxford historian Anthony Wood, who was in turn attacked by historian Gilbert Burnet. See Burnet, *History*, 1:148-49, 571-74.
30. **The condition included in the Cambridge opinion:** The Cambridge opinion was subject to a condition that the marriage of Catherine to Arthur had been consummated: '*cognitam a priori viro per carnalem copulam* [who had been known by her prior husband through sexual intercourse]'. Burnet, *History*, 6:32 [doc. 16].
31. **Henry's third letter to Oxford:** Burnet, *History*, 6:39 [doc.17(iii)].
32. **Henry's plan to obtain support of Sorbonne faculty:** *CSP-Spain*, vol. 4, part 1, #270, 16 March 1530, Eustace Chapuys to the Emperor, 472-91.
33. **Francis helped Henry to obtain favourable opinions:** Fisher, *History*, 302.
34. **Why Francis helped Henry:** Harpsfield, *Treatise*, 209.
35. **England's widespread bribery:** Ibid., 208-9. The English Angel was a gold coin originally issued by King Edward IV in 1464. It had enriched the Crown because it contained less gold than the old Noble coin that it replaced. See Knight, *Popular History*, 2:153-54.
36. **England's bribery in Italy:** *LP*, vol. 4, #6478, 27 June 1530, MAI to CHARLES V, 2912.
37. **England bribed using annual income awards:** *LP*, vol. 4, #6610, 11 September 1530, MAI to CHARLES V, 2979-80.
38. **England's tactics at the Sorbonne:** *LP*, vol. 4, #6399, 23 May 1530, DR. GARAY to CHARLES V, 2872.

39. **Imperial ambassador causes Venice to stop the Padua faculty from issuing opinions:** *LP*, vol. 4, #6392, 17 May 1530, RODRIGO NIÑO to CHARLES V, 2869.
40. **Henry is determined to proceed:** *LP*, vol. 4, #6514, 13 July 1530, RODRIGO NIÑO to CHARLES V. 2930.
41. **England solicits opinions from unlearned friars:** *LP*, vol. 4, #6528, July 1530, RODRIGO NIÑO to CHARLES V, 2937.
42. **Stokesley solicits unlearned faculty opinions.** *LP*, vol. 4, #6537, 30 July 1530, MAI to CHARLES V, 2941.
43. **Surprise that the Bologna faculty does not need to be bribed:** *LP*, vol. 4, #6633, 23 September 1530, STOKESLEY to HENRY VIII, 2989.
44. **Croke the Tutor:** Croke had been Greek language tutor to Henry during his childhood, and later to Henry's illegitimate son, Henry Fitzroy. See Roth, *Renaissance*, 159; Burnet, *History*, 1:148.
45. **Croke obtains the Padua opinion:** Burnet, *History*, 4:134–35 [doc. 33, July 1, 1530].
46. **Croke's payments for opinions in 1530:** See *LP*, vol. 4, 1524–1530. Under today's standards, it is dismaying that Professor Croke so readily and regularly used lies, intimidation, and especially bribery to obtain individual and faculty opinions supporting Henry. Perhaps somewhat in Croke's defence, we can note that these techniques were the typical methods used by almost all of Henry's representatives in the King's Great Matter throughout Europe. Moreover, both the pope and the emperor on their parts did not hesitate to have their agents respond in kind.

8 Why Henry's Christian Sources Failed

1. **Importance of the Judah–Tamar story:** The significance of the Judah and Tamar story is intensified because of the importance of Judah. Although Judah was not technically one of the Jewish patriarchs, he was the son of Jacob who, according to the Hebrew Bible, becomes the ancestor of the Davidic monarchy and ultimately of the Messiah. See Is. 11:1; Kaplan, *The Real Messiah*, 46. And see *Tanach* (Artscroll/Stone Edition) p. 972, note to Is. 11.1: 'The Ten Tribes, which were exiled by the Assyrians, will also be redeemed by the future Messiah, who will descend from the son of Jesse i.e., David (*Rashi*).'
2. **Deuteronomy's levirate marriage provisions hurt Henry's case:** See Katz, *History*, 20: 'The apparent contradiction between Leviticus and Deuteronomy was glaring even at the beginning of Christian biblical interpretation and attracted the attention of Augustine, whose analysis was the starting-point for later exegesis. Augustine saw the problem as not only

Notes

resolvable, but resolvable in more than one way... The biblical references to levirate marriage seemed to support Augustine's view, unpleasant as it was to Henry VIII.'

3. **Levirate marriage in the Book of Ruth:** Naomi's statement to her daughters-in-law seems to presume a basic levirate-type marriage obligation for a brother to marry his widowed sister-in-law. The Book of Ruth does not, however, completely track all the provisions of Deuteronomy as interpreted in the Talmud and rabbinic commentary. For example, Naomi's hypothetical future sons would not have dwelt 'together' with their deceased brothers: their lifetimes would not have overlapped as is required in Deut. 25:5. This suggests that the levirate-type marriage references in the Book of Ruth and the actual levirate marriage provisions of Deut. 25:5–10 might both be derived from some common source of pre-biblical practice. See Ziegler, 'The Book of Ruth and Levirate Marriage', in *Ruth, From Alienation to Authority*, 362 ff.

4. **Levirate marriage and *halitzah* in Ruth:** Compare Ruth 1.11–13; 4:1–12 with Deut. 25:5–10; see Katz, *History*, 20; cf. Ziegler 'The Book of Ruth and Levirate Marriage', in *Ruth*, 362 ff.

5. **The Genealogy of Jesus:** Compare Matthew 1:16 with Luke 3:23; see, Katz, *History* 20.

6. **Translation of *Aririm*:** *Aririm*, pl., from *ariri*, 'stripped' or 'laid bare', used in this context to denote 'childless' or 'barren'. See Brown-Driver-Briggs, *Lexicon*, 792d (Strong's ref. number 6185); and see Katz, *History*, 21–22.

7. **Robert Wakefield:** There were no Jews openly residing in Tudor England. The golden age of English Christian Hebraists, led by John Selden, would not arrive until the seventeenth century. See Rosenblatt, *Chief Rabbi*.

8. **Wakefield's translation:** Even if the Hebrew Bible had used the word that Wakefield imagined it should have used (that the couple would be without '*bonim*', sons), that word still would not have made Henry's case. Although *bonim* is the Hebrew Bible word for 'sons', biblical Hebrew grammar also uses the same word to refer to a mixed gender group, 'children'. Compare, e.g., Gen. 3:16, 'In pain shall you bear children [*bonim*]', with Gen. 5:4: 'Adam ... begot sons [*bonim*] and daughters [*bonot*].' See J. Hackett, *Biblical Hebrew*, 28 [in the essential information box entitled 'The Feminine Plural in Biblical Hebrew']: 'The masculine plural is used for groups of items that are all masculine in gender *and* for groups that are mixed in gender' [italics in original].

9. **Wakefield changed his opinion:** After first defending Catherine, Wakefield bragged that he could provide Henry with a definitive opinion for the annulment that would silence Bishop Fisher's opposition. See *LP*, vol. 4,

#3233, [July 1527], RICH. PACE to HENRY VIII, 1472; ibid., #3234, [July 1527], R. WAKFELDE to HENRY VIII, 1472. Later biographers debated whether these documents showed that Wakefield was a mercenary. See *Chalmers' Biography*, 1812, s.v. 'Robert Wakefield (?–1537) – divine', 30:485.

10. **Only the pope could change the Vulgate translation:** See Katz, *History*, p. 22, discussing Bishop John Fisher's opposition to Wakefield's attack upon the Vulgate translation. Katz also cites other prominent Catholic theologians who opposed Henry's position.
11. **Levirate marriage provisions as tribal ritual:** See ibid., 19.
12. **Catholic opposition to levirate marriage:** See ibid., 22.
13. **Gregory's answer to Augustine's question V:** See Johnson, *Laws and Canons*, 1:69–70.
14. **St Theodore imposed a more relaxed standard:** In the seventh century, a later Archbishop of Canterbury, St Theodore, appears to have approved an even laxer standard than Pope St Gregory. Theodore allowed converts who had married their widowed sister-in-law before conversion to continue marital intercourse, stating, 'Though the marriage be unlawful, yet a man may entertain himself with such as he has.' See Johnson, *Laws and Canons*, 1:71, note r.
15. **Gregory and the power of Julius to dispense:** In his 1850 collection of canon law of the Church of England, author John Johnson recognises the implications of Gregory's leniency for converts: 'Any modern pope writing on this subject, would have said that the marriage was null, without his Holiness's dispensation: but a dispensation was a thing unheard of in those days, till the twelfth century.' Johnson, *Laws and Canons*, 1:71, note r.
16. **Innocent III reduced the degrees of relationship for the Leviticus Prohibitions:** See Grayzel, *The Church and the Jews*, 89, n. 3: 'In the IV Latera [Innocent III] succeeded in limiting the prohibition to four degrees of relationship [as specified by Gregory I], instead of the eight within which marriage had been prohibited [immediately] before his time.'
17. **Innocent III and Deuteronomy:** Ibid., 100 (Latin), 101 (English translation).
18. **Innocent III 'dispensation':** See ibid.
19. **Recent papal dispensations:** See Katz, *History*, 22–23; Kelly, *Trials*, 8–14; Scarisbrick, *Henry VIII*, 177–80.
20. **Dispensation for Catherine's sisters:** See Katz, *History*, 23; Kelly, *Trials*, 14; Scarisbrick, *Henry VIII*, 177.
21. **Dispensation for Henry's ancestor:** See Katz, *History*, 23; Kelly, *Trials*, 10.
22. **Dispensations by Pope Clement VII:** See Katz, *History*, 23; Scarisbrick, *Henry VIII*, 177.

9 Henry Turns to Jewish Law

1. **Consummation no longer an active issue:** There also remained open the question of whether the marriage of Catherine and Arthur had been consummated. However, by 1530, that issue was viewed by both sides as less a matter of theology than a question of fact, or perhaps a presumption of law. Although both Henry and Catherine continued to insist upon their respective versions of the facts, neither was enthusiastic about continuing to argue the question in a legal forum. Following Cranmer's suggested strategy, Henry now wanted to end further legal disputes and focus on the basic theological issues.

2. **Did Stokesley originate the idea of consulting Jewish authorities?** On 27 December 1529, Croke wrote to King Henry from Bologna that he was waiting until the pope and the emperor left the area before he would be able to start actively soliciting opinions supporting Henry's case. Croke states that, pursuant to Stokesley's instructions, his activities will include contacting the Jews: 'On their [the pope's and the emperor's] departure, [Croke] will treat with the Jews as Stokesley advised...'. *LP*, vol. 4, #6105, 27 December 1529, CROKE to HENRY VIII, 2723. In a letter to Henry attributed to the date of 24 January 1530, Croke repeats his intention to 'treat with the Jews, as Stoxley advised' when Clement and Charles leave the area. Ibid., #6161, 24 January 1530, CROKE to HENRY VIII, 2752. See also Roth, *Renaissance*, p.159: 'Before he [Croke] left, John Stokesley, later Bishop of London, advised him to put himself in contact also with the Jews, so as to ascertain what was their view regarding the interpretation and application of the Mosaic law in this delicate matter.' And see Katz, *History*, 23: 'It would appear that the initial impetus behind the appeal to Italian rabbinical authorities came from the new bishop of London, John Stokesley, sometime towards the end of November 1529.'

3. **Jews not bound by Deuteronomy:** *LP*, vol. 4, #6149, 18 January 1530, RICHARD CROKE to [STOKESLEY], 2745.

4. **Jews barred from England:** As discussed in Chapter 1, above, the Edict of Expulsion issued by King Edward I of England on 18 July 1290, expelled all Jews from the Kingdom of England. The expulsion edict was not overturned until the time of the Protectorate almost 360 years later, when Oliver Cromwell permitted Jews to return to England in approximately 1657.

5. **Exceptions to the exclusion of Jews:** Henry VIII's royal court was renowned as a centre of culture and music, and it is reported that some of his court musicians were Italian Jews. More significantly, since the time of the Spanish and Portuguese expulsions of their Jews in 1492 and 1496, some individual Jews found their way from Iberia to England either in transit while they were traveling to other lands, or temporarily to transact trade,

or for a few, even to reside there. Jews in Tudor England tried to live as invisibly as possible, as a part of a handful of very small, covert groups of Jews. See Katz, *History*, 1–3.

We have already noted the significance of the fact that the Holy Roman Emperor at the time of the Great Matter happened to be the nephew of Catherine of Aragon. Catherine's family also played a key role in the story of the Jewish expulsion from the Iberian Peninsula. Just four years after the 1492 expulsion of Jews from Spain by King Ferdinand and Queen Isabella, Portugal followed suit. On 5 December 1496, as required under the contract of marriage between King Manuel I of Portugal and the heiress apparent to the throne of Castile, Princess Isabella, who was Queen Isabella's daughter and Catherine of Aragon's older sister, King Manuel decreed that all Jews must convert to Catholicism or leave Portugal. This was especially tragic for the Jews, as many previously exiled Spanish Jews had fled to presumed safety in Portugal.

6. **English Christian Hebraists:** By the early sixteenth century, Christian Hebraists in Italy were studying Hebrew-language books that had been printed there for several decades. In England, however, it would take another century after Henry sought his annulment before a corps of English scholars including the great John Selden transformed themselves into Christian Hebraists. Hebrew scholarship ultimately became accessible in England thanks to the new printing press technology and the Hebrew-language publishing houses in Italy and the Netherlands. However, it wasn't until the seventeenth century that Christian academics in England finally had the resources to master Hebrew and Aramaic languages and study and write about Jewish interpretations of the laws and customs found in Torah, Talmud, and the *midrash* (rabbinic commentary). See Rosenblatt, *Chief Rabbi*.

7. **Jewish divorce:** In traditional Jewish practice, a divorce decree (a *get*) is typically issued, depending upon local custom, by either a local rabbi or a rabbinic court (*bet din*) of three, whose jurisdiction is limited to determining matters of Jewish law for Jews. See Klein, *Guide*, 476.

8. **Defender of the Faith:** After Henry VIII led England out of Roman Catholicism, and even after the Church of England ultimately rejected Catholicism and became a Protestant denomination, Henry and his successors to the throne maintained the official title of Defender of the Faith. It continues today to be part of the official title of King Charles III of the United Kingdom.

9. **Most, but not all, early Jewish religious documents were written in Hebrew or Aramaic:** In Diaspora communities, some early Jewish religious works were produced in or translated into the language of the host culture, most notably the *Septuagint*, a Greek language version of the Hebrew Bible, as well as the

Notes

philosophical/theological writings of Philo of Alexandria and the historical writings of Josephus, both of which were originally written in Greek. Also, during the Dark Ages, some early Hebrew/Aramaic works were translated, typically into Latin or Greek, and preserved in monastery libraries. See Simkovich, 'Christian Monks'.

10. **Early Christian Hebraists in Italy:** As previously noted, the era of widespread Christian Hebraist scholarship would not develop in England until the seventeenth century. However, the influence of Renaissance humanism had already reached Italy in the fifteenth century and was established in force by the sixteenth century. Early Christian Hebraists developed in Italy from academic and theological exchanges between rabbis and Christian scholars, including some officials in the hierarchy of the Catholic Church. See Roth, *Renaissance*, Chapter 7, 137–164. On the beginnings of the Italian Renaissance humanist movement in the fifteenth century in general, see Greenblatt, *The Swerve*, especially 23–50.

11. **Early Hebrew printed books:** The early advent of Hebrew character mechanical printing in Italy meant that some of the most important Jewish primary sources and early commentaries were available there by 1530. The first printing of Maimonides' *Mishneh Torah* has been attributed to printers in Rome in the late 1470s. The Soncino family published a second edition of *Mishneh Torah* in 1490. And in the early sixteenth century the great Daniel Bomberg, who was not Jewish, published the first printed version of the Rabbinic Bible (*Mikra'ot Gedolot*, 1517–18), which surrounded the text with excerpts from Rashi and other medieval commentators. Bomberg went on to complete his publication of the full multi-volume collection of the *Babylonian Talmud* in 1523, the same year he completed publication of the first printed *Jerusalem Talmud*. See Canada Library and Archives, 'Incunabula, Hebraica, & Judaica' (exhibition catalogue); Sotheby's, 'The Bromberg Talmud' (auction brochure).

A set of the Bomberg Talmud (the 'Valmadonna copy') recently sold at auction on 22 December 2015 for $9,322,000, almost double the advance Sotheby's estimate. This price was obtained despite the fact that by the time of that sale, some fascinating prior rumours that Henry VIII had purchased that very copy to provide evidence in his divorce dispute had been finally discredited, as noted in the online 2015 Sotheby's Auction brochure for 'The Bromberg Talmud' cited above: 'For some time it was believed on the basis of the letters "*RB*" on its custom binding that this set derived from the royal library (*Regia Bibliotheca*) of Henry VIII, who, it was formerly posited, consulted it during divorce proceedings against his first wife, Catherine of Aragon. In truth, the Valmadonna copy is bound in leather incorporating the central cipher of Richard Bruarne, Regius Professor of Hebrew at Oxford University from 1546 to 1556.' (See Samuel, 'Provenance of the Westminster Talmud', 148–150. For some details about the life of Daniel Bomberg, see Roth, *Renaissance*, 162–163.)

12. **Babylonian Talmud:** With their conquest of Judea and the destruction of the First Temple (597 and 586 BCE), the Babylonians exiled much of the religious and national leadership of the Jewish people to Babylon. After a half-century, Babylonian dominance was overthrown by Cyrus the Great of Persia. In accordance with his less punitive policy regarding conquered peoples, Cyrus allowed the Jews to return to the Land of Israel and rebuild their Temple. Although some returned, many others did not, so that the early Jewish world developed two centres of Judaism – one in the Land of Israel and one in Babylonia.

    Unless expressly qualified, the term 'Talmud' generally refers to the Bavli, or Babylonian Talmud, compiled from the commentaries by generations of rabbis living in ancient Babylonia. The Talmud is a combination of the Mishnah, an early organised interpretation of Jewish law, and the Gemara, later rabbinic elaborations of biblical and mishnaic statements. There is also an earlier version of the Talmud, compiled from the commentaries of the rabbis living in the ancient Land of Israel (the Yerushalmi, or 'Jerusalem Talmud'). Until recently, the Jerusalem Talmud had not been as conveniently accessible to the general English-reading public.

13. **The style of Talmudic discussions:** For examples of hypothetical Talmudic discussions of levirate marriage, see BT, Yevamot 2a, 9b-10a.

14. **Authority of Rabbinic commentary:** On the power and authority of rabbinic interpretation to inform our understanding of the Bible, see *Pirke Avot*, 1:1; Kugel, *How to Read the Bible*, 679–682; Holtz, *Back to the Sources*, 16-18. For extended introductions to the study of rabbinic literature, see Neusner, *Introduction to Rabbinic Literature*; Schiffman, *Texts and Traditions*.

15. **Maimonides as court physician:** See Arbel, *Maimonides*, 136.

16. **Two thousand rabbis named in the Talmud:** In a current study applying digital humanities techniques to analyse interactions of rabbinic opinions in the Talmud, Professor Michael Satlow of Brown University has determined that 1,956 rabbis are referred to by name in the Bavli. See Satlow, 'The Rabbinic Network'.

17. **What *Mishneh Torah* included and omitted:** Although *Mishneh Torah* looked to the Mishnah portion of the Talmud for a beginning model of content, Maimonides also included the post-Talmudic development of rabbinic rules designed to put a 'fence' around the Torah laws, when the rabbis extended the express provisions of specific Torah laws in order to lessen the likelihood

of Jews' inadvertent violation of Torah law, or to lessen the likelihood of what might only appear to the outside world to be a violation. See Klein, Introduction and commentaries to *Code of Maimonides* (Book 4), xx–xxi.

Today it seems especially regrettable that in the twelfth century of Maimonides, the slowness or absence of communication often isolated various centres of Jewish learning in different parts of the world. This isolation was especially prevalent between the world of Maimonides' Spanish/North African Sephardi Judaism and the Ashkenazi Judaism of western Europe. Maimonides appears to have been unacquainted with the two great rabbinic developments of the eleventh century in Ashkenazi Judaism: the 'ban of R. Gershom', issued at the beginning of the eleventh century, which prohibited polygamy, and the extensive commentaries of Rashi (Rabbi Shlomo Yitzchaki, 1040–1105) who lived one hundred years before Maimonides. See ibid., xxi, xxvii.

18. **Early printed Hebrew books were costly:** Although the new printed versions offered by Hebrew publishers were more available and affordable than the previous handwritten copies, they were still an expensive luxury. See 'A Note About Book Prices in the Sixteenth Century' in Sotheby's, 'The Bromberg Talmud' (auction brochure).

19. **The commandment prohibiting sexual relations with a brother's wife:** See the statement in the *Mishneh Torah* of negative commandment 344 at *http://mechon-mamre.org./e/e0002.htm*.

20. **Levirate marriage provisions include three commandments:** Maimonides identifies one negative and two positive commandments regarding levirate marriage: [neg. #357:] a widow may not marry another while she is subject to levirate marriage; [pos. #216:] a surviving brother must marry the widow; and [pos. #217:] *halitzah* must be performed if the surviving brother refuses to enter into levirate marriage. See Maimonides, *Code* (Book 4), 264.

21. **Maimonides holds that levirate marriage obligation takes precedence over *halitzah* release:** Maimonides, *Code* (Book 4), 265. This clear statement by Maimonides masks a significant history of Talmudic majority positions as to the priorities of levirate marriage and *halitzah*, which that vacillated over time according to the cultural changes through the rabbinic generations. Although the law is usually decided in accordance with Maimonides, in this case it the final Talmudic rulings gave preference to *halitzah* over levirate marriage. As previously discussed in the text, we know why the position of Maimonides favouring the levirate marriage obligation over the *halitzah* release was not the majority rabbinic view in the twelfth century. Maimonides was writing as a Sephardic Jew living in a Muslim culture. The majority rabbinic preference for *halitzah* became the Ashkenazi view after

the eleventh-century prohibition of polygamy, which applied only to the Ashkenazi.
22. **Positive commandments take precedence in *Mishneh Torah*:** Maimonides, *Code*, 306.
23. **Positive commandments take precedence in Talmud:** BT, *Nazir* 41a, attributing the general principle of priority of a positive commandment over a negative commandment to R. Reish Lakish, and, in BT, *Nazir* 41b, also attributing that rule to R. Eliezer, who derives it from the adjacent commandments of Deut. 22:11 and 22:12, which are read to permit the positive commandment of *tzitzit* (attaching ritual fringes) to be an exception to the negative commandment of *shatnez* (prohibiting the mixture of different clothing materials, such as wool and linen).
24. **Even after an annulment, Jewish law would not approve of Henry marrying Anne:** See Lev. 18:18: 'Thou shalt not take thy wife's sister for a harlot, to rival her: neither shalt thou discover her nakedness, while she is yet living.' *Bible*, Douay-Rheims version, 1609.

10 Henry's Rabbis

1. **Bribing some rabbis:** Some historians seem to reserve their greatest moral indignation about English bribery for instances when rabbis were the beneficiaries. This conveniently ignores the far more widespread bribery by the English to obtain favourable opinions from Christian university faculties and individual Christian clerics.
2. **Giorgi not Jewish:** In the ensuing centuries some historians have argued that Giorgi might have come from a Jewish family because in a few surviving documents, he or others refer to Mark Raphael, a former rabbi who converted to Christianity, as his 'nephew'. But this appears to have been either a reference to another individual, or simply an honorific term used metaphorically, as when we call an unrelated close companion our brother or sister. See Kaufmann, 'Mantino', p. 52 and authorities cited there at footnote 3.
3. **Giorgi's accomplishments:** See Yates, *Occult*, p. 35, and generally Chapter 4 for Giorgi's life and achievements.
4. **Secret Jews:** The Iberian Jewish exiles included crypto-Jews, referred to as *conversos* or New Christians, who had been, or whose ancestors had been, forcibly converted to Christianity but who secretly preserved Jewish practices, beliefs, and identities in their families, often for many generations.
5. **The ten *Sefirot*:** See Kaplan, *Sefer Yetzira*, pp. 19 ff.
6. **Croke writes to Henry about Giorgi:** *LP*, vol. 4, #6229, 18 February 1530, [CROKE to HENRY VIII], 2796. The 'stranger' who was concealing his

name and country refers to Croke himself. At the outset of his search, Croke pretended that he was John [Johannes] of Flanders, who was researching a personal family inheritance matter.

7. **Halfan's family:** Halfan's grandfather was Rabbi Joseph Colon, a well-known leader of the Jewish community. Halfan's father-in-law, Kalonymus ben David, called Maestro Calo, was also from an eminent and learned family, who also agreed to support Henry's arguments for annulment. See Kaufmann, 'Mantino', p. 51; see also Katz, *History*, 24.

8. **Teaching Christians:** In earlier times the rabbis had forbidden Jews to teach the Hebrew language or Jewish interpretations of the Torah to non-Jews, in the fear that such knowledge would be distorted and used as instruments of persecution against Jews. But in 1545, Rabbi Halfan would issue a ruling that Jews were now allowed to teach Christians the Hebrew language and Jewish biblical interpretation, but not the mystical secrets of Kabbalah. The latter matter was considered so powerful and potentially dangerous that the rabbis had specifically prohibited teaching Kabbalah even to Jews until they had achieved maturity and a settled life within the Jewish community. See Katz, *History*, 24; Roth, *Renaissance*, 142–3.

9. **Croke's assurances that Jewish law did not recognise levirate marriage as an exception to the Leviticus Prohibitions:** See excerpt from *LP*, vol. 4, #6149, 18 January 1530, RICHARD CROKE to [STOKESLEY], 2745, presenting letters of support from Elijah Halfan and Mark Raphael, quoted in the text above, in Chapter 9 at note 3.

10. **The rabbi/doctor and the convert:** See ibid. See also Katz, *History*, 24, confirming that the Jewish physician was 'most certainly' Elijah Halfan. The former rabbi who converted to Christianity is identified by Croke as Mark Raphael in Croke's companion letter to Henry, #6229, quoted in the text accompanied by the following note 11.

11. **Croke's letter to Henry:** *LP*, vol. 4, #6229, 18 February 1530, [CROKE to HENRY VIII], 2796. This letter from Croke to Henry was a copy in Latin retained by Croke. In the *LP* version, its date is footnoted as having been attributed by later scholars. It might have been a later copy based upon Croke's similar letter to Stokesley, #6149, dated a month earlier, or the two letters might have been drafted at the same time but for whatever reason, the letter to Henry was not sent immediately. The Latin passage, which was not translated in the *Letters and Papers* version of this three-page Latin document, refers to two limited exceptions that permit marriages between close relatives despite the Leviticus Prohibitions: (a) The end of Numbers (Num. 36:1–12) shows God's insistence that inheritance of land for Jews must preserve ownership within the original tribe, requiring marriage within

the paternal tribe where necessary to achieve this, and (b) levirate marriage is supported in the new Testament only in the case of the fathers of St Joseph, the father of Jesus, with this reference credited to Mark Raphael.

12. **Ghinucci's role for England:** Although England was recognised as one of the world's major Catholic kingdoms, in 1530 it had no English cardinal in the Vatican representing its interests. This contrasts to France, which enjoyed a significant Vatican presence. As the nominal Bishop of Worcester, Girolamo Ghinucci received annual incomes from his position in exchange for which it was expected that he would help England in Vatican matters, including in this instance helping to obtain theological opinions supporting the annulment.

13. **Ghinucci letter to Henry:** *LP*, vol. 4, #6205, 7 February 1530, [CROKE to GHINUCCI], 2783. Attributions of authorship between Halfan and Raphael are indicated in *LP*, vol. 4, #6229, at Chapter 10, note 11 above; and #6250 at note 15 and #6266 at note 16 of Chapter 10, below. It appears that Elijah Halfan made the initial argument about Jews only applying Deuteronomy in matters of inheritance, while Mark Raphael made the initial argument that Deuteronomy's custom of levirate marriage had never been recognised in the New Testament except in the case of the grandfathers of Jesus.

14. **Copies of Documents:** In those days, it was not unusual to make multiple copies or summaries of an important document. This was frequently done in order to share it among different recipients, or in an attempt to ensure that at least one copy would be safely delivered despite the risks of international travel or the possible efforts by political opponents to block the communication. Therefore, the cover letters for important documents were often sent, perhaps with copies or summaries, by ordinary fast couriers, while the precious documents themselves might be sent separately with especially reliable diplomatic envoys even if that required some delay.

15. **Croke letter to Ghinucci:** *LP*, vol. 4, #6250, 2 March 1530, [CROKE to GHINUCCI] 2812.

16. **Croke letter to Henry:** *LP*, vol. 4, #6266, 11 March 1530, [CROKE to HENRY VIII], 2819. Reference to 'Benedict, a German' is uncertain (perhaps the kabbalist Baruch of Benevento?). 'Calo' refers to Kalonymos ben David, a scholar and translator who was Halfan's father-in-law. See Katz, *History*, 31; Kaufmann, 'Mantino', 51, 54–55; *Jewish Encyclopedia* (1906), s.v. 'Italy-Spread of the Cabala'.

17. **Support for Henry's natural law argument:** *LP*, vol. 4, #6266, March 11, 1530, [CROKE to HENRY VIII], 2819. The Chaldaic commentaries sent by Croke apparently supported Henry's arguments that Lev. 18:16 was a statement of natural law, which could not be dispensed by the pope. As an accomplished Hebraist, Francesco Giorgi would have been able to translate

Notes

texts written in Chaldaic, an early Semitic language used in the Babylonian Empire, which is related to both the Aramaic and Hebrew languages.

18. **Clement opposes the solicitation of clergy and university opinions:** *LP*, vol. 4, #6445, 9 June 1530, [CROKE to STOKESLEY], 2893–94.

19. **Christian and Jewish opinion:** The weight of Christian theological opinion was against Henry. See Katz, *History*, 22; Scarisbrick, *Henry VIII*, 179–80. Rabbinic support for Henry also withered during 1530 despite continuing English attempts at bribery. See *LP*, vol. 4, #6445, 9 June 1530, [CROKE to STOKESLEY], 2893–94. See also Katz, *History*, 40, referring to 'Halfan's extraordinary decision to write in favour of Henry VIII when all other serious Jewish commentators made it clear that it was both politically dangerous and religiously improbable to support the English king'.

20. **On Mantino's life generally,** see Kaufmann, 'Mantino' in *Review of Jewish Studies*, No. 27, Part 1, 30 ff.

21. **Mantino's recognition in Christian society:** See ibid., Part 2, 212–13 for the yellow hat exemption, and 209–219 generally.

22. **Mantino's ruling against Henry:** See ibid., Part 1, 50.

23. **Croke's first meeting with Mantino:** *LP*, vol. 4, #6165, 25 January 1530, [RICHARD CROKE to GHINUCCI], 2753.

24. **Croke concealed his identity from Mantino:** Ibid.; see also Kaufmann, 'Mantino', Part 1, 52–53.

25. **Croke's general concealment of his identity:** See *LP*, vol. 4, #6165; #6145; #6149; #6160. See also Kaufmann, 'Mantino', Part 1, 50, 53.

26. **Croke's second Mantino meeting:** See *LP*, vol. 4, #6174, 29 January 1530, [RICHARD CROKE to the BISHOP OF WORCESTER (GHINUCCI)], 2759.

27. **Mantino judged the Leviticus/Deuteronomy disputation for the pope:** See *LP*, vol. 4, #6165, 25 January 1530, [RICHARD CROKE to GHINUCCI], 2753, quoted in the text above at note 23.

28. **Weight of opinions against Henry:** See text above at note 19.

29. **Mantino's concern for the Jewish Community:** See *LP*, vol. 4, #6445, 9 June 1530, [CROKE to STOKESLEY], 2893–94): 'Jacobus [Jacob Mantino] and other Jews who came lately from Bologna report the Pope's displeasure…'. Cf. *LP*, vol. 4, #6463, 19 June 1530, [CROKE to STOKESLEY], 2905: 'He [Paul Casales] and Croke have attempted Jews here [Padua], but they say they have such advice from Venice that they dare not write.'

30. **Jewish messianic movements:** See Rabow, *50 Jewish Messiahs*.

31. **Asher Lemlein:** See Rabow, *50 Jewish Messiahs*, 57–58.

32. **Halfan–Mantino enmity over the Molkho–Reuveni messianic rivalry:** See Katz, *History*, 41: 'By the autumn of 1530 even Elijah Halfan had dropped

out [from writing in support of King Henry], either because the hopelessness of the argument was now apparent, or in order to pursue his feud with Mantino in the more fertile rabbinic hunting grounds attached to the Messianic claims of Molcho and Reubeni.'

33. **The Jewish community in Egypt ransomed Reuveni from captivity:** In the sixteenth century, one of the hazards of travel by sea or land was the risk that pirates or desert marauders would capture travellers and hold them for ransom. Jewish communities considered it a sacred obligation to ransom any Jewish captives brought to them, even if not from that community. Sometimes the cost of the ransom would later be reimbursed by the former captive's Jewish community of origin.

34. **Life of David Reuveni:** See Rabow, *50 Jewish Messiahs*, 62–69; see also the purported diary of David Reuveni, covering the first part of his life: Reuveni, 'Diary', in Adler, *Jewish Travellers*, 251–328.

35. **Molkho's flag and tunic:** The actual flag and silk tunic of Shlomo Molkho, from the early sixteenth century, can be seen at the Jewish Museum of Prague.

36. **Molkho's escape:** Molkho's bizarre escape from the fires of the Inquisition proved to be only temporary. Clement sent both David Reuveni and Shlomo Molkho on a doomed joint mission to Germany to obtain the participation of the Holy Roman Emperor Charles V for Reuveni's Christian-Jewish Crusade for the recapture of Jerusalem. Charles was not amused. He placed both these Jewish messianic figures into captivity, sending Molkho back to Italy where in 1530 he suffered the execution at the stake that he had evaded earlier. Reuveni was imprisoned, and presumably died either from natural causes or perhaps assassination in captivity. See Rabow, *50 Jewish Messiahs*, 68–69, 74–76.

37. **Life of Shlomo Molkho:** See Rabow, *50 Jewish Messiahs*, 70–77.

11 Henry's Search for Additional Rabbinic Support

1. **Henry's focus on rabbinic support:** *LP*, vol. 4, #6353, [February?] 1530, THE KING'S LETTERS, 2851; cf. Pocock, *Records*, doc. no 105 (Latin), 1:296. Pocock dates this document as 'Probably of the date of February 1530', but *LP* prints it with the documents of April 1530.

2. **Quality of English support:** *LP*, vol. 4, #6353 ii, [February?] 1530, THE KING'S LETTERS, 2851–52.

3. **English payments for helpful rabbinic opinions:** See the following documents in *LP*, vol. 4, for 1530: #6156, 22 January 1530, [RICHARD CROKE to GHINUCCI], 'Asks what reward he is to give. Mark Raphael, a learned Jew, has written most plainly on our side, and offers to defend his writings';

#6250, 2 March 1530, [CROKE to GHINUCCI], 'We can have three or four more Rabbis, but they cannot be hired for less than 24 [cr.]'; #6287, 26 March 1530, [CROKE to GHINUCCI], 'Will give a few gold pieces to Hebrews who have promised to write'; #6375, 10 May 1530, [CROKE'S EXPENSES], 'To two Jews, for coming home to you daily and writing ... To a Jew when he subscribed ... For a concordance and another book from a Jew, 2 cr. To Helias the Jew, for 3 copies, 4 cr. ... To Mark Raphael, a Hebrew, 5 ducats'; #6541, July 1530, PAYMENTS, 'London, 17th. The King's reward to Mark Raphaell, 40/'; #6739, 28 November 1530, MAI [Imperial ambassador to the Vatican] to CHARLES V, 'Among those here who have given opinions in the King's favour is a converted Jew, named Marc Gabriel [Raphael], and the King has provided to give him as much money as he requires, and to send him thither'; #6786 December 1530, [CROKE'S EXPENSES], 'To Hebrews. To Mark Raphael, a Christian, 6 cr. To Helias, a Jew, and his companions, 8 cr.'

4. **Failure to mention reliance upon the rabbis:** Little or no mention of Henry's search for rabbinic opinions can be found in many of the prominent academic and popular histories cited herein, including those by Elton, Friedmann, Francis Hackett, Ives, Kelly, and Starkey. For a significant exception, see Scarisbrick, *Henry VIII*, 256: 'They [Henry's agents] argued with Scripture scholars, Hebrew scholars, canonists, doctors of medicine, rabbis, friars, laymen ... They gathered lists of signatories, collected copies of rare letters of Fathers and rabbinical writings.'

5. **H. A. L. Fisher's description of the rabbis:** Fisher, *History*, 303. These words were quoted almost a half-century later in Hughes, *Reformation in England*, 216, published in 1950 with the imprimatur and approval of a deputy censor and vicar general for the Catholic Church. It may not be surprising to find such a charged antisemitic verbal attack in a 1906 English academic history, but it is distressing to see it recirculated in a 1950 text. As additional context, however, we can note that there is probably some corresponding measure of philo-Semitic selectivity bias in the succinct but detailed discussion about the English search for rabbinic opinions in Roth, *Jews in the Renaissance*, 160, which is accurate as far as it goes, but which conveniently omits reference to any English bribes for Jewish support.

6. **Paying only for favourable opinions:** *LP*, vol. 4, #6353, [February?] 1530, THE KING'S LETTERS, 2851–52. See also ibid., #6207, 9 February 1530, FRANCISCO GEORGIUS to _____, 2786: 'Would not wish to give money to those who think the Pope can dispense, but to those who think the opposite, and agree with our writings...' See also ibid., #6209, 11 February 1530, [GHINUCCI to CROKE], 2787: 'Croke had better try, if

he thinks there is any hope, but he must not let him have the money until he gets what he wants.'

7. **The English ignored negative opinions:** Herbert, *History*, 456; see also ibid., 448, for the parliamentary declaration of 30 July 1530.

8. **Ortiz confirms English misuse of university opinions:** *LP*, vol. 5, #342, 19 July 1531, [DR ORTIZ to CHARLES V], 162, [summarising the arguments of Bishop Fisher].

9. **Importance of R. Jacob Raphael responsum adverse to Henry:** The few historians who discuss this responsum recognise the importance of Jacob Raphael having concluded adversely to Henry VIII. The British Library online catalog states: 'The question proposed is whether the law of levirate as given in Deuteronomy 25:5, 6 was originally understood to limit the prohibition of Leviticus 18:16, or not. The answer is in favour of the first alternative, and thus adversed to the contention of Henry VIII'. British Library, 'Arundel MS 151' in *Catalogue of Digitised Manuscripts*, 190. See also the blog article by Miriam Lewis, 'Hebrew Manuscripts Digitisation Project': 'This letter is the reply of Jacob Rafael of Modena, who did not give the answer the king was looking for. He stated that the law of levirate marriage overrode the prohibition in Leviticus, and therefore Henry VIII's marriage to Catherine of Aragon was valid and could not be annulled on those grounds.' See also Kaufmann, 'Opinion of Jacob Raphael', *Review of Jewish Studies*, 30:311: 'Far from being favorable to the King of England, he [Jacob Raphael] argues, [in accordance] with Nahmani [Nachmanides], that the levirate is an ancient institution, which must be observed in case the brother died without descendants. ... The Consultation [responsum] of Jacob Rafael therefore did not excuse the act [annulment] of Henry VIII.' Kaufmann not only provides an explanation of how he came to possess a copy of the Jacob Raphael responsum, but he also briefly summarises it and includes, in an appendix to his article, a full transcription of the text in standard printed Hebrew. (For a new English translation of the responsum, see Appendix C.)

10. **The original responsum document:** The responsum by Rabbi Jacob Raphael of Modena was acquired by the British Museum Library in 1831 as part of a purchase from the Royal Society of London of 550 manuscripts in the Arundel collection. The document is dated 1530 (5290 in the Hebrew Calendar). Recognising the historical significance and exceptional beauty of this original manuscript, the British Museum Library has made a high-resolution digitisation image of Jacob Raphael's *Responsum* freely accessible for public viewing online at: *http://www.bl.uk/manuscripts/Viewer.aspx?ref=arundel_ms_151_ff_190-191v_f190r#* [accessed 5/2/22].

Notes

11. **Francesco da Corte:** See Roth, *Renaissance*, 160.
12. **Responsum by Rabbi Jacob Raphael:** The original 30 January 1530 responsum was one of forty major manuscripts featured in a recent exhibition by the British Library.
13. **Image and translation of the original 30 January 1530 responsum:** Please see Figs 26–28 for images of the original document, and see Appendix C for a new English translation of the text. For a transliteration of the calligraphed text into printed Hebrew, see Kaufmann, 'Opinion of Jacob Rafael Peglione', *Review of Jewish Studies*, 30:311–313.
14. **Henry abandons other arguments:** Another argument that Henry tried to hold onto was his insistence that Catherine and Arthur had consummated their marriage. The king's position was that, once it was established that Catherine's prior marriage to Arthur had been consummated, the Leviticus Prohibitions absolutely barred Henry from marrying his sister-in-law. Henry ultimately stopped arguing the factual consummation issue in response to Catherine's consistent and rigorous denials of consummation with Arthur, together with Pope Clement's support for her on this issue.
15. **Mark Raphael arrives in London:** See *LP*, vol. 5, #70, 31 January 1531, [CHAPUYS to CHARLES V], 31: 'The Jew sent for by the King arrived six days ago, notwithstanding all the efforts made by [Imperial ambassador] Mai to prevent his passage.'
16. **Before his conversion, Mark Raphael was a chief rabbi:** Richard Croke refers to Mark as a former chief rabbi who had converted to Christianity. See *LP*, vol. 4, #6229, 18 February 1530, [CROKE to HENRY VIII], 2796: '[Mark] Raphael, who is now converted to Christ, was at one time a chief rabbi.' See also ibid., #6288, [March 1530], [CROKE to ____], 2826.
17. **Anne as 'the lady':** See *LP*, vol. 5, #112, 21 February 1531, [CHAPUYS to CHARLES V], 49–50; see also *LP* V, for many other Chapuys reports referring to Anne as 'the lady'. In 1536, after Catherine's death at the beginning of the year, and continuing through Anne's downfall, trial, and execution, Chapuys resorted to repeatedly referring to her as 'the Concubine'. See, e.g., *LP*, vol. 10, #199, 29 January 1536, Chapuys to Charles V, 70–71; ibid. #909, 19 May 1536, Chapuys to Granvelle, 380–81.
18. **Ambassador Mai tries to stop Mark Raphael going to England:** See *CSP-Spain*, vol. 4 (i), #513, 28 November 1530, Miçer Mai to the Emperor, 816–31; see also ibid., #533, 13 December 1530, Miçer Mai to the Emperor, 831–47.
19. **Mark Raphael's first recommendation to Henry:** See *CSP-Spain*, vol. 4 (ii), #619, 31 January 1531, Eustace Chapuys to the Emperor, 31–47; cf. *LP*, vol. 5, #70, 31 January 1531, [CHAPUYS to CHARLES V], 32.

20. **Henry rejects taking Anne as a second wife:** *CSP-Spain*, vol. 4 (ii), #619, 31 January 1531, Eustace Chapuys to the Emperor, 31–47.
21. **Antisemitism at high levels of government:** In the three Chapuys reports from early 1531 being considered here (*CSP-Spain*, vol. 4 (ii), #619, and *LP*, vol. 5, #70 and #120), he refers to Mark Raphael, a converted New Christian, as 'the Jew'. As a mark of personal disfavour, Chapuys does not mention Raphael by name, just as he would not mention Anne Boleyn by name. Because of their lack of blood purity (*limpieza de sangre*), New Christians like Mark Raphael were not always fully accepted by members of the Catholic faith, sometimes for many years or even for generations. Years earlier, Catherine of Aragon, her duenna Doña Elvira Manuel, Ambassador Don Pedro de Ayala, and others complained to Ferdinand and Isabella about the Spanish ambassador to London, Doctor Don Roderigo De Puebla, a *converso*. Their complaints likewise included antisemitic elements such as vicious and unjustified attacks on De Puebla's character, breeding, and sincerity of conversion. Ambassador Ayala seems to have instigated many of these attacks against his political rival. For a detailed refutation of many of the charges against De Puebla, including their antisemitic nature, see Mattingly, 'The Reputation of Doctor De Puebla', 27–46.
22. **Chapuys's antisemitic attack on Mark Raphael:** *LP*, vol. 5, #70, 31 January 1531, [CHAPUYS to CHARLES V], 32.
23. **Levirate marriage requires intent to create issue for the deceased brother:** See Klein, 'Introduction', in Maimonides, *Mishneh Torah*, Book 4, xxvii.
24. **Mark Raphael's revised advice:** *LP*, vol. 5, #120; 1 March 1531, [CHAPUYS to CHARLES V], 59.
25. **Redefining 'childless':** See discussion of Robert Wakefield and the translation of *aririm* in the text above in Chapter 8 at note 8.
26. **Mark Raphael in business:** See grant of import licence to Raphael on 24 May 1532 at *LP*, vol. 5, #1065, item 29, Grants in May 1532, 485: '29. Mark Raphael of Venice. Licence to import 600 tuns of Gascon wine and Toulouse woad. *Del.* Westm., 24 May 24 Hen. VIII.'

    The ability to enter into an import business required royal permission, so this venture could have been one of the means used by Henry to provide living expenses to Raphael.
27. **Mark Raphael's Stipend from Venice:** It is not clear whether Raphael's income from Venice was a reward for inventing a new type of invisible ink for secret diplomatic or military dispatches (see Roth, *Renaissance*, 160), or, as sometimes occurred for Jewish converts at the time, he received funds from the government for his costs of living during the period between his leaving Judaism and finding employment now open to him in the Christian world.

28. **Mark Raphael planning to serve the emperor:** *LP*, vol. 5, #216, 29 April 1531, [CHAPUYS to CHARLES V], 101. Mark Raphael's loyalty to the king's cause had been questioned a year earlier by Bishop Ghinucci, when the bishop warned that Raphael was actually in the service of the pope. See *LP*, vol. 4, #6414, 31 May 1530, [CROKE to HENRY VIII], 2879.
29. **Dancing in France:** *LP*, vol. 5, #1484, 29 October 1532, The King's Visit to Calais, 624.
30. **Anne's elevation to Marchioness of Pembroke:** For further discussion of the Pembroke title, see Chapter 13 at note 15.
31. **Mark Raphael in France:** See *LP*, vol. 5, #1429, 14 October 1532, [Chapuys to Charles V], 605.

12 *Why Jewish Law Failed to Help Henry*

1. **Christian Hebraist movement not yet developed in England:** See Rosenblatt, *Chief Rabbi*; and see Chapter 9, note 6.
2. **Two principal steams of Judaism:** The two early streams of Judaism continue today: Ashkenazi Jews and Sephardi Jews. The latter group may also refer to the Mizrahi Jews who either did not leave or eventually returned to the Muslim Middle East, and who follow many of the Sephardi laws and customs. These cultural identities are not directly reflected by any particular group resulting from the evolution of modern Judaism, beginning in the nineteenth century, into several formal self-governing denominational branches – initially Orthodox, Reform, and Conservative, and subsequently also Modern Orthodox, Reconstructionist, and others.
3. **Polygamy banned in State of Israel:** The State of Israel's first chief rabbis banned polygamy for all Jewish communities in Israel in 1950. Conforming state criminal laws were adopted beginning in 1959 to make polygamy a crime in Israel. However, prior to those changes, Jewish communities often utilised special provisions in the Jewish marital contract (*ketubah*) to protect a bride against the husband's subsequent polygamy without her permission. See *Jewish Virtual Library*, s.v. Bigamy and Polygamy.
4. **Jews observed both Leviticus and Deuteronomy:** See Klein, 'Introduction', in Maimonides, *Mishneh Torah*, Book 4, xxvii.
5. ***Halitzah:*** The *halitzah* ceremony, intended to be a humiliation for the surviving brother, not only has the legal effect of freeing him from his obligation to marry his widowed sister-in-law, but it also liberates her to marry, if she wishes, anyone not having an otherwise prohibited relationship with her.
6. **Jews had abandoned levirate marriage under Deuteronomy:** *LP*, vol. 4, #6229, 18 February 1530, [CROKE to HENRY VIII], 2796.

7. **Jews who had fled from Iberia to other cultures often retained Sephardi customs:** As an example, Maimonides came from the Sephardi tradition and had fled to Muslim lands. He stated that Jewish law preferred performance of levirate marriage over the *halitzah* release of that obligation, following the Sephardi view: 'The commandment to contract levirate marriage has precedence over the commandment to perform [*halitzah*].' Maimonides, *Code*, Book Four, p. 265.
8. **Henry was unconcerned with the quality of supporting opinions:** *LP*, vol. 4, #6353, [February ?] 1530, THE KING'S LETTERS, 2851, quoting Ghinucci: 'What I wrote about learned theologians, who you say are rare in Italy has been provided for by the King, who does not wish so much to obtain excellent ones, as all.'
9. **Levirate marriage in Rome, 1530:** *CSP-Spain*, vol. 4 (i), #446, 2 October 1530, Miçer Mai to the Emperor, 734–53; *LP*, vol. 4, #6661, 2 October 1530, MAI to CHARLES V, 2999–3013.
10. **Timing of Rome wedding is suspicious:** See Katz, *History*, 41: 'But the perfect mistiming of the match leaves open the question of whether it was arranged by someone such as Jacob Mantino ...'; Bernard, *The King's Reformation*, 18 '... the event may have been specially staged'. Some commentators have been able to resist seeing anything suspicious: see Guy and Fox, *Hunting the Falcon*, 203: 'It was coincidental but perhaps unfortunate ...'

13 Henry's Final Tactics

1. **Excommunication enforced by inviting invasion:** Henry VIII well understood how popes could try to enforce an excommunication by summoning other Catholic leaders to invade the land and force cooperation from or punish a recalcitrant Catholic king. In 1512, Pope Julius II attempted to punish King Louis XII by declaring Henry VIII King of France, conditional upon his successful military invasion of France. However, notwithstanding some relatively minor English battles in France, Henry was never able to mount a serious military invasion that threatened France. See Scarisbrick, *Henry VIII*, 33–40.
2. **Henry ultimately wins supremacy:** The major parliamentary Acts empowering the king as Supreme Head of the Church in England were enacted after 1530. See the Acts of 1532–1534 regarding Annates, Appeals, Clergy Submission, Heresy, Succession, Supremacy, and Treason. What can be seen as Henry's first significant manoeuvre in this struggle for formal dominance over the clergy resulted in the Pardon of the Clergy in 1531. See Scarisbrick, *Henry VIII*, 274–281.
3. **Henry tries to bribe Clement:** *LP*, vol. 5, #327, 10 July 1531, [Henry VIII to Benet], 154.

Notes

4. **Henry does not fear excommunication:** *CSP-Spain*, vol. 4 (ii), #739, 6 June 1531, Eustace Chapuys to the Emperor, 168–89; cf. *LP*, vol. 5, #287, 6 June 1531, Chapuys to Charles V, 134: Henry 'did not care three straws' about excommunication; ibid., #148, 22 March 1531, Chapuys to Charles V, 70: the Duke of Norfolk said: '... if the Pope issued 10,000 excommunications, he [Henry] would not care a straw for them'.
5. **Confiscation of Church property:** *LP*, vol. 5, #326, 10 July 1531, Henry VIII to Ghinucci, Benet, and Casale, 153.
6. **Reformation of the English Church:** For some recent histories of the English Reformation, including the role of the King's Great Matter, as approached from different religious views, compare Bernard, *The King's Reformation* (neutral historian); Holmes, *Episcopal Church* (Protestant); and Hughes, *Reformation* (Catholic).
7. **The 25 January 1533 wedding date:** See Friedmann, *Anne Boleyn*, Appendix Note D: 'The Date of Anne's Marriage', 299–300.
8. **Royal supremacy over the Church in England:** In March 1532, the Commons sent Henry its Supplication against the abuses of the Vatican, asserting that in England the king was the supreme ruler of the church. The clergy did not dare to contest this. Parliament enacted enabling legislation in 1533 and 1534. See the Parliamentary Acts of Supplication, Restraint of Appeals, Succession, Dispensations, and Submission of the Clergy, culminating with the 1534 Act of Supremacy recognising Henry VIII as the Supreme Head of the Church in England, and also imposing a loyalty oath by all Henry's subjects to confirm that his marriage to Anne Boleyn was valid.
9. **Anne became pregnant sometime around the end of 1532:** See Scarisbrick, *Henry VIII*, 309 (December); Weir, *Six Wives*, 173 (the autumn of 1532); Archer, *Henry VIII*, L-904 (by Christmas 1532); Francis Hackett, *Henry VIII*, 229 (perhaps as early as November); cf. Bernard, *The King's Reformation*, 67 (no later than January 1533).
10. **Pregnancy disclosed in early 1533:** See Mattingly, *Catherine of Aragon*, 354 (Anne hints in February 1533); cf. Francis Hackett, *Henry VIII*, 226–7; see also *CSP-Spain*, vol. 4 (ii), #1059, 21 April 1553, Count of Cifuentes to the Emperor, 628–46 (in April 1533, Pope Clement heard about the pregnancy); ibid., #1061, 15 April 1533, Eustace Chapuys to the Emperor, where Henry hints to Chapuys in April 1533 about his prospects of having more children: 'Am I not a man like others?'
11. **Was the wedding just a story?** On 28 May 1533, Henry had Archbishop Cranmer validate the marriage to Anne, suggesting some lingering need for legitimisation. See Kelly, *Trials*, 213. And on 17 June 1533, Cranmer denied that he had personally married the couple. He claimed that he wasn't sure

of the date, saying he had learned of it only two weeks later. See ibid. Even after 25 January, Anne was saying that she expected there to be only 'a little' wait before she celebrated her marriage to the king. *LP*, vol. 6, #142, 9 February 1533, Chapuys to Charles V, 66. But by early March 1533 Henry gave instructions that King Francis be told that he had married and that the royal succession 'to all appearance, is in a state of advancement already...' *LP*, vol. 6, #230, [11 March?] 1533, Instructions to Lord Rochford, 103.

12. **Warham protests Parliament limiting powers of the Pope and the Archbishop of Canterbury:** See *LP*, vol. 5, #818, 24 February 1532. Archbishop Warham, 386–87.
13. **Anne's social class:** See Ridgway online blog, 'Was Anne Boleyn a Commoner?' See *https://www.youtube.com/watch?v=NCmmt9ZqvlI*.
14. **Henry planning Calais meeting and the coronation:** *LP*, vol 5, #1202, 29 July 1532, [Chapuys to Charles V], 526; see also ibid., #1232, 18 August 1532, The King's Visit to Calais, 537.
15. **Anne receives title and wealth:** See *LP*, vol. 5, #1274, 1 September 1532, Anne Boleyn, 552–53; ibid., #1370 (1), Grants in September 1532, 585; ibid. #1499 (23), Grants in October 1532, 633–34. Note that in #1370 (1), the Pembroke title was granted expressly 'in tail male', so that it could be inherited only by Anne's male descendants, matching what Henry hoped would be the succession to his throne by their male descendants – and perhaps to make it clear to Anne exactly what was included in her new job description.
16. **Anne is invited to the conference.** *LP*, vol. 5, #1316, 15 September 1532, Chapuys to Charles V, 571.
17. **Appointment of Cranmer:** *LP*, vol. 6, #89, 27 January 1533, Chapuys to Charles V, 35.
18. **Threat of withholding the annates:** Ibid.; and cf. ibid., #101, 31 January 1533, Boner to Benet, 40, also reporting Henry's threat to withhold 90 per cent of all the English annates, and additionally threatening that the pope should reduce ('gently handle') the particular annates for Cranmer's appointment: 'If the Pope could gratify the King, he will do all that he can to please his Holiness. If not, the Pope will be in great danger here. As my lord elect of Canterbury, Dr Cranmer, a man of singular good learning, virtue, and all good parts, sends his Bulls, it would be advisable that he should be gently handled in the charges, and especially the annates[,] otherwise the matter of the annates, which is now only stayed by the King's goodness, will be determined to the disadvantage of the court of Rome.'
19. **Cranmer's secret precondition:** See *LP*, vol. 6, #291, 30 March 1533, Archbishop Cranmer, 126.

14 Why Henry's Quest Failed

1. **Limits to imperial military influence:** Charles V was not above using his political and military power to extract great wealth from Pope Clement and from King Francis as the price of setting them free, but at least he did not seek to push his advantage over either of them to totally destroy their respective positions of leadership over the Church and over France.
2. **Building of St Peter's:** The construction of St Peter's Basilica in the Vatican was begun in 1506, during the reign of Julius II, ten years before Luther's 95 Theses. The building project took more than a century to complete.
3. **Clement's delays:** In the end, it was Clement who blinked, not Henry. Perhaps in an attempt to at least reframe the resolution of the dispute, Clement agreed to Henry's request to designate Thomas Cranmer as Archbishop of Canterbury. It must have been obvious to Clement that Cranmer would use his new authority to grant Henry the annulment and permit the marriage to Anne. But perhaps that was Clement's goal at that point. Clement may have concluded that England was already lost to the Church, and that having Henry act on his own was the best path to minimise and slow the spread of the Reformation while at the same time avoid a clash with Charles V.
4. **The women's response:** The women of England felt special empathy for Catherine. They could appreciate the risks and costs of her decade of almost annual pregnancies and the devastation of repeated miscarriages and infant deaths. Moreover, like most people in England at that time, they presumed that only a male heir would likely be an acceptable successor to the crown. The women of England might therefore have additionally felt the injustice of how little their country and their king valued his surviving daughter Princess Mary.
5. **Catherine's character:** Catherine of Aragon consistently displayed many admirable personal qualities, including fortitude, loyalty, and bravery. But like all of the actors in this drama, she was not free from human shortcomings. In relation to anti-Semitism, Catherine may have been in some respects a product of her family and the times. Henry inherited an England without Jews, but Isabella and Ferdinand took the initiative of embracing the Inquisition and expelling Spain's Jews. At their insistence, another daughter's marriage contract with the King of Portugal required Portugal to follow suit. Catherine herself seems to have followed the bad example of Doña Elvira and Don Pedro de Ayala, Spanish ambassador to Scotland, to repeatedly complain that her father's ambassador to England, Roderigo De Puebla, a New Christian convert, was untrustworthy and incompetent – apparently because he was still regarded as a Jew. See Starkey, *Six Wives*, 99; Mattingly, *Catherine of Aragon*, 33; Mattingly, 'Reputation of Doctor De Puebla', *English Historical Review*, vol. 55, no. 217 (Jan., 1940), 27–46.

6. **The Tudor Dynasty:** For further details of the Tudor succession after Henry VIII, see the Afterword and Appendix E.

Afterword: Henry Crafts the Tudor Dynasty

1. **Anne displays arrogance:** LP, vol. 5, #216, 29 April 1531, [CHAPUYS to CHARLES V], 101.
2. **Anne's 1534 pregnancy:** LP, vol. 7, #556, 27 April 1534, Geo. Tayllour to Lady Lisle, 221, (Anne visibly pregnant); see *CSP-Spain*, vol. 5 (i), #6, 23 January 1534, Count of Cifuentes to Charles V, 37 (news had reached Rome); ibid., #19, 26 February 1534, Eustace Chapuys, 53–70 (Henry stated that Parliament would confirm that Mary was illegitimate and could not succeed to the throne: 'There was no other princess in his kingdom than his daughter, Elizabeth, until he himself had a son, which he thought would shortly happen.'); see also, for the silver cradle apparently made in readiness for the birth of the king's son, LP, vol. 7, Appendix: Miscellaneous, #1668, [1534], Goldsmiths' Work [Cornelys Hayes, goldsmith], 615: 'A silver cradle, price 16*l.* For making a silver plate, altering the images, making the roses underneath the cradle, the roses about the pillars, and new burnishing, 13*s.* 4*d.* For the stones that were set in gold in the cradle, 15*s.*; for fringes, the gold about the cushions, tassels, white satin, cloth of gold, lining, sypars and swadylbands, 13*s.* 6*d.* Total, 18*l.* 1*s.* 10*d.* The silver that went to the dressing of the Adam and Eve, the making of all the apples, the gilding of the foot and setting of the currall, 33*s.* 4*d.* To Hance, painter, (fn. 19) for painting the same Adam and Eve, 20*s.* A silver and gilt dial, 16*l.* 4*s.* The garnishing of two books with silver-gilt, 66 oz., at 6*s.* For the books and binding, 4*l.* To Mr. Loke, for the velvet that covered the books, 43*s.* 9*d.* Total, 62*l.* 18*s.* 11*d.*, whereof 20*l.* is received.'
3. **Anne's 1534 miscarriage:** LP, vol. 7, #1193, 27 September 1534, Chapuys to Charles V, 463. For a detailed analysis of the miscarriage and the deterioration of the royal marriage in 1534, see Ives, *Anne Boleyn*, 235-55.
4. **Catherine of Aragon's death:** Some, like Catherine's physician and Ambassador Chapuys, quickly voiced their suspicions that Henry and Anne had arranged for Catherine to be poisoned. However, the consensus today is that the crude post-mortem examination showed evidence of advanced cancer. See *CSP-Spain*, vol. 5 (ii), #9, 21 January 1536, Eustace Chapuys to the Emperor, 11–29 (cancer of the heart); see also Ives, *Anne Boleyn*, 341 (cancer); Guy and Fox, *Hunting the Falcon*, 341 (stomach cancer).
5. **Yellow costumes to mark Catherine's death:** *CSP-Spain*, vol. 5 (ii), #9, 21 January 1536, Eustace Chapuys to the Emperor, 11–29; see Ives, *Anne Boleyn*, 341–42.

Notes

6. **Anne's fear of ending up like Catherine:** *CSP-Spain*, vol. 5 (ii), #13, 29 January 1536, Eustace Chapuys to the Emperor, 11–29.
7. **Jane Seymour:** Ibid., #21, 17 February 1536, Eustace Chapuys to the Emperor, 39–52.
8. **Anne's Miscarriage:** Ibid.
9. **Adultery trial and executions:** See Fisher, *History*, 386–88.
10. **Betrothal and marriage to Jane Seymour:** See ibid., 388.
11. **Tudor succession:** For further details of the Tudor succession after Henry VIII, see Appendix E.

Conclusion: Who Was Henry VIII?

1. **Henry's political achievements:** Fisher, *History*, 482–83.
2. **Henry's conviction that he was right:** Elton, *Tudors*, 101.
3. **Henry's complex character:** Mattingly, *Catherine of Aragon*, 368.
4. **Henry's narcissism:** Guy and Fox, *Hunting the Falcon*, 412.
5. **The Jewish belief in weighing morality:** Like many other ancient religions, early Judaism used the image of the divine weighing of morality on a balance scale. See Howes, 'My Soul on the Scale' in *Old Testament Essays* 27/1 (2014), 102: 'The idea of psychostasia [divine weighing of the soul] spread from [ancient] Egypt to many other peoples and religions of the time.' Later, the rabbis elaborated on the theme in Judaism that both the good inclination (*yetzer tov*) and the evil inclination (*yetzer harah*), are necessary for human welfare. See *Bereishit Rabbah*, 9:7–8: 'But without the Evil Desire, however, no man would build a house, take a wife and beget children.' See also Eccl 4:4: '... all labor and skillful enterprise come from men's envy of each other...'

Appendix A: Summaries of Henry VIII's Love Letters to Anne Boleyn

1. **Dates and full text editions of the love letters:** The dates and ordering of Henry VIII's love letters in these summaries are based upon the recent analysis in Jasper Ridley's *Love Letters*. Ridley also provides an updated translation of the full text of the original letters into modern English. Other convenient sources for full-text editions of the letters include Halliwell, *Letters*, 1:297–320 (available online at *archive.org*); Luce, *Love Letters*, 1906 Edition (available online at *archive.org*); and Norton, *The Anne Boleyn Papers*, 52–61.
2. **The unprintable expurgated language in Letter IX:** See Chapter 4 at note 18, above, analysing the bowdlerised version of Letter IX in James Orchard Halliwell's 1848 edition of his collection of letters of the kings of England. Halliwell, *Letters*, 1:310, n. 1.

3. **Complicity of Anne's father and brother:** By the latter half of 1528, Henry and Anne's communications and meetings were being facilitated by her father Thomas Boleyn, and her brother George Boleyn. Both relatives enjoyed good relations with the king and received honours and advancements in their positions of royal service.
4. **Dukkys:** See Chapter 4, note 19, above, for the term 'dukkys' and the moral judgement expressed by mid-nineteenth century author James Orchard Halliwell in his collection of letters of the kings of England at Halliwell, *Letters*, p. 318, n. 1.

Appendix B: Canon Law Governing Annulments

1. **The King was no longer the absolute ruler of England:** In addition to the powers over ecclesiastical matters that were retained by the Church in the early sixteenth century, the King of England was by then no longer an absolute ruler even with regard to civil law and governance. Starting with the Magna Carta (1215), the Crown began to grant certain rights and liberties to the feudal barons and eventually to the nobility of England. Over the next three centuries, the English parliamentary system gradually evolved, extending civil representation and power in government to a broader segment of local landowners and leaders, including high Church officials. In large measure, this development was driven by the pragmatic necessity of obtaining popular support and consent to taxation for the Crown's wars and other financial needs in a post-feudal society.
2. **Joining a religious order might not terminate a marriage:** Kelly strongly questions whether taking religious orders that require a pledge of celibacy would qualify for terminating an existing marriage, calling such possible grounds for divorce for Henry VIII and Catherine of Aragon a 'highly dubious and revolutionary expedient'. Kelly, *Trials*, 232. See also *LP*, vol. 4, #5344, 3 March 1529, PETER VANNES to WOLSEY, 2351–2368: 'The most learned of the advocates consulted thinks that the Pope cannot give a dispensation that the King may marry again on the Queen entering a religion. Rome, 3 March 1528.'
3. **'Bull' and 'Brief':** Besides his Bull of dispensation, Pope Julius also issued at least one other dispensation in the form of a Brief. For the differences between a Bull and a Brief, and details about Julius's Spanish Brief, see Chapter 6 of this text at the section 'The Spanish Brief'.
4. **Henry's technical objections to the Bull:** For a fourteen-item list of Catherine's counsel's response to Henry's formal objections to the Bull from the court records of the Blackfriars trial, see Kelly, *Trials*, 105–108.

Notes

5. **Prince Henry's Protestation of the marriage contract:** See *LP*, vol. 1, #435, 27 June 1505, [Henry, Prince of Wales. His protestation against his marriage with Princess Katharine of Spain] for a summary of Prince Henry's formal protestation against the contract for his marriage to Catherine. The complete text of Henry's Protestation in Latin and English is provided in Herbert, *History*, 387–89.
6. **Discovery of the Spanish Brief:** The Spanish claimed that in late 1528 the Spanish Brief (Pope Julius's private summary of his dispensation for Prince Henry to marry Catherine, dated 26 December 1503) had been discovered in the papers of former Spanish ambassador Dr Roderigo de Puebla by the ambassador's family, who sent it to the emperor. See *LP*, vol. 4, #5486, 24 April 1529 [extract from the letters of the Bishop of Worcester (Ghinucci) to Nicolas Rusticus, dated Saragossa, 21 April, in cipher]. By the beginning of March 1529, Emperor Charles had sent a transumpt (a copy with technical language simplified for the reader) to Catherine. Henry, Wolsey and the Privy Council studied its contents. See ibid., #5346, 3 March 1529, [Charles V to Mai]; ibid., #5375, 14 March 1529 [Wolsey to Gardiner, Brian, Gregory Casale, and Vannes]. Charles refused to give up possession of the original Brief to Henry, so Henry sent various envoys to Charles to examine and obtain a verified copy of the original Brief. See *CSP*, vol. 3, #563, 1 October 1528 [Instructions to Miçer Miguel Mai, going as ambassador to the Pope], pp. 805–823; *LP*, vol. 4, #5471, 20 April 1529 [Ghinucci and Lee to Wolsey], 2400–2414.
7. **The English received only limited access to examine the Spanish Brief:** See *LP*, vol. 4, #5471, 20 April 1529 [Ghinucci and Lee to Wolsey], 2400–2414.
8. **English arguments that the Spanish Brief was a forgery:** See ibid.; see also some of Henry's specific objections to the Spanish Brief discussed in Chapter 6, in the section 'The Spanish Brief'.
9. **'Uncover the nakedness' refers to sexual intercourse:** See Brown-Driver, 788d (Strong's #6172); 166c (Strong's #1566).
10. **Affinity incest requires 'One Flesh' from consummation of the first marriage:** See Gen. 2.24. And see Chapter 5, note 5, above.
11. **Was Arthur too sickly to consummate his marriage?** Some historians argue that Arthur may have been sickly since early childhood, perhaps from tuberculosis or other lung disease. See Starkey, *Six Wives*, 76–77.
12. **Was Arthur too young to consummate his marriage?** See Starkey, *Six Wives*, 62.
13. **Catherine's parents were initially uncertain if Arthur had consummated her marriage:** See *CSP-Spain*, vol. 1, #325, 16 June 1502, Ferdinand and Isabella to Ferdinand Duke de Estrada, 269–71.

14. Catherine's parents were soon convinced that there had been no consummation: See ibid., #327, 12 July 1502, Queen Isabella to Ferdinand, Duke de Estrada, 272–76.
15. Henry and Catherine's marriage treaty confirms Arthur's consummation of her first marriage: *CSP-Spain*, vol. 1, #364, 23 June 1503, 306–308.
16. The Pope's dispensation should follow the statement in the marriage treaty that Catherine's first marriage had been consummated: See the 23 August 1503 letter from King Ferdinand to his ambassador to Rome, acknowledging that a chapter in the treaty with England for the marriage of Catherine of Aragon to Prince Henry recites that the parties must obtain a dispensation confirming that Catherine's prior marriage to Arthur had been consummated. Ferdinand goes on to explain: '… but the truth is that it was not consummated, and that the said princess our daughter was as intact as before the wedding, and this is very true and well known where she is; but it has seemed to the lawyers in England, that those scruples and doubts that the people of that Kingdom often put in things, that even though it being the truth that the said Princess, our daughter, was left intact, and that even though she and prince Arthur veiled themselves the marriage was not consummated, that for removing all doubt for later in the succession of the children that, our Lord willing, will be born from this marriage, which now will be affirmed, you have to say in the dispensation that they consummated the marriage, and that upon this your Holiness dispense, consistent with the content of the said chapter, so that this marriage is binding.' [Author's translation of the original Spanish version in Pocock, *Records of the Reformation*, document no. 322, 2:426.] Compare the English-language summary in *CSP-Spain*, vol. 1, #370, 23 August 1503, Ferdinand to Francisco de Rojas, his ambassador at Rome, 309–10; see also ibid., #364, 23 June 1503, Treaty between Ferdinand and Isabella and Henry VII [Joint commission of the monarchs to their respective ambassadors], 306–8.
17. Julius's Bull dated 26 December 1503 stated that Catherine and Arthur did perhaps consummate their marriage: Herbert, *History*, 371–2 (English), 373 (Latin).
18. Julius's Brief dated 26 December 1503 stated that Catherine and Arthur did consummate their marriage: Herbert, *Life and Reigne*, 239 (Latin); Herbert, *History*, 373 (Latin). Note the typographical error in the English translation of the Brief at Herbert, *History*, 372. And see note 38 to Chapter 6, above.
19. Possible legal presumption of consummation if insufficient proof of the actual fact: See the ninth in the list of the fourteen disputed issues in the booklet (*libellus*) presented by Catherine's counsel in the Blackfriars trial, translated and summarised from the court records in Kelly, *Trials*, 107: '9. Should the

marriage between Catherine and Arthur be presumed consummated from their having lived and slept together?' See also ibid., 122–23, concluding that it was the testimony of the witnesses in the Blackfriars trial (primarily 'that Catherine and Arthur were seen going to the same be, or actually in bed together'), which provided in that trial 'and in later years the presumptive evidence for consummation in the queen's first marriage'. See also *LP*, vol. 6, #142, 9 February 1533, Chapuys to Charles V, pp. 56–68: Henry asserted 'that to prove the consummation, besides the presumption' Henry had found an instrument by Ferdinand and Henry VII acknowledging consummation.

20. **Henry and his advisors were aware of the potential public honesty argument:** Professor Scarisbrick concludes that the issue of public honesty was overlooked by the king and his counsel. However, Henry and his legal team were quite aware of the possible technical strengths of the public honesty argument, even though they ultimately abandoned that tactic. As reported in October 1529 by Chapuys, Henry told Catherine in a private argument about the matter: 'You wish to help yourself and defend the validity of the dispensation by saying that your former husband, Prince Arthur, my brother, never consummated marriage. Well and good, but no less was our marriage illegal, for the bull does not dispense *super impedimento publicæ honestatis*, and, therefore, I intend disputing and maintaining against all people that a dispensation thus conceived is insufficient.' (*CSP*, vol. 4, Part 1, #182, 8 October 1529, [Eustace Chapuys, Imperial Ambassador in England, to the Emperor], 260–281.) Chapuys accompanied this report with his opinion that Henry's position would be found to rest on thin ice ['*la glace d'une nuyt*', the ice of one night]. See also Kelly, *Trials*, 130, n. 62 [quoting the version of this report in the Vienna Archives].

21. **Dispensation of public honesty was express condition in the 1503 marriage treaty for Henry and Catherine:** Rymer, *Foedera*, vol. XIII, 'Confirmation of the Treaty of Marriage', p. 81 (Latin). Compare the summary and translation of this document in *CSP-Spain*, vol. 1, 23 June 1503, #364, 'Treaty between Ferdinand and Isabella and Henry VII', which omits from its summary the treaty provision regarding dispensation of public honesty and justice.

22. **Clement was willing to dispense retroactively the technical shortcomings in the Bull of Pope Julius:** See Kelly, *Trials*, 139–40.

Appendix C: Responsum of Rabbi Jacob Raphael

NOTE: *All notes for the translation of the Responsum have been produced by the translator.*

1. Apparently: an expression of extreme humility.
2. I.e. a teaching from the period of the Mishna, but not included in the Mishna itself. This *baraitha* is preserved in Babylonian Talmud, Ḥullin 101b.

3. In his commentary on Babylonian Talmud, Ḥullin 100b.
4. Babylonian Talmud, Yevamoth 4a.
5. Babylonian Talmud, Makkoth 23a.
6. I.e., there is great wisdom behind the placement of the commandments in the Torah; but if we do not see the wisdom, and we see it as 'empty', this emptiness is due only to our own inadequacy. This statement is based on Deuteronomy 32:47 (For it is no vain thing for you), as interpreted in the Palestinian Talmud, Peah 1:1.
7. Isaiah 44:18.
8. Babylonian Talmud, Nidda 70a. The author's point here is that the counterfactual question is not at all practical or relevant, because in fact the rule of levirate marriage is written in Deuteronomy.
9. Babylonian Talmud, Sanhedrin 51b.
10. Not engagement in the modern sense, but the first, and more important, legal stage of marriage.
11. Babylonian Talmud, Kethubboth 47a.
12. Babylonian Talmud, Sanhedrin 51b.
13. Genesis Rabba 88:6.
14. In the Book of Ruth.
15. The Jewish date corresponding to 1530. Note that the month and date are stated according to the Roman calendar, but the year according to the Jewish calendar.

Appendix E: The Tudor Succession
1. **Mary Queen of Scots was a potential rival to Elizabeth for the throne:** See Ellis, *Original Letters*, Letter #188, Mary, Queen of Scots to Elizabeth's Council, 18 2:224–28, including the introductory note by Ellis.

BIBLIOGRAPHY AND ONLINE RESOURCES

The following selected bibliography lists the works cited in this book, together with some additional helpful sources consulted. Readers interested in pursuing further research will find especially valuable Conyers Read's *Bibliography of British History: Tudor Period 1485–1603*, which includes some annotations, descriptions, and evaluations for many of the significant titles in the over 6,500 listed works about the Tudor period published through 1956.

Researchers comfortable with English-language sources will appreciate the accessibility of the British public records archives, particularly the relatively modern translations or partial translations in the following three series for the reigns of Henry VII and Henry VIII, which are conveniently available to the public without charge at British History Online: *Letters and Papers*; *Calendar of State Papers-Spain*; and *Calendar of State Papers-Venice*.

Access to particular works from the Tudor era or from subsequent centuries of histories and commentaries can present challenges for researchers. Local public and university libraries may have copies of some of these resources on their reference shelves. Many libraries are in the process of converting such collections into digital format.

The following Bibliography provides online sites for many older books and periodicals. Many of these works can be found at *archive.org* and similar sites. At the end, I have listed several of the websites which I found helpful in searching for relevant works, especially for older and out-of-print books.

For citation abbreviations used for the most frequently cited book and journal titles, see the list of abbreviations at the beginning of the Notes section, above.

Books, Articles, and Online Works

Abrahams, B. Lionel. 'The Condition of the Jews of England at the Time of their Expulsion in 1290'. In *The Jewish Historical Society of England: Transactions*. Session 1894-5, vol. 2, 76-84 and Appendix, 85-105. Available online at *archive.org*.

Abrahams, Israel. *Jewish Life in the Middle Ages* (Philadelphia: Jewish Publication Society, 1896, 1993).

Adelman, Howard Tzvi. 'Custom, Law, and Gender: Levirate Union among Ashkenazim and Sephardim in Italy after the Expulsion from Spain'. In *The Expulsion of the Jews: 1492 and After*. Ed. Raymond B. Waddington and Arthur H. Williamson, 107-25. (New York: Garland Publishing, 1994).

Adelman, Howard Tzvi. 'Jewish Women and Family Life, Inside and Outside the Ghetto: Henry VIII and Jewish Marriage Law in Venice, 1527-1533'. In *The Jews of Early Modern Venice*. Ed. Robert C. Davis and Benjamin Ravid, 143-167. (Baltimore: John Hopkins University Press, 2001).

Adler, Elkan Nathan, ed. *Jewish Travellers in the Middle Ages: 19 Firsthand Accounts*. (New York: Dover Publications, 1987).

Antiquarian Repertory. Vol. 2. Francis Grose and Thomas Astle, comps. (London: Edward Jeffery, 1808). Available online at *archive.org*.

Aquinas, St Thomas. *The Summa Theologica*. Second Part of Second Part, Question 154, Article 9. Trans. Fathers of the English Dominican Province. Available online at *newadvent.org*.

Arbel, Ilil. *Maimonides: A Spiritual Biography*. (NY: Crossroad Publishing Co., 2001).

Archer, Abigail. *Henry VIII*. Kindle edition. (New Word City, 2015).

Augustine of Hippo, 'Questions on Leviticus'. In *Patristic Bible Commentary*, Question 61. Available online at *sites.google.com/site/aquinasstudybible*.

Babylonian Talmud ('BT'). See 'Talmud'.

Beccatelli, Lodovico. *The Life of Cardinal Reginald Pole*. Trans. Benjamin Pye. (London: C. Bathurst, 1766). Available online at *archive.org*.

Bibliography and Online Resources

Belkin, Samuel. 'Levirate and Agnate Marriage in Rabbinic and Cognate Literature'. In *The Jewish Quarterly Review*, vol. 60 (1969–1970), 275, 327–29. (Philadelphia: Dropsie Univ. 1970).

Bereishit Rabbah. Available online at *sefaria.org*.

Bernard, G. W. *The King's Reformation: Henry VIII and the Remaking of the English Church*. (New Haven: Yale Univ. Press, 2005).

Biale, David. *Eros and the Jews: From Biblical Israel to Contemporary America*. (New York: Basic Books, 1992).

Bible (The Holy Bible). Douay-Rheims 1610 version. Trans. the English College of Doway. (Printed by John Cousturier, 1635). Available online at *archive.org/details/1610A.d.DouayOldTestament1582A.d.RheimsNewTestament_176/*.

Bible (The Holy Bible). Douay-Rheims 1609 (modern spelling and translation version). Available online at *archive.org/details/1609TheCatholicDouayRheimsBible/*.

Bible (The Holy Bible). Vulgate (Latin) version. Available online at *vulgate.org*.

Bible (The Holy Bible). King James 1611 version. Available online at *kingjamesbibleonline.org*.

Bible (The Holy Bible). See *JPS Hebrew-English Tanakh*; *Pentateuch and Haftorahs* (Hertz); *Tanach* (Artscroll/Stone).

Bonfil, Robert. 'A Cultural Profile'. In *The Jews of Early Modern Venice*. Ed. Robert C. Davis and Benjamin Ravid, 169–90. (Baltimore: John Hopkins University Press, 2001).

Borman, Tracy. *The Private Lives of the Tudors*. Kindle edition. (New York: Grove Press, 2016).

Brachman, Eli. 'Henry VIII, Oxford's Hebraists and the Rabbis of Venice in the 16th Century'. Available online at *oxfordchabad.org*.

Brandi, Karl. *The Emperor Charles V: The Growth and Destiny of a Man and of a World-Empire*. Trans. C. V. Wedgwood. (London: Jonathan Cape, 1939, 1965).

Brewer, J. S. *The Reign of Henry VIII: From his Accession to the Death of Wolsey*. Ed. James Gairdner. Vol. 1–4. (London: John Murray, 1884).

Bridgett, Thomas Edward. *Life of Blessed John Fisher*. (New York: Catholic Publication Society, 1890). Available online at *archive.org*.

British Library. 'Arundel MS 151'. (Responsum of R. Jacob Raphael, 1530.) In *Catalogue of Digitised Manuscripts*. Available online at *bl.uk/manuscripts*.

British Library. 'Hebrew Manuscripts: Journeys of the Written Word'. (Online announcement of August 2020-June 2021 exhibition). Available online at *bl.uk/events/Hebrew-manuscripts#*.

Brooks, Andrée Aelion. *The Woman Who Defied Kings: The Life and Times of Dona Gracia Nasi – a Jewish Leader During the Renaissance.* (St. Paul, MA: Paragon House, 2002).

Brown, Francis, S. R. Driver, and Charles A. Briggs. *Brown-Driver-Briggs Hebrew and English Lexicon.* (Peabody, MA: Hendrickson Pub., 1906).

Brown, Jeremy. 'Polydactyly', in *Science, Medicine, and the Talmud.* Available online at *Talmudology.com, Kiddushin* 25a, 7 September 2023.

Burnet, Gilbert. *History of the Reformation of the Church of England.*, Ed. Nicholas Pocock. Rev. Edition. 7 vols. (Oxford: Clarendon Press, 1865). Available online at *archive.org*.

Calendar of State Papers-Spain. Vol. 1–5, 1485–1538. Ed. G. A. Bergenroth and Pascual de Gayangos. (London: Her Majesty's Stationery Office 1862–1888). Available at British History Online (*british-history.ac.uk*).

Calendar of State Papers Relating to English Affairs in the Archives of Venice. Vol. 1–5, 1202–1554. Ed. Rawdon Brown. (London: Her Majesty's Stationery Office 1864–1873). Available at British History Online (*british-history.ac.uk*).

Canada Library and Archives. 'Incubala, Hebraica & Judaica'. Exhibition catalog. (Ottawa: 1981, 1997). Available online at *collectionscanada.gc.ca*.

Cavendish, George. *The Life of Cardinal Wolsey.* Ed. Samuel Weller Singer. Second edition. (London: Harding and Lepard, 1827). Available online at *archive.org*.

Cavendish, George. 'The Life and Death of Cardinal Wolsey'. In *Two Early Tudor Lives.* Ed. Richard S. Sylvester and Davis P. Harding. (New Haven: Yale Univ. Press, 1962).

Chalmers' Biography. S.v. Robert Wakefield. 1812. Available online at *words.fromoldbooks.org*.

Chalmers, C. R., and E. J. Chaloner. '500 years later: Henry VIII, leg ulcers and the course of history'. In *Journal of the Royal Society of Medicine.* 2009 Dec 1; 102(12), 514–517. Available online at *ncbi.nlm.nih.gov*.

Cleland, Elizabeth, and Adam Eaker. *The Tudors: Art and Majesty in Renaissance England.* (New York: The Metropolitan Museum of Art, 2022).

Bibliography and Online Resources

Cooper, T. P. *The History of the Castle of York*. (London: Elliot Stock, 1911). Available online at *archive.org*.

Dickens, A. G. *The English Reformation*. (New York: Schocken Books, 1964).

Dodd's Church History of England. Vol. 1. Ed. M. A. Tierney. (London: Charles Dolman, 1737, 1839). Available online at *archive.org*.

Edinburgh Review. Vol. 142, No. 240, April 1863, 195. [Review of *Calendar of State Papers-Spain* (Simancas records). Vol. 1. Henry VII. 1485–1509. Ed. G. A. Bergenroth.] (New York: Leonard Scott, 1863). Available online at *play.google.com/books*.

Ellis, Henry, ed. *Original Letters, Illustrative of English History*. Second ed., vol. 2. (London: Harding, Thriphook, and Lepard, 1885).

Elton, G. R. *England Under the Tudors*. (London: Putnam, 1955).

Encyclopaedia Judaica, 2nd ed., vol. 12. S.v. Levirate Marriage and Halizah, 725–729. (San Francisco: Thompson Gale, 2007). Available online at *archive.org*.

Epstein, Louis M. *Marriage Laws in the Bible and the Talmud*. (Cambridge, MA: Harvard Univ. Press, 1942).

Falk, Ze'ev W. *Jewish Matrimonial Law in the Middle Ages*. (Oxford: Oxford Univ. Press, 1966).

Fiddes, Richard. *The Life of Cardinal Wolsey*. Second ed. (London: Knapton, et al., 1726). Available online at *archive.org*.

Fisher, H. A. L. *The History of England: From the Accession of Henry VII to the Death of Henry VIII (1485–1547)*. Vol. 5 of *The Political History of England*. (New York: Greenwood Press, 1906).

Fletcher, Catherine. *Our Man in Rome: Henry VII and his Italian Ambassador*. (London: The Bodley Head, 2012).

Foxe, John. *Book of Martyrs* (orig. *Acts and Monuments*). Ed. Paul Wright. London: Alex Hoag, 1784. First pub. in English by John Day, 1563. Available online at *globalgreyebooks.com*.

Frankel, Jonathan. *The Damascus Affair: "Ritual Murder," Politics, and the Jews in 1840*. (New York: Cambridge University Press, 1997).

Friedmann, Paul. *Anne Boleyn*. First pub. 1884. Ed. Josephine Wilkinson. (Gloucestershire: Amberley Publishing, 2010).

Froude, James Anthony. *The Divorce of Catherine of Aragon: The Story as Told by the Imperial Ambassadors Resident in the Court of Henry VIII*. (New York: Longman Green, 1897). Available online at *archive.org*.

Gairdner, James. 'New Lights on the Divorce of Henry VIII', Parts 1, 2, and 3. In *The English Historical Review*. Vol. 11, no. 44 (October 1896), 673–702; 12, no. 45 (January 1897). 1–16; and 12, no. 46 (April 1897), 237–53. Available online at *archive.org*.

Gairdner, James ed. *Letters and Papers Illustrative of the Reigns of Richard III and Henry VII*. Two vols. (London: Longman, Green, 1861, 1863).

Gasquet, Francis A. *The Eve of the Reformation*. (New York: G. P. Putnam's Sons, 1900). Available online at *archive.org*.

Genesis Rabbah. See *Bereishit Rabbah*.

Giustinian, Sebastian. *Four Years at The Court of Henry VIII*. (2 vols). Trans. Rawdon Brown. (London: Smith, Elder, & Co., 1854). Available online at *archive.org* (Vol. 1) and *google.com/books* (Vol. 2).

Graetz, H. *History of the Jews*. Vol. 3. (Philadelphia, Jewish Publications Society, 1902).

Grayzel, Solomon. *The Church and the Jews in the Thirteenth Century*. (Philadelphia: Dropsie College, 1933). Available online at *archive.org*.

Grayzel, Solomon. *A History of the Jews: From the Babylonian Exile to the Present*. (New York: New American Library, 1947).

Greenblatt, Stephen. *The Swerve*. (New York: W. W. Norton, 2011).

Gregory, Brad S. *The Unintended Reformation: How a Religious Revolution Secularized Society*. Kindle edition. (Cambridge, MA: Belknap Press of Harvard Univ. Press, 2012).

Guy, John. *Queen of Scots: The True Life of Mary Stuart*. Kindle edition. (Boston: Mariner Books-Houghton Mifflin, 2004).

Guy, John and Julia Fox, *Hunting the Falcon: Henry VIII, Anne Boleyn, and the Marriage That Shook Europe*. (originally published in Great Britain by Bloomsbury Press, 2023; New York: HarperCollins, 2023).

Hackett, Francis. *Henry the Eighth*. (New York: Liveright, 1929).

Hackett, Jo Ann. *A Basic Introduction to Biblical Hebrew*. (Peabody, MA: Hendrickson Pub., 2010).

Halliwell (Halliwell-Phillipps), James Orchard. *Letters of the Kings of England*. Vol. 1, 297-320. (London: Henry Colburn, 1848). Available online at *archive.org*.

Hall's Chronicle. (London: J. Johnson et al., 1809). Originally *The Union of the Two Noble and Illustre Famelies of Lancastre & Yorke*, 1548. Available online at *archive.org*.

Bibliography and Online Resources

Hardy, Thomas Duffus. *Syllabus of Documents: Rymer's Foedera*. Vol. 2. (London: Longmans, 1873). Available online at *archive.org*.

Harpsfield, Nicholas. *A Treatise on the Pretended Divorce Between Henry VIII and Catherine of Aragon*. Ed. Nicholas Pocock. (Oxford: The Camden Society, 1878). Available online at *google.com/books*.

Haynes, Samuel, comp. *A Collection of State Papers, Relating to Affairs in the Reigns of King Henry VIII ... Left by William Cecill Lord Burhley*. (London: William Bowyer, 1740). Available online at *archive.org*.

Henry VIII, *The Love Letters of Henry VIII*. Ed., trans. and introduction by Jasper Ridley. (London: Cassell, 1988).

Henry VIII, *Love Letters of Henry VIII to Anne Boleyn*. (Boston: John W. Luce Company, 1906). Available online at *archive.org*.

Henry VIII, 'Love-Letters of Henry VIII'. See Halliwell, *Letters*.

Henry VIII, 'The Love Letters of Henry VIII & Anne Boleyn'. See Norton, ch.3.

Herbert, Lord Edward. *The Life and Raigne of King Henry the Eight*. (London: Thomas Whitaker, 1649) Available online at *archive.org*.

Herbert, Lord Edward. *The History of England Under Henry VIII*. Reprint of Kennet's Fol. Edition, 1719. (London: Alexander Murray, 1870). Available online at *archive.org*.

Historical Portraits Image Library (Philip Mould Ltd). Commentary on the Drewe Portrait of Queen Elizabeth I. Available online at *historicalportraits.com/Gallery*.

Holmes, David L. *A Brief History of the Episcopal Church: With a Chapter on the Anglican Reformation and an Appendix on the Quest for an Annulment of Henry VIII*. (Harrisburg, PA: Trinity Press, 1993).

Holmes, Oliver Wendell. 'Natural Law'. *Harvard Law Review*. Nov. 1918, 40–44. Available online at *jstor.org/stable/i257017*.

Holtz, Barry W., ed. *Back to the Sources*. (New York: Summit Books, 1984).

Hope, Mrs. *The First Divorce of Henry VIII: As Told in the State Papers*. Ed. Francis A. Gasquet. (London: Kegan Paul, Trench, Trubner, 1894). Available online at *archive.org*.

Horowitz, Elliott. 'Processions, Piety, and Jewish Confraternities'. In *The Jews of Early Modern Venice*. Ed. Robert C. Davis and Benjamin Ravid, 231. (Baltimore: John Hopkins Univ. Press, 2001).

Howes, Llewellyn. 'Who Will Put My Soul on the Scale?' In *Old Testament Essays*, 27/1(2014) 100–122. Available online at *researchgate.net/publication/303237463*.

Hughes, Philip. *The Reformation in England*. Vol. 1, 'The King's Proceedings'. (London: Hollis & Carter, 1954).

Hume, David. *History of England from the Invasion of Julius Caesar to the Revolution in 1688*. (London: Robert Bowyer, 1806).

Innes, Arthur D. *A History of England and the British Empire*. Vol. 2, 1485–1688. (New York: Macmillan Co., 1913). Available online at *archive.org*.

Ives, Eric. *Anne Boleyn*. (New York: Basil Blackwell, 1986).

Jacobs, Joseph. *The Jews of Angevin England: Documents and Records*. (London: David Nutt, 1893). Available online at *archive.org*.

Jewish Encyclopedia. Isidor Singer, ed. 12 vols. S.v. 'Italy-Spread of the Cabala'. (New York: Funk and Wagnalls, 1906). Available online at *jewishencyclopedia.com*.

Jewish Historical Society of England. *Transactions*. See Abrahams, B. Lionel.

Jewish Virtual Library. S.v. 'Bigamy and Polygamy'. Available online at *jewishvirtuallibrary.org*.

Johnson, John. *A Collection of the Laws and Canons of the Church of England*. Vol. 1. (Oxford: John Henry Parker, 1850). Available online at *archive.org*.

Jones, Dan. *The War of the Roses: The Fall of the Plantagenets and the Rise of the Tudors*. Kindle Edition. (New York: Penguin Books, 2014).

Jones, Philippa. *The Other Tudors: Henry VIII's Mistresses and Bastards*. (New York: Metro Books, 2009).

Josephus, Flavius. *The Wars of the Jews*. Vol. 1 of *The Works of Flavius Josephus*. Tr. William Whiston. (Grand Rapids, MI: Baker Book House, 1974).

JPS Hebrew-English Tanakh, Second Ed. (Philadelphia: Jewish Publication Society, 1999).

Kaplan, Aryeh. *Sefer Yetzira*. (Northvale, NJ: Jason Aronson, 1995, 1990).

Kaplan, Aryeh. *The Real Messiah? A Jewish Response to Missionaries*. (Toronto: Jews for Judaism, 1976). Available online at *jewsforjudaism.ca*.

Katz, David S. *Philo-Semitism and the Readmission of the Jews to England, 1603-1655*. (Oxford: Clarendon Press, 1982).

Katz, David S. *The Jews in the History of England, 1485-1850*. (Oxford: Clarendon Press, 1994).

Katz, Jacob. 'Post-Zoharic Relations Between Halakhah and Kabbalah'. In *Jewish Thought in the Sixteenth Century*. Ed. Bernard Dov Cooperman, 283. (Cambridge, MA: Harvard Univ. Press, 1983).

Kaufmann, David. 'Jacob Mantino – A Page of the History of the Renaissance'. In *Review of Jewish Studies [Revue Des Etudes Juives]* (Paris). Vol. 27 (1893): 30-60, 207-219. Original in French. Available online at *archive.org*.

Kaufmann, David. 'Opinion of Jacob Rafael Peglione of Modena on the Divorce of Henry VIII'. *Review of Jewish Studies [Revue Des Etudes Juives]* (Paris). Vol. 30 (1895): 309-13. Original in French and Hebrew. Available online at *archive.org*.

Kelly, Henry Ansgar. *The Matrimonial Trials of Henry VIII*. (Stanford, CA: Stanford Univ. Press, 1976).

Klein, Isaac. *A Guide to Jewish Religious Practice*. (New York: Jewish Theological Seminary, 1979).

Klein, Isaac. Trans. Introduction and commentaries to *The Code of Maimonides [Mishneh Torah]. Book 4: The Book of Women [Nashim]. Treatise 1: Laws Concerning Marriage*. Yale Judaica Series. (New Haven: Yale Univ. Press, 1972).

Knight, Charles. *The Popular History of England*. Vol. 2. (Boston: Estes and Lauriat, 1874). Available online at *archive.org*.

Kugel, James. *How to Read the Bible*. (New York: Free Press, 2007).

Letters and Papers, Foreign and Domestic, Henry VIII, 1509-1536. 11 vols. (London: His Majesty's Stationery Office, 1888-1920). Available at British History Online at *british-history.ac.uk*.

Lewis, John. *The Life of Dr. John Fisher, Bishop of Rochester in the Reign of King Henry VIII*. 2 vols. (London: Joseph Lilly, 1855). Available online at *archive.org*.

Lewis, Miriam. 'Hebrew Manuscripts Digitisation Project Phase 1 completed'. In *British Library, Asian and African studies blog*. September 19, 2016. Available online at *blogs.bl.uk/asian-and-african/2016/09*.

Linder, Douglas O. 'Leviticus & The King's Great Matter'. In *Famous Trials*. Available online at *famous-trials.com/thomasmore*.

Linder, Douglas O. 'The Trial of Sir Thomas More: An Account'. In *Famous Trials*. Available online at *famous-trials.com/thomasmore*.

Lingard, John. *The History of England*. 6th ed. Vol. 4. (Dublin: James Duffy & Sons, 1874). Available online at *archive.org*.

Loades, David. *Henry VIII*. (Gloucestershire: Amberley Publishing, 2011).

Maimonides, *The Code of Maimonides [Mishneh Torah]. Book 4: The Book of Women [Nashim]. Treatise 1: Laws Concerning Marriage*. Trans. and commentary Isaac Klein. Yale Judaica Series. (New Haven: Yale Univ. Press, 1972).

Maimonides, *Mishneh Torah. Sefer Nashim: Yibbum v Chalitzah*. Trans. Eliyahu Touger [Hebrew and English]. Available online at *Chabad.org*.

Malamud, Bernard. *The Fixer*. (New York: Dell Publishing, 1966).

Marcus, Jacob R. *The Jew in the Medieval World: A Source Book: 315–1791*. (New York: Athenium, 1978).

Margolis, Max L. and Alexander Marx. *A History of the Jewish People*. (New York: World Publishing and Jewish Publication Society, 1927).

Mattingly, Garrett. *Catherine of Aragon*. (New York: Book-of-the-Month Club, 1941).

Mattingly, Garrett. 'The Reputation of Doctor De Puebla'. In *English Historical Review*, vol. 55, No. 217, Jan. 1940, 27–46. Oxford University Press. Available online at *jstor.org/stable/554029*.

Murphy, Beverly A. *Bastard Prince: Henry VIII's Lost Son*. Kindle edition. (Gloucestershire: The History Press, 2011, 2001).

Nadler, Steven. *Menasseh ben Israel: Rabbi of Amsterdam*. (New Haven: Yale Univ. Press, 2018).

Nalson, John. *An Impartial Collection of the Great Affairs of State from the Beginning of the Scotch Rebellion in the year 1639 to the Murther of King Charles I*. 2 vols. (London: Mearne, Dring, et al., 1682). Available online at *archive.org*.

Neale, J. E. *Queen Elizabeth I*. (Garden City, NY: Doubleday Anchor, 1934).

Neusner, Jacob. *Introduction to Rabbinic Literature*. (New York: Doubleday, 1994).

Norton, Elizabeth. *The Anne Boleyn Papers*. (Gloucestershire: Amberley Publishing, 2011).

Bibliography and Online Resources

Norwich, John Julius. *Four Princes: Henry VIII, Francis I, Charles V, Suleiman the Magnificent, and the obsessions that Forged Modern Europe.* Kindle edition. (New York: Atlantic Monthly Press, 2016).

Pentateuch and Haftorahs. 2d ed. Ed. and commentaries by J. H. Hertz. (London: Soncino Press, 1936).

Pirkei Avot (Ethics of the Fathers). Available online at *sefaria.org*.

Pirkei Avot. (Sayings of the Fathers). Trans and commentary by Joseph H Hertz. (New York: Behrman House 1945).

Prescott, H. F. M. *Mary Tudor: The Spanish Tudor.* (London: Orion/Phoenix, 1940).

Pocock, Nicholas. *Records of the Reformation: The Divorce 1527–1533.* 2 vols. (Oxford: Clarendon Press, 1870). Available online at *archive.org*.

Pole, Reginald. *Pole's Defense of the Unity of the Church.* Translated with introduction by Joseph G. Dwyer. (Westminster, MD: The Newman Press, 1965). Available online at *archive.org*.

Pollard, A. F. *Henry VIII.* (London and New York: Goupil & Co., 1902). Available online at *archive.org*.

Prescott, William H. *History of the Reign of Ferdinand and Isabella.* Vol. 1. (New York: A. L. Burt, 1837). Available online at *archive.org*.

Pumfrey, Liz. 'History of Fractions'. Univ. Cambridge Faculty of Mathematics NRICH project. Available online at *nrich.maths.org/2515*.

Rabow, Jerry. *50 Jewish Messiahs.* (New York and Jerusalem: Gefen Publishing House, 2002).

Raphael, Jacob. *Responsum.*1530, Available online as *Arundel MS 151* at *bl.uk/manuscripts*.

Read, Conyers. *Bibliography of British History: Tudor Period 1485–1603.* 2d ed. (Oxford: Clarendon Press, 1959).

Reubeni, David. 'Diary'. In *Jewish Travellers in the Middle Ages.* Ed. Elkan Nathan Adler. (New York: Dover Publications, 1987. Reprint of *Jewish Travellers*, 1930). 251-328.

Reuveni, David. See Reubeni, David.

Ridgeway, Claire. 'Was Anne Boleyn a Commoner?' In *Questions About Anne Boleyn* (blog series). Available online at youtube.com.

Ridley, Jasper. See Henry VIII. *The Love Letters of Henry VIII.*

Roach, J. P. C., ed. 'The University of Cambridge: The Middle Ages'. In *A History of the County of Cambridge and the Isle of Ely: Vol. 3*. (London: Victoria County History, 1959). Available at British History Online (*british-history.ac.uk*).

Rosenblatt, Jason P. *Renaissance England's Chief Rabbi: John Selden*. (London: Oxford Univ. Press, 2006).

Roth, Cecil. *The Jews in the Renaissance*. (New York: Harper & Row, 1959).

Rymer, Thomas. *Foedera*. Vol. 13. (London: Tonson, 1727). Available online at *archive.org*.

Samuel, Edgar. 'The Provenance of the Westminster Talmud'. In *Transactions and Miscellanies (Jewish Historical Society of England)*. Vol 27 (1978–1980). 148–150. Available online at *jstor.org/stable/29778903*.

Sander, Nicolas. *Rise and Growth of the Anglican Schism*. Translated with introduction and notes by David Lewis. (Original published 1585; London: Burns and Oats, 1877.) Available online at *archive.org*.

Sanford, Vera. 'La Disme of Simon Stevin – The First Book on Decimals'. In *The Mathematics Teacher*. Vol 14 (October 1, 1921). 321-333. Available online at *archive.org* (*jstor-27950351*).

Sarna, Jonathan D. and Dvora E. Weisberg. 'A Writ of Release from Levirate Marriage (Shtar Halitzah) in 1807 Charleston'. In *The American Jewish Archives Journal*, vol. 63, no.1 (2011), 38–56. Available online at *sites.americanjewisharchives.org*.

Satlow, Michael. 'The Rabbinic Network'. In *Tablet Magazine*, 2 May 2021. Available online at *tabletmag.com*.

Scarisbrick, J. J. *Henry VIII*. (Berkeley and Los Angeles: Univ. of California Press, 1968).

Schiffman, Lawrence H., ed. *Texts and Traditions*. (Hoboken, NJ: KTAV Publishing House, 1998).

Selden, John. *John Selden on Jewish Marriage Law: The Uxor Hebraica*. Trans. and notes by Jonathan R. Ziskind. (Leiden: Brill, 1991).

Simkin, John. 'Was Henry FitzRoy, the illegitimate son of Henry VIII, murdered?' Spartacus Blog post, 31 May 2015. Available online at *spartacus-educational.com*.

Simkovich, Malka. 'The Christian Monks Who Saved Jewish History. Lehrhaus Blog post, 11 May 2017. Available online at *thelehrhaus.com/scholarship*.

Simon, Ed. '"Rabbi" John Selden and the Restoration of the Jews to England'. In *Tablet Magazine.* 15 December 2017. Available online at *tabletmag.com* (251506).

Sothebys. 'The Bromberg Talmud'. 2015 auction brochure for the Valmadonna Trust Library. Available online at *sothebys.com/en/auctions.*

State Papers, Published under the Authority of His Majesty's Commission. Vol. 1. King Henry VIII's correspondence with Cardinal Wolsey and with his other ministers, 1509-1547. (London: G. Eyre and A. Strahan, 1830). Available online at *archive.org.*

Starkey, David. *Six Wives.* (New York: HarperCollins, 2003).

Stevin, Simon. See Sanford, Vera. See also *Wikipedia.org,* s.v. Simon Stevin.

Stow, Kenneth R. 'The Church and the Jews'. In *The New Cambridge Medieval History.* Ed. David Abulafia. Vol. 5. C. 1198–c. 1300. 204–219. (New York: Cambridge University Press, 1999). Available online at *archive.org.*

Strype, John. *Ecclesiastical Memorials.* Vol. 1, part 2. (Oxford: Clarendon Press, 1822). Available online at *archive.org.*

Surtz, Ed. Edward and Virginia Murphy. *The Divorce Tracts of Henry VIII.* (Angers, France: Moreana, 1988).

Talmud (Babylonian Talmud, or *BT).* Tractate 'Yevamot'. Available online at *sefaria.org.*

Tanach. (Artscroll/Stone Edition). (Brooklyn, NY: Mesorah Publications, 1996).

Vergil, Polydore. *The Anglica Historia of Polydore Vergil, A.D. 1485–1537.* Book 27. Translated by Dana F. Sutton. (London: Royal Historical Society, 1950). Available online at *philological.bham.ac.uk.*

Walsh, William Thomas. *Philip II.* (New York: Sheed & Ward, 1937).

Warnicke, Retha M. *The Rise and Fall of Anne Boleyn.* (New York: Cambridge Univ. Press, 1989).

Weir, Alison. *The Children of Henry VIII.* Kindle edition. (New York: Ballentine Books, 1996, 2008).

Weir, Alison. *The Lady in the Tower: The Fall of Anne Boleyn.* (New York: Ballantine Books, 2009).

Weir, Alison. *The Six Wives of Henry VIII.* Kindle edition. (New York: Grove Press, 1991).

Weisberg, Dvora E. *Levirate Marriage and the Family in Ancient Judaism.* (Waltham, MA: Brandeis Univ. Press, 2009).

Wertman, Janet. *Jane the Quene.* Kindle edition. 2016.

Wertman, Janet. *The Path to Somerset.* Kindle edition. 2018.

Wyatt, George. 'Extracts from The Life of Anne Boleigne'. In Appendix to Cavendish, George. *The Life of Cardinal Wolsey,* Second ed., by Samuel Weller Singer. (London: Harding and Lepard, 1827). Available online at *archive.org.*

Yates, Frances. *The Occult Philosophy in the Elizabethan Age.* (New York: Routledge Classics, 1979). Available online at *archive.org.*

Yoffie, Adina M. 'Refusal of the Levirate Marriage'. In *Conservative Judaism,* vol. 52 No. 3, Spring 2000, 22.

Ziegler, Yael. *Ruth, From Alienation to Monarchy.* Kindle edition. (New Milford, CT: Maggid Books, 2015).

Online Resources

Interested readers and researchers may want to browse some of the following online resources for additional information and background about the Tudor period in general and Henry VIII's Great Matter in particular:

Internet Archive: *archive.org*

This is an extremely helpful source for free access to older books, some going back to the beginnings of movable type book printing. The site includes a powerful search engine, a convenient online reader, and multiple choices for download formats. For books printed in modern type fonts, download format options often include searchable PDF, facilitating searching for individual words or passages without the need for further OCR applications.

Alternate online archives

If a particular work cannot be located on the Internet Archive site, you can also search several similar sites that also offer free viewing and downloading of scanned early books, including Google Books (*books.google.com*), which can store your downloaded selections in your Google Books Library; Digital Public Library of America (*dp.la*); and Hathi Trust Digital Library (*HathiTrust.org*). These sites have considerable overlap in the works offered, but sometimes what you are looking for might be available on only one of these archive sites.

World-wide Library Catalog: *worldcat.org*
Search this huge catalogue to see what university libraries or other public libraries have a physical copy or an ebook copy of a particular book. Your access to the real or virtual book will depend upon the particular library's policy.

British History online: *british-history.ac.uk*
This British government archive provides free public online access to a vast number of official government records, including three series of documents that are centrally important to the study of Henry VIII:

Letters and Papers: In the very extensive series of *Letters and Papers* for the reign of Henry VIII, volumes 1–11 cover the earlier years, 1509–1536. These are the most relevant to Henry's marriage to Catherine, the Great Matter of his annulment, and his marriage to Anne Boleyn.

Calendar of State Papers-Spain: The first ten books of the *Calendar of State Papers-Spain* are numbered through volume 5, part 2 because some of the 'volumes' include multiple parts or supplements. These ten books cover essentially the same period as the *Letters and Papers* series mentioned above. In addition, the first volume of the *CSP-Spain* series covers the reign of King Henry VII. When, as sometimes occurs, descriptions of the same event or even the same documents appear in both *Letters and Papers* and *CSP-Spain*, it can be helpful to compare the two sources, because wording, extent of translation, and the relative amounts of summary rather than direct quotation can differ between these sources.

Calendar of State Papers-Venice: This series is similar to but more limited than the *Calendar of State Papers-Spain*. However, the Venetian documents include some detailed and perhaps more unbiased observations of English affairs in the diplomatic reports submitted to the government of Venice by various Venetian ambassadors.

Luminarium Anthology of English Literature: *luminarium.org*
In addition to providing an anthology of English literature, including links to works by various contemporaries of Henry VIII, this site includes an encyclopaedia, with indexed entries to many Tudor characters, events, portraits, biographies, letters, and speeches.

Regular online blogs and podcasts for Henry VIII and Tudor History: If you would prefer to continue your learning about Henry VIII and Tudor history in periodic, small doses, you can subscribe to online blogs or podcasts (frequent online newsletters or video or audio programs) from one of many available sources. Three of the most established and popular offerings are by Claire Ridgway (*theanneboleynfiles.com*), Janet Wertman (*janetwertman.com*), and Heather Teysko (*englandcast.com*). They can also be followed on YouTube or similar platforms. Blogs and podcasts differ in their precise format, focus, and citation of sources, but they can be interesting and convenient secondary sources for continuing to learn about Tudor historical facts and interpretations.

Purchasing Used Books
Some older or out-of-print books can be very expensive to purchase, but you may be surprised to find the occasional book that you are looking for in relatively good used condition and very modestly priced. Visit your local used bookstore in person or online, or search *abebooks.com* or similar sites, which list offerings from independent booksellers throughout the world. New and recently published used books may also be found at *amazon.com*.

INDEX

advocation *see* Blackfriars trial: suspension and advocation of
affinity incest
   consummation of first marriage, requires 93, 102, 105–7, 227–9, 322–3 n. 19
   Deuteronomy, conflict with 78, 102, 117, 121–2, 130, 131, 138
   dispensation of 62, 73, 75–6, 77–8, 119–20, 121–2, 123–4, 138
   in-law relationship causes 73
   punished by childlessness 76
annates 193–4, 316 n.18
Anne Boleyn, queen of England *Fig. 5*
background
   beauty, opinions about 47–8, 198, 271–2 n.3, 272 n.4
   Catholic conservatives, unpopular with 108
   commoners, unpopular with 198
   George Boleyn, and 271 n.2, 320 n.3
   Liberal clergy and members at court support 199
   Mary Boleyn, different from 46–7
   personal qualities 47, 117, 214
   physical features 48, 272 n.4

before marriage to Henry VIII
   Chapuys opposes 168, 311 n.17
   French royal court, experiences in 47, 271 n.2
   Henry VIII, gains influence over him 85
   Henry VIII, pursued by 45, 46, 49
   Henry VIII, meeting with Francis, attends with 172–3
   Henry VIII, sexual relationship with 53–5, 57–8, 278 n.29
   Henry Percy, romantic relationship with 48–9, 273 n.6
   Leviticus issue because of her sister 139–40, 285 n.9, 304 n.24
   love letters from Henry VIII 50–3, 54, 216–21
   Pembroke, elevated to Marchioness of 173, 192, 316 n.15
   pregnant before marriage: 189–0, 200–1, 315 n.9, 315 n.10
   Wolsey, her enmity towards 49, 273–4, n.8
after marriage to Henry VIII
   coronation at Westminster 194
   Elizabeth, gives birth to 189

Henry VIII, displeases him 205, 277 n.27, 318 n.1
Henry VIII, marriage ends in three years 204
Henry VIII, wedding to 189, 315 n.7, 315–16 n. 11
male heir, she fails to produce 206, 207
trial and execution 208
Anne of Cleves, queen of England Fig.18 (see 262–3 n.Fig. 18), 240–2, 277 n.25, 278 n.35
annulment vs. divorce 67–8, 72–3, 223–4, 279 n.1, 320 n.2
antisemitism 23–6, 169, 264 n.1, 309 n.5, 312 n.21
Arthur, prince of Wales 32–4, 43–4, 266 n.4–5, 278 n.30, *see also* consummation of Arthur's marriage
Ashkenazi vs. Sephardi 20, 145, 176–9, 302–3 n.17, 303–4 n. 21, 313 n.2
Augustine of Hippo, St 280 n.5, 296–7 n.2

Babylonian Talmud *see* Talmud
Bavli *see* Talmud
Beaufort, John, Earl of Somerset 32, 124, 244, 265 n.1
Beaufort, Margaret 124, 244
betrothal 48, 135, 208, 235, 240, 241, 262, 273 n.6, 285–6 n.9, 319 n.10
Bible, Christian 78, 89, 117, 118, 122, 130, 147, 260 n.Fig. 2, 305–6 n.11, 306 n. 13
Bible, Hebrew 78, 79, 89, 117, 118, 130, 134, 143, 152, 169, 296 n.1, 297 n.8, 300–1 n.9
bigamy 88, 89, 90, 169, 170
Blackfriars trial *Fig. 13* (see 261 n.Fig. 13)

Catherine, actions and speech at 93, 107, 288–9 n.28
Catherine, public support for 93
Fisher advocates for Catherine 93, 94, 289 n.32
hall where held 92
Henry, positions taken at 93–4, 289 n.29, 320 n.4
judges 91, 92
suspension and advocation of 94, 97
Wolsey, personal statement at 273 n.7
see also Campeggio; Cavendish; Consummation; Fisher, John; Spanish Brief
Blood Libel 24–5, 264 n. 1–3
Blount, Elizabeth (Bessie) 43, 44, 56, 190
Boleyn, Anne *see* Anne Boleyn, queen of England
Boleyn, George 217, 220, 320 n.3
Boleyn, Mary
children 44, 270 n.8
French court, reputation in 46–7, 271 n.1, 285 n.9
Henry VIII, mistress to 44, 56, 139–40, 285 n.9
Henry VIII, not supported by 44
William Carey, married to 44
Boleyn, Thomas 44, 46, 47, 273 n.8, 320 n.3
Bomberg, Daniel 136, 301 n.11
Bosworth Field, Battle of 32, 245
bribery and fraud by the English 102, 109, 111–12, 113–15, 142, 159–60, 161–3, 187, 296 n.46, 304 n.1, 308–9 n.3, 309–10 n.5–6
brief, papal *See* Julius II, Spanish brief
British Library 163, 165, 311 n.12
Buckmaster, William 102–3, 104, 107, 109
Bull, papal *See* Julius II, Bull of Dispensation

342

Index

Cabalism (Christian) 141, 143–4, 145
Calais 172, 191, 192, 252
Cambridge (city) 264 n.4, 291–2 n.3–4
Cambridge University 55, 100, 102–05, 107–10, 291–2 n.3–4, 294 n.21, 294 n.25, 295 n.30
Campeggio, Lorenzo, cardinal *Figs. 12–13* (see 261 n.Fig 12–13)
  Arthur failed to consummate 289 n.28
  Blackfriars trial, and 52–3, 90, 94
  Blackfriars trial, delay of 92–3, 95, 287 n.25
  Clement, loyalty to 91
  dispensation, offer to cure defects 284 n.21
  emperor, support for 95, 97–8
  health 92
  Henry VIII theological knowledge 282 n.11
  love letters searched for 274–5 n.12
  payment for English bishoprics 91, 287 n.23
  religious order, attempt to have Catherine join 92, 288 n.27
  Secrecy of commission 92, 94, 287 n.24
Casale, Gregory, ambassador 60, 70, 88, 131, 144, 286 n.13
Casale, John, prothonotary and ambassador 150, 151, 160, 271 n.12, 307 n.29
Casali *see* Casale
Castel Sant'Angelo *Fig. 11*, 82, 83
Catherine Howard, queen of England 242
Catherine of Aragon, queen of England *Figs. 2, 12, 13* (see 260 n.Fig. 2, 261 n.Fig. 12–13)
  Antisemitism, shown by 317 n.5
  Arthur Tudor, marriage to 33–4
  beauty, loss of 59–60, 278 n.34–5
  Blackfriars trial, speech at 93
  Chapuys, support from 167–8
  Charles V, support from 196
  children and pregnancies 42, 76, 269–70 n.2
  claim to throne of England 265 n.2
  consummation by Arthur, denies 93, 107, 227, 283 n.16, 288–9 n. 28, 294 n.20, 322–3 n. 19
  convent, refuses to retire to 92, 288 n.26–7, 320 n.2
  death 206, 318 n.4
  exile from court and separation from daughter 204, 250
  finances as widow 267 n.8
  Henry VIII, annulment of marriage to 194
  Henry VIII, ceases sexual relations with 44–5, 59, 270–1 n.11–12
  Henry VIII, wedding to 40–1
  Henry VIII, wedding treaty 39–40, 62
  hero of the Great Matter, as 215
  Leviticus Prohibitions and dispensation 37–9, 62, 69–70, 71, 285–6 n.9
  popular with the people 33, 68, 69, 93, 198, 280 n.3, 317 n.4
  queen, summary of reign 239
  supported by conservative clergy 199
  Wolsey is blamed by 72
  See also Blackfriars trial, Spanish Brief, Westminster trial
Catholicism 20, 67–8, 108, 133, 138, 154–5, 156–7, 173, 197, 251, 253–4, 294 n.24
Cavendish, George 273 n.7, 281 n.9, 288–9 n.28
Chapuys, Eustace
  Anne Boleyn, opposed to 168, 192, 205, 206, 273–4 n.8
  Catherine of Aragon, support for 167–8, 229

Charles V, reports to 167
Cranmer, Thomas, warns
   against 193
fraud by English, warns
   about 111–12, 169, 193
Henry VIII, relationship with and
   reports about 167, 213
Raphael, Mark, antisemitic
   comments about 312 n.21
Raphael, Mark, warns against 169,
   172
Charles V, holy Roman emperor *Fig. 10*
   Catherine of Aragon, support
      for 196
   Clement VII, conflict with 82, 83
   Clement VII, reconciliation
      with 97–8, 196
   Francis I, conflict with 82, 111, 317
      n.1
   Henry VIII, conflict with 84, 112
   Ottoman Turk army, threatened
      by 186
   Spanish Brief, and 97, 226, 290–1
      n.40, 321 n.6
   Mary Tudor, support for 249
   Wolsey, conflict with 72
   see also Sack of Rome
Clement VII, pope *Fig. 8*
   advocation of annulment trial to
      Vatican 97
   bribery attempt by Henry,
      declines 187
   Cardinals, purports to rely upon
      advice of 76, 284 n.20
   Church property, allows surrender
      of 63
   Cranmer as Archbishop, agrees to
      appoint 193–4, 201, 317 n.3
   decretal commission, grant of 87–8,
      91–2, 287–8 n.24–5
   dispensation to marry Anne,
      grants 285–6 n.9
   excommunication, threatens Henry
      VIII with 186, 187

general commission, makes grant
   of 90–1
Henry should marry Anne as a
   second wife 89–90
Henry should marry Anne without
   dispensation 39–40, 88
illegitimacy reversed by cousin Pope
   Leo X 265 n.1
Jewish Messiah figures, sponsors
   two 154–5, 156, 157–8, 308 n.36
Julius II dispensation, offers to cure
   defects 74
Julius II dispensation, reluctance to
   reverse 74, 284 n.21
Knight's dispensation petition,
   rewrites 86
Leviticus Prohibitions, previously
   dispensed by 122–4
Mantino, Jacob, contact with 150
natural law argument,
   opposes 77–8
motivations and character, analysis
   of 196–7, 214
procrastination 68, 74, 283 n.15
Protestant Reformation, threatened
   by 69
Sack of Rome, flight from 82, 83
Cloth of Gold, Field of *see* Field of
   Cloth of Gold
consummation of Arthur's marriage 96,
   105, 107, 227, 229, 283 n.16,
   288–9 n.28, 289 n.31, 290 n.38,
   292 n.10, 293 n.15, 299 n.1, 311
   n.14, 321 n.10, 322 n.14–15, 322–3
   n.19
conversos 154, 155, 157, 304 n.4
Coronation Riot *See* London: Richard
   I coronation and riots
Corte, Francesco de *See* Curtiso,
   Francesco
Cranmer, Thomas *Fig. 15* (*see also*
   262 n.Fig. 15)
   Archbishop of Canterbury, appointed
      as 193–4, 316 n.18, 317 n.3

Index

Anne Boleyn crowned queen of England by 194
Anne Boleyn marriage annulled by 208
Anne Boleyn marriage declared valid by 194
Cambridge University, liberal faculty leader of 100, 108
Catherine of Aragon marriage annulled by 194, 209
levirate marriage never applied to Christians 122
rabbinic opinions, possible source of strategy for 129
secret oath that he would follow English law 194
university opinions, source of strategy for 99–100
Croke, Richard 115–16, 130–1, 132, 133–4, 142, 145, 150–1, 178
Cromwell, Oliver 26
Cromwell, Thomas *Figs. 18, 19* (see 262–3 n.Fig. 18), 188, 208, 239, 240–1
Curtis, Francesco *see* Curtiso, Francesco
Curtiso, Francesco 163–4, 232

decretal commission 87–8, 90, 91–2, 274–5 n.12, 287–8 n.24
Deuteronomy *see* levirate marriage
Diaspora 20, 145, 175, 300 n.9
dispensation *see* Julius II: Bull of dispensation
divorce *see* annulment vs. divorce
dowry 33, 35–7, 39, 40, 293 n.14
Dudley, John, duke of Northumberland 246–8

Edmunds, John 103, 104, 107
Edward I, king of England 26, 299 n.4
Edward III, king of England 32, 61, 124, 244–5

Edward VI, king of England *Fig. 21*, 34, 44, 201, 210, 240, 245–6, 247, 249, 255, 270 n.6, 278 n.30
Elizabeth I, queen of England *Fig. 24*
accepted by the people 210
Anne Boleyn, differentiated self from 271–2 n.3
birth and legitimacy 189–90, 204, 209
Mary, Queen of Scots, conflict with 253–4
Queen Mary I, conflict with 250–1, 252–3
succession, in line of 210, 252, 278 n.32
Elizabeth of York, queen of England *Fig. 3*, 32, 35
Elton, G. R. 15, 212, 309 n.4
English sweating sickness *see* sweating sickness
excommunication 186, 187, 314 n.1, 315 n.4

Father Francis *see* Giorgi, Francesco
Ferdinand and Isabella, monarchs of Spain *Fig. 4* (*see* 260–1 n.Fig. 4), 32, 36, 62, 106, 228, 231, 268–9 n.12, 293, n.14–15, 299–300 n.5, 317 n.5, 321 n.13, see also Ferdinand II, King of Aragon, Isabella, Queen of Castile
Ferdinand II, king of Aragon *Fig. 4* (*see* 260–1 n.Fig. 4), 33, 36, 38, 73, 106–7, 229, 268–9 n.12, 269 n.13, 280–1 n.8, 322 n.16, 322–3 n.19, *see also* Ferdinand and Isabella, monarchs of Spain
Field of Cloth of Gold 172
Fisher, H. A. L. 15, 112, 160, 211–12, 309 n.5
Fisher, John, Bishop *Fig. 14* (*see* 261–2 n.Fig. 14), 93, 94, 121, 180, 191, 199, 204, 215, 282 n.12, 285 n.3, 289 n.32, 297–8 n.9–10

Fitzroy, Henry 34, 43–4, 59, 190, 270 n.5, 270 n.7, 278 n.30, 296 n.44
Fox, Edward 88, 99–100, 101, 109, 283 n.15, 291–2 n.2–3
Foxe, John 281, 291 n.1–2
France
 Boleyn, Mary and Anne in royal court of 46–7, 271 n.1–2
 Charles V, conflict with 112
 England, allied with 186
 England, Norman-French invasion of 23
 Henry VIII invades 280 n.3, 314 n.1
 Jews, massacred in Blois 264 n.3
 League of Cognac, leader of 82
 love letters taken to 52
 Mary I, queen of England, invades 251–2
 military world power, as 33, 38, 82
 opinions supporting Henry sought from 111–12
 Raphael, Mark, in 173
 Vatican influenced by 84
 Wolsey goes to negotiate with 84
Francis I, king of France 60, 80, 82, 84, 111, 112, 172, 192, 271 n.1, 317 n.1

Gardiner, Stephen 88, 99–100, 102, 103, 104, 283 n.15, 291–2 n.2–4, 294 n.25
Gershom, rabbi 177, 302–3 n.17
Ghinucci, Girolamo, bishop 89, 131, 144, 146, 159, 160, 161, 164, 285 n.5, 306 n.12, 309–10 n.6, 313 n.28, 314 n.8, 321 n.7
Giorgi, Francesco 142, 143, 144–5, 145, 146, 150–1, 304 n.2, 306–7 n.17
Georgius, Francesco *see* Giorgi, Francesco
Great Matter *see* Henry VIII: seeking an annulment

Gregory I, Pope *Fig. 16* (*see* 262 n.Fig. 16), 75–6, 122–3, 298 n.13–15
Grey, Lady Jane *Fig. 22*, 201, 246–8

Halfan, Elijah Menahem, rabbi 131, 145–6, 147–9, 152, 156–8, 166, 178, 305 n.7–8, 307 n.19
halitzah 78, 118, 131, 138–9, 177–8, 303–4 n.21, 313 n.5, 314 n.7
Hapsburg 63, 82, 97, 186, 196
Hebraist 121, 134, 136, 142, 145, 297 n.7, 300 n.6, 301 n.10, 306–7 n.17
Helias *see* Halfan
Helyas *see* Halfan
Henry VII *Fig.3*, 32, 33–4, 35–6. 38, 39, 62, 73, 74, 106, 124, 228, 244–5, 265 n.1, 268–9 n.11–13, 278 n.30
Henry VIII *Figs. 1, 7, 13* (*see* 261 n.Fig.7, 261 n.Fig. 13)
as Prince Henry Tudor
 birth 32
 Arthur's wedding, escorts Catherine at 33, 40
 heir apparent, becomes 35
 marriage treaty 35, 36, 62, 229, 231, 268 n.11, 293 n.14, 322 n.16, 323 n.21
 marriage treaty, renounces 39, 268 n.11
marriage to Catherine
 Catherine, romantically attracted to 40
 Coronation, jointly with Catherine 40–1
 Leviticus Prohibitions 37–8
 marriage dispensation by Pope Julius II 38
 marriage, financial considerations for 35–6, 39
 marriage treaty, reaffirmation by Henry 39–40
 Mary Tudor, only child surviving infancy, as 42

346

Index

mistresses 43, 44, 49, 57, 85, 190, 216, 277 n.5
paternity of Henry Fitzroy, acknowledged by 43
paternity of Mary Boleyn's children, not acknowledged by 44
sons both ultimately die as teenagers 34, 43–4
wedding ceremony is private 40

public image and appearance
appetite 56
body 56
character of 211–13
hunting 55
jousting 55–6
leg injury 56
musician, as 55
royal court 55
strength 55
weight and shape, changes in 56, 276–7 n.23

courtship of Anne Boleyn
Anne becomes pregnant 189–90, 315 n.10
Anne controls the love relationship 57, 58
sexual prowess of Henry mocked by Anne 57
sexual relations with Anne Boleyn before marriage 57–8

seeking an annulment
Church wealth as motive for 62–3, 187–8
Cranmer appointed archbishop and grants annulment 194
dispensation of Julius II, problems with 73–7
head of Church in England, Henry as 186, 188, 191, 201
levirate marriage rules of Deuteronomy, problems with 77–8
levirate wedding in Rome 179–81
love for Anne as motive for 58–9, 60–1, 86, 192, 195
moral scruples as motive for 51–2, 61, 70–1, 72, 280–1 n.8, 282 n.12
moral scruples, origin of 61, 71–2
motivations for, other 43, 52, 59, 62–3
Parliament and clergy controlled by 186, 188, 191, 193, 208, 209, 314 n.2, 315 n.8
succession concerns as motive for 43, 52, 59, 60–1, 88, 185, 190, 191, 192–3, 226, 231

Jewish law and rabbinic authorities
Babylonian Talmud on levirate marriage 135
Bribery and threats for rabbinic opinions 159–60
Halfan–Mantino dispute 152, 156–8
Jews excluded from England during Tudor era 26, 132
Jewish Messianic figures, role of 152, 156–8
Leviticus–Deuteronomy dispute 75–8
Maimonides's *Mishneh Torah* 136–8
Mark Raphael as Henry's Jewish law advisor 167, 170–1
opinions sought from Jewish sources 129–30
opinions sought from universities and clerics 100
rabbinic authorities not understood by English 177, 178–9
responsum of Rabbi Jacob Raphael of Modena 163, see 163–5 for summary, see also Appendix C for full English translation

after Henry marries Anne
Anne fails to provide a male heir 207
Anne is executed 208
Catherine dies 206
Jane Seymour is courted by Henry 207, 208
six wives of see Appendix D
succession, Henry names Mary and Elizabeth to 209

Henry Tudor, prince *see* Henry VIII: as Prince Henry Tudor
Hever Castle 51, 273 n.6, 274 n.12

impediment 38, 62, 68, 73, 75–6, 77, 230
incest *see* affinity Incest
infallibility doctrine *see* papal infallibility
Innocent III, pope *Fig 16* (*see* 262 n.Fig 16), 123
Inquisition 143, 154, 156–7, 308 n.36
Isabella, queen of Castile *Fig. 4* (*see* 260 n.Fig. 4), 74, 268–9 n.12, 269 n.15, 278 n.32, 280 n.3, 293 n.16, *see also* Ferdinand and Isabella, monarchs of Spain
Israel 18, 77–8, 153, 154, 171, 177, 236, 302 n.12, 313 n.3
Italy
  Christian Hebraists in 134, 142, 145, 300 n.6, 301 n.10, 306 n.17
  Hebrew books printed in 134, 136, 301–2 n.10–11
  Jewish messianic figures in 153, 154, 155–8
  Knight's mission to 85–6, 286 n.10
  levirate wedding in 180–1
  Mark Raphael in 166
  rabbis in 130–1, 145, 147–8, 149–50, 159, 160, 163
  responsum of Rabbi Jacob Raphael 163–5
  university opinions for Henry VIII 111, 113, 114–15, 116
  wars in 82, 196
  see also Inquisition

Jane Seymour, queen of England *Fig.* 20, 201, 207, 208, 210, 240, 277 n.27
Jerusalem 131, 135, 146, 155, 178, 308 n.36

Jewish law and rabbinic authorities *see* Henry VIII: *Jewish law and rabbinic authorities*
Jewish Messiahs *see* messianic figures
Jews expelled from England 26
Jews return to England 26
John III, king of Portugal 154–5
John of Flanders *see* Croke, Richard
Julius II, Pope *Fig. 9*
  Blackfriars Trial, and 87, 95, 96, 97
  Bull of Dispensation 38, 39, 71, 73–5, 77, 81, 87, 95–6, 97, 101, 107, 114, 225–6, 229, 282–3 n.14, 283–4 n.16–17
  Catholic opinions about dispensation 121, 122–5, 298 n.15
  Clement willing to cure technical problems of Bull 74, 231, 284 n.21
  consummation, issue of 106–7, 230, 322 n.16
  objections to Bull 74, 81, 121–2, 230
  papal infallibility 73–4, 282–3 n.14
  public honesty, issue of 230
  Spanish Brief 95–6, 229, 290 n.34–5, 321 n.6
  Westminster trial, and 81
Judah and Tamar 117–18, 165, 235–6, 296 n.1
Judaism and Jewish law 20, 132–3, 134, 135, 137, 143–4, 156, 158, 167, 168, 169, 175, 176, 179, 302 n.12, 302–3 n.17, 313 n.2, 319 n.5, *see also* Henry VIII: *Jewish law and rabbinic authorities*

Kabbalah, Kabbalism (Jewish) 143–4, 152, 153, 156, 179, 305 n.8
Katherine Parr, queen of England 342–3
Knight, William 85–6, 286 n.10

Lancaster, House of 31, 32, 244

Index

League of Cognac 82, 84
Lemlein, Asher 153
Leo X, Pope 133, 265 n.1, 285 n.1
levirate marriage
  Christians, applicable to 119–20, 121–2, 122–4
  consummation, requirement of 105
  Deuteronomy, requirements for 78, 119–20
  Jesus' grandfathers, example of 118–19, 296–7 n.2
  Jewish law, contemporaneous rabbinic opinions of 145, 147–8, 151, 163, 178, 307 n.19
  Jewish law, interpretation under 134–5 (Talmud), 137–8, 139 (Maimonides), 303–4 n.20–1, 304 n.23
  Judah and Tamar, example of 117–18, 165
  levirate wedding in Rome 180–1, 314 n.10
  Leviticus Prohibitions apply to widow 280 n.5
  Leviticus Prohibitions, conflict with 101–2, 117, 119–20, 122
  Leviticus Prohibitions, papal power to dispense 101, 104–5, 122–4
  Leviticus Prohibitions, punishment for violating 120
  motivation, requirement of 119, 170–1, 177
  Ruth and Boaz, example of 118, 165
  see also Ashkenazi vs. Sephardi; Gregory I; Halfan; Innocent III; Mantino; Raphael, Jacob; Raphael, Mark
Leviticus Prohibitions Anne Boleyn, could apply to 139–40, 285 n.9
  Catholic interpretation of 70, 73, 75, 78, 119–20, 298 n.15
  consummation of first marriage required for: 94, 96, 102, 105
  Gregory I and 75–6, 122–3, 298 n.15
  Henry VIII's scruples about see Henry VIII: seeking an annulment: moral scruples as motive for
  Innocent III and 123–4
  Julius II's dispensation of 73
  Mary Tudor legitimacy, effect upon 250
  natural law, indispensable as 75–6, 78, 81, 100–1, 101, 104–5, 112, 117, 118, 123–4, 165, 306 n.17
  widow of brother, applies to 70, 280 n.5
  See also levirate marriage
London
  Boleyn family wealth from 198
  Catherine and Arthur's wedding 33
  Catherine and Henry's coronation 41
  Eustace Chapuys arrives at 167–8
  Jewish communities begin in 23
  Mark Raphael arrives at 168, 171
  Mary Tudor's victory march and coronation 248
  Richard I Coronation and Riot 25, 264 n.4
Longland, John 61, 72, 109, 295 n.26
Louis XII, king of France 266 n.5, 288 n.26, 314 n.1
love letters
  authenticity 51
  expurgated version of 276 n.18
  French, early letters written in 50, 274 n.10
  Henry's complaints and desires revealed in 58
  history of 52
  motive for seeking annulment disclosed in 55, 195
  secrecy and privacy for 50, 274 n.11
  sexual activities discussed in 52, 54, 276 n.18–19

sincerity of 53, 58
survival of 51–2, 274–5 n.12
themes of 52
undated 53, 275 n.15
see also Summaries of Love Letters in Appendix A
Luther, Martin 69, 108, 133, 197
Lutheran see Protestantism; Reformation, Protestant

Mai, Miguel 113, 115, 168, 180, 308–9 n.3
Maimonides 136–7, 137–8, 139, 139–40, 265 n.5, 303–4 n.20–1, 314 n.7
Mantino, Jacob, rabbi 149–50, 150–1, 152, 156, 157, 158, 308–9 n.32
Manuel, Doña Elvira 106, 228, 293 n.15, 312 n.21, 317 n.5
Manuel I, king of Portugal 124, 299–300 n.5
Marriage treaty of Henry and Catherine see Henry VIII: *marriage to Catherine*: marriage treaty
matzo See Blood Libel
Mary Queen of Scots *Fig. 25*, 253–4
Mary Tudor, queen of England *Fig. 23*
  Anne of Cleves and 242
  annulment dispute and 89, 209, 248, 250
  birth of 42
  Catholicism and anti-Protestantism 249, 251
  false pregnancies and emotional instability 249, 252
  John Dudley, Duke of Northumberland and 247–8
  Katherine Parr and 242–3
  Lady Jane Gray and 247–8
  Philip II of Spain, husband of 249–50, 251, 252, 253
  Princess Elizabeth and 250–1, 252
  popularity 201, 210, 248, 249, 250–1, 251–2

succession issues 59, 210, 252, 278 n.32
messianic figures
  Charles V and 308 n.36
  Clement VII and 154, 155–6, 157–8, 308 n.36
  Halfan and 156, 157, 158, 307–8 n.32
  Mantino and 156, 157, 158
  see also Lemlein, Asher; Molkho, Shlomo; Reuveni, David
Mishneh Torah see Maimonides
mistresses see Blount, Elizabeth; Boleyn, Mary; Boleyn, Ann; see also Henry VIII: *marriage to Catherine*: mistresses
Mizrahi see Ashkenazi and Sephardi
Molkho, Shlomo 155–6, 156–7, 157–8, 308 n.36
Molko, Shlomo see Molkho, Shlomo
More, Thomas 199, 204, 215, 289 n.32
Muslim, Muslims 20, 24, 130, 136, 154, 155, 177, 178, 303 n.21, 313 n.2, 314 n.7

Nachmanides 165, 310 n.9
Naḥmanides see Nachmanides
natural Law 75–6, 76–7, 81, 100–1, 101–2, 104, 112, 120, 123–4, 138, 165, 284 n.21, 306 n.17
Northumberland see Dudley, John
Norwich 24–5, 264 n.1

Orvieto 83, 84
Oxford (city) 109, 295 n.26
Oxford University 55, 102, 109–10

papal infallibility 73–4, 282–3 n.14
Paris 52, 111–12, 114, 162–3, 173
Parliament 162, 186, 188, 191, 193–4, 208, 209, 223, 245, 251, 278 n.32, 314 n.2, 315 n.8, 318 n.2, 320 n.1
Paul III, pope 149, 261–89 n.32 n.Fig. 14

Index

Pembroke, marchioness of *see* Anne Boleyn, queen of England
Percy, Henry 48–9, 85, 273 n.6, 285–6 n.9
Pires, Diogo *see* Molkho, Shlomo
Plantagenet 32, 61, 244
Pole, Reginald, cardinal 61
pollicitation 90, 287 n.20
polygamy 169, 177, 178, 302–3 n.17, 303–4 n.21, 313 n.3
Portugal 124, 143, 153, 154, 177, 299–300 n.5, 317 n.5
positive law 75
printing with Hebrew type fonts 134, 136, 301–2 n.11, 318 n.18
Protestant Reformation *see* Reformation, Protestant
Protestantism 197, 201, 246, 251, *see also* Reformation, Protestant
public honesty 73, 226–7, 230–1, 283 n.16, 323 n.20–21

Rambam *see* Maimonides
Raphael, Mark 131, 146, 147–8, 166–7, 168–72, 172–4, 178, 179, 287 n.19, 304 n.2, 305–6 n. 10–11, 306 n.13, 308–9 n.3, 311 n.15–16, 312 n.21, 312–13 n.26–8
Raphael, Jacob, rabbi *Figs. 17, 26–8* (*see* 263 n.Figs. 26, 27, and 28), 163, 164–5, 215, 232, 310–11 n.9–10, 311 n.12
Rashi 233, 296 n.1, 301 n.11, 302–3 n.17
Reformation, English 17, 62, 108, 188, 201, 209, 238, 254, 263 n.1, 294 n.24
Reformation, Protestant 62, 69, 76, 108, 152, 197, 199, 317 n.3
Reuveni, David 153–4, 154–5, 155, 307–8 n.32–3, 308 n.36

Richard I (the Lionheart), king of England 25, 365 n.5, *see also* London: Richard I Coronation and Riot
Richard III, king of England 32, 244–5
Ritual Murder Libel *see* Blood Libel
Roman Catholic Church *see* Catholic Church
Rome 51, 82, 83, 84, 87, 93, 97, 149, 154, 155, 157, 180–1, 223, 274–5 n.12, 301–2 n.11, 314 n.10
Rota 97, 223
Ruth and Boaz 118, 131, 165, 297 n.3

Sack of Rome 82
sandal removal ceremony *see halitzah*
Scarisbrick, J. J. 160, 270 n.10, 281–2 n.11, 291 n.1, 295 n.26, 309 n.4, 323 n.20
shoe removal ceremony *see halitzah*
Soncino family 136, 301 n.11
Spain 33, 36, 38, 39, 41, 62, 74, 82, 97, 106, 229, 249, 251–2, 267 n.7–8, 278 n.32
Spanish Brief *see* Julius II: Spanish Brief
Starkey, David 23, 266 n.4–5, 274 n.11, 277 n.26, 278 n.35, 283 n.15
Stokesley, John, bishop 115, 130, 145, 299 n.2
Succession to the English throne 31, 34, 38, 229, 278 n.32, *see also* Henry VIII: seeking annulment: succession concerns.
Sweating Sickness 34, 43, 52, 100, 218, 219, 228, 266 n.4

Talmud 130, 135–6, 137, 139, 140, 164, 297 n.3, 301–2 n.11–12, 303 n.18, 303–4 n.21, 304 n.23
Tower of London 40, 131, 204, 208, 252
tuberculosis 34, 43, 321 n.11

Tudor dynasty 31–2, 35, 41, 43, 60–1, 209, 210, 244, 254–5
Tudor, Arthur, prince of Wales *see* Arthur, prince of Wales

Vatican 82, 97, 154, 157–8, 274 n.9, 274–5 n.12, 290 n.34, 306 n.12, 317 n.2
Venice 82, 114, 136, 142, 145, 149–50, 153, 154, 156, 160, 312 n.27

Wakefield, Robert 121, 297–8 n.8–10
War of the Roses 31, 32
Warham, William, archbishop 81, 190–1, 199, 215, 280–1 n.8
Wedding of Henry VIII and Anne Boleyn *see* Anne Boleyn: *after marriage to Henry VIII*: Henry VIII, wedding to
Westminster trial 81, 82, 84, 87, 200
Wolsey, Thomas, cardinal Figs. 6, 12, 13 (see 261 n.Figs. 12, 13)
   Anne Boleyn, and 48, 49, 84–5, 86–7, 199, 204, 219, 273–4 nn.7–8, 274–5 n.12
   Blackfriars trial 52–3, 91, 92
   career end and death 131, 188
   Catherine of Aragon, and 60, 72, 92, 93, 271 n.12, 281 n.9, 288 n.26
   character 214
   Charles V, and 72, 84
   Clement VII, and 86, 91, 92, 287–8 n.24
   decretal commission sought 87, 90–1, 91–2, 287 n.21
   deputy pope, seeks to become 83, 285 n.5
   Francis I, and 84
   Henry VIII's moral scruples, as source of 61, 70, 71–2, 281 n.9, 282 n.12
   papal legatee, as 81, 285 n.1
   Westminster trial 81–2
Worcester, bishop of *see* Ghinucci, Girolamo, Bishop

Yevamot 135, 234
Yevamoth *see* Yevamot
York (city) 264 n.4
York (House of) 31–2, *see also* Elizabeth of York, queen of England
York Castle massacre 25

Zelophehad 146, 147
Zohar 143
Zorzi, Francesco *see* Giorgi, Francesco